I0015723

Hands-On ROS for Robotics Programming

Program highly autonomous and AI-capable mobile robots powered by ROS

Bernardo Ronquillo Japón

Packt>

BIRMINGHAM - MUMBAI

Hands-On ROS for Robotics Programming

Copyright © 2020 Packt Publishing

All rights reserved. No part of this book may be reproduced, stored in a retrieval system, or transmitted in any form or by any means, without the prior written permission of the publisher, except in the case of brief quotations embedded in critical articles or reviews.

Every effort has been made in the preparation of this book to ensure the accuracy of the information presented. However, the information contained in this book is sold without warranty, either express or implied. Neither the author, nor Packt Publishing or its dealers and distributors, will be held liable for any damages caused or alleged to have been caused directly or indirectly by this book.

Packt Publishing has endeavored to provide trademark information about all of the companies and products mentioned in this book by the appropriate use of capitals. However, Packt Publishing cannot guarantee the accuracy of this information.

Acquisition Editor: Rohit Rajkumar
Content Development Editor: Ronn Kurien
Senior Editor: Richard Brookes-Bland
Technical Editor: Dinesh Pawar
Copy Editor: Safis Editing
Project Coordinator: Neil Dmello
Proofreader: Safis Editing
Indexer: Rekha Nair
Production Designer: Joshua Misquitta

First published: February 2020

Production reference: 1250220

Published by Packt Publishing Ltd.
Livery Place
35 Livery Street
Birmingham
B3 2PB, UK.

ISBN 978-1-83855-130-8

www.packt.com

Packt.com

Subscribe to our online digital library for full access to over 7,000 books and videos, as well as industry leading tools to help you plan your personal development and advance your career. For more information, please visit our website.

Why subscribe?

- Spend less time learning and more time coding with practical eBooks and Videos from over 4,000 industry professionals
- Improve your learning with Skill Plans built especially for you
- Get a free eBook or video every month
- Fully searchable for easy access to vital information
- Copy and paste, print, and bookmark content

Did you know that Packt offers eBook versions of every book published, with PDF and ePub files available? You can upgrade to the eBook version at www.packt.com and as a print book customer, you are entitled to a discount on the eBook copy. Get in touch with us at customercare@packtpub.com for more details.

At www.packt.com, you can also read a collection of free technical articles, sign up for a range of free newsletters, and receive exclusive discounts and offers on Packt books and eBooks.

Contributors

About the author

Bernardo Ronquillo Japón is an Internet of Things (IoT) and robotics expert who has worked for top technology companies since 1995, including Instituto de Astrofísica de Canarias, Gran Telescopio Canarias, Altran, and Alestis Aerospace.

Using his skills and experience, he founded The Robot Academy, where he develops open source hardware and software solutions for engineers and makers: Social Robot IO (2015), for the stimulation of children with autistic spectrum disorder; Robot JUS (2016), which helps engineers get deeper technical insights with the **Robot Operating System** (**ROS**) when using low-complexity hardware; and IIoT All-in-One (2018) as an industrial IoT training package for assisting companies in their digital transformation process.

Special thanks to Nicole Parrot, Director of Engineering at Modular Robotics, the company that manufactures GoPiGo3. They provided the hardware, software libraries, and prompt answers to every technical question I had while writing and testing practical examples. Also, my thanks go to Open Robotics and the ROS open source community, who support all of the ROS packages upon which the ROS wrappers for GoPiGo3 are written.

About the reviewers

Lentin Joseph is an author, roboticist, and robotics entrepreneur from India. He runs a robotics software company called Qbotics Labs in Kochi, Kerala. He has 8 years of experience in the robotics domain, primarily in ROS, OpenCV, and PCL.

He has authored several books on ROS, including *Learning Robotics Using Python – First Edition* and *Second Edition, Mastering ROS for Robotics Programming – First Edition* and *Second Edition, ROS Robotics Projects,* and *Robot Operating System for Absolute Beginners, Published by Packt.*

He gained his master's in robotics and automation in India and has worked at the Robotics Institute, CMU, USA. He is also a TEDx speaker.

> *I dedicate this book to my parents, C. G. Joseph and Jancy Joseph, for giving me the strong support make this project happen.*

Ramkumar Gandhinathan is a roboticist and researcher by profession. He started building robots in sixth grade and has been in the robotics field for over 15 years. He has personally built over 80 robots of different types. With 7 years of professional experience (4 years full time and 3 years part time/internship) in the robotics industry, he has 5 years of experience with ROS in particular. In his career, he has built over 15 industrial robot solutions using ROS. He is also fascinated by building drones and he himself pilots drones. His research interests include **simultaneous localization and mapping** (**SLAM**), motion planning, sensor fusion, multi-robot communication, and systems integration.

Packt is searching for authors like you

If you're interested in becoming an author for Packt, please visit `authors.packtpub.com` and apply today. We have worked with thousands of developers and tech professionals, just like you, to help them share their insight with the global tech community. You can make a general application, apply for a specific hot topic that we are recruiting an author for, or submit your own idea.

Table of Contents

Section 2: Robot Simulation with Gazebo

Section 3: Autonomous Navigation Using SLAM

Section 4: Adaptive Robot Behavior Using Machine Learning

Preface

Why a new book about learning robotics with ROS? Well, programming is but a small part of what it takes to work with robots. If you want to become really good at robotics, you'll need skills in other areas as well: electromechanics, robot simulation, autonomous navigation, and machine learning/reinforcement learning. Each of these four topics is a building block that you will need to master on your path to acquiring full robotics skills. This book is divided into four parts, each one being devoted to each of these building blocks.

Part 1, *Physical Robot Assembly and Testing*, focuses on electromechanics and describes each hardware part of the robot, providing practical demonstrations of how to test every sensor and actuator that it is equipped with. This part of the book should provide you with a good understanding of how a mobile robot works.

Part 2, *Robot Simulation with Gazebo*, deals with robot simulation. It is here where we introduce ROS and develop a two-wheeled robot simulation that emulates both the physical aspects and the behavior of an actual robot. We will explore the concept of the digital twin, a virtual robot that is the twin of a physical one. This is a fundamental part of developing robotic applications, as it cuts the costs associated with testing real hardware. The digital twin allows us to speed up the development process and save testing with the physical robot for the advanced stages of development.

Part 3, *Autonomous Navigation Using SLAM*, is devoted to **robot navigation**, the most common task for mobile robots. State-of-the-art algorithms and techniques are explained in a practical manner, first in simulation and then with a physical robot.

Part 4, *Adaptive Robot Behavior Using Machine Learning*, focuses on **machine learning** and **reinforcement learning**, the most active fields in robot research and real-world robotic applications. By using this technology, a robot is able to transition from pure automatism – where every possible behavior or answer is coded – to being a flexible behavior machine, where the robot is capable of reacting in a smart way to environmental demands by learning from data. This data can be obtained from the robot's previous experience or gathered from the experience of similar robots.

To build a state-of-the-art robot application, you will first need to master and then combine these four building blocks. The result will be what is commonly known as a **smart robot**. This is your task – this is your challenge.

Who this book is for

If you are an engineer who wishes to build AI-powered robots powered using ROS, then this book is for you. Technicians and hobbyists who wish to develop their own ROS robotics projects will also find this book to be a useful resource.

What this book covers

`Chapter 1`, *Assembling the Robot*, provides the key concepts and the practical assembly guidelines about the mobile robot on which all the content in this book is based. With a very practical approach in mind, we dive deep into the characteristics of GoPiGo3 that makes it an ideal and cost-effective platform to learn robotics. By completing the GoPiGo3 assembly, you will have acquired the first manual skills necessary for manipulating typical components in robotics. To purchase GoPiGo3 kit, you can visit `https://www.dexterindustries.com/gopigo3/` and apply the coupon code `BRJAPON@PACKT` to get a 10% discount.

`Chapter 2`, *Unit Testing of GoPiGo3*, provides you with a practical insight into how GoPiGo3 works. We do so by introducing the JupyterLab environment, a friendly interface that takes the structure of a notebook composed of human-readable paragraphs followed by Python code snippets. You will produce two versions of each test program: the JupyterLab notebook and the pure Python script. Using these programming tools, you will test each sensor/actuator individually and check that it's working properly, as well as gain an understanding of the technology behind.

`Chapter 3`, *Getting Started with ROS*, explains the basic concepts of ROS. It introduces you to the framework using easy-to-understand language, avoiding very technical descriptions. This is because our primary goal is to show you exactly what ROS is in a conceptual sense. It will be in the following chapters that deep technical descriptions are provided so that you are finally able to integrate ROS into your projects.

`Chapter 4`, *Creating a Virtual Two-Wheeled ROS Robot*, describes how to build a simple two-wheeled robot, a digital twin of GoPiGo3. The model is written in the **Unified Robot Description Format** (**URDF**) and the result is checked with RViz, an ROS tool that provides a configurable **Graphical User Interface** (**GUI**) to allow the user to display the specific information they are after. RViz may be used both for global robot visualization and for debugging specific features while building a model.

`Chapter 5`, *Simulating Robot Behavior with Gazebo*, teaches you how to plug the digital definition of your robot (the URDF file) into the simulation environment of Gazebo, which is powered with a physics engine able to emulate realistic behaviors. You will also develop your understanding of how to check and test a digital robot to ensure that its behavior represents well what should happen in the reality.

`Chapter 6`, *Programming in ROS Commands and Tools*, introduces you to command-line interaction with ROS and explains the types of ROS commands. We will explore the most frequently used communication patterns in ROS, including the publish-subscribe model. To deal with all of your ROS data, you will be introduced to rqt, which eases the process of developing and debugging applications. Also, ROS parameters are introduced to give you an overview of their power to manage robot configuration at a high level.

`Chapter 7`, *Robot Control and Simulation*, teaches you how to set up an ROS environment for a real robot, using GoPiGo3. We will start by looking at remote control using the keys of your laptop keyboard, then progress to the more technical method of using ROS Topics. This chapter will start you on your path from manual keyboard- and Topic-based control to internal programming logic, so that your robots can be capable of executing tasks autonomously.

`Chapter 8`, *Virtual SLAM and Navigation Using Gazebo*, explores the technique of **Simultaneous Localization and Mapping** (**SLAM**) using a practical approach and the digital twin of GoPiGo3. You will be taught why SLAM is required prior to proper navigation. The simulation will be run in Gazebo, the ROS-native simulation tool with a physics engine that offers realistic results.

`Chapter 9`, *SLAM for Robot Navigation*, shifts the focus to the real world with the physical GoPiGo3 robot. The chapter highlights the many details and practical questions that arise when you face a robotic task in a real environment. Simulation is good to start with, but the real proof that your robot performs as expected is gained by executing tasks in an actual scenario. This chapter is the starting point for you to get deeper into robot navigation and will be vital to your knowledge base if this is a field that you want to pursue.

`Chapter 10`, *Applying Machine Learning in Robotics*, intends to be a gentle introduction to the topic of machine learning in robotics, favoring intuition instead of complex mathematical formulations and putting the focus on understanding the common concepts used in the field. The practical example used in this chapter will involve the Pi camera of GoPiGo3 recognizing objects.

`Chapter 11`, *Machine Learning with OpenAI Gym*, gives you the theoretical background on reinforcement learning based on simple scenarios. This chapter allows you to better understand what happens under the hood in classical reinforcement training tasks. We will continue using practical examples to explore the concepts presented and will use the open source environment OpenAI Gym, which lets us easily test different algorithms from training agents, also driving robots in ROS.

`Chapter 12`, *Achieve a Goal through Reinforcement Learning*, goes a step further than computer vision for object recognition and shows that GoPiGo3 not only perceives things but can also take steps to achieve a goal. Our robot will have to decide what action to execute at every step of the simulation to achieve the goal. After executing each action, the robot will be provided with feedback on how good the decision it made was in the form of a reward. After some training, the incentive of the reward will enforce and reinforce good decision making.

To get the most out of this book

The book takes a practical approach to things and will encourage you to practice what you are learning with a physical robot. We choose GoPiGo3 (`https://www.dexterindustries.com/gopigo3/`) because of its modularity, moderate cost, and the fact that it's based on the Raspberry Pi. You can acquire a Raspberry Pi board from online stores worldwide. Before purchasing any component of the kit, we recommend that you first read `Chapter 1`, *Assembling the Robot*, to get basic information on all the components that you will need to purchase. To purchase GoPiGo3 kit, you can visit `https://www.dexterindustries.com/gopigo3/` and apply the coupon code `BRJAPON@PACKT` to get a 10% discount.

Some knowledge of Python and/or C++ programming and familiarity with single-board computers such as the Raspberry Pi are required to get the most out of this book.

Finally, you will need a laptop with Ubuntu 16.04 Xenial Xerus or Ubuntu 18.04 Bionic Beaver. The code of the book has been tested using both operating systems. If you have to start from scratch, we recommend that you use Ubuntu 18.04 because it is the latest **Long-term Support** (**LTS**) version provided by Canonical and will be supported until April 2023.

All the installation instructions you'll need are given in the *Technical requirements* section at the beginning of each chapter.

Download the example code files

You can download the example code files for this book from your account at `www.packt.com`. If you purchased this book elsewhere, you can visit `www.packtpub.com/support` and register to have the files emailed directly to you.

You can download the code files by following these steps:

1. Log in or register at `www.packt.com`.
2. Select the **Support** tab.
3. Click on **Code Downloads**.
4. Enter the name of the book in the **Search** box and follow the onscreen instructions.

Once the file is downloaded, please make sure that you unzip or extract the folder using the latest version of:

- WinRAR/7-Zip for Windows
- Zipeg/iZip/UnRarX for Mac
- 7-Zip/PeaZip for Linux

The code bundle for the book is also hosted on GitHub at `https://github.com/PacktPublishing/Hands-On-ROS-for-Robotics-Programming`. In case there's an update to the code, it will be updated on the existing GitHub repository.

We also have other code bundles from our rich catalog of books and videos available at `https://github.com/PacktPublishing/`. Check them out!

Download the color images

We also provide a PDF file that has color images of the screenshots/diagrams used in this book. You can download it here: `http://www.packtpub.com/sites/default/files/downloads/9781838551308_ColorImages.pdf`.

Code in Action

Visit the following link to check out videos of the code being run:
`http://bit.ly/2PrRpXF`

Conventions used

There are a number of text conventions used throughout this book.

`CodeInText`: Indicates code words in text, database table names, folder names, filenames, file extensions, pathnames, dummy URLs, user input, and Twitter handles. Here is an example: "It seems that only the last line is executed, which is `my_gopigo.left()`."

A block of code is set as follows:

```
msg_range.header.frame_id = "distance"
msg_range.radiation_type = Range.INFRARED
msg_range.min_range = 0.02
msg_range.max_range = 3.0
```

When we wish to draw your attention to a particular part of a code block, the relevant lines or items are set in bold:

```
std_msgs/Header header
uint8 radiation_type
float32 field_of_view
float32 min_range
```

Any command-line input or output is written as follows:

```
$ cd./Chapter2_Unit_Tests/drivingAround
$ python <name_of_script.py>
```

Bold: Indicates a new term, an important word, or words that you see onscreen. For example, words in menus or dialog boxes appear in the text like this. Here is an example: "Check the vital signs by clicking **Check Vital Signs**."

Warnings or important notes appear like this.

Tips and tricks appear like this.

Get in touch

Feedback from our readers is always welcome.

General feedback: If you have questions about any aspect of this book, mention the book title in the subject of your message and email us at `customercare@packtpub.com`.

Errata: Although we have taken every care to ensure the accuracy of our content, mistakes do happen. If you have found a mistake in this book, we would be grateful if you would report this to us. Please visit `www.packtpub.com/support/errata`, selecting your book, clicking on the Errata Submission Form link, and entering the details.

Piracy: If you come across any illegal copies of our works in any form on the Internet, we would be grateful if you would provide us with the location address or website name. Please contact us at `copyright@packt.com` with a link to the material.

If you are interested in becoming an author: If there is a topic that you have expertise in and you are interested in either writing or contributing to a book, please visit `authors.packtpub.com`.

Reviews

Please leave a review. Once you have read and used this book, why not leave a review on the site that you purchased it from? Potential readers can then see and use your unbiased opinion to make purchase decisions, we at Packt can understand what you think about our products, and our authors can see your feedback on their book. Thank you!

For more information about Packt, please visit `packt.com`.

1

Section 1: Physical Robot Assembly and Testing

This section focuses on describing and setting up the hardware that will be used alongside this book. Mechanical parts, including sensors and actuators, microcontrollers, and embedded computers, are the core hardware features of any mobile robot. Installation instructions for the required software in order to run GoPiGo3 with ROS will be included.

This section comprises the following chapters:

- `Chapter 1`, *Assembling the Robot*
- `Chapter 2`, *Unit Testing of GoPiGo3*
- `Chapter 3`, *Getting Started with ROS*

1
Assembling the Robot

This chapter will provide you with a variety of practical assembly guidelines about the mobile robot that the content of this book is based on. With a very practical approach in mind, we'll deep dive into the characteristics of GoPiGo3 and what makes it an ideal platform to learn robotics.

First, we will focus on the hardware and talk about the components that every robot is composed of including the mechanical parts and embedded system, sensor, and motors.

After completing the GoPiGo3 assembly section, you will be acquiring manual skills so that you can start manipulating typical components in robotics. You will also be driven to adopt a systematic approach of applying partial verification tests while assembling your robot, also known as **unit tests**.

After introducing the GoPiGo3 robot in the first section of this chapter, we will explain these concepts in depth, including the embedded controller, the GoPiGo3 board, and the embedded computer, the Raspberry Pi.

Next, we will describe the sensors and actuators that the robot will use, grouped into what we will call the **electromechanics**.

Finally, we will provide you with some useful guidelines so that assembling the robot is straightforward. Then, we will test the GoPiGo3 robot using its easy-to-start software, DexterOS. Even though we will adopt Ubuntu as an operating system for running ROS later in this book, it is recommended that you start with DexterOS so that you familiarize yourself with the hardware while avoiding specific software programming tasks, which is something that will be left for later chapters.

In this chapter, we will cover the following topics:

- Understanding the GoPiGo3 robot
- Getting familiar with the embedded hardware – GoPiGo3 board and Raspberry Pi

- Deep diving into the electromechanics – motors, sensors, and 2D camera
- Putting it all together
- Hardware testing using Bloxter (visual programming) under DexterOS

Understanding the GoPiGo3 robot

GoPiGo3 is a Raspberry Pi-based robot car manufactured by Dexter Industries. It is intended to be used as an educational kit for learning about both robotics and programming, two complementary perspectives that clearly show the transversal knowledge you should acquire to become a robotics engineer. We'll explain what this means by letting Nicole Parrot, Director of Engineering at Modular Robotics, explain it in her own words:

> *"The GoPiGo originated from a Kickstarter campaign in early 2014 when the Raspberry Pi was still somewhat new. The first users were hobbyists, but soon teachers and coding club volunteers were sharing their GoPiGo with their students. This lead to various changes being made to the board to make a classroom-ready robot. It's robust, it has a full list of features, and it's still based on the Raspberry Pi! The latest iteration has been around since 2017 and is a stable platform.*
>
> *A Raspberry Pi-based robot offers quite a few advantages in the classroom. It can be programmed in an array of languages, it can be independent of the school Wi-Fi while not requiring Bluetooth, and it can perform advanced applications right on the board, such as computer vision and data collection. The GoPiGo with DexterOS comes with scientific libraries all preinstalled. The GoPiGo with Raspbian for Robots allows the user to install whatever libraries and tools are required for the project at hand. It comes with two Python libraries: easygopigo3.py and gopigo3.py. Both of these offer high-level control of the robot and low-level control, depending on the user's technical skills.*
>
> *The GoPiGo has become the premier go-to robot for universities, researchers, and engineers seeking a simple, well-documented robot for the Raspberry Pi."*

Ready to dive into robotics? Let's go!

The robotics perspective

From the robotics perspective, you will learn how to work with the basic parts:

- **Motors**, which allow the robot to move from one point to another. In GoPiGo3, we have DC motors with built-in encoders that provide a precise motion. This is one of the main upgrades from GoPiGo2, where the encoders were external to the motors and not very accurate.
- **Sensors**, which acquire information from the environment, such as the distance to near objects, luminosity, acceleration, and so on.
- The **controller**—that is, the GoPiGo3 red board—handles the physical interface with sensors and actuators. This is the real-time component that allows GoPiGo3 to interact with the physical world.
- A **single-board computer** (**SBC**) Raspberry Pi 3B+, which provides processing capacity. As such, it works under an operating system, typically a Linux-based distribution, providing wide flexibility from a software point of view.

Most educational kits stop at a level-3 controller; they do not include a level-4 single-board computer. The software in the controller is a small program (only one) that is embedded in the board. Every time you want to modify the code for the robot, you have to fully replace the existing program and flash the new version from an external computer while using the serial connection over a USB port.

A classic example of this is an Arduino-controlled robot. Here, the Arduino board plays the role of our GoPiGo3 board, and if you have worked with it, you will surely remember how you needed to transfer the new program from the Arduino IDE on your laptop to the robot through a USB cable.

The programming perspective

From the programming perspective, GoPiGo3 allows you to start easy by learning a visual programming language, Bloxter, a fork of the open source Google Blockly, that was specifically developed for GoPiGo3. This is a very comfortable prerequisite when it comes to learning about the basic concepts of writing software programs.

But if you are reading this book, we are sure you already know how to program in one of the many available languages, that is, C, C++, Java, JavaScript, or Python. Dexter Industries provides various open source libraries (`https://github.com/DexterInd/GoPiGo3/tree/master/Software`) that you can use to program GoPiGo3. Some of them are as follows:

- C
- C#
- Go
- Java
- Node.js (JavaScript)
- Python
- Scratch

In any case, in this first chapter, we encourage you to only use Bloxter to emphasize the robotics perspective and become familiar with the hardware you have in your hands. After that, you may use your choice of language, given the many GoPiGo3 **application programming interfaces** (**APIs**) that are available.

In this book, we will focus on Python as the primary language to program in ROS. The Python language is easier to learn while still being very powerful and predominant in robotics and computer science. After going through some Python examples in `Chapter 2`, *Unit Testing GoPiGo3*, we will get started with the **Robot Operating System** (**ROS**), which isn't an actual programming language but a development application framework for robots. As such, we will show you how to adapt your Python programs with wrappers so that they can also run within ROS as pieces for building high-level functionalities.

You will appreciate the added value of such a jump to ROS when you discover how many more things GoPiGo3 can do when its Python base of code is wrapped with ROS. This software upgrade provides GoPiGo3 with a toolkit that allows students, creators, and engineers to understand how robots work. Furthermore, you should be aware that the ROS is commonly used in professional environments.

Robot kit and resources

At a high level, we can group the hardware of the robot into two sets:

- **Electromechanics**: This refers to the sensors and actuators that allow it to interact with the physical world.

- **Embedded hardware**: The electronic boards that allows it to acquire a signal from the sensors, convert it into a digital signal, and provide the processing logic and send commands to the actuators. Here, we typically have two types of electronic boards:
    - The **controller**, which serves as the physical interface with the sensors and actuators—that is, the GoPiGo3 board. The controller deals with both analog and digital signals from the electromechanical devices, transforming them into digital signals that can be processed by a CPU.
    - The **computer**, which provides us with the means to implement intelligent logic. In most robots, this is an SBC. In the case of GoPiGo3, this is the Raspberry Pi running a Linux OS distribution, such as Raspbian or Ubuntu.

Although you could directly connect digital devices to the Raspberry Pi through its **general purpose input/output** (**GPIO**) pins, from a functional point of view, it is better to interface all the sensors and actuators through the controller—that is, the GoPiGo3 board: keep the interface with the physical world at the controller level and do the processing and computation at the computer level.

If you are a regular Raspberry Pi user and own the board, you only need to purchase the GoPiGo3 Robot Base Kit (`https://www.dexterindustries.com/product/gopigo3-robot-base-kit/`). This kit includes the following:

- GoPiGo3 board (red board)
- Chassis (frame, wheels, hardware)
- Motors
- Encoders
- Power battery pack and cable
- Screwdriver for assembly

The following image shows all the parts that are included:

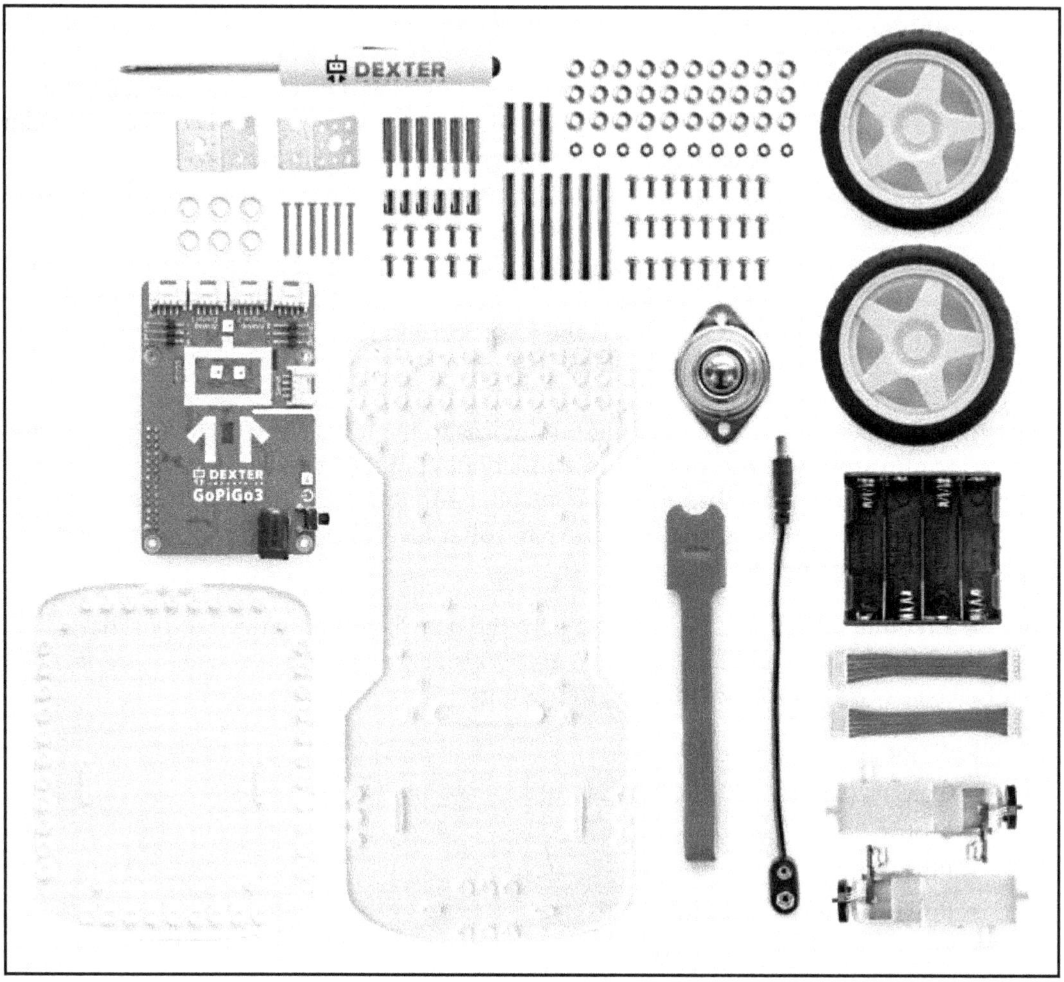

Image courtesy: Dexter Industries:
https://shop.dexterindustries.com/media/catalog/product/cache/4/thumbnail/1800x2400/9df78eab33525d08d6e5fb8d27136e95/g/p/gpg3_components_rgb.jpg

The following image shows the assembled kit (without the Raspberry Pi):

Image courtesy: Dexter Industries: https://32414320wji53mwwch1u68ce-wpengine.netdna-ssl.com/wp-content/uploads/2017/05/GPG3_BaseKit_2.jpg

The batteries (8 AA 1.2 V) are not included. Although you can use cheaper replaceable units, it is strongly advised that you use rechargeable batteries. In the long term, it will be cost-effective and environmentally friendly.

Apart from the kit, you will need to add a Raspberry Pi 3 and its Micro SD card; otherwise, especially if you are new to the Raspberry Pi world, you would be better off buying the GoPiGo3 Beginner Starter Kit (`https://www.dexterindustries.com/product/gopigo-beginner-starter-kit/`), which includes the Raspberry Pi 3 and its accessories, as well as an orientable distance sensor equipped with a servo-motor, allowing it to cover a 180° field of view. This sensor set is composed of the following:

- The distance sensor (`https://www.dexterindustries.com/product/distance-sensor/`)
- The servo package (`https://www.dexterindustries.com/product/servo-package/`)

The following image shows the final aspect of the Beginner Starter Kit, once it's been assembled. The same result can be obtained with the Robot Base Kit by adding the Raspberry Pi and the orientable distance sensor:

Image courtesy: Dexter Industries:
https://www.robotshop.com/media/catalog/product/cache/image/380x380/9df78eab33525d08d6e5fb8d27136e95/g/o/gopigo3-beginner-starter-kit.jpg

Now that we've looked at the GoPiGo3 robot, it's time to cover the technical details regarding the embedded hardware and the electromechanics.

Getting familiar with the embedded hardware

Do you remember which hardware is for what? The GoPiGo3 board is for interfacing with sensors and actuators, while Raspberry Pi is used for computing tasks. We will cover these topics in detail here.

The GoPiGo3 board

This customized board (`https://www.dexterindustries.com/GoPiGo/learning/hardware-port-description/`) provides the general features that are expected from a controller:

- Real-time communication with sensors and actuators.
- Interface **input/output** (**I/O**) through a **serial peripheral interface** (**SPI**) that feeds the data from the sensors to the Raspberry Pi and may also receive commands for the actuators (also from the Raspberry Pi, after running the logic in its CPU for every step of the control loop).
- One single program loaded on board, known as the firmware. Since the goal of this software is to implement a communication protocol while the computer implements the logic, it doesn't need to be changed unless you decide to upgrade it when a new version is available.

Let's briefly explain the input/output interface protocol that we mentioned in the preceding bullet point list. SPI is a bus that's used to send data between microcontrollers and external devices, which are sensors, in our case. It uses separate clock and data lines, along with a select line to choose the device to talk to. The side of the connection that generates the clock is called the master, which is the Raspberry Pi in our case, while the other side is called the slave, which is the GoPiGo3 board. This way, both boards are synchronized, resulting in a faster form of communication than asynchronous serial, which is the typical communication protocol in general-purpose boards such as Arduino.

You can find out more about the SPI protocol in an easy-to-follow tutorial at `https://learn.sparkfun.com/tutorials/serial-peripheral-interface-spi`. Communication over SPI with the Raspberry Pi occurs through the headers interface, which can be seen in the top part of GoPiGo3 board in the following image. Only five out of the 40 GPIO pins are needed for such an interface:

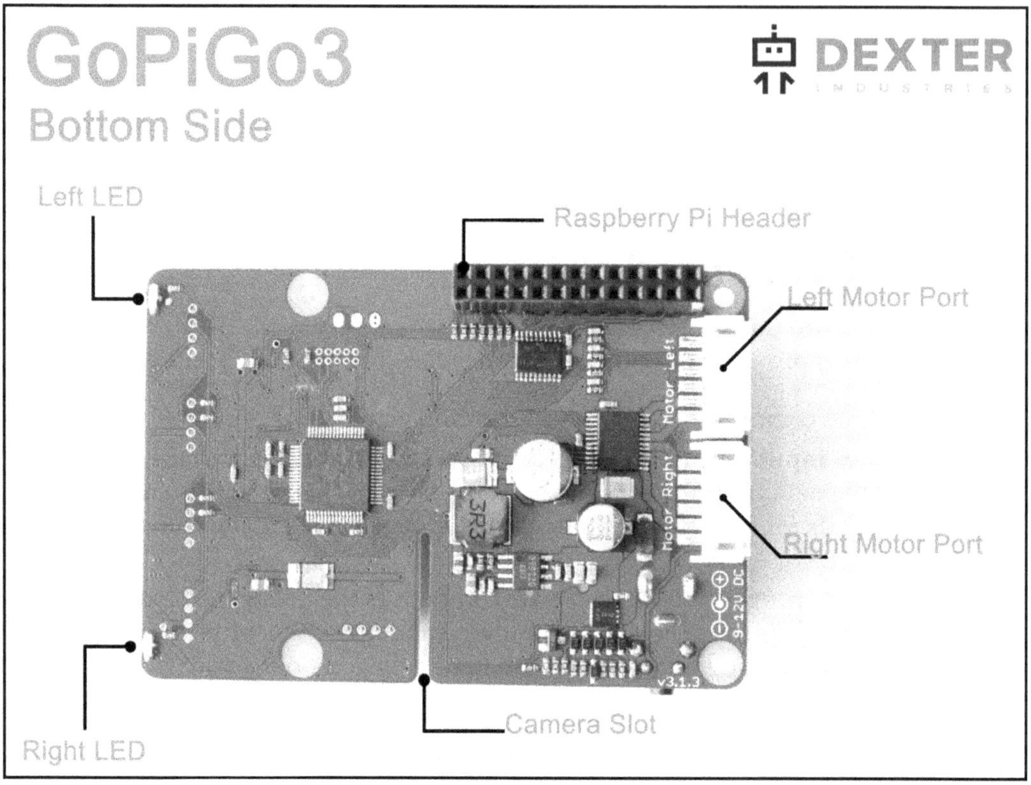

Image courtesy: Dexter Industries: https://32414320wji53mwwch1u68ce-wpengine.netdna-ssl.com/wp-content/uploads/2014/07/GoPiGo3-Bottom_annotated-600x441.jpg

For interfacing with devices, the board provides the following (a top view of the board can be seen in the next diagram):

- Two I2C ports—two Grove ports connected to the Raspberry Pi I2C bus through a level-conversion chip
- One serial port—one Grove port connected to serial pins on the Raspberry Pi through a level-conversion chip

- Two analog-digital ports—two Grove ports connected to the GoPiGo3 microcontroller
- Two servo ports for the PWM type servomotor:

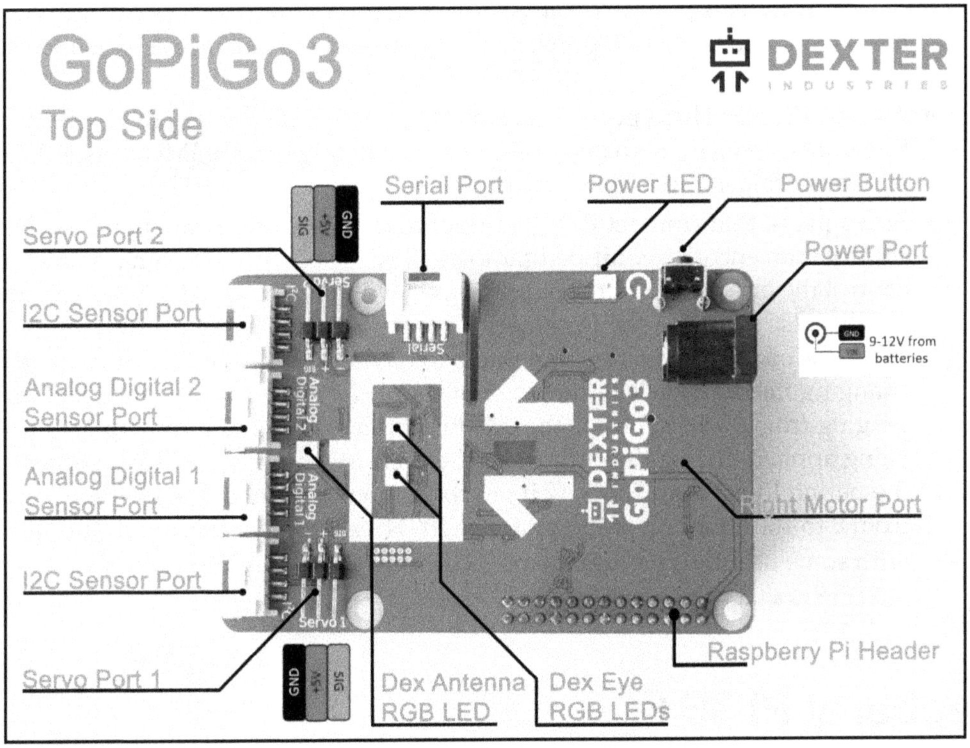

Image courtesy: Dexter Industries: https://32414320wji53mwwch1u68ce-wpengine.netdna-ssl.com/wp-content/uploads/2014/07/GoPiGo3-Top-768x565.jpg

Let's explain these new concepts:

- **Serial port**: This is the complimentary communication protocol we mentioned previously when we talked about the SPI. While the last is synchronous (it needs five interface pins), the serial port is asynchronous—that is, there is no clock signal to follow and only two pins are needed: **Tx** for data transmission and **Rx** for data reception. In GoPiGo3, this port is directly connected to the Raspberry Pi serial pins through a level-conversion chip.

- **I2C ports**: As its name suggests, this uses the I2C communication protocol. Just like SPI, it is a synchronous protocol, faster than asynchronous serial. I2C uses two lines, **SDA** for data and **SCL** for the clock signal. The third and fourth wires are for the power supply: **VIN** at 5V and the **GND** ground—that is, a 0V reference. **SDA** is bidirectional, so any of the connected devices can send or receive data. In these two ports, you will connect the distance sensor and the line follower sensor.
- **Analog-digital**: These ports can connect to analog, digital, or I2C Grove devices. We will be connecting to one of the analog-digital port, the IMU sensor. We will talk about this in more detail later.
- **Servo ports, that connect PWM servomotors**: These are cheaper and easier to control than encoder-equipped motors, all while offering enough accuracy to control the orientation of the support they will hold. In GoPiGo3, we can attach the distance sensor or the Pi camera to a servo motor. **Pulse Width Modulation** (**PWM**) technology refers to having control in a continuous range by changing the duty cycle of the voltage supply, resulting in an equivalent output ranging from 0V to 5V: 0V is the 0% duty cycle, while 100% corresponds to 5V being applied during the entirety of the cycle. By applying 5V for a percentage of the period lower than 100%, you get continuous control of the position, ranging from 0 to 180° rotation of the motor shaft. For an explanation about this, along with some useful figures, go to `https://www.jameco.com/jameco/workshop/howitworks/how-servo-motors-work.html`.

Raspberry Pi 3B+

Raspberry Pi has the largest community both in terms of education and the industry, which makes it the best single-board computer of choice when developing embedded software for robots or for **Internet of Things** (**IoT**) devices. The following image shows the Raspberry Pi 3B+, the most common model that powers GoPiGo3:

Image courtesy: https://en.wikipedia.org/wiki/File:Raspberry_Pi_3_B%2B_(39906369025).png, License CC BY-SA 2.0

The main characteristics of Raspberry Pi 3B+ are as follows:

- A **Central Processing Unit** (**CPU**) composed of four Cortex-A53 1.4 GHz.
- A **Graphics Processing Unit** (**GPU**) is a Broadcom VideoCore IV at 250 MHz.
- The **Synchronous Dynamic Random-Access Memory** (**SDRAM**) is 1 GB, which is shared with the GPU.
- On-board storage is provided through a MicroSDHC slot. You can choose whatever micro SD card size fits your needs. In any case, the general recommendation is to use a class-10 micro SD of 16 GB capacity—10 means that it is able to be written at 10 Mb/second.

Let's go over the functionality of each of these components:

- The CPU provides the computation capacity to run all kinds of algorithms. This is where the intelligence of our robot resides.
- The GPU's mission is to handle computer graphics and image processing. In our case, it will mostly be devoted to processing the images from the Pi camera and providing computer vision capabilities.
- SDRAM has 1 GB volatile storage that's shared with the GPU, so this is a balance of how much memory you assign to the GPU (by default, it takes up to 64 Mb). RAM is where the program is loaded so that it can be executed.
- On-board microSD card is the persistent storage that contains the operating system as well as all the installed software.

Raspberry Pi runs an operating system, typically a Linux-based distribution such as Debian or Ubuntu.

Although Raspbian—the Debian-based distro by the Raspberry Pi Foundation—is the official distribution, we will be using Ubuntu—supported by Canonical—because it's the platform that Open Robotics (`https://www.openrobotics.org`) uses to deliver a version of ROS every year, synchronized with the yearly versions of Ubuntu.

Why does a robot need a CPU?

Apart from the fact that this book's goal is to get you some hands-on experience with ROS—and for that, you need a Linux OS to install the software on—if you really want to create a smart robot, you need the processing capacity to run compute-intensive algorithms, and that is what a CPU such as Raspberry Pi provides.

Why is this computation needed? Because a smart robot has to integrate information from the environment with the logic of the task at hand to be able to complete it successfully. Let's use the example of carrying one object from its current position to a target destination. To do so, devices such as a laser distance sensor, a 3D camera, and/or a GPS provide the robot with information from the environment. These sources of data have to be combined so that the robot is able to locate itself in the environment. By supplying a target destination, it also has to compute the optimum path to carry the object on, something that it is called *path planning*. When executing such a path plan, it has to detect obstacles that may appear along the path and avoid them without losing focus of the goal. Hence, every step of the task involves executing an algorithm in the CPU of the robot.

This is one of the many practical scenarios that you will learn to solve using ROS, which is currently the *de facto* industry standard for the development of robotics applications.

Deep diving into the electromechanics

As explained in GoPiGo's official documentation (`https://www.dexterindustries.com/GoPiGo/learning/technical-specifications-for-the-gopigo-raspberry-pi-robotics-kit/`), the specifications of the GoPiGo3 robot are as follows:

- **Operating voltage**: 7V-12V
- **External interfaces**:
    - **I2C ports**: Two Grove ports connected to the Raspberry Pi I2C bus through a level-conversion chip
    - **Serial ports**: One Grove port connected to the serial pins on the Raspberry Pi through a level-conversion chip
    - **Analog digital ports**: Two Grove ports connected to the GoPiGo3 microcontroller
- **Encoders**: Two magnetic encoders with six pulse counts per rotation (with 120:1 gear reduction for a total of 720 pulses per wheel rotation)
- **Wheels diameter**: 66.5 mm
- **Distance between wheels**: 117 mm
- **More:** Design information is available at the official GitHub repository (`https://github.com/DexterInd/GoPiGo3`)

This is just a summary of what we explained in the section titled *The GoPiGo3 board*. In this section, we will concentrate on describing the devices that are connected to the GoPiGo3 board.

The most useful sensors

The sensors we are going to mount onto the GoPiGo3 are the ones that we need in order to accomplish the top-level task of the robot—that is, navigation with motion planning, while keeping costs low. These sensors are as follows:

- Distance sensor
- Line follower
- **Inertial Measurement Unit** (**IMU**) sensor
- 2D camera

In the case of using the line-follower sensor, since the robot will follow a marked path on the floor (usually painted in black), the motion-planning part can be skipped and navigation will be much easier. If there is an obstacle on the path, you will have to apply an algorithm to move around the obstacle and return to the path—that is, place the line-follower sensor above the black line again.

Now, we should take the time to understand what information each sensor provides. Later in this book, you will encounter such a navigation problem and the algorithms that can be used to implement it.

Distance sensor

The simple distance sensor allows us to measure the distance to the object in front of it. It has a small laser that measures the distance to an object. The sensor applies the time of flight method for a very fast and accurate distance reading. The product page can be viewed at `https://www.dexterindustries.com/product/distance-sensor/`:

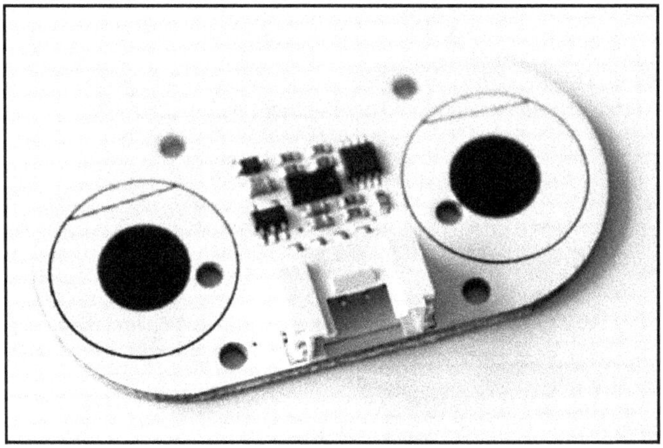

Image courtesy: Dexter Industries: https://shop.dexterindustries.com/media/catalog/product/cache/4/image/1800x2400/9df78eab33525d08d6e5fb8d27136e95/d/e/dexter-industries-raspberry-pi-robot-distance-sensor-for-robots-front-of-sensor-1.jpg

You can connect the distance sensor to any of the two I2C ports. Be aware that the GoPiGo3 software libraries will not ask you to specify which of the two ports you are using. This will be detected automatically.

You can mount the sensor onto a servo package to scan a wide angle of about 180°. The servomotor can be connected to either servo port 1 or servo port 2. The product page can be viewed at `https://www.dexterindustries.com/product/servo-package/`:

Image courtesy: Modular Robotics: https://www.dexterindustries.com/wp-content/uploads/2019/09/GoPiGo3-Molded-Servo-Frontal-300x200.jpg

In `Chapter 2`, *Unit Testing of GoPiGo3*, there is a specific test you can run with your robot to check that this unit works properly.

Line follower

The line follower of GoPiGo3 is composed of six pairs of LED phototransistors. The LED emitter is the right-most part of each pair when you position the sensor in front of you to read the letters. This can be seen in the following photograph, which is a picture of the powered sensor, although you cannot yet see the LED light beams:

Why don't you see them in the picture? Because LEDs emit infrared light, which can't be detected by your eyes; however, it can be revealed by a phone camera (by default, the optics of these cameras do not include infrared filters). So, if, later on, you find that the line follower does not work properly, the first thing you must check is the hardware. To do this, simply take a photo with the camera app that ships with your smartphone.

In the following image, the sensor view has been intentionally blurred so that you can see the rays and confirm that the light beams come from the right-hand side of the LED phototransistor. The receiving part—that is, the phototransistor—is the component that detects whether there is reflected light coming from the LED emitter. The product page for this component can be viewed at `https://www.dexterindustries.com/product/line-follower-sensor/`:

Now, you are in a position to understand the working principles of the line-follower sensor:

- If the rays are reflected off the floor because it is white, the phototransistor receives the mirrored beam and provides this information in the data sensor stream.
- If the sensor is over a black surface, the phototransistor does not receive any reflected light and lets the robot know.

Reflection makes the sensor electronics report a signal close to 1 (white surface), while absorption provides a value close to 0 (black surface). But what if the sensor is far away from the floor or not facing it? Well, from the point of view of the sensor, absorption is equivalent to the lack of reflection. Therefore, the reported signal is close to zero. This property allows GoPiGo3 not only to follow a black path on the ground, but also to walk along edges avoiding drops that could damage the robot.

Since you have six pairs, you will have six signals, where each reports 0 or 1. These six numbers will allow us to infer how well centered the robot is over a black line. The sensor's specifications are as follows:

- I2C sensor with a Grove connector.
- Six analog sensors, each giving a value between zero and one, depending on how much light it receive from the floor, with 0 indicating black and 1 indicating white.
- The sensor can be polled up to 120 Hz.
- An easy library (`https://di-sensors.readthedocs.io/en/master/api-basic.html#easylinefollower`) and a driver-level library (`https://di-sensors.readthedocs.io/en/master/api-advanced.html#linefollower`) are available and fully documented. The easy library provides methods that do the heavy lifting for you.

The following is a bottom view of the emitter-receiver. This face is the one that has to be a few millimeters above the floor to ensure a proper reflection of the LED's emission:

Image courtesy: Modular Robotics: https://shop.dexterindustries.com/media/catalog/product/cache/4/thumbnail/1800x2400/9df78eab33525d08d6e5fb8d27136e95/l/i/linefollower_bottom.jpg

The following image shows the line follower sensor mounted on the GoPiGo3 at the proper position—that is, above the floor:

Image courtesy: Modular Robotics: http://www.dexterindustries.com/wp-content/uploads/2019/03/linefollowerinaction.jpg

For instructions on how to assemble and calibrate the sensor, go to `https://www.dexterindustries.com/GoPiGo/line-follower-v2-black-board-getting-started/`. For connecting, you can use either of the two available I2C connectors on the line-follower sensor. Remember that one of them will be in use by the distance sensor.

The line follower can also be connected to one of the AD ports if you are using Raspbian For Robots (`https://www.dexterindustries.com/raspberry-pi-robot-software/`). It's for more advanced use, and coding for this setup is slightly different.

For the purposes of introducing robotics, we will take it easy by connecting the sensor to an I2C port and use the more friendly DexterOS (`https://www.dexterindustries.com/dexteros/`). In `Chapter 2`, *Unit Testing of GoPiGo3*, we will go over a specific test you can run with your robot to check that this unit works properly.

IMU sensor

The IMU sensor allows us to measure the orientation of the robot, as well as obtain an estimation of its position as it moves. The product page of the Dexter Industries IMU can be viewed at `https://www.dexterindustries.com/product/imu-sensor/`. The respective aspect of the sensor can be seen in the following image:

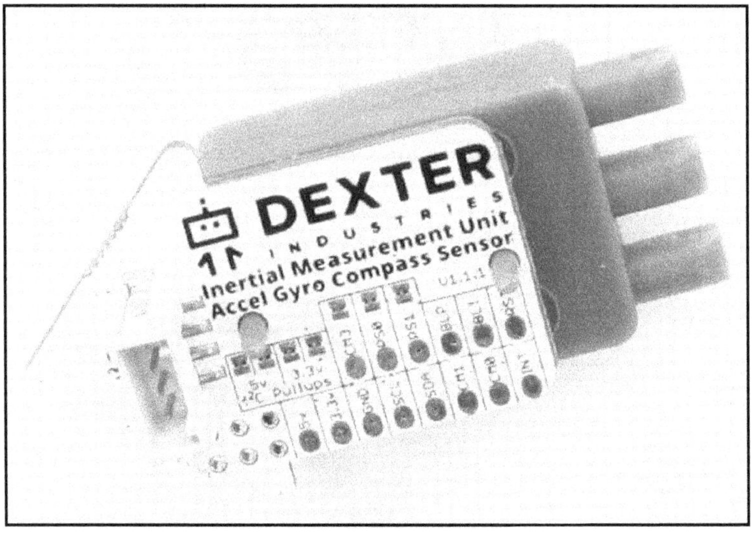

Image courtesy: Dexter Industries: https://shop.dexterindustries.com/media/catalog/product/cache/4/thumbnail/1800x2400/9df78eab33525d08d6e5fb8d27136e95/i/m/imu-sensor_mount2-800x800.jpg

In the following image, you can see it mounted on the GoPiGo3. To connect to the robot, you only have to plug it into either AD1 or AD2 on the GoPiGo board:

Image courtesy: Dexter Industries:
https://shop.dexterindustries.com/media/catalog/product/cache/4/thumbnail/1800x2400/9df78eab33525d08d6e5fb8d27136e95/i/m/imu-sensor_gpg3_3.jpg

This IMU has nine **degrees of freedom** (**DOF**), plus temperature measurement capabilities. Let's talk about each sensor of the IMU and what kind of data they provide:

- Let's start with the simpler one, the temperature. This provides the ambient room temperature and can be used in combination with the rest of the sensors to create, for example, a temperature map of a room, by taking measurements at several locations as the GoPiGo3 covers the surface.
- The accelerometer is an absolute sensor because its value is always referred to as zero acceleration (static object). It provides a value for each of the three axes, *X*, *Y*, and *Z*:
    - It is good for measuring the inclination of the robot (an angle whose cosine is the vertical acceleration divided by the value of gravity = 9.81 m/s^2) and the free-fall condition, which is equivalent to a 90° ramp and is a vertical wall (gravity is continuously detected by the sensor—that is, 9.81 m/s^2, if the object stays in a horizontal plane).
    - The accelerometer is not as accurate for the measurement of velocity because this value is not directly provided by the sensor. We can obtain it by performing the integral of the acceleration signal over time, which produces cumulative errors (drift), mainly coming from the sensor noise (electronics) and the measurement error itself. This is where the gyroscope comes into the picture to provide an accurate speed measurement.

- The gyroscope is a differential sensor that provides the three rotations (*X*, *Y*, and *Z* axes) with respect to an arbitrary reference. What they really provide is the rotation velocity. This means that they are accurate for measuring rotation velocities, but not good for measuring angular position (you have to integrate of the speed signal over time, accumulating measurement errors and sensor noise, thereby producing drift).

A six-DOF IMU will be one that combines the accelerometer (three DOFs) and gyroscope (three DOFs):

- The accelerometer accurately measures the inclination with respect to the vertical. It does not have drift in the medium/long term, but is not accurate for short-term measurements.
- The gyroscope accurately measures rotation velocities, but they have drift. This means that they are not good for medium/long-term measurements.

By combining the six values from the accelerometer and gyroscope, it is possible to obtain an improved measurement of the orientation. This is expressed by means of the Euler angles—α, β, γ—as shown in the following diagram:

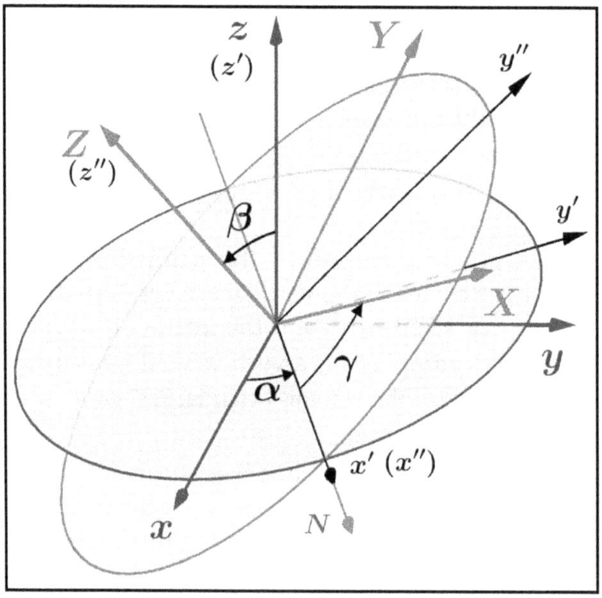

Image courtesy: https://commons.wikimedia.org/wiki/File:Euler_angles_zxz_int%2Baxes.png, License CC BY-SA 4.0

Something's that's more commonly used than the Euler angles are the Tait-Bryan version or navigation angles, roll-pitch-yaw, which can be defined as follows:

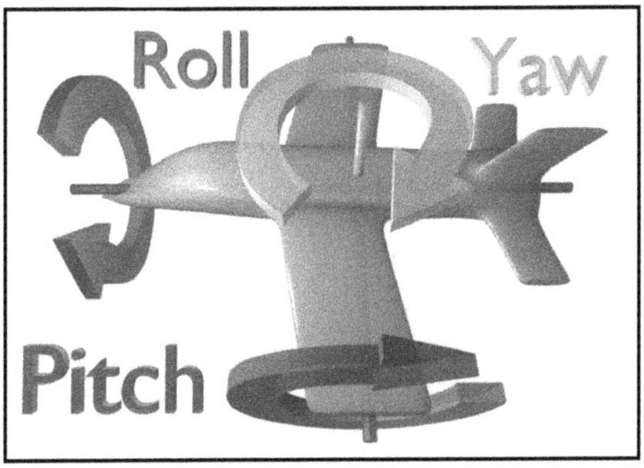

Image courtesy: https://es.m.wikipedia.org/wiki/Archivo:Flight_dynamics_with_text.png, License CC BY-SA 3.0

These angles are obtained by applying a special filter, called a **complimentary filter**, to the sensor's signals. It works like this:

- For the signal from the accelerometer, it behaves as a low-pass filter since we trust its medium/long-term measurement.
- For the signal from the gyroscope, it behaves as a high-pass filter since we trust its short-term measurement.

Mathematically, the complimentary filter is expressed as follows:

$$\theta = A \cdot (\theta_{prev} + \theta_{gyro}) + B \cdot \theta_{accel}$$

Here, *A* and *B* has to sum 1. These constants are determined by the calibration of the sensor, and typical values include *A* = 0.98, *B* = 0.02. The complimentary filter offers very similar results to the Kalman filter, which is the **best linear (unbiased) estimator** (**BLE**) but more computationally intensive.

Now, we have three rotations (about the *X*, *Y*, *Z* axes), but they are not absolute angles just yet:

- Thanks to the accelerometer, the orientation with respect to the vertical is an absolute reference, but for the orientation on the horizontal plane we are lacking such a reference because the gyroscope is a differential sensor.
- This is where the magnetometer appears to give us the orientation (three axes *X*, *Y*, *Z*) of the Earth's magnetic field.

Therefore, with our 6 + 3 = 9 DOFs IMU, we have the absolute orientation of our robot, with the gravity and the magnetic field vectors as references. In `Chapter 2`, *Unit Testing of GoPiGo3*, we'll go over a specific test you can run with your robot to check that this unit works properly.

Pi Camera

The Pi Camera is a custom 2D camera with a **Camera Serial Interface** (**CSI**). The following image shows the two physical components—that is, the camera's electronic board and a ribbon cable:

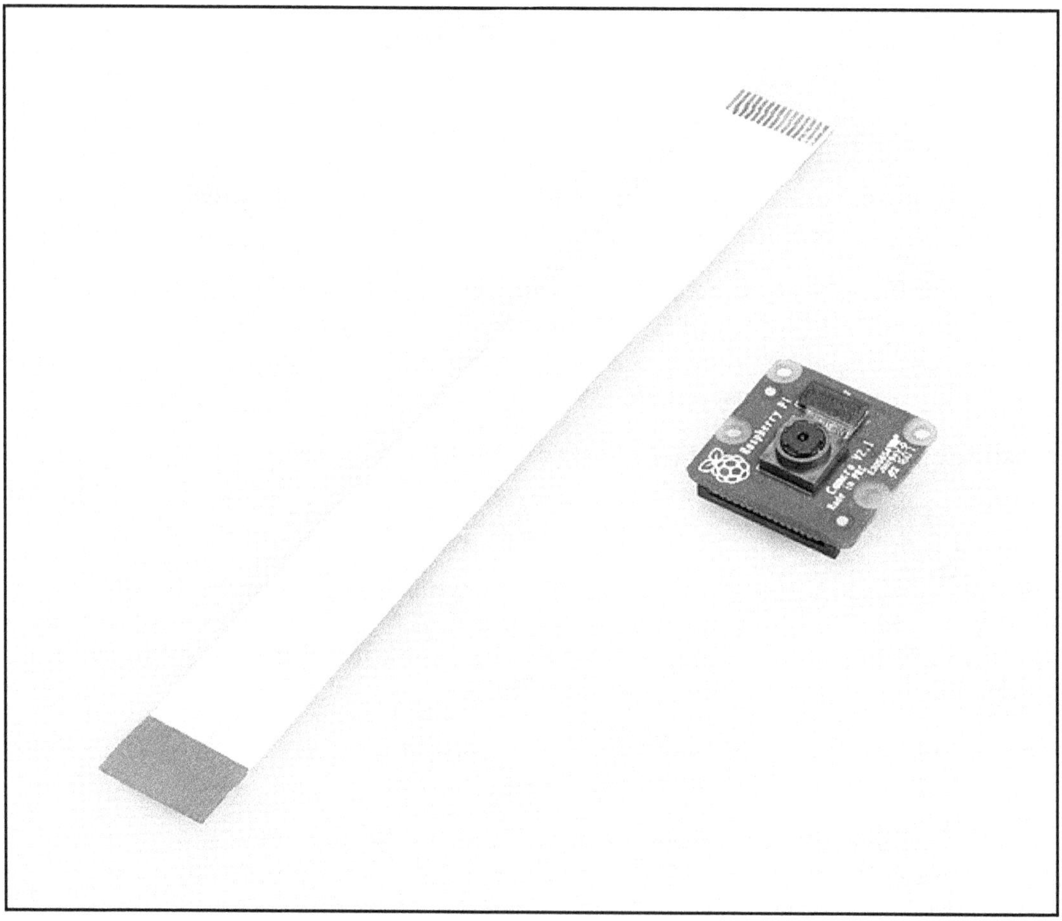

Image courtesy: https://commons.wikimedia.org/wiki/File:Raspberry_Pi_Camera_Module_v2_with_ribbon.jpg, License CC BY-SA 4.0

In the following image, we can see how the ribbon is connected to the CSI port of the Raspberry Pi:

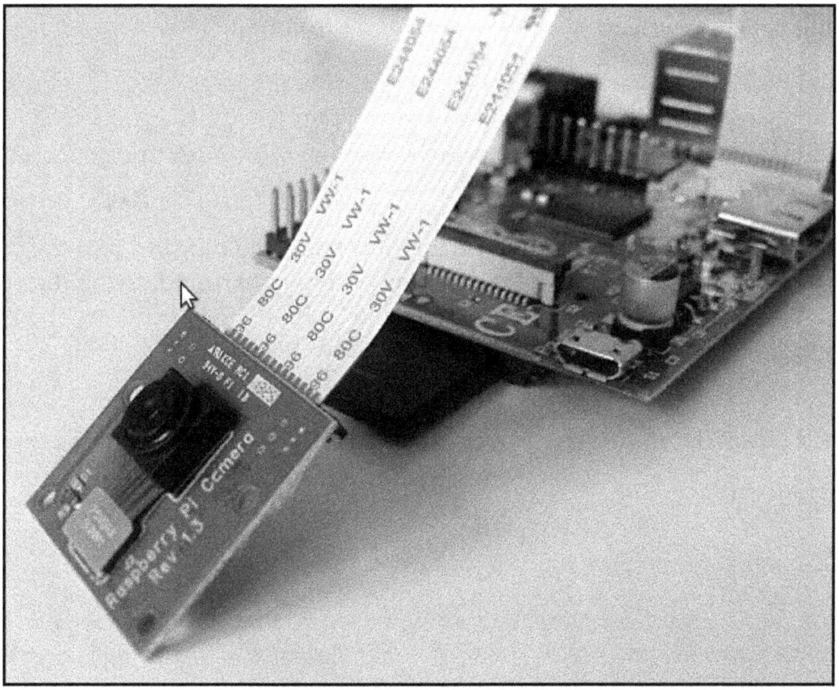

Image courtesy: https://www.flickr.com/photos/nez/9398354549/in/photostream by Andrew, License: CC BY-SA 2.0

The Pi Camera is able to provide an HD resolution (1920 x 1080 pixels) up to a frame rate of 30 **frames per second** (**FPS**). You can find the possible configurations for this in the documentation at `https://picamera.readthedocs.io/en/release-1.12/fov.html`. In `Chapter 2`, *Unit Testing of GoPiGo3*, we'll go over a specific test that you can run with your robot to check that this unit works properly.

Putting it all together

Now that you are familiar with the hardware, it is time to put everything together, connect it, and run a quick test to check that GoPiGo3 works properly. The assembly process is very well documented in a step-by-step guide in the official documentation, along with plenty of figures and photos; you can find this documentation at `https://www.dexterindustries.com/GoPiGo/get-started-with-the-gopigo3-raspberry-pi-robot/1-assemble-gopigo3/`.

Alternatively, you can use the Workbench training environment at `https://edu.workbencheducation.com/` and register a personal account for free to go through the same assembly process while registering your progress. If you do, then follow the two assembly stages that are covered in the official documentation from the manufacturer:

- **GoPiGo3 assembly stage 1**: `https://edu.workbencheducation.com/cwists/preview/26659-build-your-gopigo3-stage-1x`
- **GoPiGo3 assembly stage 2**: `https://edu.workbencheducation.com/cwists/preview/26655-build-your-gopigo3-stage-2x`

> Be aware that the cable of each motor has to be plugged into the connector on the same side. If you do this the other way around, then when you command a forward motion with the GoPiGo3 API libraries, the robot will go backward, and vice versa. If you find this happens to you, you just have to exchange the connectors so that it works properly.

To attach the Pi Camera, follow the instructions at `https://www.dexterindustries.com/GoPiGo/get-started-with-the-gopigo3-raspberry-pi-robot/4-attach-the-camera-and-distance-sensor-to-the-raspberry-pi-robot`. These extend upon the Raspberry Pi part.

Once you've assembled the base kit, you can proceed with the sensors:

- For the line follower, you can follow the instructions at `https://www.dexterindustries.com/GoPiGo/line-follower-v2-black-board-getting-started/`.
- For mounting the distance sensor, you can watch the video at `https://www.youtube.com/watch?v=R7BlvxPCll4`. This mounts the Pi camera on top of the Sero package, but you can mount the distance sensor instead.
- For the IMU sensor, plug it into one of the analog-digital Grove connectors (AD1 or AD2) and make sure that you fix its orientation, as shown in the following images (see the orientation of the *X*, *Y*, and *Z* axes).

The following image shows the GoPiGo3 with the three sensors attached to it:

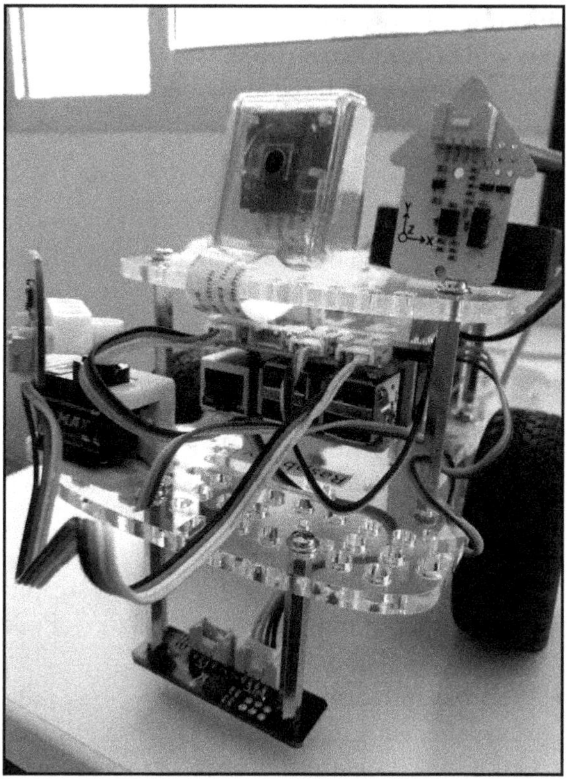

Be aware that the *Z* axis of the IMU sensor should point in the forward direction, the *X* axis should point to the left wheel, and—as a consequence—the *Y* axis should be along the vertical axis and pointing up. When properly calibrated and placed on a horizontal surface, the two angles, *pitch* and *roll*, will be zero, and if *Z* points to the magnetic south, the *yaw* angle will be zero too.

Quick hardware test

To perform a quick test and focus on the hardware at hand, we will use DexterOS, the Raspbian-based distro created by Dexter Industries to allow the user to get started quickly. Details of the operating system are provided at `https://www.dexterindustries.com/dexteros/`. Instead of having to deal with a full Linux desktop, Dexter Industries has simplified the interface by providing a simple web environment.

You can access it by connecting to the Wi-Fi access point called GoPiGo (a password won't be needed). This way, you will be connected directly to the robot with your laptop. Before installing it, let's review the resources we have available.

Resources

There are at least three sites/repositories that you will manage while working with the robot:

- The official libraries by Dexter Industries hosted in GitHub. These are as follows:
    - **GoPiGo3 official library**: `https://github.com/DexterInd/GoPiGo3`. This repository contains not only the API for several languages (Python, Scratch, C, Javascript, Go, and so on), but also examples and complete projects, some of which we will use in the next chapter to extend them to ROS.
    - **DI sensors library**: `https://github.com/DexterInd/DI_Sensors`. This repository covers all the sensors supplied by Dexter Industries, not only the ones used in GoPiGo3. There are APIs for Python, Scratch, C#, and Node.js.
    - **Web-based learning platform**: `https://edu.workbencheducation.com/`. This is a guided training site for GoPiGo3 if you are starting from scratch.

Getting started with DexterOS

After going through stages 1 and 2 of the *Putting it all together* section, you should go through the steps at `https://www.dexterindustries.com/dexteros/get-dexteros-operating-system-for-raspberry-pi-robotics/`, where you can download the image file of the operating system and follow the instructions to burn a micro SD card with the Etcher app (`https://www.balena.io/etcher/`). Follow these steps to get started with DexterOS:

1. Once you have placed the card in the slot of the Raspberry Pi, switch the GoPiGo board on and connect to the Wi-Fi network it creates (its SSID is GoPiGo, without a password).

2. After that, go to to `http://mygopigo.com` or `http://10.10.10.10` to gain access to the robot's enviroment, where the landing page looks as follows. You can find the step-by-step procedure at `https://edu.workbencheducation.com/cwists/preview/26657x`:

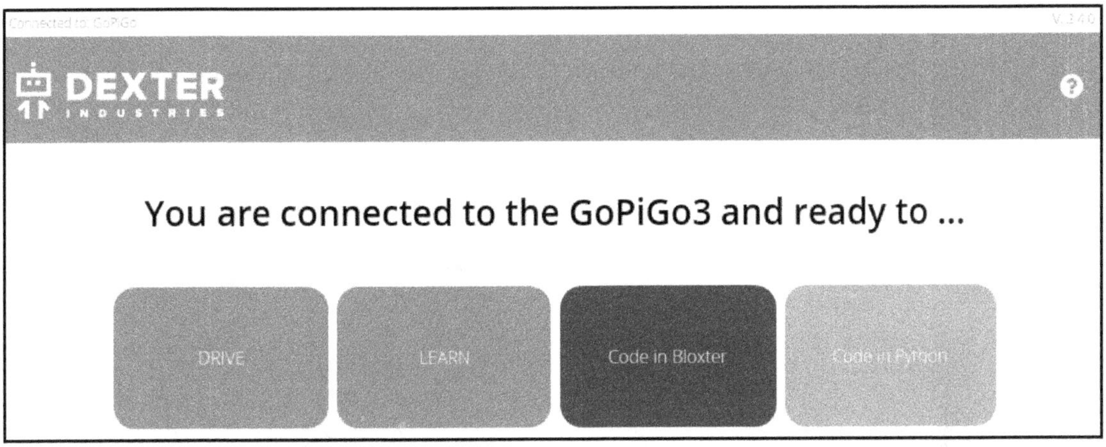

Be aware that if you keep your laptop's internet connection (wired), then you should connect to the robot IP address `http://10.10.10.10`. If you need help, you can visit the DexterOS forum at `https://forum.dexterindustries.com/c/DexterOS`.

From this point on, as you saw on the landing page, you can do the following:

- **DRIVE**: thereby moving the robot in all directions with a basic control panel.
- **LEARN**: by following the guided tutorials in Bloxter—one of the languages of choice—or Python using Jupyter Lab notebooks.
- **Code in Bloxter**: the visual programming language based on the open source Blockly by Google (`https://github.com/google/blockly`).
- **Code in Python**: the main environment that we will use to develop our training in robotics.

Next, we will start coding with Bloxter.

Coding with Bloxter

Of the available programming languages, **Bloxter** gives you the opportunity to learn about robotics without the complexities of typing out code. Using a visual interface, you can arrange and connect blocks and quickly develop basic programs to control GoPiGo3. Let's get started:

1. By clicking **LEARN** in the landing page and then clicking **Lessons in Bloxter**, you can access the available lessons, as shown in the following screenshot:

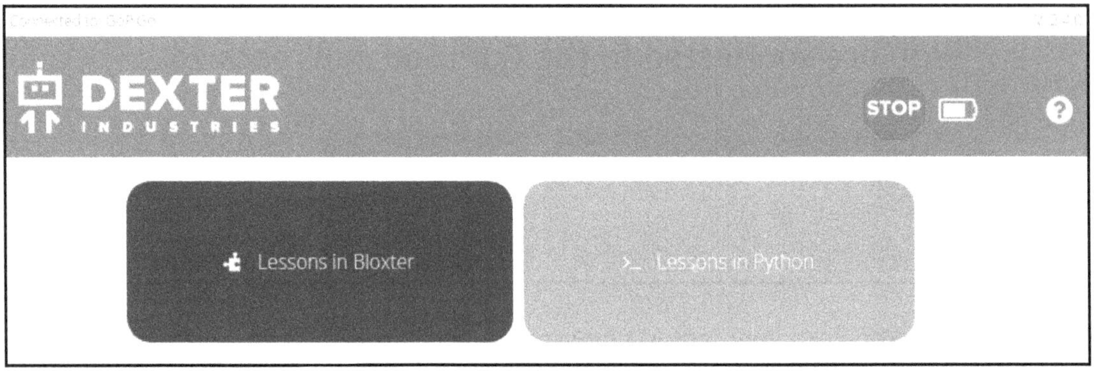

2. Select the one you prefer, taking into account that they are ordered by increasing difficulty:

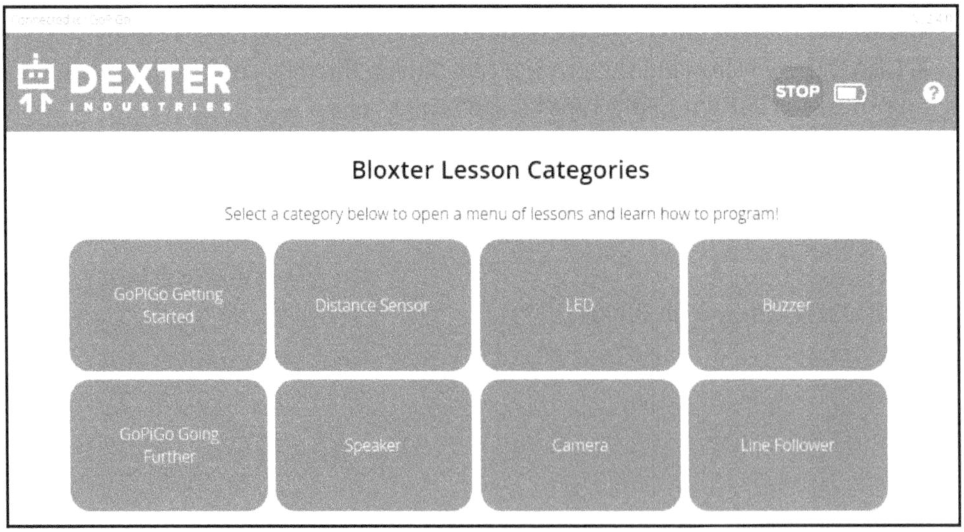

You are encouraged to complete the **LEARN** section for the Bloxter part before starting `Chapter 2`, *Unit Testing of GoPiGo3*. The lessons are easy to follow, and they teach you more about GoPiGo3 than what you could get by simply reading the documentation.

Calibrating the robot

Follow these steps to calibrate the robot:

1. Get back to the main page, `http://mygopigo.com/`, and click on the upper right-hand icon of the landing page. A help screen will pop up with two buttons, one for calibration and another for checking the battery status, as shown in the following screenshot:

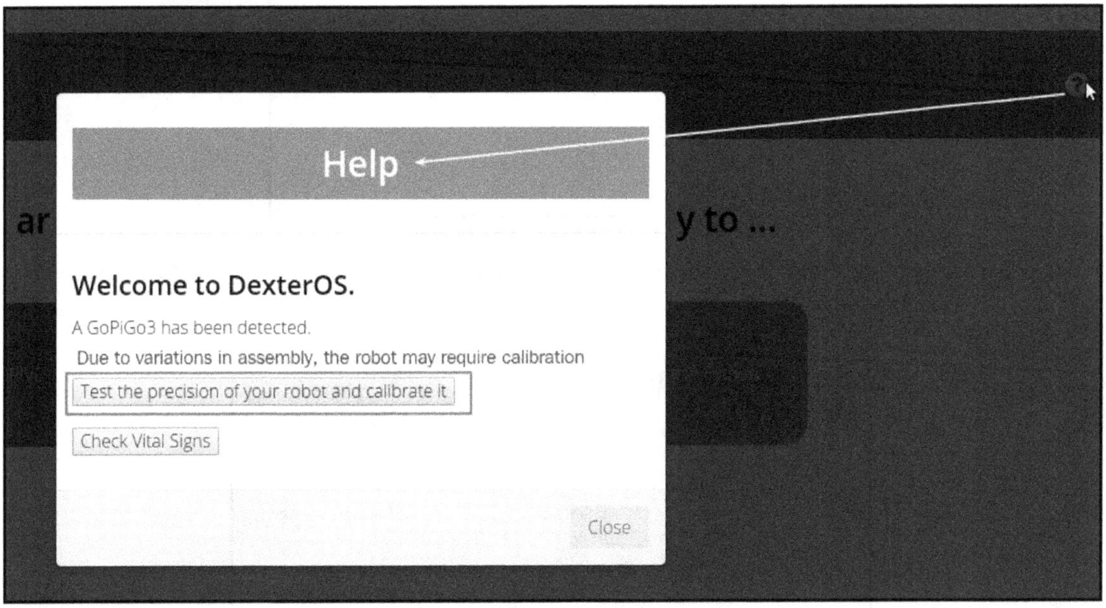

2. Check the vital signs by clicking **Check Vital Signs**:

3. Now, click the former button, **Test the precision of your robot and calibrate it**. You will see the following screen:

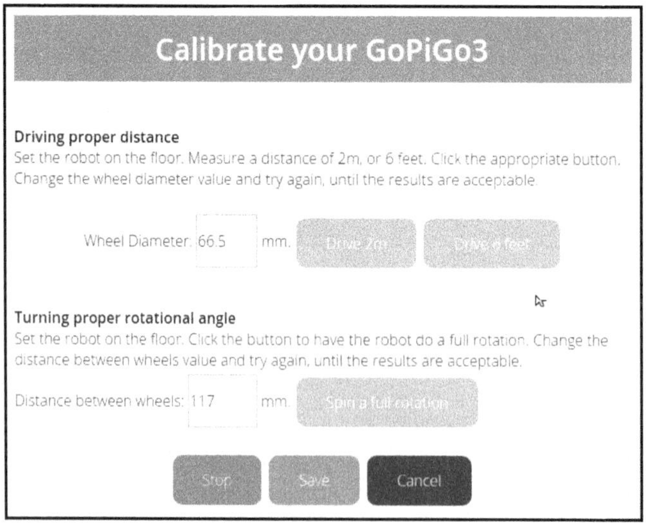

4. Adjust the dimensions so they match those of your robot:
    - **Wheel Diameter**: Mark a distance of 2 meters on the floor and click the **Drive 2m** button. If GoPiGo3 arrives just at the finish line, 66.5 mm is OK. If it does not arrive, you should increase the diameter a bit; if it goes past the finish line, you should reduce it. Test this again. By trial and error, you will find the diameter that best fits your own robot.
    - **Distance between wheels**: This procedure is very similar, with the only difference, that, in this case, the robot will rotate about itself when you press **Spin a full rotation**. If GoPiGo3 gives a complete turn of 360°, 117 mm is OK. If it does not complete the turn, you should reduce the distance; if it turns more than 360°, you should increase it instead. Test this again. By trial and error, you will be able to adjust this distance, just like in the case of the wheel diameter.

Driving the robot

To drive the robot, follow these steps:

1. Close the help window and select the **DRIVE** item on the main page.
2. By clicking this button, you gain access to a panel where there are controls to move the robot forward/backward and rotate it right/left. Go ahead and check that GoPiGo3 moves as expected.
3. Whenever you need to stop the motion, press the spacebar of the keyboard:

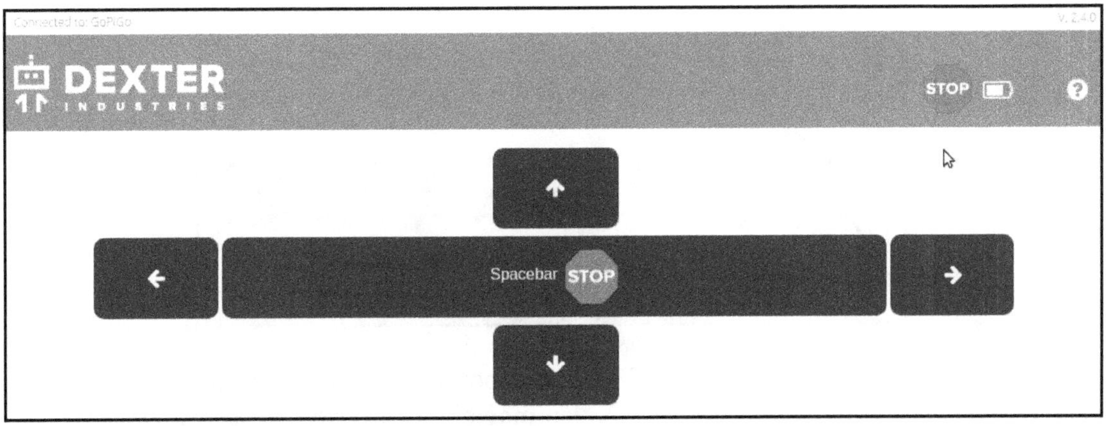

Next, we will check the sensors.

Checking the sensors

Follow these steps to check the sensors:

1. Go back to the main page and click **Code in Bloxter**.
2. On the right-hand side of the screen, you will see a sliding window, where you can indicate what port you have connected to each sensor. For the purposes of our example, we have set this arrangement:
    - The **distance sensor** plugged to I2C-1, the I2C on the left-hand side of GoPiGo3
    - The **line follower** to I2C-2, the I2C on the right-hand side
    - The **IMU** sensor to AD1 (on the left-hand side)
3. As soon as you select a port in DexterOS, you will be able to make a selection for each drop-down menu that appears, which is all about the real-time data coming from the sensors, as shown in the following screenshot:

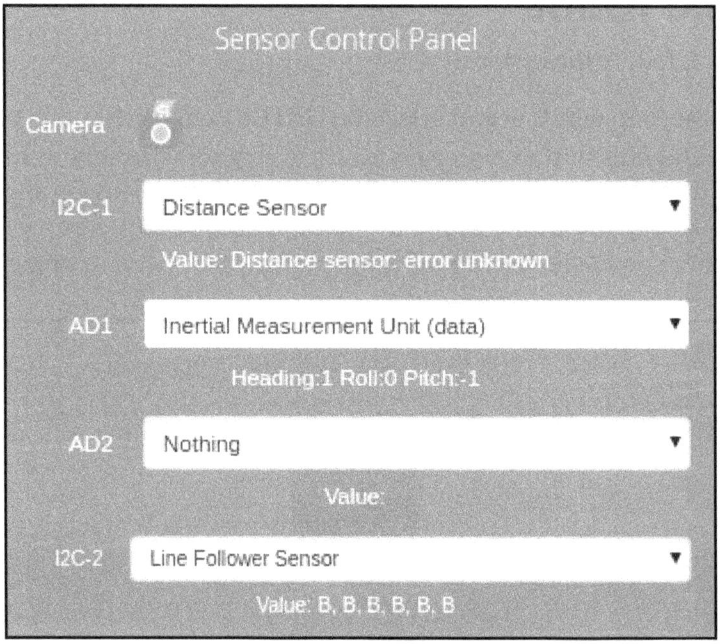

4. Check all three—that is, the distance sensor, line follower, and IMU—to provide readings. In the distance sensor, you may obtain an *error unknown* message. Don't worry about that; the sensor isn't damaged, it's just a software bug. When we use Python in the next chapter, you will definitely obtain good readings.

5. Finally, let's take a look at the data of the more complex sensor, the IMU. After setting its connection to AD1, the window will prompt you—when you select either **Inertial Measurement Unit** or **Inertial Measurement Unit (data)—**to spin the robot in the air for 3 seconds to calibrate its orientation. This way, we obtain the absolute orientation reference by combining Earth's gravity and magnetic fields. Then, if we select **Inertial Measurement Unit** from the drop-down list, we will see the Euler angles that were reported in real time. If they've been calibrated properly, we should find the following:
    - All three angles of the Euler heading (yaw, roll, and pitch) are zero when GoPiGo3 is on a horizontal surface and facing east. In this situation, the *Z* axis (painted in the sensor) is pointing South.
    - In this position, if you rotate GoPiGo3 with your hands over 90° around the *Z* axis, then the roll angle will be 90° and the *X* axis will be pointing up (to the cenith).
    - Getting back to the original position, if you rotate GoPiGo3 with your hands +90° around the *X* axis, the pitch angle will be 90° and the *Y* axis will be pointing south.

The physical position of the IMU in GoPiGo3 can be seen in the following image:

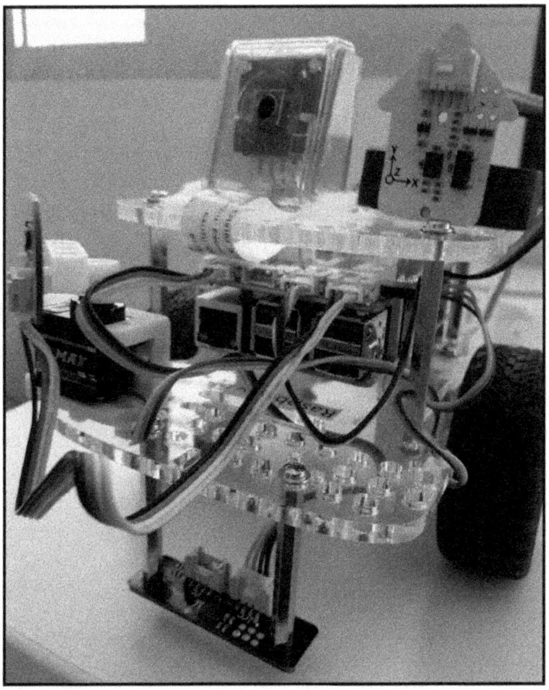

We will learn how to use the Pi Camera in the next chapter, when we make use of Python to program the robot.

Shutting down the robot

To finish your first journey with GoPiGo3, just long-press the black button of GoPiGo's red board. After a few seconds, the red LED will stop blinking, meaning that the shutdown process has completed.

Summary

In this chapter, we familiarized ourselves with the GoPiGo3 hardware by learning about the physical principles of the sensors and the motor the kit has. We checked that they worked properly by running some quick tests so that we can start programming tasks.

In the next chapter, we will learn how to program GoPiGo3 with Python while we execute some unit tests for each of its main components: the servomotors, distance sensor, line follower, IMU, and the Pi Camera.

Questions

1. Is it mandatory for a robot to have a computer such as Raspberry Pi?

   A) Yes, because the computer powers the controller board.
   B) No, because the computer is only needed for visualizing the software code on a screen. It may work alone with the controller if a program has been flashed to it.
   C) Not really; you could write a small program that controls the robot and flash it to the chip of the controller. Every time you power the robot, it will execute the program in an endless loop.

2. What kind of radiation is emitted by the distance sensor of GoPiGo3?

   A) Laser
   B) Infrared
   C) Ultrasound

3. Why can't you see the light being emitted by the line-follower sensor?

   A) Because the sensor has to be previously activated with a software command
   B) It does not emit light but a magnetic field
   C) It does not emit anything in the visible range of light

4. What is the purpose of the serial port of the GoPiGo red board?

   A) To allow us to program it in the same manner that you would use with an Arduino board, where you use the serial port to flash a program to the chip of the microcontroller.
   B) To synchronously transmit data from the sensor to the board.
   C) To access the serial pins of the GPIO from Raspberry Pi.

5. Does an IMU sensor provide an absolute orientation of the robot?

   A) Yes, since this is the goal of putting an accelerometer and a gyroscope together.
   B) Only if the IMU includes a magnetometer.
   C) Only in the case of IMU sensors with six degrees of freedom.

Further reading

You can find out more about the features of GoPiGo3 by reading the extensive official documentation provided by the manufacturer:

- Dexter Industries GoPiGo3 documentation: `https://gopigo3.readthedocs.io`
- Dexter Industries DI-Sensors documentation: `https://di-sensors.readthedocs.io`
- Pi Camera documentation: `https://picamera.readthedocs.io/`

2
Unit Testing of GoPiGo3

After finishing the assembly of the hardware, in this chapter, you will get familiar with how GoPiGo3 works using the JupyterLab environment, a friendly interface that takes the structure of a notebook composed of human-readable paragraphs followed by Python code snippets. You will produce two versions of each test program: the JupyterLab notebook and the pure Python script.

Using these programming tools, you will test each sensor/actuator individually and check that they're working properly while learning about the technology behind each of them.

We will be covering the following topics:

- Getting started with Python programming under the user-friendly environment Jupyterlab
- Testing the robot perception: distance sensor, line follower, and 2D
- Testing the robot actuation: motors and encoders

If you follow the practical exercises, you'll learn how the different packages (sensors, motors, and so on) build up the whole robot, what is measured with sensors, and how to systematically test sensors and actuators at the unit level.

Technical requirements

The code for the first section, *Getting started with Python and Jupyterlab,* is included within the image of *DexterOS,* the custom operating system supplied by the manufacturer of GoPiGo3. In `Chapter 1`, *Assembling the Robot,* we explained how to get this image and burn it to an SD card. This was explained in the *Quick hardware testing* section in the *Getting started with DexterOS* sub-section.

The code for this chapter is in the GitHub repository of the book, located at `https://github.com/PacktPublishing/Hands-On-ROS-for-Robotics-Programming/tree/master/Chapter2_Unit_Tests`. At the beginning of the *Unit testing of sensors and drives* section, we explain how to clone the code locally in the Raspberry Pi.

Getting started with Python and JupyterLab

JupyterLab is a very extensive tool in the Python community because it lets you write a program as if you were solving a mathematics problem in a school class. That is to say, you write the heading, then the problem statement and the initial data. After this declaration, you write a paragraph explaining the operation that you are going to perform, and then you write the Python line(s) that perform such operation in a *code cell.* For every operation you repeat the same steps:

1. A human-readable paragraph explaining the next operation, which is formatted with the well-known *markdown syntax* `https://commonmark.org/help/`.
2. A code cell with the lines of Python that perform the operation.
3. Repeat steps 1 and 2 for every code snippet that perform a single operation. The final one will provide the solution to the problem..

Here's a self-explaining example for reading the distance sensor of GoPiGo3:

Problem statement:

You want to read the distance sensor every 1 second and provide the real time output reading in three units: centimeters, milimeters and inches

Solution:

Import required Python modules

- **EasyDistanceSensor** for accessing the distance sensors readings
- **time** to set the interval between consecutive readings

```
from di_sensors.easy_distance_sensor import EasyDistanceSensor
from time import sleep
```

Instantiate the distance object

Create the object *my_sensor*, which is of the *EasyDistanceSensor* class

```
my_sensor = EasyDistanceSensor()
```

Read the sensor

Launch an infinite loop that is executed one time per second. You use the 3 methods provided by the *EasyDistanceSensor* class to obtain the reading:

- *.read()* for centimeters
- *.read_mm()* for milimeters
- *.read_inches()* for inches

```
while True:
  read_distance = my_sensor.read()
  read_distance_mm = my_sensor.read_mm()
  read_distance_inch = my_sensor.read_inches()

  print("distance from object: {} cm or {} mm or {} in".format(read_distance,read_distance_mm,read_distance_inch))

  sleep(1)
```

```
distance from object: 15 cm or 149 mm or 5.5 in
distance from object: 9 cm or 90 mm or 3.5 in
distance from object: 14 cm or 146 mm or 5.9 in
distance from object: 20 cm or 213 mm or 8.7 in
```

Next, we are going to explain how to launch JupyterLab for GoPiGo3.

Launching JupyterLab for GoPiGo3

In DexterOS, you have two lessons that explain both Jupyter notebooks and controlling the robot with Python:

1. You can access them by navigating to `http://mygopigo.com` or `http://10.10.10.10`, and click on **LEARN**, then **Lessons in Python**:

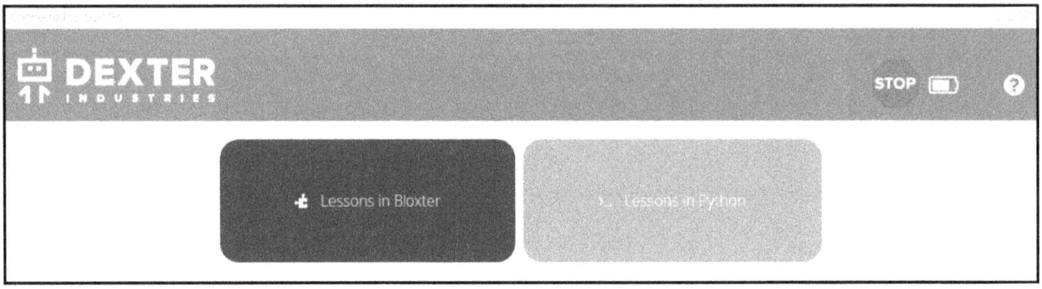

   The JupyterLab environment is then launched, and in the left part of the window you will see two files:

   - `1_Moving_Around.ipynb` is a Jupyter notebook that explains step-by-step how to move the robot forward and rotate it. Follow the instructions given in the notebook to execute the commands.
   - `2_The_Environment.ipynb` is another example that explains how to deal with JupyterLab: run a cell, stop the execution, and so on. If you got stuck in the previous notebook, follow this one and return to the first afterward.

2. Now let's try `1_Moving_Around.ipynb`. The following command makes the robot go forward 10 cm:

```
my_gopigo.drive_cm(10)
```

3. If you prefer to work in inches, use this command:

```
my_gopigo.drive_inches(10)
```

4. If you execute both in the same code cell, you will notice a small gap before the execution of the second command:

```
my_gopigo.drive_cm(10)
my_gopigo.drive_inches(10)
```

Now let's perform a physical test with the robot:

1. Mark a sign on the floor in the starting point, drive 10 cm forward and 10 cm backward and find how precise the motion is:

```
# Forward
my_gopigo.drive_cm(10)
my_gopigo.drive_inches(10)

# Backward
my_gopigo.drive_cm(-10)
my_gopigo.drive_inches(-10)
```

   You should find that it returns exactly to the starting point. Errors that we measured with a micrometer (three times) were +1.29 mm, -0.76 mm, and +2.16 mm. Positive means that it passed over the starting point when driving back, and negative means that it did not arrive at the starting point.

2. If you add the distances (10 cm + 10 inches = 35.4 cm) into one forward command, and then make another command for moving back the same distance, the errors we measured were (again, we did it three times) -0.01 mm, -1.40 mm, and -0.72 mm:

```
# Forward
my_gopigo.drive_cm(+35.4)

# Backward
my_gopigo.drive_cm(-35.4)
```

   You can see that the pause caused by using two commands introduces an error that is in the order of 1 mm. Using only one command for forward and one for backward substantially reduces the error.

3. We can perform a similar test for turning:

```
# Turn clockwise (right)
my_gopigo.turn_degrees(90)

# Turn counterclockwise (left)
my_gopigo.turn_degrees(-90)
```

4. Other useful commands are as follows:

```
my_gopigo.forward()
my_gopigo.backward()
my_gopigo.right()
my_gopigo.left()
```

5. To stop the robot, use this command:

   ```
   my_gopigo.stop()
   ```

6. It is crucial to note that software flow may not be compatible with robot physics. Try this sequence and observe what GoPiGo3 does:

   ```
   my_gopigo.forward()
   my_gopigo.backward()
   my_gopigo.right()
   my_gopigo.left()
   ```

It seems that only the last line is executed, which is `my_gopigo.left()`. What is actually happening is that the commands execute so quickly (a few milliseconds each) that the robot's inertia does not allow enough time for GoPiGo to move forward, backward, or right. Remove the last line to check it: the only command you see physically executed is now `my_gopigo.right()`.

> TIP: One of the most challenging issues when programming a robot is understanding its dynamics, because something that may seem to be a software bug may be an unexpected physical response of the robot. So, prior to developing the software, you must make sure you understand the physics of the problem, including its mass (inertia), friction forces, the maximum load on the motors, the power supply limit, and the battery level. The list of variables coming from the physical world can be endless, and you should apply your knowledge of mechanics and electricity to successfully develop functional software.

A possible solution for this simple case is to specify in the sequence the distance or angle you want it to move:

```
my_gopigo.drive_cm(-10) # Forward
my_gopigo.drive_cm(10) # Backward
my_gopigo.turn_degrees(90) # Right (clockwise)
my_gopigo.turn_degrees(-90) # Left (counterclockwise)
```

To save your work in DexterOS, you have to do it from the `~/.lessons_python` folder. This is owned by `pi:users`, while the DexterOS user is `jupyter` (issue the `$ whoami` command in a terminal or just see it in the prompt). Go one level above in the tree, and create a folder there with any name you wish. Then save your changes in that location with **File | Save Notebook As...**.

Hardware testing

To access these notebooks in DexterOS outside of the LEARN environment, navigate to `http://mygopigo.com` or `http://10.10.10.10`, and click on **Code in Python**. JupyterLab will be launched:

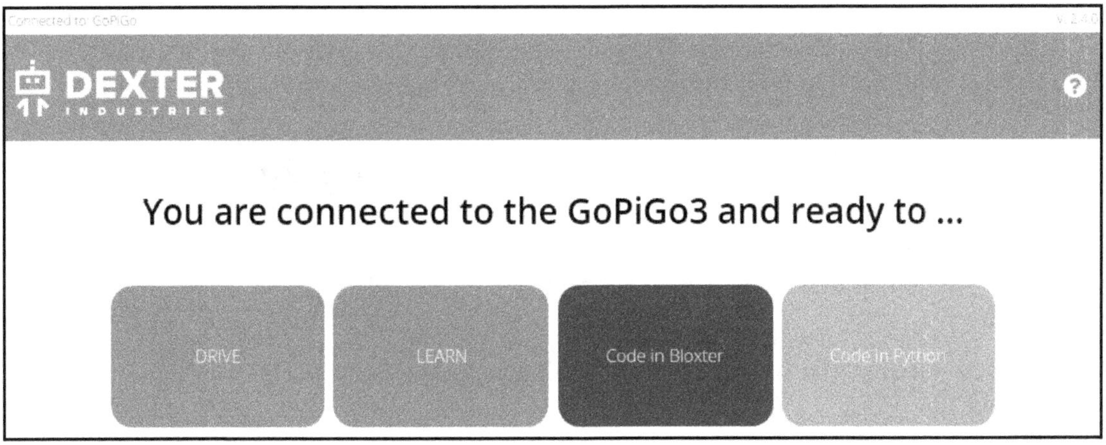

In the file manager view on the left side of the screen, you will find these two notebooks:

- One of them is `First Ride Around.ipynb`, which provides a widget to drive the robot with a visual panel:

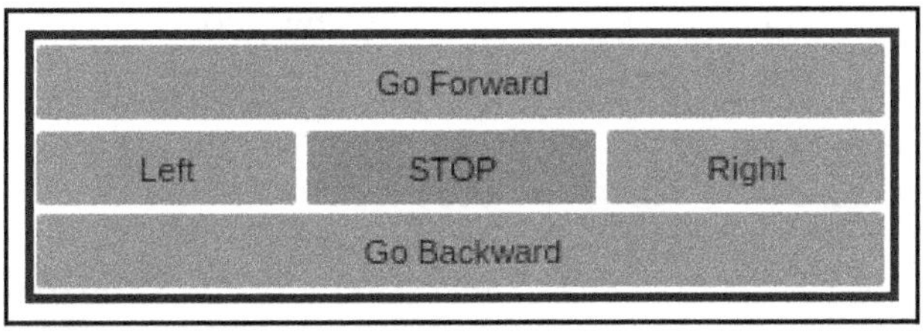

- The other notebook is `Hardware Testing.ipynb`, which runs specific tests for batteries, LEDs, and encoders. What we should expect in terms of GoPiGo3's behavior is addressed in the following subsection.

Testing battery, LEDs, and motors/encoders

Open the notebook and go through each cell to understand what it does.

Battery level

The following command reads and displays the current battery voltage. It should be above 9 V for GoPiGo3 to work properly. When the batteries are not charged enough, you will lose the Wi-Fi connection with the robot and you will have to recharge them or replace them with new batteries:

```
print("Battery voltage : ", GPG.get_voltage_battery() )

OUTPUT ===> Battery voltage : 9.114
```

Next, we will look at hardware information and voltage levels.

Hardware information and current voltage levels

The next block of commands prints information of the manufacturer, hardware and firmware versions, and battery levels. The following relates to the output:

- *Battery voltage* is the same as before. The measurement gives a slightly different value, 9.294V, and it is OK.
- *5V voltage* is that of the power supply to the Raspberry Pi through its GPIO. GoPiGo red board has a power regulator that transforms the 9V raw input to a regulated 5V. If the batteries are properly charged, this value should be very close to 5V as shown here:

```
print("Manufacturer : ", GPG.get_manufacturer() )
print("Board : ", GPG.get_board() )
print("Serial Number : ", GPG.get_id() )
print("Hardware version: ", GPG.get_version_hardware())
print("Firmware version: ", GPG.get_version_firmware())
print("Battery voltage : ", GPG.get_voltage_battery() )
print("5v voltage : ", GPG.get_voltage_5v() )

OUTPUT ===>
Manufacturer     :  Dexter Industries
Board            :  GoPiGo3
Serial Number    :  F92DD433514E343732202020FF112535
Hardware version:  3.x.x
Firmware version:  1.0.0
Battery voltage :  9.294
5v voltage       :  4.893
```

Next, we will check the LEDs and blinkers.

LEDs and blinkers

There are two LEDs on top of the board that simulate GoPiGo3's eyes. By running the following block of code, they will change their color:

```
colors = [ (255,0,0), (255,255,0), (255,255,255), (0,255,0), (0,255,255),
(0,0,255), (0,0,0)]
for color in colors:
    GPG.set_eye_color(color)
    GPG.open_eyes()
    time.sleep(0.5)
```

The blinkers are two small red LEDs underneath the red board at the front. The following code makes them blink 5 times:

```
for i in range(5):
 GPG.led_on("left")
 GPG.led_on("right")
 time.sleep(0.5)
 GPG.led_off("left")
 GPG.led_off("right")
 time.sleep(0.5)
```

Check it visually, and be aware that no message appears in the console.

Motors and encoders test

The following cell will run for approximately 5 seconds and will report encoder readings:

```
GPG.set_motor_dps(GPG.MOTOR_LEFT | GPG.MOTOR_RIGHT, 100)
start = time.time()
lapse = 0

while lapse < 5:
   lapse = time.time() - start
   time.sleep(0.5)
   print("LEFT: {}
RIGHT:{}".format(GPG.get_motor_status(GPG.MOTOR_LEFT),GPG.get_motor_status(
GPG.MOTOR_RIGHT)))

passed_test = GPG.get_motor_status(GPG.MOTOR_LEFT)[0]==0 and
GPG.get_motor_status(GPG.MOTOR_RIGHT)[0]==0
GPG.set_motor_dps(GPG.MOTOR_LEFT | GPG.MOTOR_RIGHT, 0)

if passed_test:
```

```
    print("Test passed.")
else:
    print("Test failed.")
```

And these are the results:

```
LEFT: [0, 26, 3095, 101]  RIGHT:[0, 26, 4806, 101]
LEFT: [0, 26, 3146, 101]  RIGHT:[0, 28, 4856, 101]
LEFT: [0, 26, 3196, 101]  RIGHT:[0, 28, 4906, 101]
LEFT: [0, 26, 3246, 101]  RIGHT:[0, 26, 4957, 96]
LEFT: [0, 26, 3296, 101]  RIGHT:[0, 26, 5007, 101]
LEFT: [0, 26, 3347, 101]  RIGHT:[0, 28, 5057, 101]
LEFT: [0, 24, 3397, 105]  RIGHT:[0, 26, 5107, 96]
LEFT: [0, 21, 3447, 96]  RIGHT:[0, 26, 5158, 101]
LEFT: [0, 26, 3497, 101]  RIGHT:[0, 21, 5208, 101]
LEFT: [0, 28, 3547, 96]  RIGHT:[0, 28, 5258, 96]
LEFT: [0, 33, 3598, 101]  RIGHT:[0, 33, 5308, 101]
Test passed.
```

We should see the message at the end telling if the test has passed. Do not worry at the moment about understanding the numbers: it is an internal test in which GoPiGo3 checks itself and reports whether it passed or failed.

If it's successful, you can go ahead with the following test. GoPiGo3 will drive forward for 10 cm and the output value at the end should be approximately 10. Should this test fail, you can stop the robot by clicking the red **Stop** button at the top:

```
GPG.reset_encoders()
#GPG.set_speed(GPG.DEFAULT_SPEED)
GPG.drive_cm(10)
encoders_read = round(GPG.read_encoders_average())
print("Drove {:.2f} cm".format(encoders_read))
if encoders_read == 10:
 print("Test passed.")
else:
 print("Test failed.")
```

If everything goes well, you will obtain this message:

```
Drove 10.00 cm Test passed.
```

Again, should this test fail you can stop the robot by pressing the red **Stop** button at the top. After these basic tests, we have enough understanding of GoPiGo3's hardware and software to perform the unit testing, which is the main goal of this chapter.

Unit testing of sensors and drives

In this section, we will run some simple scripts in Python by using Jupyter Notebooks. From a terminal in your laptop, clone the book repository and go into the `Chapter2_Unit_Tests` folder to access the files for this chapter:

```
$ git clone
https://github.com/PacktPublishing/Hands-On-ROS-for-Robotics-Programming
$ cd Hands-On-ROS-for-Robotics-Programming/Chapter2_Unit_Tests
```

For completeness, we have included the notebooks used in the previous section inside the `lessons_GettingStarted` folder.

Quick start with sensors and motors

To enter the Python environment of your robot, switch on the red board and connect to the *GoPiGo* Wi-Fi network from your laptop. Then, visit the following URL in the browser:

`http://10.10.10.10/python`

In JupyterLab, focus on the left-hand side, where the file storage is shown. To run any of the examples, you will have to manually upload to the location where you want to place it in the robot storage. Create a folder named `Chapter2_Unit_Tests` and upload the required files. We will indicate at the beginning of each exercise which file we will use.

Driving around

The files in this sub-section are in the `./Chapter2_Unit_Tests/drivingAround` folder of the repository. You can upload them one by one. Afterward, launch a shell session in JupyterLab by opening a launcher tab:

1. Select the **Terminal** icon from the tab, as shown in the following screenshot:

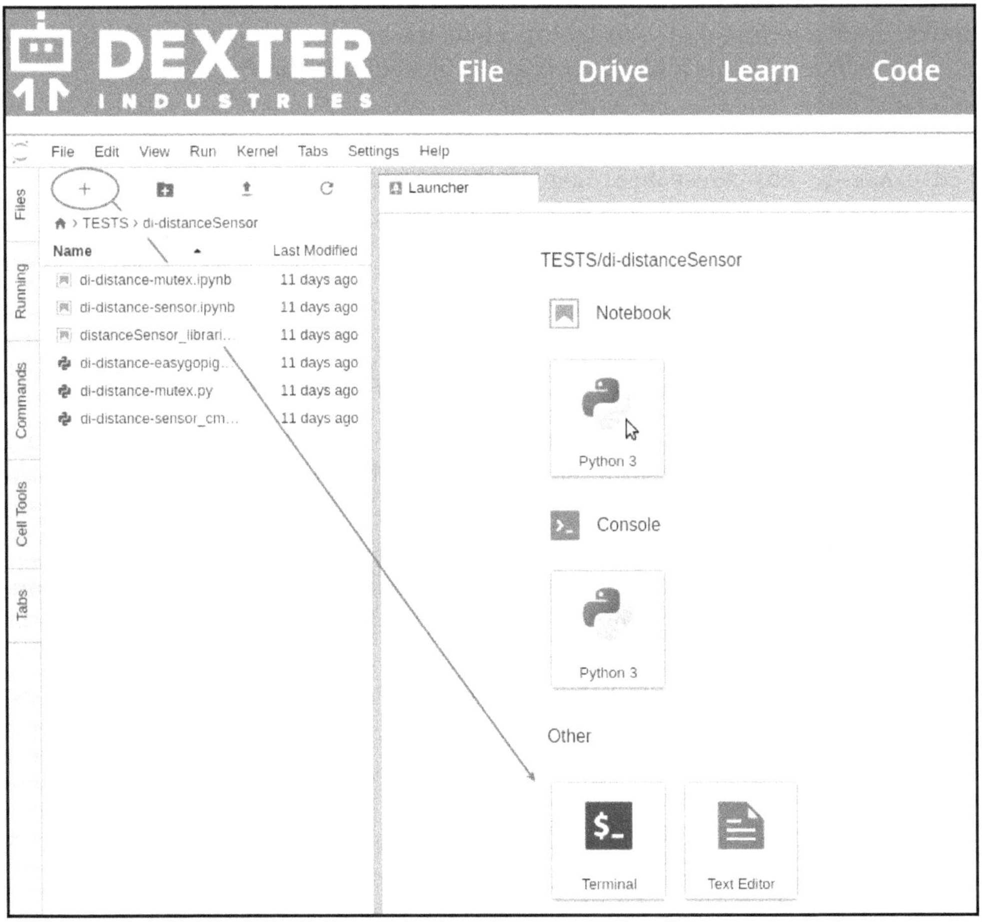

2. Execute the scripts from the terminal by changing to their location:

```
$ cd./Chapter2_Unit_Tests/drivingAround
$ python <name_of_script.py>
```

The first script is `1-easyMotors.py`, and it plays a very simple sequence:

1. Move the motors forward for 1 second.
2. Stop the motors for 1 second.
3. Drive the robot for 50 cm and then stop.
4. Turn right for 1 second.
5. Turn left for 1 second.
6. Stop.

You can see the first part of the script in the following code listing, which shows the commands to move forward for 1 second, and then stop for another second:

```
# import the time library for the sleep function
import time
# import the GoPiGo3 drivers
from easygopigo3 import EasyGoPiGo3

# Create an instance of the GoPiGo3 class.
# GPG will be the GoPiGo3 object.
gpg = EasyGoPiGo3()

print("Move the motors forward freely for 1 second.")
gpg.forward()
time.sleep(1)
gpg.stop()
print("Stop the motors for 1 second.")
time.sleep(1)
```

The second part is shown here, and it includes the commands to drive forward 50 cm, then turn right for 1 second, and then turn left for 1 second:

```
print("Drive the motors 50 cm and then stop.")
gpg.drive_cm(50, True)
time.sleep(1)

print("Turn right 1 second.")
gpg.right()
time.sleep(1)
print("Turn left 1 second.")
gpg.left()
time.sleep(1)

print("Stop!")
gpg.stop()
print("Done!")
```

The next script is `2-driveSquare.py`, and it does what it says: it draws a square on the floor. If we use a `for` loop that makes a 90º rotation after each 30 cm drive, we get a program with very few lines:

```
from easygopigo3 import EasyGoPiGo3

gpg = EasyGoPiGo3()
length = 30

for i in range(4):
  gpg.drive_cm(length) # drive forward for length cm
  gpg.turn_degrees(90) # rotate 90 degrees to the right
```

The `3-circularMoves.py` Python script makes GoPiGo3 travel a semicircle in one direction, and then in the opposite, returning to the starting point:

```
from easygopigo3 import EasyGoPiGo3

gpg = EasyGoPiGo3()

gpg.orbit(180, 50) # draw half a circle
gpg.turn_degrees(180) # rotate the GoPiGo3 around
gpg.orbit(-180, 50) # return on the initial path
gpg.turn_degrees(180) # and put it in the initial position
```

The program `4-drawEight.py` combines arcs and straight paths to draw an 8 shape on the floor:

```
from easygopigo3 import EasyGoPiGo3

gpg = EasyGoPiGo3()
radius = 30

gpg.orbit(-270, radius) # to rotate to the left
gpg.drive_cm(radius * 2) # move forward
gpg.orbit(270, radius) # to rotate to the right
gpg.drive_cm(radius * 2) # move forward
```

Finally, the program `5-accelerateForward.py` illustrates how to accelerate the robot. The sequence is pretty simple:

1. Set an initial speed and an end speed.
2. Calculate a step by dividing the interval between them by 20.
3. Run a loop that increases the speed in the step value in each iteration.
4. Perform one iteration every 0.1 seconds.
5. After 2 seconds, GoPiGo3 will reach the end speed and will stop:

```
from easygopigo3 import EasyGoPiGo3
from time import time, sleep

gpg = EasyGoPiGo3()

# setting speed to lowest value and calculating the step increase in speed
current_speed = 50
end_speed = 400
step = (end_speed - current_speed) / 20
gpg.set_speed(current_speed)

# start moving the robot at an ever increasing speed
gpg.forward()
while current_speed <= end_speed:
  sleep(0.1)
  gpg.set_speed(current_speed)
  current_speed += step

# and then stop it
gpg.stop()
```

Let's now test all of the sensors with which we have equipped the robot.

Distance sensor

To communicate with the sensors, we will use the DI-sensors Python library `https://github.com/DexterInd/DI_Sensors`.

First of all, we need to revise the port connections. This is what we will review now.

Check port connections

The following diagram should be of great help when connecting sensors to GoPiGo3 ports, in order to make sure that the hardware is correctly wired:

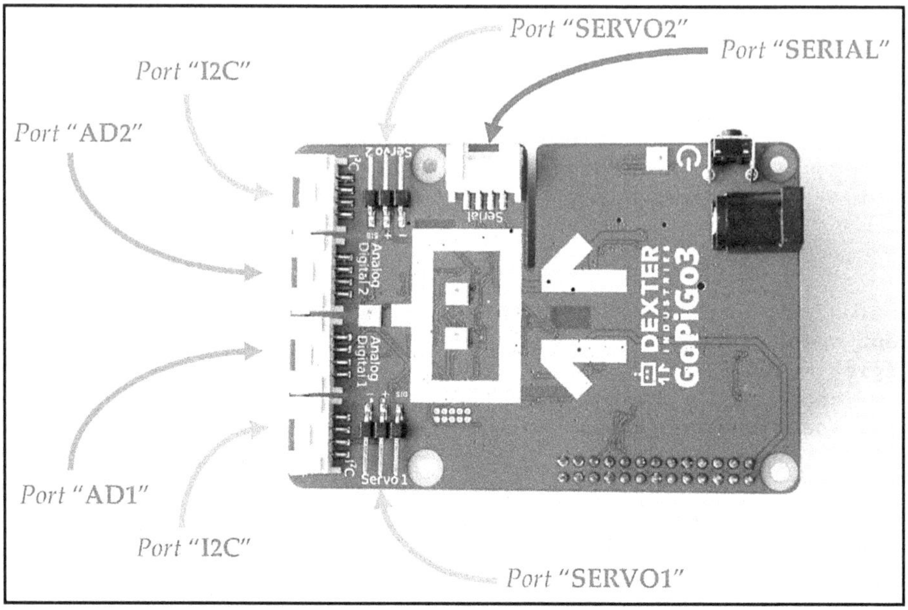

Image courtesy: Dexter Industries: https://gopigo3.readthedocs.io/en/master/_images/gpg3_ports.jpg

From the previous chapter, you should remember the purpose of each port:

- Ports **AD1** and **AD2** are general-purpose *input/output* ports.
- Ports **SERVO1** and **SERVO2** are the servo controller ports.
- The **I2C** ports are where you connect *I2C-enabled* devices.
- The **SERIAL** port is where you can connect *UART-enabled* devices.

Given this description, check that sensors are connected as we described in the first chapter:

- The **Distance sensor** should be plugged into **I2C-1**, the I2C port on the left side of GoPiGo3.
- The Servo package should be connected to **SERVO1**.
- The **Line follower** should be plugged into **I2C-2**, the I2C port on the right side.
- The **IMU** sensor should be connected to **AD1** (on the left side).

Distance sensor unit test

Although you have connected the distance sensor to the **I2C-1** port, be aware that GoPiGo3 software libraries will not require you to specify in the script which of the two ports you are using. It will be automatically detected.

The files for testing are located in the `./Chapter2_Unit_Tests/DI-distance` folder of the repository. You can upload them one by one to DexterOS:

- `di-distance_cm.py`
- `di-distance-easygopigo_mm.py`

Afterward, open a shell session in JupyterLab by opening a launcher window and selecting the terminal icon from it. Execute the scripts from the terminal by moving to their location:

```
$ cd./Chapter2_Unit_Tests/DI-distance
$ python <script.py>
```

The first script is `di-distance_cm.py`. It takes a reading at a fixed time rate:

```
# import the modules
from di_sensors.easy_distance_sensor import EasyDistanceSensor
from time import sleep

# instantiate the distance object
my_sensor = EasyDistanceSensor()

# and read the sensor iteratively
while True:
  read_distance = my_sensor.read()
  print("distance from object: {} cm".format(read_distance))

  sleep(0.1)
```

The publishing interval is 0.1 seconds, as specified in the line `sleep(0.1)`. The detailed specification of the distance sensor API can be found at `https://di-sensors.readthedocs.io/en/master/api-basic.html#easydistancesensor`. The `my_sensor.read()` method provides the distance in centimeters, but there are an other two methods if you prefer to use other units:

- `my_sensor.read_mm()` is for millimeters.
- `my_sensor.read_inch()` is for inches.

The second script, `di-distance-easygopigo_mm.py`, imports the GoPiGo3 library as per `https://github.com/DexterInd/GoPiGo3`, which implicitly includes the sensor library, `https://github.com/DexterInd/DI_Sensors`. You can see that it uses the same class methods to take readings. In this case, the function that reads the distance in millimeters is used:

```
# import the GoPiGo3 drivers
import time
import easygopigo3 as easy

# This example shows how to read values from the Distance Sensor

# Create an instance of the GoPiGo3 class.
# GPG will be the GoPiGo3 object.
gpg = easy.EasyGoPiGo3()

# Create an instance of the Distance Sensor class.
# I2C1 and I2C2 are just labels used for identifyng the port on the GoPiGo3
board.
# But technically, I2C1 and I2C2 are the same thing, so we don't have to
pass any port to the constructor.
my_distance_sensor = gpg.init_distance_sensor()

while True:
    # Directly print the values of the sensor.
    print("Distance Sensor Reading (mm): " +
str(my_distance_sensor.read_mm()))
```

For completeness, we have included in the folder of this chapter the two libraries:

- `easysensors.py` for the sensors
- `easygopigo3.py` for the robots

If you inspect the latter, you will see this `import` line at the beginning of the file:

```
import easysensors
...
try:
 from di_sensors import easy_distance_sensor
```

This way, we can incorporate the DI sensors you need to increase the perception capabilities of your robot. Let's go through an example to better understand the libraries provided by Dexter Industries.

GoPiGo3 API library

The main class of the robot is `GoPiGo3`, and you can see the class structure in the following diagram. The **easysensors** library is imported (inherited) by the `EasyGoPiGo3` class, and so has access to all sensor methods. The class structure is shown in the following diagram:

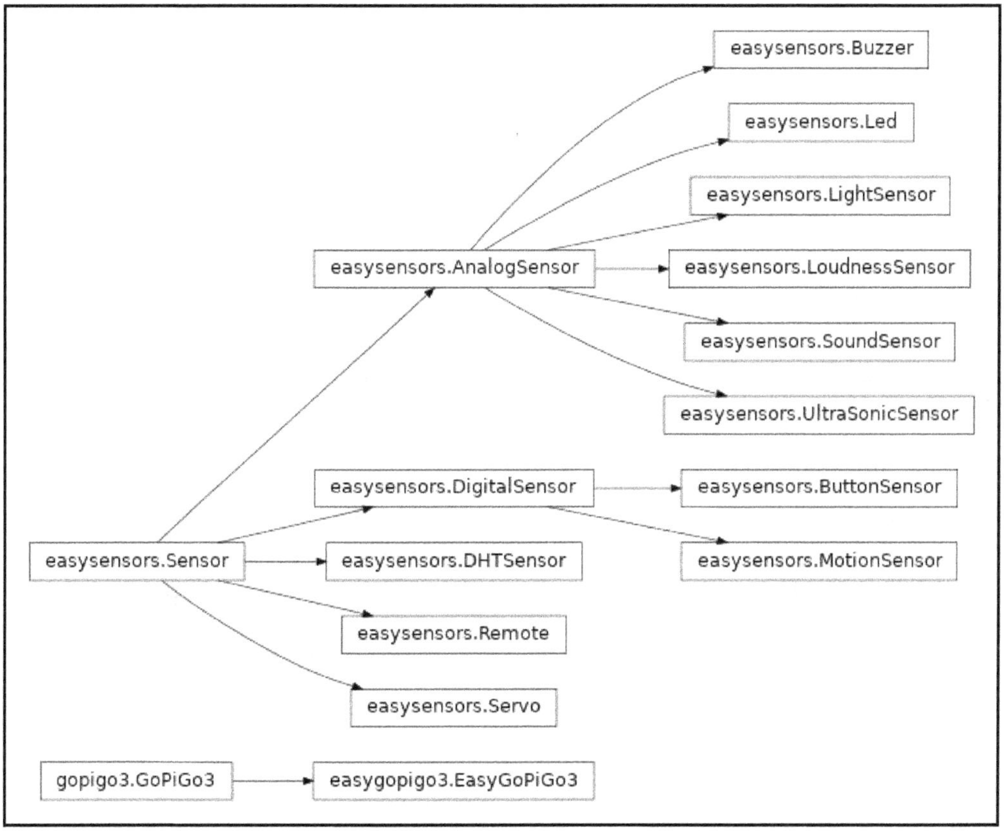

Image courtesy: Dexter Industries: https://gopigo3.readthedocs.io/en/master/_images/inheritance-e4cb3d2ae1367b2d98aab1a112a1c8e1b7cd9e47.png

A summarized table with all the functions of the class is available at https://gopigo3.readthedocs.io/en/master/api-basic/structure.html#functions-short-list. The API library is covered in detail at https://gopigo3.readthedocs.io/en/master/api-basic/easygopigo3.html

Hence, using the easygopigo3.py library, you create an instance of your robot and initialize the sensors you need. For example, the distance sensor is initiated with this method of the class:

```
easygopigo3.EasyGoPiGo3.init_distance_sensor([port])
```

In our script, this is accomplished in three lines:

```
import easygopigo3 as easy
gpg = easy.EasyGoPiGo3()
my_distance_sensor = gpg.init_distance_sensor()
```

In the first line, you import the easygopigo3 library. In the second line, you instantiate a robot object, and in the third line, you initialize the distance sensor. Then you are ready to acquire data from the sensor:

```
my_distance_sensor.read_mm()
```

In short, if you use the easygopigo3.py library, *the top-level object is the robot itself.* On the other hand, if you were using the sensors in a custom project that doesn't deal with GoPiGo, the top-level object is yet to be created unless you already have the corresponding library available. If you don't, it is your task to define a class that represents that entity (a weather station, for example) and import the DI sensors library. This is the topic of the next sub-section.

DI sensors API library

Each sensor type has its own class and methods. In the `./Chapter2_Unit_Tests/DI-distance/di-distance_cm.py` script, we were using the DI-sensors library. The class structure is shown in the following screenshot and explained at `https://di-sensors.readthedocs.io/en/master/structure.html#library-structure`:

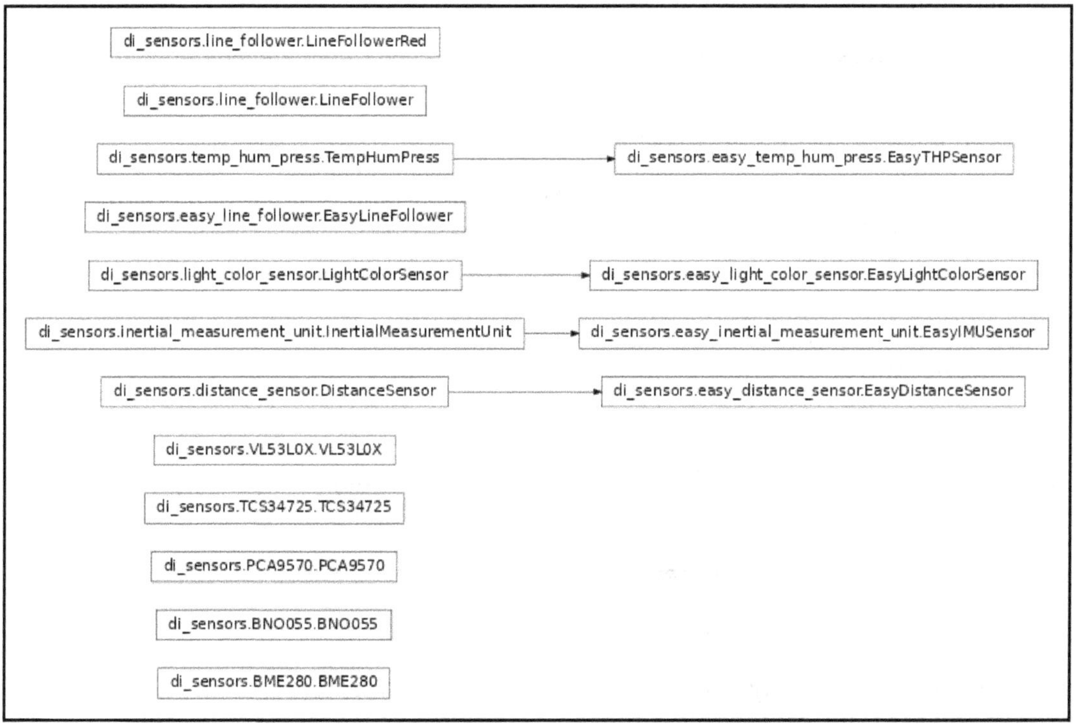

Image courtesy: Dexter Industries: https://di-sensors.readthedocs.io/en/master/_images/inheritance-a8243413ad98ddae26cdf121c775ad137c7f2e30.png

Summarized tables with methods for all DI sensors are shown at `https://di-sensors.readthedocs.io/en/master/structure.html#functions-short-list`. You will find two alternatives of usage for each sensor:

- The **easy methods** – prepended with the `easy` prefix – are for quick usage and provide top-level functionalities. You can see the syntax on the right-hand side of the preceding diagram.

- The **advanced methods** without the `easy` prefix are for developer use and provide low-level control.

The distance sensor is managed with the following class:

```
di_sensors.easy_distance_sensor.EasyDistanceSensor([...])
```

In our script,the sensor is initialized as follows::

```
from di_sensors.easy_distance_sensor import EasyDistanceSensor
my_sensor = EasyDistanceSensor()
```

The preceding lines are described as follows:

- On the first line, you import the class of the distance sensor. Be aware that you need to import just the `EasyDistanceSensor` class from `di_sensors.easy_distance_sensor`.
- On the second line, you instantiate the distance sensor object with the `Easy` class.

Then you are ready to acquire data from the sensor:

```
read_distance = my_sensor.read()
```

Compare with the case of not using the `easy` option. The syntax is similar, the only difference being the removal of the `_easy` and `Easy` prefixes:

```
from di_sensors.distance_sensor import DistanceSensor
my_sensor = DistanceSensor()
read_distance = my_sensor.read()
```

The same scheme will apply to the other sensors we will cover later, specifically, the line follower and the IMU.

Servo package

The servo package consists of a **Pulse Width Modulation** (**PWM**) servomotor. It is controlled in an open loop by applying a voltage that produces a proportional rotation of the motor shaft in a 180° amplitude coverage. In the following image there is a small rod that lets us visualize the rotation. In our GoPiGo3 assembly, we will see rotating the distance sensor:

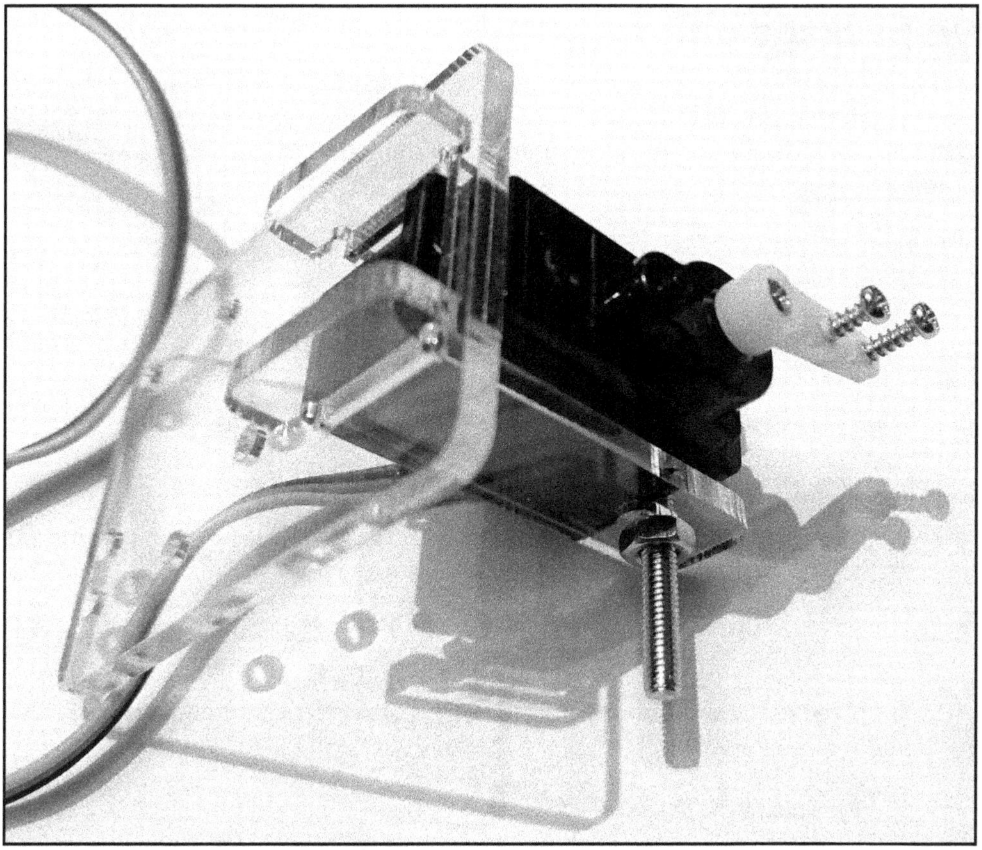

Image courtesy: Dexter Industries: https://www.dexterindustries.com/wp-content/uploads/2017/06/GoPiGo3-Servo-Assembly-11-600x338.jpg

The servo package is part of the GoPiGo3 API library described in the *Distance sensor unit test* section. Its API methods are detailed at `https://gopigo3.readthedocs.io/en/master/api-basic/sensors.html#servo`.

Next, we will carry out some unit tests to check that it rotates properly. Since we have mounted the distance sensor with the servo package, we can measure the distance to obstacles in a 180º field of view by rotating the servo. In the test, we will also calibrate the actual field of view your robot will be able to cover.

Servo package unit test

The test consists of placing the distance sensor with respect to the servomotor shaft in an angular position that covers the entire front view of GoPiGo3, from left to right. All the explanations and code are in a Jupyter notebook located at `./Chapter2_Unit_Tests/DI-servo_package/servoCalibration.ipynb`:

1. First, we create the servo object from the `EasyGoPiGo3` class. To do this, we need to import the library and instantiate `GoPiGo3`:

    ```
    import easygopigo3 as easy
    my_gpg3 = easy.EasyGoPiGo3()
    ```

2. Then we initiate the servo:

    ```
    servo = my_gpg3.init_servo()
    ```

3. We check that we are able to fully rotate the servo. You should have unmounted the sensor to prevent collisions with the robot's chassis:

    ```
    servo.rotate_servo(0)   # This is 0º position
    servo.rotate_servo(180) # This is 180º position
    ```

4. Then, move the servo to the middle of the interval, 90º, and attach the sensor so that it faces forward:

    ```
    servo.rotate_servo(90)
    ```

5. Adjust the angle so that the sensor faces exactly forward. In our case, this angle is 95°. You should find out what yours is:

    ```
    servo.rotate_servo(95)
    ```

6. Once we have checked the reference position, let's set up the actual limits. To do that, find the angles that preclude any interference with the sensor by the robot chassis. In our case, these angles are 30º and 160º. Again, you should find what yours are:

    ```
    servo.rotate_servo(30)
    servo.rotate_servo(160)
    ```

That's all for the setup of the servo package with sensor distance.

For advanced users, there is another API library, **gopigo3**, that provides low-level access to the hardware in order for you to take full control of it. Although covering such low-level programming is not in the scope of the book, you are provided with a Python script, `Servo.py`, that briefly illustrates the usage of one of its methods. This script sets the rotation in terms of *counts* instead of *rotation angle*. We perform a loop when the counts go from 1000 to 2001.

This way, you have access to the full resolution of the servomotor, and you should have an idea of the size of the rotation steps it can provide.

Line follower

As mentioned in the first chapter, the line follower is composed of six pairs of emitter-receivers to sense six aligned points on the floor in order to determine how decentered the robot is with respect to the black line it will be following.

The line follower is also part of the GoPiGo3 API library. Its methods are detailed at `https://di-sensors.readthedocs.io/en/master/api-basic.html#easylinefollower`. The unit test we are going to perform consists of validating that the sensor can tell which side of a black line the robot is.

Line follower unit test

The Jupyter notebook for the test is `./CH2-uniTests/di-lineFollower/lineFollower_libraries.ipynb`. This notebook also shows you both the easy library, `di_sensors.easy_line_follower`, and the advanced version, `di_sensors.line_follower`, in action.

When the sensor reports *center*, this is because the robot is well centered on the black line, as shown in the next image. This means that the two external emitter-receiver pairs report *white*, while the pairs between them report *black*:

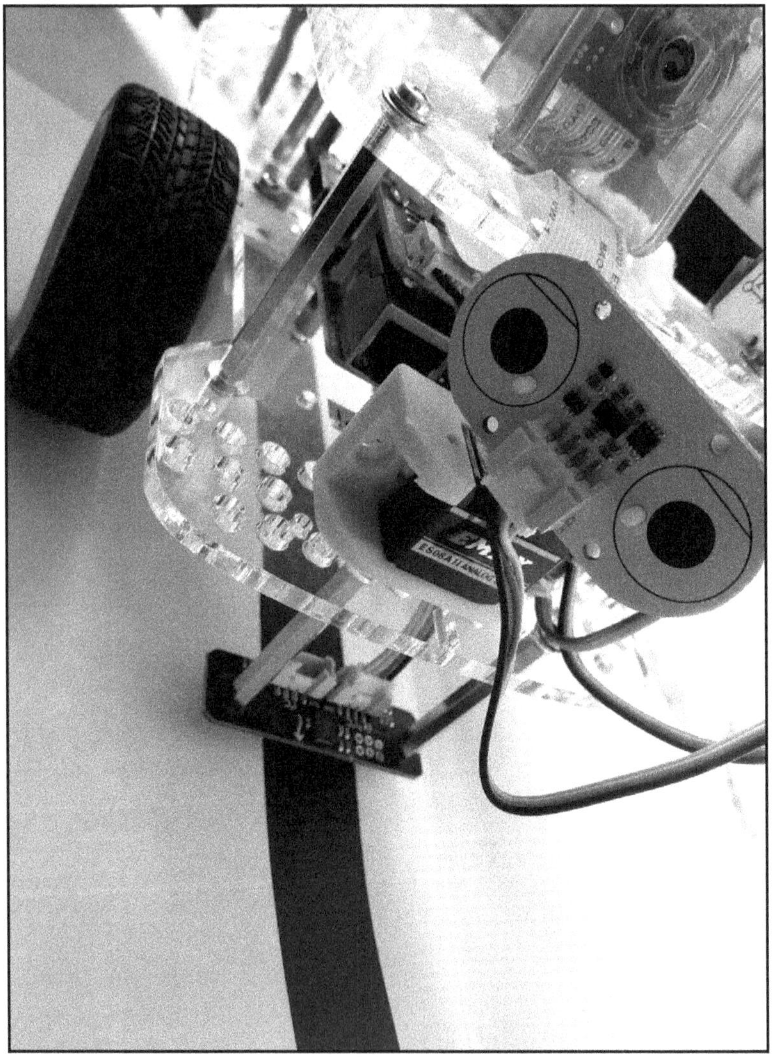

When the sensor reports *left*, it means that the line is slightly to the left of the robot, as shown in the following photo. This means that the left-most pair reports *black*, the central ones *black*, and the rest *white*:

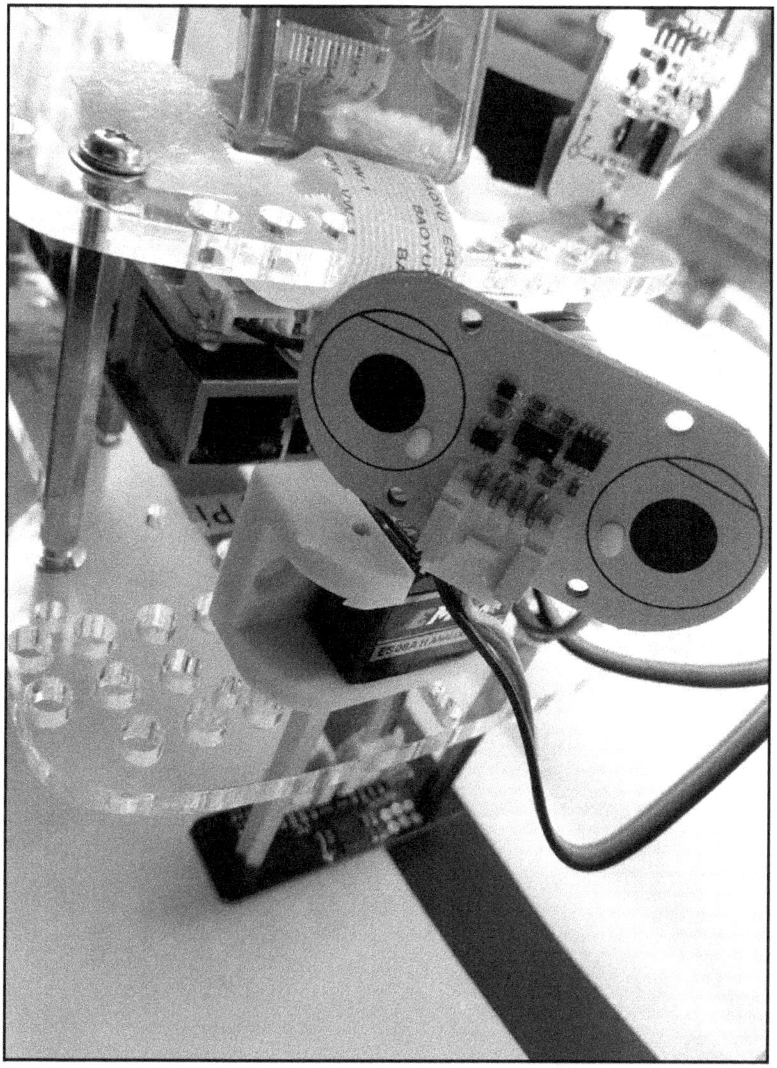

If the robot ends up completely off the line, all the pairs report *white* and the line follower throws *white* overall. The opposite is also true: if all the pairs report *black*, it may be because the black line is too wide or the robot has been placed on a dark surface.

Inertial Measurement Unit (IMU)

With the supplied IMU, we have the following sensors:

- Magnetometer, three axes
- Gyroscope, three axes
- Accelerometer, three axes

As explained in the previous chapter, with these three sensors – once their calibration setup is complete – it is possible to obtain the absolute orientation of the robot in the 3D space, quantified in terms of Euler angles. Additionally, we also have the temperature because the DI IMU ships with a temperature sensor.

IMU unit test

The Jupyter notebook for the test is `./Chapter2_Unit_Tests/DI-IMU/IMU_reading.ipynb`. The corresponding DI sensor API library is documented at `https://di-sensors.readthedocs.io/en/master/examples/imu.html`.

When running the notebook, you can check that the reported Euler angles are OK.

Raspberry Pi

Pi is an essential perception device for any robot. Take into account that about 80% of the perception data that the human brain processes comes from vision. In this section, we are only going to test that Pi is able to take photos to check that it works properly. In `Chapter 10`, *Applying Machine Learning in Robotics*, we will use object recognition algorithms on images captured by the camera. Hence, the robot will exhibit smarter behavior and will be able to recognize colors, shapes, faces, and so on.

Pi unit test

The Jupyter notebook for the test is `./Chapter2_Unit_Tests/PiCamera/Taking_Photos.ipynb`. This simple example takes a photo and creates a histogram, that is, a chart showing how many colors and the amount of each color that is present in the image.

So, let's take an image with few colors to make it easier to understand the information from the histogram. The following photo, taken with the GoPiGo3 , has the characteristics we need:

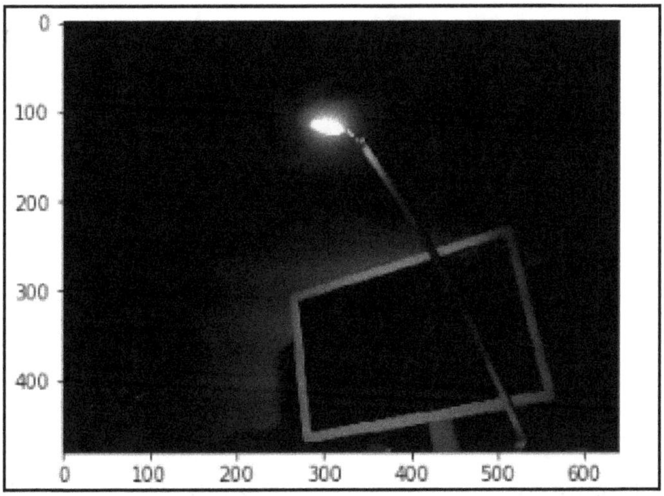

This is accomplished with the following code snippet:

1. First, we take the photo. Then we convert it to a JPG image format and save it, and, finally, we show the result on the screen:

```
with picamera.PiCamera() as camera:
 camera.resolution = (640, 480)
 camera.capture(output, format = 'rgb', use_video_port = True)

img = Image.fromarray(output)
img.save("../photo.jpg")

plt.imshow(output)
```

2. Finally, we draw the histogram with this simple command:

```
img = Image.open("../photo.jpg")
histogram = img.histogram()
plt.plot(histogram)
```

And this is the result:

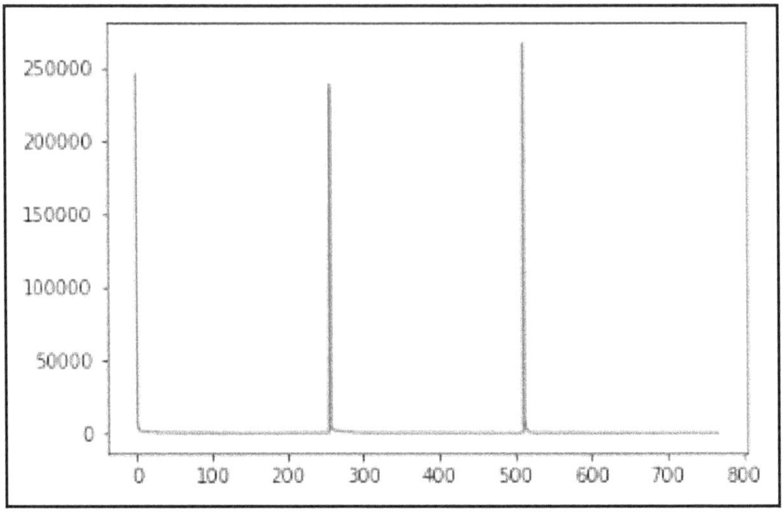

You may see that colors are concentrated into three points. The scale of the x axis goes from 0 (black) to 768 (white). This interval is explained by taking into account that 24-bit RGB pixels have values that go up to 768. Let's see what each vertical line means:

- The line at $x = 0$ represents the zones that are black.
- The line at $x = 525$ represents the more shiny area, which is the light bulb.
- Finally, it is easy to infer that $x = 250$ corresponds to the lighter areas around the monitor, which appear to have a gray tone.

With this last test, we have validated that our robot has all of its sensors and drives working properly and we are ready to proceed to the next step, building functional behaviors.

GoPiGo3 projects

The official GoPiGo3 software hosted on Github at `https://github.com/DexterInd/GoPiGo3` provides several interesting projects. At this point, we recommend you clone the repository and upload some of these projects to the robot running DexterOS. The projects are located in this folder of the repository: `https://github.com/DexterInd/GoPiGo3/tree/master/Projects`.

You can try, for example, the *Basic Robot Control* project, located at `https://github.com/DexterInd/GoPiGo3/tree/master/Projects/BasicRobotControl`. You have the means to get full control of the drives, LEDs, and blinkers using the keys of your wireless keyboard that's connected to the robot:

```
[key w ] : Move the GoPiGo3 forward
[key s ] : Move the GoPiGo3 backward
[key a ] : Turn the GoPiGo3 to the left
[key d ] : Turn the GoPiGo3 to the right
[key <SPACE> ] : Stop the GoPiGo3 from moving
[key <F1> ] : Drive forward for 10 centimeters
[key <F2> ] : Drive forward for 10 inches
[key <F3> ] : Drive forward for 360 degrees (aka 1 wheel rotation)
[key 1 ] : Turn ON/OFF left blinker of the GoPiGo3
[key 2 ] : Turn ON/OFF right blinker of the GoPiGo3
[key 3 ] : Turn ON/OFF both blinkers of the GoPiGo3
[key 8 ] : Turn ON/OFF left eye of the GoPiGo3
[key 9 ] : Turn ON/OFF right eye of the GoPiGo3
[key 0 ] : Turn ON/OFF both eyes of the GoPiGo3
[key <INSERT>] : Change the eyes' color on the go
[key <ESC> ] : Exit
```

Up to this point, you may argue that the method we have used to put new files in the robot is tedious. We have used DexterOS so that you be able to start quickly, without having to deal with Linux issues.

From the next chapter, we will use Ubuntu 16.04 on your laptop and a full Linux desktop, Ubuntu 18.04, inside GoPiGo3 . This will allow the robot to connect to the internet, and this will let you clone repositories directly into the robot.

Summary

In this chapter, we have familiarized ourselves with the GoPiGo3 Python environment by running simple programs that allow us to test robot sensors and actuators. We have checked them one by one in what is formally known as *unit testing*. This has served two goals: getting started with Python programming and functionally validating your robot hardware.

Next, we will leave the robot for one chapter, and we will discuss the core software concepts of ROS that we will later use to program GoPiGo3.

Questions

1. If you have this sequence of Python commands, what will GoPiGo3 do?

```
my_gopigo.drive_cm(10)
my_gopigo.turn_degrees(90)
```

A) It will drive 10 cm forward and then turn 90º to the right
B) It will drive 10 cm forward and then turn 90º to the left
C) It will turn 90º

2. What is the battery level required for GoPiGo3 to work properly?

A) Slightly above 9V is enough.
B) 5V, the same that the Raspberry Pi needs.
C) There is no minimum. If the voltage is low, the robot will drive slowly.

3. Which set of commands will make GoPiGo3 draw a right angle arc 60 cm in diameter?

A) `gpg.orbit(90, 60)`
B) `gpg.orbit(90, 30)`
C) `gpg.orbit(180, 30)`

4. What combination of the six sensor signals of the line follower does not correspond to GoPiGo3 being to the right of the black line? (w: white, b: black)

A) b-b-b-b-w
B) w-b-b-b-w
C) b-b-b-w-w

5. If you have a histogram of an image that consists of two vertical lines of equal height at $x = 0$ and $x = 768$, given that the color range of x is from 0 to 768, what colors are present in the image?

A) Gray, because it is the result of mixing black and white in equal proportions.
B) Half of the image is black and the other half is white.
C) It is not possible to get a histogram like that.

Further reading

To delve deeper into the technical aspects of GoPiGo3, you have very detailed information in the official guides listed here:

- Dexter Industries GoPiGo3 Documentation: `https://gopigo3.readthedocs.io`
- Dexter Industries DI-Sensors Documentation: `https://di-sensors.readthedocs.io`
- Pi camera documentation: `https://picamera.readthedocs.io/`

3 Getting Started with ROS

Robot Operating System (**ROS**) is an open source piece of software. Its development started at Willow Garage, a technology incubator and robotics research laboratory. Its origin dates back to several projects at Stanford University from the mid-2000s, where researchers found themselves reinventing the wheel every time they had to build the software for each project.

In 2007, Willow Garage took the lead and gave rise to ROS. The main goal was to reuse existing code and make it possible to prototype new robot designs quickly, focusing on high-level functionality and minimizing the need for editing code. If you are curious about how ROS has become the *de facto* standard for robot application development, you can view an interactive page at `https://www.ros.org/history`.

ROS is intended for the development of applications where different devices have to talk to each other in order to create a flexible and scalable environment. This chapter explains the basic concepts of ROS. It will introduce you to the framework using an easy language while avoiding very technical descriptions. This is because our first goal is to neatly show you what ROS is in a conceptual sense. In the following chapters, we will have the opportunity to cover technical descriptions; the ones that, in any case, you will need later in order to be able to use ROS in your projects.

In the first section of this chapter, we will cover how ROS works under the hood, and why it should not be simply considered as a specific-purpose programming language, but a framework for developing robotics apps. You will dive into the core concepts of the ROS graph and the asynchronous communication between nodes.

In the second section, you will be guided step by step to configure the ROS environment on your laptop.

In the third section, guided with a practical exercise, you will learn how to exchange simple messages between nodes using the command line.

Finally, we will give you an overview of the many available ROS packages that have been contributed by the open source community.

In this chapter, we will cover the following topics:

- ROS basic concepts and the ROS graph
- Configuring your ROS development environment
- Communication between ROS nodes: messages and topics
- Using publicly available packages for ROS

Technical requirements

The practical aspects of this chapter require you to have access to a desktop computer or laptop with either of these two Ubuntu versions:

- Ubuntu 16.04 Xenial
- Ubuntu 18.04 Bionic

Long-term support (**LTS**) Ubuntu versions are maintained by Canonical for the next 5 years. Also, these kind of versions are released in even years. Hence, Ubuntu 16.04- released in 2016- will be maintained up to 2021, while Ubuntu 18.04- released in 2018- will be maintained up to 2023. We will not consider odd-year versions, that is, Ubuntu 17 or Ubuntu 19 because they are development releases that are not LTS.

Open Robotics releases a new version of ROS every year coinciding with every Ubuntu version. The correspondence is as follows:

- ROS Kinetic running under Ubuntu 16.04 Xenial
- ROS Melodic running under Ubuntu 18.04 Bionic

The most used version as of the writing of this book is ROS Kinetic. The practical examples provided in the following chapters are valid for both Ubuntu 16.04 and Ubuntu 18.04. Hence, they will work for ROS Kinetic as well as for ROS Melodic.

When we don't make any distinction between Ubuntu or ROS versions, you should assume that they work for the two versions covered. If there is some difference in the commands or scripts to be run depending on the version, we will mention it explicitly.

The code for this chapter can be found in `Chapter3_ROS_basics` of the book repository, which is hosted on GitHub at `https://github.com/PacktPublishing/Hands-On-ROS-for-Robotics-Programming/tree/master/Chapter3_ROS_basics`. In the *Setting up the ROS package* section, you will learn how to download the code and make it work with your ROS installation.

ROS basic concepts

Early on, researchers of robotics at Stanford University found that prototyping software for robots was an intensive programming task, as they had to start coding from scratch for every project. There was a time in which programming languages such as C++ and Python were used for robotics as the general programming languages they are, and that fact required great efforts to build every piece of software to provide a robotic level of functionality, such as navigation or manipulation.

It was not only a question of the reusability of the code, but it was also a matter of how things worked in robotics. In procedural programming, the typical flow of a program executes one step after another, as shown in the following diagram:

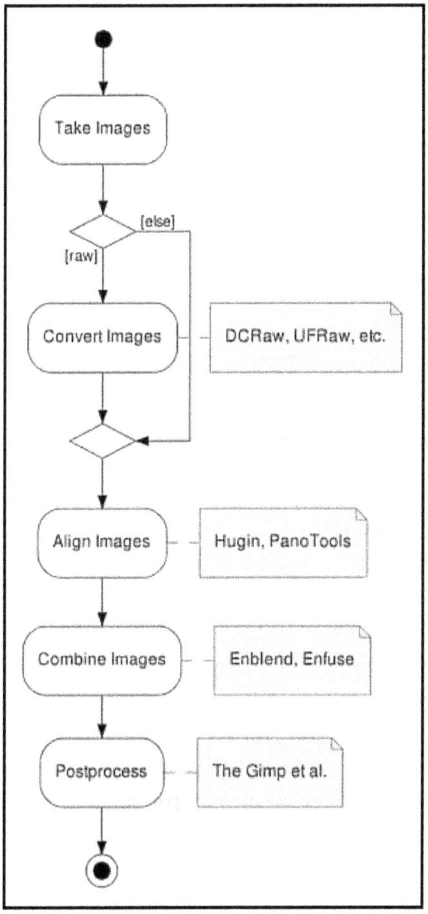

The task that this program executes is to combine multiple images into one, as can be easily inferred. From our robotic point of view, the main drawback of a process working like this is that, if some steps fail to execute, then the process cannot go on and, therefore, fails to deliver its results, that is, a combined image. If we use the analogy of robotics, this would mean that a humanoid robot transporting a light object (for example, a paper book) from one place to another may fail in its task if one of its arms does not work properly (the motor that drives the articulation of its elbow is broken, for example). The humanoid should be able to do the task with the other arm for sure. And this is what ROS does!

Let's take a look at the following example of a ROS graph.

The ROS graph

This graph is to ROS what a workflow diagram is to procedural programming:

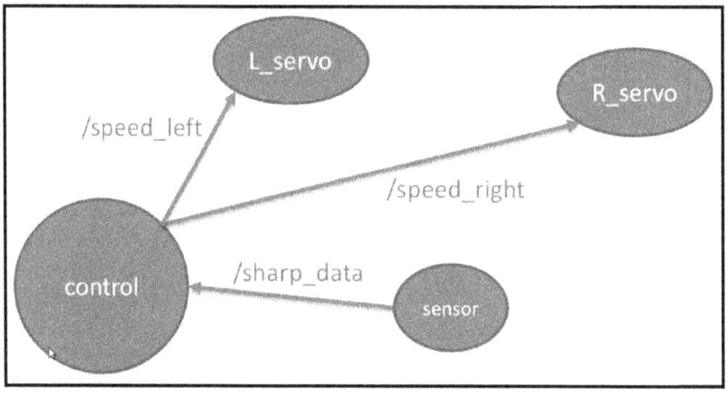

In the preceding graph, each circle—called a **node**—represents an independent program (this can be written in Python, Java, C++, Ruby, Node.js, or any of the other programming languages that ROS has implemented). The connections between them—called **edges**—represent the exchange of information. The meaning behind the direction of the arrows is self-explanatory: the emitter of data is the node where the arrow starts, and the receiver node is the one where the arrow points to. The words that appear above the edges are what ROS calls **topics**, and they constitute the channels through which flows the information exchanged between the nodes. When a node needs to use the information of a topic, it does so by subscribing to it and this operation adds a new arrow to the graph from the producer (of the data for such topic) to the subscriber node.

So, what does this graph do from the point of view of the robot? Remember that GoPiGo3 is a classical differential drive robot, where each wheel can be turned independently, and the sensor—for example, a distance sensor—provides the robot with information about how far away the obstacle is while moving:

Image courtesy: Dexter Industries https://32414320wji53mwwch1u68ce-wpengine.netdna-ssl.com/wp-content/uploads/2017/05/GPG3_FullServoDistanceGoogly_1-800x800.jpg

Therefore, you might have already guessed that in the preceding ROS graph, the `L_servo` node is the program that controls the left servomotor (by rotating that wheel) and the `R_servo` node does the same with the right wheel.

The `sensor` node is the one that takes the readings from the distance sensor and makes them available to the `control` node through the edge that is connected to it, that is, by using the `/sharp_data` topic.

Within the `control` node resides the program that takes the decision of what to do if GoPiGo3 is facing an obstacle. For example, it can rotate the robot until it finds a direction without any obstacles. Rotating means that the `control` node sends opposite commands to the `L_servo` and `R_Servo` nodes.

These signals are the ones that flow through the corresponding edges of the graph: the `/speed_left` topic or the left servo and `/speed_right` for the other one. In the ROS language, we say that the `control` node publishes the command for the left servo in the `/speed_left` topic.

roscore

roscore is the mandatory and first node that has to be launched so that the ROS environment can be running. This allows every node to be capable of finding any other node by subscribing to the topics it publishes. roscore also manages the database for ROS parameters—the values that define the robot configuration. As a result, if the roscore process dies, the master node fails, and the robot stops working. You may guess that this single point of failure is a clear limitation for a distributed computed framework such as ROS. For this reason, ROS2 has addressed this issue, and the running software no longer requires a master node. Communication between the nodes relies on the **DDS** (short for **Data Distribution Service**) architecture for real-time systems.

Can you see how different programming a robot is from writing a software application? In robotics, you focus on the top-level functionalities of your application and integrate premade software pieces written by others.

Do take into account that not all software in robotics follows this approach. In fact, among its many uses, we selected ROS because its philosophy adapts very well to the *learn-through-practice* methodology that we have adopted for this book.

These pieces of software, which consist of code blocks grouped into nodes, form what we call a **ROS package**. Several related nodes constitute a ROS package that delivers a specific functionality, for example, object recognition with a camera.

Workspaces and catkin

A workspace in ROS is an isolated environment for building and running your software. You may use different workspaces to manage different projects. The workspace will contain all the ROS packages you will need for your project.

Physically, it is a folder in your home directory that contains all of the specific files of your application in such a way that deploying this workspace in another machine with ROS preinstalled will work properly and do the same as it did on the original computer.

Tightly attached to the concept of the workspace is catkin, the build system of ROS that combines CMake macros and Python scripts to provide functionality on top of CMake's normal workflow. At this point, it is enough that you are aware that this is a tool used to build the software each time you include new packages in your workspace. You can find an in-depth conceptual explanation of catkin at `http://wiki.ros.org/catkin/conceptual_overview`.

Configuring your ROS development environment

In this section, we will guide you on how to install and configure the tools that you will need to work comfortably with ROS on your laptop. In short, these are the steps you need to complete before starting the practical exercises in this chapter:

1. Make sure that your computer runs **Ubuntu 16.04** or **Ubuntu 18.04**. Both are the LTS releases that have the most extensive collection of ROS packages at the time of writing this book.
2. Install and set up **ROS** on your laptop. You will also be provided with the guidelines to install ROS in the Raspberry Pi, the CPU of the GoPiGO3 robot. However, in part 2 of the book, you will only need your laptop, since we will be dealing with a virtual model of the robot. The inclusion of the physical robot is left for part 3 of the book.
3. For the *Integrated Development Environment* (**IDE**) we will use **RoboWare Studio**, which is based on the general purpose IDE by Microsoft called **Visual Studio Code**. We provide the instructions to set it up in the *Installing RoboWare Studio* section below.

So, provided your laptop has the required operating system, let's now move on to the second step of the configuration.

Installing ROS

If you work under Ubuntu 16.04, you will need to install the Kinetic distribution of ROS. On the other hand, if you have Ubuntu 18.04, the corresponding version of ROS to install is called Melodic. Remember that these choices were explained in detail in the *Technical requirements* section.

Before installing the software, make sure that you have the two basic `curl` and `git` tools. If this is not the case, then run the following command to install the missing ones:

```
$ sudo apt update
$ sudo apt install curl git
```

The instructions on the **ROS Kinetic** installation page (`http://wiki.ros.org/kinetic/Installation/Ubuntu`) are pretty clear and straightforward. They are the same for your laptop (*amd64/i386*) and for the Raspberry Pi (the *armhf* architecture). They are included here for the completion of the description.

> **ROS Melodic** also has an installation page at `http://wiki.ros.org/melodic/Installation/Ubuntu`. There, you will find that the commands are the same as those for Kinetic, because they are written in such a way that are not dependent on the Ubuntu version of choice.

Following the next steps you will get ROS up and running in your laptop:

1. First, add the source repository for ROS:

```
$ sudo sh -c 'echo "deb http://packages.ros.org/ros/ubuntu
$(lsb_release -sc) main" > /etc/apt/sources.list.d/ros-latest.list'
```

   This command adds ROS repository sources to your system. Since such a source is dependent on the Ubuntu version, the inner command `$(lsb_release -sc)` in the snippet above outputs the version, i.e. **xenial** for Ubuntu 16.04 and **bionic** or Ubuntu 18.04.

2. Then, set up your keys:

```
$ sudo apt-key adv --keyserver 'hkp://keyserver.ubuntu.com:80' --
recv-key C1CF6E31E6BADE8868B172B4F42ED6FBAB17C654
```

   Alternatively, you can use `curl` instead of the `apt-key` command. This is useful if you are behind a proxy server:

```
$ curl -sSL
'http://keyserver.ubuntu.com/pks/lookup?op=get&search=0xC1CF6E31E6B
ADE8868B172B4F42ED6FBAB17C654' | sudo apt-key add -
```

> If you do not get the key to be validated, then it may have been changed for security reasons (as of February 2020, the key remains active). If it is not the case at this moment, go to the official installation page at `http://wiki.ros.org/melodic/Installation/Ubuntu` and find the section, where the key value `0xC1CF6E31E6BADE8868B172B4F42ED6FBAB17C654` needs to be replaced.

3. Update your sources:

```
$ sudo apt update
```

4. If you have Ubuntu 16.04 on your laptop, install the full stack of ROS Kinetic, including the simulator called **Gazebo**, navigation, and robot perception packages (recommended):

```
$ sudo apt install ros-kinetic-desktop-full
```

If you are working in Ubuntu 18.04, perform the installation of ROS Melodic instead:

```
$ sudo apt install ros-melodic-desktop-full
```

Alternatively, you may install the desktop version, which only includes the ROS GUI tools (`rqt`, `rviz`). Later on, you can add the packages for simulation (Gazebo), navigation, and perception when needed (remember that these are installed with full version outlined in step 4 above):

```
$ sudo apt install ros-kinetic-desktop
```

Alternatively, if you are in Ubuntu 18.04, you can use the following:

```
$ sudo apt install ros-melodic-desktop
```

5. Initialize `rosdep`. This is the component that enables you to easily install system dependencies for the source code to compile. It is also required in order to run some core components in ROS:

```
$ sudo rosdep init
$ rosdep update
```

6. Set up the ROS environment for your interactive shell session:

```
$ source /opt/ros/kinetic/setup.bash
```

Alternatively, if you are in Ubuntu 18.04, use the following:

```
$ source /opt/ros/melodic/setup.bash
```

To avoid having to run this command each time you open a new terminal, include it at the end of your `.bashrc` file with the following command:

```
$ echo "source /opt/ros/kinetic/setup.bash" >> ~/.bashrc
$ source ~/.bashrc
```

The second command in the snippet above executes the **.bashrc** file refreshing your custom setup. If in Ubuntu 18.04, just replace `kinetic` for `melodic`:

```
$ echo "source /opt/ros/melodic/setup.bash" >> ~/.bashrc $ source
~/.bashrc
```

7. Finally, install `rosinstall`, the command-line tool that enables you to easily download many source trees for ROS packages:

```
$ sudo apt install python-rosinstall python-rosinstall-generator
python-wstool build-essential
```

Bear in mind that, as you become more familiar with the communication between the Raspberry Pi in the robot and your laptop, you can make all the desktop interactions from your computer and let the Raspberry Pi execute only robotics-specific tasks. This approach will make GoPiGo3 more responsive because you will have a minimal Ubuntu server in the Raspberry Pi and the ROS base version, which excludes the GUI tools and has only the core packages, as well as the build and communication libraries.

You can refer to the next section for specific details on how to prepare the ROS environment for the robot.

Ubuntu and ROS in the Raspberry Pi

Since you will be using only the core ROS packages in your Raspberry Pi, it is recommended that you install the latest Ubuntu LTS version, that is, Ubuntu Mate 18.04 Bionic (`https://ubuntu-mate.org/download/`). This is because, although almost all contributed ROS packages are available for ROS Kinetic, it is also true that core packages are already available in the 2018 version of ROS Melodic. Therefore, it is safe to install this release in the Raspberry Pi under Ubuntu 18.04.

As mentioned already, the instructions on the ROS Melodic installation page (`http://wiki.ros.org/melodic/Installation/Ubuntu`) are pretty clear and straightforward.

Follow the next guidelines to decide which version to install:

- If installing ROS Desktop (which is recommended for beginners and for covering the contents of this book), use the following command:

```
$ sudo apt-get install ros-melodic-desktop
```

- If you wish to install the bare-bones version, that is, ROS Base, and so get a better performance from your Raspberry Pi, then use this command (this is only recommended for advanced users; at the moment, there is no desktop GUI):

```
$ sudo apt install ros-melodic-ros-base
```

As mentioned at the beginning of the section, for this chapter you will only need a laptop. The physical robot is left for part 3 of the book, starting from `Chapter 6`, *Programming in ROS – Commands and Tools*. In that chapter, we will provide the necessary details to correctly set up the software in the Raspberry Pi.

Integrated Development Environment (IDE)

In the section of ROS wiki devoted to *Integrated Development Environments* (`http://wiki.ros.org/IDEs`) are described the currently available IDEs for ROS—a total of 15 IDEs exist at the time of writing this book. Out of all of these options, we have selected to work with RoboWare Studio because of the following factors:

- It is a fork of **Visual Studio Code** (**VSC**), the general-purpose and customizable IDE by Microsoft that is extensively used in the developer community. It is open source, light, easy to use and offers lots of contributed plugins, making it possible to customize the IDE environment to your own specific needs. **RoboWare Studio** is built on top of VSC code to provide ROS development functionalities. Furthermore, the plugin panel of the IDE is customized so that you can easily install ROS packages on demand. The current version is 1.2.0, which was issued in June 2018. Its code is open source and it is publicly available in GitHub at *TonyRobotics/RoboWare-Studio* (`https://github.com/TonyRobotics/RoboWare-Studio`).
- **RoboWare Studio** out-of-the-box features allow you to start working with all of ROS's main characteristics: workspaces, packages, nodes, messages/services/actions, and more.

For all of the explanations in this book, we will always give you the commands to be executed in `bash`, as this is the native way of commanding ROS.

IDEs such as RoboWare Studio may be of help in at least two scenarios:

- When beginning with ROS, to avoid dealing with the complexity of the command line if you are not very familiar with it
- When developing projects, where the IDE facilitates the management of the large number of files that are spread along with the ROS packages that make up your application. Such packages provide functionalities such as coordinate transformations, computer vision, robot navigation, and so on.

In any case, our advice is that you do the first round of this book using RoboWare Studio, and, for the second round, go directly to `bash`. If you want to skip one of them, then discard the IDE option and keep learning with the command line. Practicing `bash` commands is the best way to really understand how ROS works, and you surely know that this applies not only for ROS but for any other software tool running under Linux OS.

Therefore, from now on, use the IDE of your choice for editing files, and always work with the ROS command line (or RoboWare if you prefer to keep working with a GUI interface).

Installing RoboWare Studio

Provided that you have already installed ROS on your computer, execute the following block of commands in a terminal to install the required dependencies, as indicated in the manual of RoboWare Studio available at `https://github.com/TonyRobotics/RoboWare/blob/master/Studio/RoboWare_Studio_Manual_1.2.0_EN.pdf`:

```
$ sudo apt-get update
$ sudo apt-get install build-essential python-pip pylint
```

Then, install the `clang-format-3.8` package:

```
$ sudo apt-get install clang-format-3.8
```

Binaries are hosted in GitHub at `https://github.com/TonyRobotics/RoboWare/blob/master/Studio`. You can download the latest version of RoboWare Studio in your Ubuntu OS for AMD64 from this link: `https://github.com/TonyRobotics/RoboWare/raw/master/Studio/roboware-studio_1.2.0-1524709819_amd64.deb`. You also have the source code available in GitHub at `https://github.com/tonyrobotics/roboware-studio`.

Installation is pretty easy; execute the following command from the location where you got the `.deb` file:

```
$ sudo dpkg -i roboware-studio_1.2.0-1524709819_amd64.deb
```

After finishing, you can launch the IDE by clicking on the RoboWare Studio icon.

Communication between ROS nodes – messages and topics

We will accomplish the goal of getting two nodes talking to each other by going step by step. First, you need to create a personal workspace, and then you will pull the book repository at `https://github.com/PacktPublishing/Hands-On-ROS-for-Robotics-Programming`, and go into the `Chapter3_ROS_basics` folder to follow the exercises by yourself.

Creating a workspace

Follow these steps to create a workspace from the command line:

1. First, create the folders that you will need later to place your ROS packages:

```
$ mkdir -p ~/catkin_ws/src
```

The following are the folder descriptions:

- `catkin_ws` will be the root location of your workspace.
- `src` is where you will place your code, that is, inside the ROS packages.

> Be aware that ~ is equivalent to the home folder, that is, `/home/bronquillo`.

2. Move to this last folder and issue the following command to initialize the workspace:

```
$ cd ~/catkin_ws/src
$ catkin_init_workspace
```

The last command will generate the `~/catkin_ws/src/CMakeLists.txt` file, which contains the definition and configuration of the workspace. That file really is a symlink to a location in the ROS installation folder where the workspace configuration is defined:

```
/opt/ros/melodic/share/catkin/cmake/toplevel.cmake
```

3. Build the workspace for the first time; it does not matter that the folder is empty at this time:

```
$ cd ~/catkin_ws
$ catkin_make
```

By listing the content, you will see two new folders:

- `build` contains the result of the compilation of our workspace, and makes available all the code you will place later when creating a package for its execution with ROS commands.
- `devel` contains the configuration of the workspace, and it will be sourced every time you open a terminal (refer to the following steps).

Be aware that compilation has to be done at the root folder, `~/catkin_ws`, while workspace initialization was done in the application code folder, `~/catkin_ws/src`.

4. To add the workspace to your ROS environment, you need to source the generated `setup` file:

```
$ source ~/catkin_ws/devel/setup.bash
```

5. To avoid having to run this command each time you open a new terminal, include it in your `.bashrc` file:

```
$ echo "source ~/catkin_ws/devel/setup.bash" >> ~/.bashrc
$ source ~/.bashrc
```

6. Then, you should have the following two lines added to your `.bashrc` file:

```
source /opt/ros/kinetic/setup.bash
source ~/catkin_ws/devel/setup.bash
```

Remember that the first line accounts for the ROS system configuration and the second for your workspace settings.

Creating a workspace and building it using RoboWare

The following instructions allow you to use the RoboWare IDE to create the workspace, avoiding the use of the command line:

1. Launch RoboWare and click on the **New Workspace...** item:

2. In the pop-up window, indicate the name of the workspace and select the folder where you want to place it:

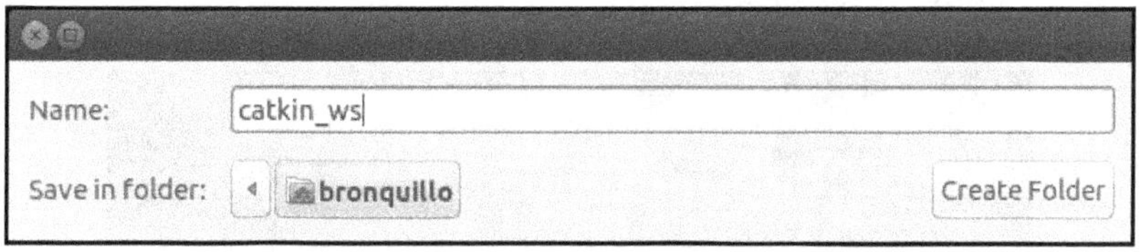

After setting the folder name, RoboWare executes `catkin_init_workspace` transparently for the user, and you will see a new file and a new folder on the left-hand side of your IDE window. They are the `src` folder and the file inside, `CMakeLists.txt`, which contains your workspace definition and configuration:

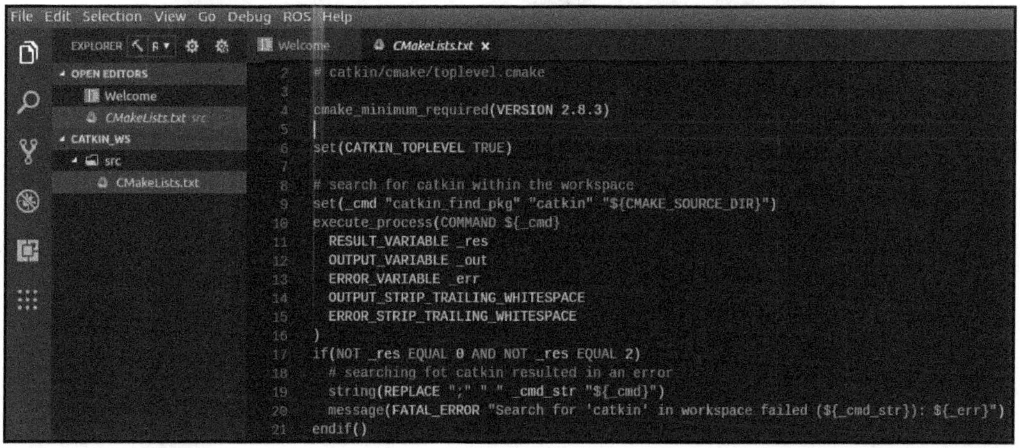
File Edit Selection View Go Debug ROS Help
EXPLORER
OPEN EDITORS
Welcome
CMakeLists.txt src
CATKIN_WS
src
CMakeLists.txt
Welcome
CMakeLists.txt
# catkin/cmake/toplevel.cmake
cmake_minimum_required(VERSION 2.8.3)
set(CATKIN_TOPLEVEL TRUE)
# search for catkin within the workspace
set(_cmd "catkin_find_pkg" "catkin" "${CMAKE_SOURCE_DIR}")
execute_process(COMMAND ${_cmd}
RESULT_VARIABLE _res
OUTPUT_VARIABLE _out
ERROR_VARIABLE _err
OUTPUT_STRIP_TRAILING_WHITESPACE
ERROR_STRIP_TRAILING_WHITESPACE
)
if(NOT _res EQUAL 0 AND NOT _res EQUAL 2)
# searching fot catkin resulted in an error
string(REPLACE ";" " " _cmd_str "${_cmd}")
message(FATAL_ERROR "Search for 'catkin' in workspace failed (${_cmd_str}): ${_err}")
endif()

For now, it is enough that you notice that the file has a symlink to a ROS system file located in the ROS installation folder, `/opt/ros/kinetic`. This folder contains the common configuration for all the workspaces you may create.

You can open a terminal in RoboWare and list all files with the `ls -la` command from the specific `~/catkin/src` location:

```
drwxrwxr-x 2 bronquillo bronquillo 4096 may 11 13:08 .
drwxrwxr-x 3 bronquillo bronquillo 4096 may 11 13:07 ..
lrwxrwxrwx 1 bronquillo bronquillo   50 may 11 13:08 CMakeLists.txt -> /opt/ros/kinetic/share/catkin/cmake/toplevel.cmake
```

Such a terminal is accessed from the top-bar menu, by clicking on the **View** item, and then selecting **Integrated terminal** (*Ctrl* + `) from the drop-down menu.

3. Select the build mode and set it to **Debug**, as shown in the following screenshot:

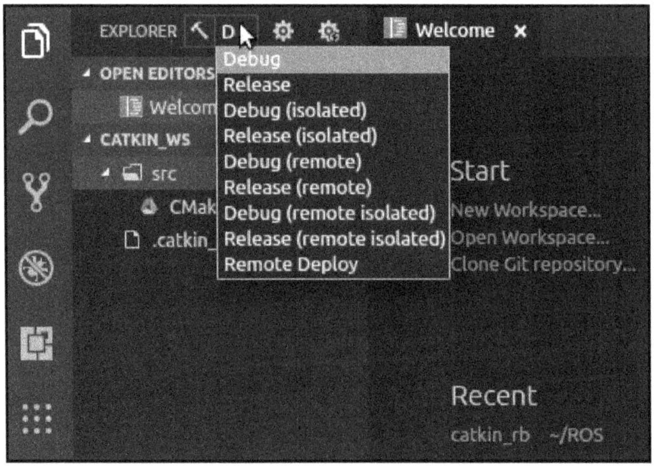

4. Then, from the top-bar menu, select **ROS** | **Build**:

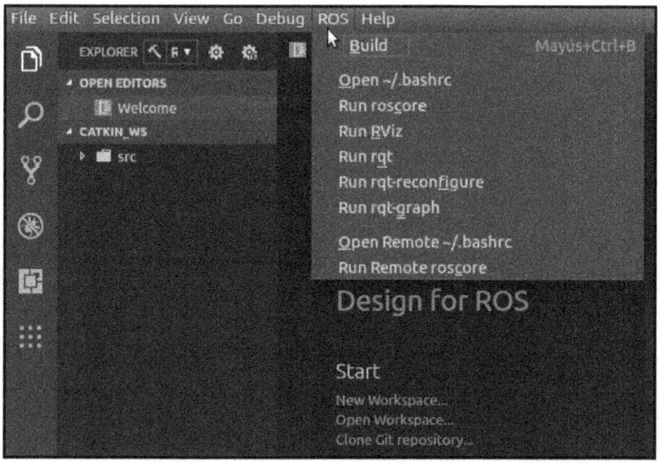

You will see the following log in the **OUTPUT** window at the bottom of the screen:

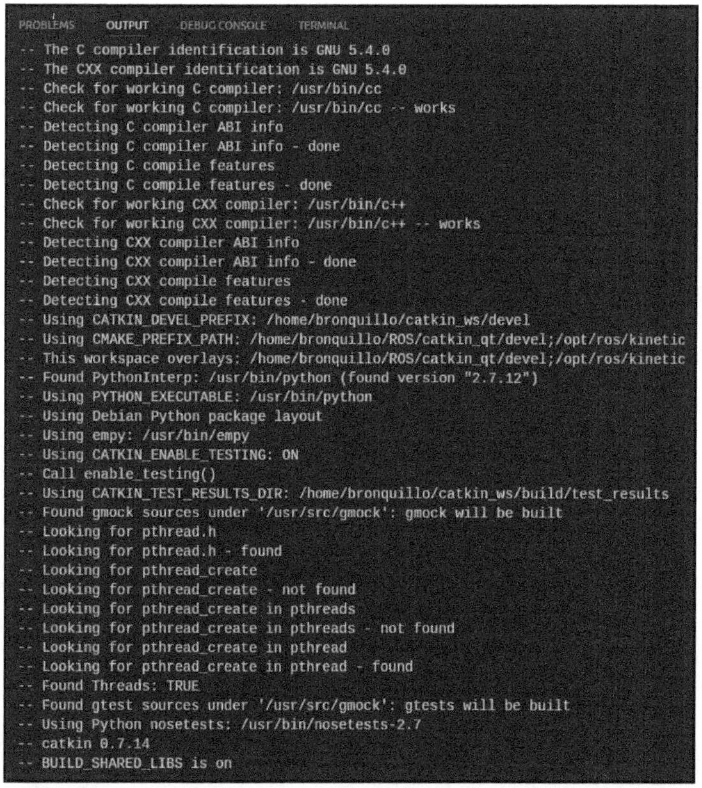

The last lines should look like this if successful:

```
-- BUILD_SHARED_LIBS is on
-- Configuring done
-- Generating done
-- Build files have been written to: /home/bronquillo/catkin_ws/build
Base path: /home/bronquillo/catkin_ws
Source space: /home/bronquillo/catkin_ws/src
Build space: /home/bronquillo/catkin_ws/build
Devel space: /home/bronquillo/catkin_ws/devel
Install space: /home/bronquillo/catkin_ws/install
####
#### Running command: "cmake /home/bronquillo/catkin_ws/src -DCMAKE_BUILD_TYPE=Debug
-DCATKIN_DEVEL_PREFIX=/home/bronquillo/catkin_ws/devel -DCMAKE_INSTALL_PREFIX=/home/bronquillo/catkin_ws/install -G Unix
Makefiles" in "/home/bronquillo/catkin_ws/build"
####
####
#### Running command: "make -j8 -l8" in "/home/bronquillo/catkin_ws/build"
####
```

Next, let's set up the ROS package.

Setting up the ROS package

Follow these steps for setting up the ROS package:

1. From a terminal, clone the book repository, `https://github.com/PacktPublishing/Hands-On-ROS-for-Robotics-Programming`, into your home folder:

```
$ cd ~
$ git clone
https://github.com/PacktPublishing/Hands-On-ROS-for-Robotics-Progra
mming
```

2. We are going to copy the code of this chapter into the ROS workspace. That way, you will have a cleaner ROS environment:

```
$ cp -R ~/Hands-On-ROS-for-Robotics-Programming/Chapter3_ROS_basics
~/catkin_ws/src
```

TIP

Do not add a backslash, `\n`, after the `src` folder name. If you do, the files will be copied directly into the `src` folder, not under `src/Chapter3_ROS_basics`.

3. Within the `Chapter3_ROS_basics` folder, you can find the files of this chapter belonging to the first ROS package you will play with. Its configuration is contained in the `package.xml` file. Be aware that the package name is defined within the `<name>ros_basics</name>` tags. You can find it inside the following code file:

```
<?xml version="1.0"?>
<package format="2">
    <name>ros_basics</name>
    <version>0.0.0</version>
    <description>Code samples for "Chapter 3: Getting started with
ROS"</description>
    <maintainer email="brjapon@therobotacademy.com">Bernardo R.
Japon</maintainer
    <license>GNU v3.0</license>
    <buildtool_depend>catkin</buildtool_depend>
    <build_depend>rospy</build_depend>
    <build_export_depend>rospy</build_export_depend>
    <exec_depend>rospy</exec_depend>
</package>
```

4. Then, go to the workspace root and build again:

```
$ cd ~/catkin_ws
$ catkin_make
$ source ~/catkin_ws/devel/setup.bash
```

In general, you will have to rebuild the workspace in at least two cases:

- Each time you include a new package
- If your code contains pieces written in a compilable language such as C++

In this book, we will be working mainly with Python, the widely used open source language that makes it easier to get started with ROS. Since Python is an interpreted language, you will not need to rebuild the workspace each time you modify the code base of the package. Hence, the rebuild will only be necessary when adding or removing ROS packages. The way to check whether the newly added package—`ros_basics`—is known to ROS is to execute this simple command:

```
$ rospack list | grep ros_basics
```

The output should look like this:

```
ros_basics /home/bronquillo/catkin_ws/src/book/Chapter3_ROS_basics
```

Although here, we will be working from a premade ROS package, it is relevant that you know at this point how to create your own package from scratch. Issue this command from the `src` location of your workspace (`$ cd ~/catkin_ws/src/`):

```
$ catkin_create_pkg <YOUR-PACKAGE-NAME> <DEPENDENCIES>
```

`<YOUR-PACKAGE-NAME>` stands for the name you want to assign to your package. `<DEPENDENCIES>` refers to the list of ROS packages you will need for your code to run. For example, if your package is going to contain code in Python and C++, you will need `rospy` for the former and `roscpp` for the latter. Then, the command will be as follows:

```
$ catkin_create_pkg <YOUR-PACKAGE-NAME> rospy roscpp
```

This will create a folder with the name given to the package and two files:

- `package.xml`: The package configuration as shown previously
- `CMakelists.txt`: The input to the CMake build system for building software packages

`CMakelists.txt` also contains the reference to `<YOUR-PACKAGE-NAME>`. For our case, this file is as simple as follows:

```
cmake_minimum_required(VERSION 2.8.3)
project(ros_basics)

find_package(catkin REQUIRED COMPONENTS rospy)

###################################
## catkin specific configuration ##
###################################
catkin_package()

###########
## Build ##
###########
include_directories()
```

Accessing package files and building the workspace using RoboWare

Here's an alternative method. The following demonstrates that you can clone a package repository and build the workspace using RoboWare.

After cloning and placing the code of the chapter, as explained in the *Setting up the ROS package* section, you can explore the content in the file tree view on the left-hand side of the IDE window. Clicking on any of the files will let you see the content in the main window:

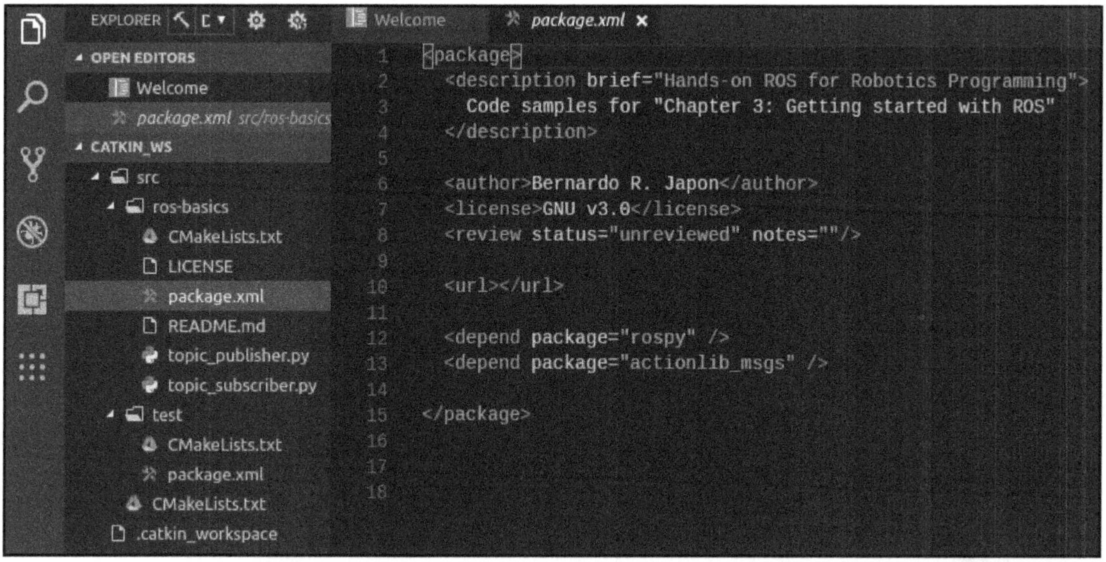

Finally, build the workspace; note that this is something you will have to do each time you create a new package on your own or when you clone an external one. To do that, go to the top bar menu, select **ROS**, and then click on **Build** as before.

A node publishing a topic

For the next steps, since we will need to deal with several simultaneous terminals, we will make use of a very handy tool, Terminator, that allows you to simultaneously handle several terminals. Launch these commands to install it on your system:

```
$ sudo apt-get update
$ sudo apt-get install terminator
```

Launch Terminator and divide the screen into four terminals (you can right-click on the mouse to divide the windows successively). We will reference them as `T1`, `T2`, `T3`, and `T4`, as shown in the following screenshot:

Launch the roscore node in terminal 1 (the top-left window):

```
T1 $ roscore
```

You should be able to see this output in `T1`:

roscore http://rosbot:11311/ 84x27
... logging to /home/bronquillo/.ros/log/01d977f2-7401-11e9-9b19-d46d6d44d91e/roslaunch-rosbot-28763.log
Checking log directory for disk usage. This may take awhile.
Press Ctrl-C to interrupt
Done checking log file disk usage. Usage is <1GB.
started roslaunch server http://rosbot:45803/
ros_comm version 1.12.14
SUMMARY
========
PARAMETERS
* /rosdistro: kinetic
* /rosversion: 1.12.14
NODES
auto-starting new master
process[master]: started with pid [28775]
ROS_MASTER_URI=http://rosbot:11311/
setting /run_id to 01d977f2-7401-11e9-9b19-d46d6d44d91e
process[rosout-1]: started with pid [28788]
started core service [/rosout]

This is the root process of ROS. roscore launches a node and starts the master service, as ROS is a centralized system. The master node is always needed so that other nodes may execute and it has to be launched prior to any other node.

In the next terminal, `T2`, run this command to launch the publisher node:

```
T2 $ rosrun ros_basics topic_publisher.py
```

This launches the `topic_publisher` node, but nothing happens! That's right. A publisher is just that, a publisher. We need a listener to know what data is being sent.

Go to terminal 3 and list the topics currently declared:

```
T3 $ rostopic list
/counter
/rosout
/rosout_agg
```

In the listing, it appears that `/counter` is the topic that updates an incremental counter every 0.5 seconds. The other two topics, `/rosout` and `/rosout_agg`, are the console log-reporting (`http://wiki.ros.org/rosout`) mechanisms in ROS.

This line of the `topic_publisher.py` file is the one that sets up the `/counter` topic publisher:

```
pub = rospy.Publisher('counter', Int32, queue_size=10)
```

To watch the published messages, launch this command in the terminal:

```
T3 $ rostopic echo counter -n 5
```

This will output the next five messages that will be published in the `/counter` topic:

```
data: 530
---
data: 531
---
data: 532
---
data: 533
---
data: 534
---
```

Finally, we will show a live view that will print the real-time frequency at which the messages are sent:

```
T3 $ rostopic hz counter

average rate: 2.000
min: 0.500s max: 0.501s std dev: 0.00020s window: 146
average rate: 2.000
min: 0.500s max: 0.501s std dev: 0.00020s window: 148
average rate: 2.000
min: 0.500s max: 0.501s std dev: 0.00020s window: 150
average rate: 2.000
min: 0.500s max: 0.501s std dev: 0.00020s window: 152
average rate: 2.000
min: 0.500s max: 0.501s std dev: 0.00020s window: 154
average rate: 2.000
min: 0.500s max: 0.501s std dev: 0.00020s window: 156
average rate: 2.000
```

Press *Ctrl* + *C* to stop the log in `T3`. Bear in mind that, if you do this in any of the two previous terminals, the process that each one controls will die with the following consequences:

- **Terminal T2**: The publisher process will end and no more messages will be sent through the `/counter` topic.
- **Terminal T1**: Pressing *Ctrl* + *C* in this terminal will kill roscore, making it evident that this process is a single point of failure in ROS, that is, all related processes (including nodes and messages) will die.

A node that listens to the topic

As there is one node that publishes the incremental counter in the `/counter` topic, we will now launch a node that subscribes to this topic.

To start, let's visualize the current ROS graph by issuing the following command in `T3`:

```
T3 $ rqt_graph
```

A window pops up and shows this:

There is a single node, that is, the one we launched in `T2`. The `/counter` topic does not appear because no other node is listening to it. In order to make the topic show, launch the listener in `T4`:

```
T4 $ rosrun ros_basics topic_subscriber.py
```

You will see this log in the bottom-right terminal window, a neverending live data stream unless you kill (press *Ctrl* + *C*) any of `T1` or `T2`, that correspond to `roscore` and `topic_publisher` respectively.

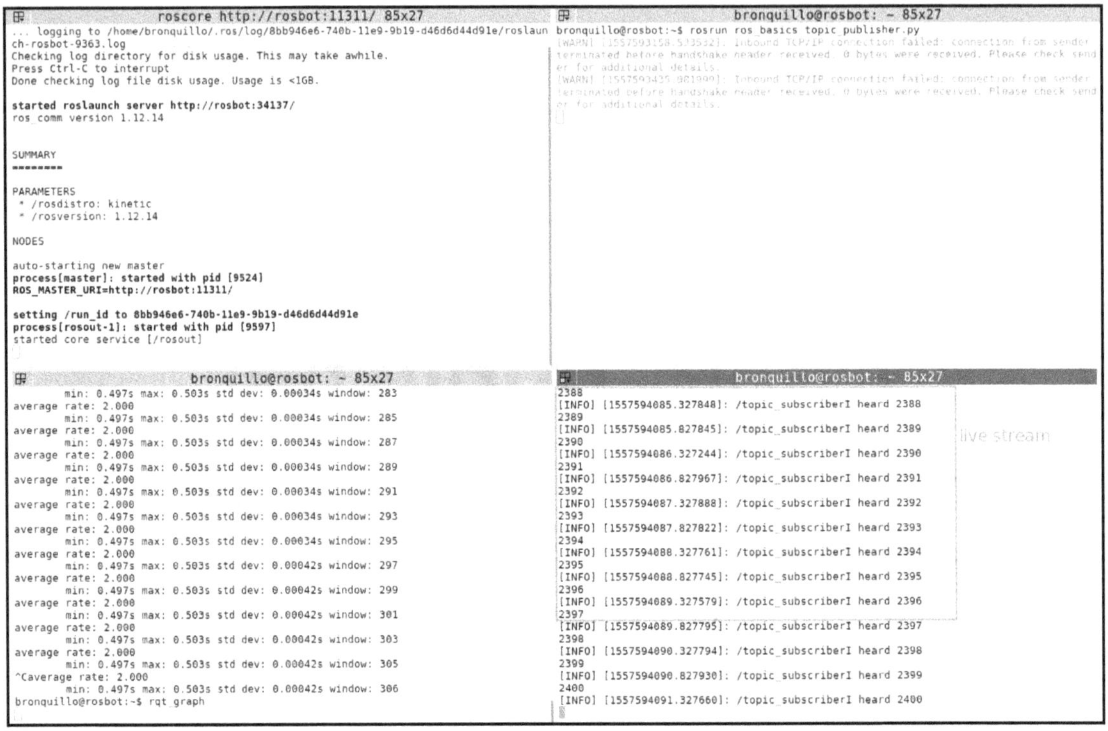

If you go back to the ROS graph window and click on the update icon, you will see the `/topic_publisher` node, the `/counter` topic that routes the messages, and the `/topic_subscriber` listening node:

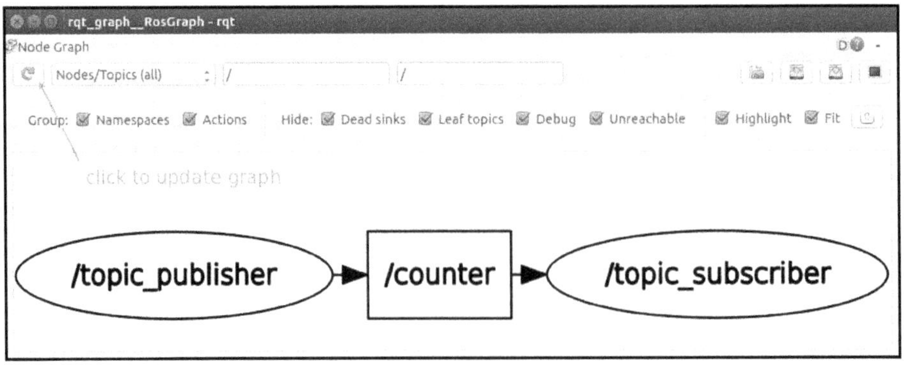

This simple example illustrates the publish/subscribe architecture of communication in ROS. You can already appreciate how it works and how simple the underlying communication principle is, which is in the base of the ROS framework. We will now do something practical.

Let's make our counter behave like a chronometer. How can we do this? Well, you just need to modify the script `topic_publisher.py`, by changing the parameter that specifies the number of times per second that a message is sent to the topic, a concept known as the publishing **frequency**, whose units are *Hertz* (= number of times/second). In the script, the Python object that accounts for this behavior is:

```
rate = rospy.Rate(2)
```

In the loop below in the script, the configured behavior is achieved by applying the **rospy** method `sleep` method to the defined `rate` object:

```
rate.sleep()
```

Remember that **rospy** is the ROS library that allows us to run nodes whose code is written in Python. **rospy** defines a set of methods to make useful stuff in ROS, such as setting a publishing frequency in this way.

The line above states that two messages are published every second, that is, one message every 0.5 seconds. Hence if `rate` is set to 1 Hz, the frequency will be one message per second, therefore emulating a chronometer. You can modify such script `topic_publisher.py` without needing to stop ROS, and, as soon as you execute it again, the node is back in the graph. Let's show you how to do it step by step:

1. Hit *Ctrl* + C in terminal `T2` to stop the execution of the node.
2. Modify the file to publish at a rate of 1 Hz, as shown previously.
3. Then, relaunch the node:

```
T2 $ rosrun ros_basics topic_publisher.py
```

You will see the effect in terminal `T4` from where `topic_subscriber.py` was launched. Therefore, the speed of new lines appearing (that is, counts) will be double compared to before when the rate was 2 Hz. This will produce one counter update (+1) per second, which corresponds to the rate of 1 Hz.

Combining the publisher and subscriber in the same node

Can a node talk and listen at the same time as a real human does? Well, if ROS is a framework for robotics, it should be possible. Let's explore this:

1. Launch these two commands in the first two terminals, with each one in an independent terminal:

   ```
   T1 $ roscore
   T2 $ rosrun ros_basics doubler.py
   ```

   `/doubler` is a node that subscribes to the `/number` topic, as specified in these two lines of the `doubler.py` script:

   ```
   rospy.init_node('doubler')
   ...
   sub = rospy.Subscriber('number', Int32, callback)
   ...
   ```

   Additionally, `/doubler` publishes its result in the `/doubled` topic:

   ```
   ...
   pub = rospy.Publisher('doubled', Int32, queue_size=10)
   ```

   You will notice that nothing happens, because it needs to be fed with a number that can be multiplied by 2, as shown in the callback of `topic_subscriber.py`:

   ```
   def callback(msg):
     doubled = Int32()
     doubled.data = msg.data * 2
   ```

2. Launch a terminal for listening to the `/doubled` topic:

   ```
   T3 $ rostopic echo doubled
   ```

   Then, let's publish a `/number` topic by hand:

   ```
   T4 $ rostopic pub number std_msgs/Int32 2
       publishing and latching message. Press ctrl-C to terminate
   ```

   The output in terminal `T3` is `4`, as expected:

   ```
   data: 4
   ---
   ```

3. Try sending other numbers in `T4` and check that the double is shown immediately in `T3`.

If you issue `rqt_graph` in a fifth terminal, you will see something like this:

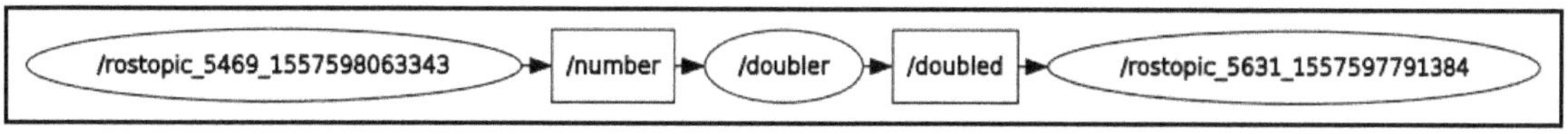

Here, you can see the `/number` and `/doubled` topics, the `/doubler` node, and two other nodes with large machine names whose correspondence are as follows:

- The node on the left of the preceding diagram, `/rostopic_5469_`, is created from the command in `T4`:

```
T4 $ rostopic pub number std_msgs/Int32 2
```

- The node on the right, `/rostopic_5631_`, is created from the command in `T3`:

```
T3 $ rostopic echo doubled
```

4. To finish this exercise, we will feed the number to the `/counter` topic, not from the command line, but from the script of the publisher node we saw in the last section: `topic_publisher.py`. For the script to work properly, you have to modify the topic name in `doubler.py`, renaming it from `number` to `counter`:

```
sub = rospy.Subscriber('counter', Int32, callback)
```

Then, after stopping all of the terminals, execute each of the following lines in an independent terminal:

```
T1 $ roscore
T2 $ rosrun ros_basics doubler.py
T3 $ rosrun ros_basics topic_publisher.py
T4 $ rostopic echo doubled
```

In this terminal, you will see the result of `counter` * 2 every time `/counter` is published. Take a look at the ROS graph (remember to click on the refresh button) and you will find that it reflects what is happening:

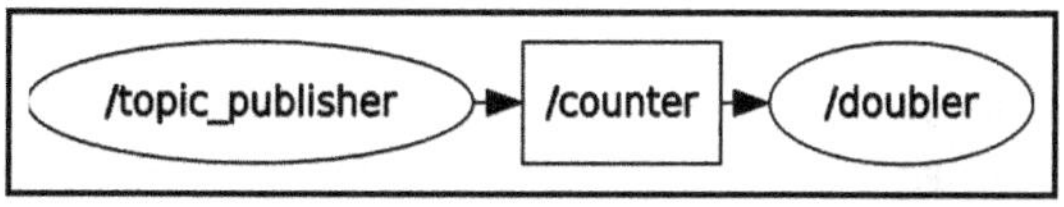

Bear in mind that `rqt_graph` will give you very useful information when debugging the code, for example, detecting any mistakes in the topic names. Take a look at the following figure, where multiplication by 2 does not work because `/topic_publisher` is subscribed to the `count` topic (note that the end `r` character is missing). The nodes are disconnected from one another, and the wrongly typed topic, which is not listened to by anyone, does not appear:

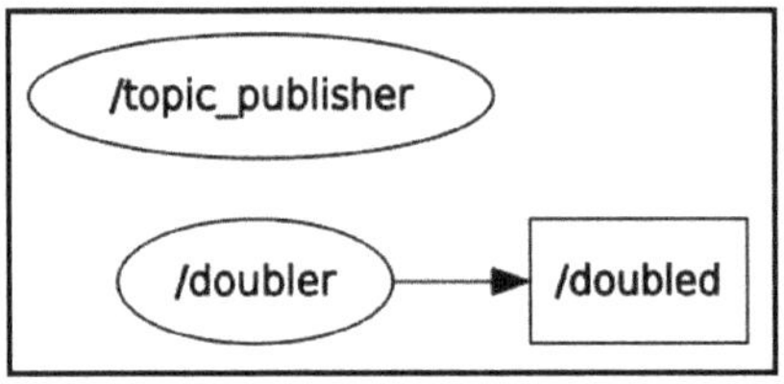

In the next section, we will provide an overview of the extension of the ROS package system.

Using publicly available packages for ROS

ROS-contributed packages are indexed on the official website at `http://www.ros.org/browse/list.php`.

As of July 2018, ROS Indigo (the distribution released for Ubuntu 14.04 LTS) has more than 2,900 packages, while ROS Kinetic (2016, Ubuntu 16.04 LTS) has over 1,600. Some of the more popularly downloaded ones include the following:

- `rviz` (`http://wiki.ros.org/rviz`): The 3D visualization tool for ROS. You will start using this in `Chapter 4`, *Creating the Virtual Two-Wheeled ROS Robot.*
- `gazebo_ros_pkgs` (`http://wiki.ros.org/gazebo_ros_pkgs`): This allows you to use the Gazebo 3D simulator from inside ROS. We will introduce Gazebo in `Chapter 5`, *Simulating Robot Behavior with Gazebo.*
- `sensor-msgs` (`http://wiki.ros.org/sensor_msgs`): This is a package that defines messages for commonly used sensors, such as cameras and scanning laser rangefinders.
- `tf2` (`http://wiki.ros.org/tf2`): This is the package that deals with the transformation of coordinates between the many reference systems used in the environment.
- `laser-geometry` (`http://wiki.ros.org/laser_geometry`): This makes it possible to transform a 2D laser scan into a point cloud for use in navigation.

This should give you a neat view of what programming in ROS will mean for you. In other words, integrate software developed by others (that is, packages) and make them work together—by designing a coherent ROS graph—to build up the functionality you wish your robot to have.

Summary

In this chapter, we introduced ROS and practiced with simple examples in order to help you understand the architecture of ROS. The top-level entity is the workspace, which is an isolated environment for building and running your software.

The workspace is constituted by ROS packages, that is, premade pieces of software that provide specific functionalities to integrate into your robot. Following this, catkin is the tool used to build the software each time you include new packages in your workspace.

The node is the basic entity in ROS and holds the functional pieces of code that make the robot work. A collection of related nodes providing specific functionalities constitute a ROS package. **roscore**, the process that runs the master node, is the one that allows each node to be capable of finding others by subscribing to the published topics. **roscore** also manages the database for the ROS parameters.

Communication between nodes is possible thanks to topics, the channels—edges of the ROS graph—through which the exchanged information flows. When a node needs to use the information of a topic, it does so by subscribing to it.

In the next chapter, you will learn how to build a virtual model of a differential drive robot, one that emulates GoPiGo3 characteristics. The chapter will also provide you with the methodology to test your code first with the virtual robot, and then install and execute it in the physical robot.

Questions

1. What is the top-level component in a ROS environment?

   A) Package
   B) Workspace
   C) ROS graph

2. What is the purpose of the roscore process?

   A) To allow a node to communicate with others and manage the robot parameters
   B) To provide a master node for driving all other nodes in the graph
   C) To allow ROS nodes to be found from outside of the LAN

3. Mark the correct sentence: A node can __ .

   A) only publish topics or only subscribe to topics
   B) publish topics and subscrib to topics at the same time
   C) publish topics and/or subscribe to other topics

4. What happens if one node fails to execute its program?

   A) Some functions of the robot will fail
   B) The robot will not work
   C) The topics it publishes will be set to undefined

5. Mark the incorrect sentence: The way to identify a message in a published topic is __.

   A) to launch a node that publishes data in such topic
   B) to issue the `$ rostopic echo </topic_name>` command
   C) to write a node that subscribes to that topic

Further reading

To go deeper into the concepts we have explained in this chapter, you can follow the links and tutorials:

- ROS tutorials: `http://wiki.ros.org/ROS/Tutorials` (sections 1 through 6)
- *ROS Robotics By Example, Second Edition, Fairchild C., Harman, Packt Publishing*, T. L. (2017), *Chapter 1, Getting Started with ROS:* `https://www.packtpub.com/hardware-and-creative/ros-robotics-example-second-edition`.
- *Programming Robots with ROS, Quigley M., Gerkey B., Bill Smart B.* (2015), *First Edition, O'Reilly*: `http://shop.oreilly.com/product/0636920024736.do` (*Chapter 2, Preliminaries*, and *Chapter 3, Topics*).

2
Section 2: Robot Simulation with Gazebo

This section is the digital counterpart of `Section 1`, *Physical Robot Assembly and Testing*, where you dealt with the physical robot. In this section, you will build a digital twin of the GoPiGo3 robot and complete the testing campaign in a virtual environment in the Gazebo simulator.

This section comprises the following chapters:

- `Chapter 4`, *Creating the Virtual Two-Wheeled ROS Robot*
- `Chapter 5`, *Simulating the Robot's Behavior with Gazebo*

4
Creating the Virtual Two-Wheeled ROS Robot

RViz is a 3D visualization tool that can display robot models. It provides a configurable **Graphical User Interface** (**GUI**) that allows the user to display any information they may request for the task being carrying out. RViz can be used for both robot visualization and for debugging specific features while building the **Unified Robot Description Format** (**URDF**) model. This format uses XML to simulate the robot.

To illustrate how to use RViz and URDF, in this chapter, you will build a simple two-wheeled robot, which is the digital twin of GoPiGo3. You will create the URDF file that describes the robot's main components. This file acts as the input for visualization in several ROS tools – not only RViz, but also the Gazebo simulation tool, which also includes a physics engine. Gazebo will be covered in the next chapter, while in this one, you will concentrate your efforts on getting familiar with RViz.

This chapter will teach you how to understand the syntax of URDF files and acquire the skills you'll need in order to systematically test/check features with RViz while building the robot model.

In this chapter, we will be covering the following topics:

- Getting started with RViz for robot visualization
- Building a differential drive robot with URDF
- Inspecting the GoPiGo3 model in ROS with RViz
- Robot frames of reference in the URDF model
- Using RViz to check results while building

Technical requirements

In the previous chapter, you were told how to clone this book's code repository so that it's in the home folder of your laptop. If you didn't do this, from a Terminal on your laptop, clone the repository into your home folder like so:

```
$ cd ~
$ git clone
https://github.com/PacktPublishing/Hands-On-ROS-for-Robotics-Programming
```

Next, only copy the code for this chapter into the ROS workspace. This way, you will have a cleaner ROS environment:

```
$ cp -R ~/Hands-On-ROS-for-Robotics-Programming/Chapter4_RViz_basics
~/catkin_ws/src/
```

Move to the path of the new files and check that the files are present:

```
$ cd ~/catkin_ws/src/Chapter4_RViz_basics
$ ls -la
```

This chapter contains a new ROS package named `rviz_basics`, so rebuild the workspace so that it is known to your ROS environment:

```
$ cd ~/catkin_ws
$ catkin_make
```

Check that the package is installing correctly by selecting it and listing its files:

```
$ roscd rviz_basics
$ ls -la
```

Now, you are ready to complete this chapter.

Getting started with RViz for robot visualization

RViz provides a configurable GUI so that you can display specific information about the robot.

To make sure RViz loads a default configuration, place the `default.rviz` file inside the `~/.rviz/` folder. You will find `Chapter4_RViz_basics` in this folder.

You can open the RViz GUI with the following commands:

```
T1 $ roscore
T2 $ rviz
```

The `T2` command, `rviz`, is an abbreviation of the official `$ rosrun rviz rviz` declaration, where first `rviz` refers to the package and the second refers to the node with the same name.

At the moment, the RViz window will be empty, so it will only show a grid at the floor level. In the next section, we will teach you how to build the robot model and get ready to visualize it. Once you've launched it, you will see a window similar to the one shown in the following screenshot:

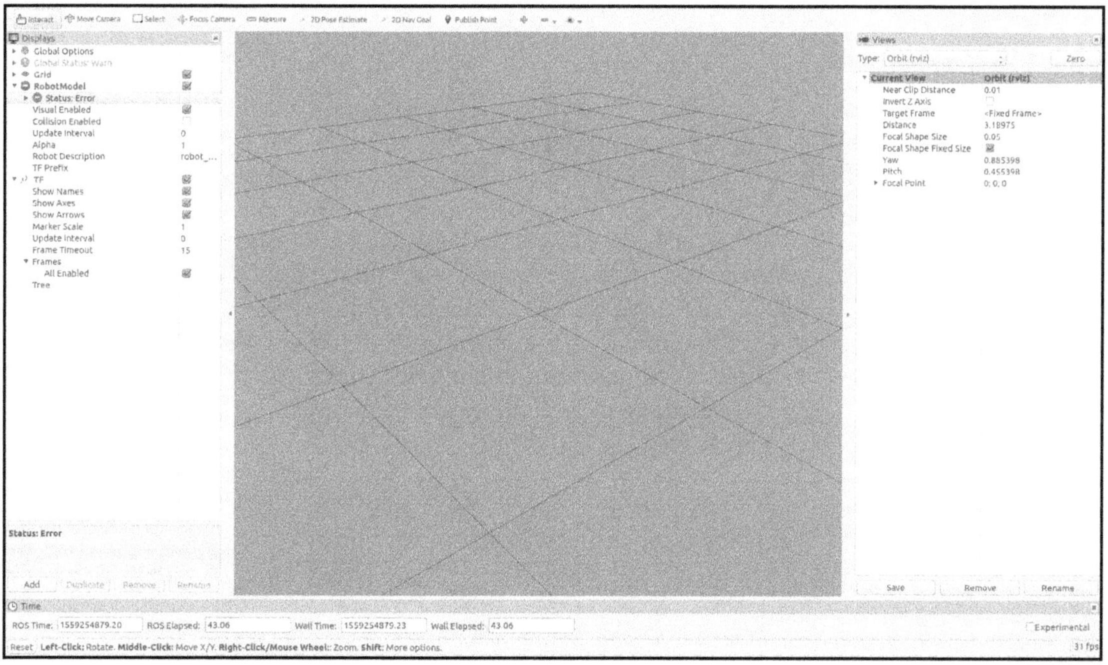

If you look carefully at the preceding screenshot, you'll see an error message in the left-hand pane. This is due to the fact that a robot model hasn't been loaded. We will develop this model in the next section.

Building a differential drive robot with URDF

The GoPiGo3 kit is composed of four several subassemblies:

- The chassis, which is the main structure that all the parts are attached to. This includes the following:
    - Raspberry Pi and GoPiGo3 board
    - Motors
    - Battery package
    - Wheels
    - Caster
- Two wheels – left and right, each one driven by one motor.
- A caster, which is a small freewheel attached to the rear part of the chassis that keeps the robot supported on three points: the left and right wheels and the caster itself. Be aware that one freewheel is the minimum to keep the robot rolling on the floor:
    - If the caster were not present, the system would be underconstrained. Then, you would have a self-balancing robot that would have to be continuously actuated by its motors to stay in equilibrium. This is a *closed-loop* control problem that needs the **Inertial Measurement Unit** (**IMU**) data from its accelerometers and gyroscopes to actuate the motors and keep the robot in equilibrium:

Image courtesy: Dexter Industries https://shop.dexterindustries.com/media/catalog/product/cache/4/thumbnail/1800x2400/9df78eab33525d08d6e5fb8d27136e95/b/a/balancebot_remote2-150x150_1_1.jpg

- If there were two casters, the system would be overconstrained. The robot would be supported on four points – two wheels and two casters – and the position of the second caster would be determined by the other caster and the two wheels. If one of the four wheels/the caster were not in contact with the floor, you would have a lame robot.

From the point of view of a simulated model, a differential drive robot such as GoPiGo3 is composed of three parts, each one being a rigid body. Therefore, we will divide the robot into mobile parts:

- The robot body, which includes the chassis and all the fixed parts attached to it (Raspberry Pi, GoPigo3 board, motors, and the battery package)
- Left and right wheels
- Caster

Going back to ROS, you are going to build a simulated GoPiGo3 with URDF. This is an XML format description that represents robot models at the component level. ROS contains a URDF package (`http://wiki.ros.org/urdf`) in order to accept this format of the robot description for simulation purposes.

In the upcoming sections, we are going to illustrate how to describe the four mobile parts of GoPiGo3 in URDF.

Overview of URDF for GoPiGo3

First, we're going to give you an overview of building the model, after which we'll walk you through the process step by step. The URDF model of our robot will render like this in RViz:

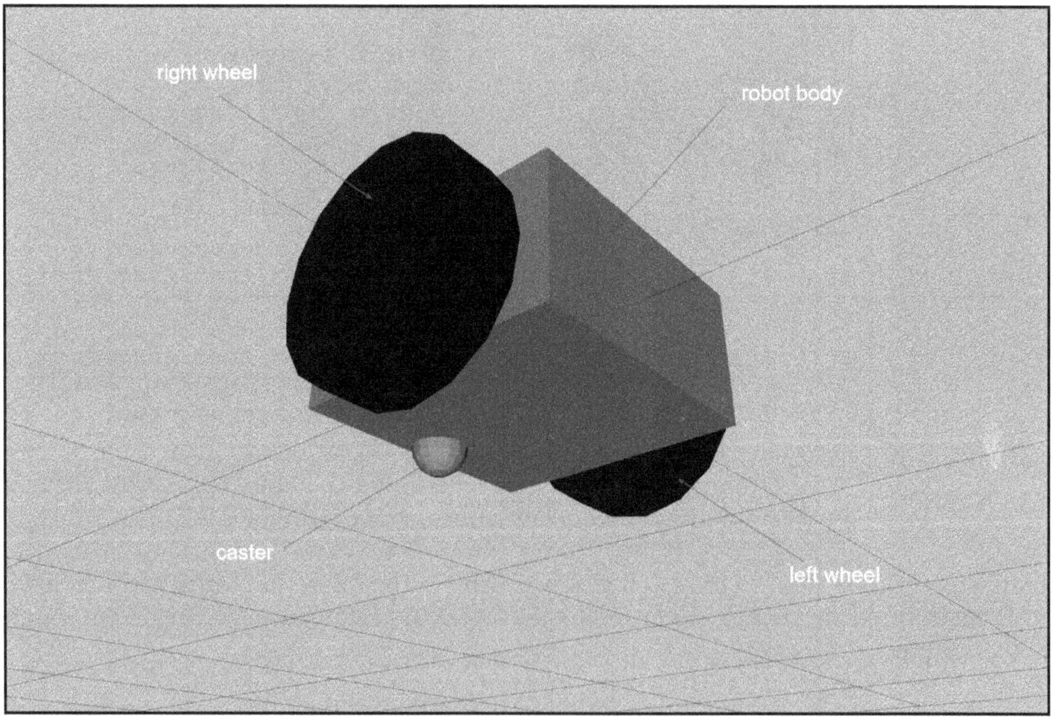

This model corresponds to the following URDF description:

```
<?xml version='1.0'?>
<robot name="GoPiGo3">

  <!-- Base Link (robot body) -->
  <link name="base_link">
    <visual>...
    </visual>

    <!-- Caster -->
    <visual name="caster">...
    </visual>

  </link>

  <!-- Right Wheel -->
  <link name="right_wheel">...
  </link>

  <joint name="joint_right_wheel" type="continuous">...
  </joint>

  <!-- Left Wheel -->
  <link name="left_wheel">...
  </link>

  <joint name="joint_left_wheel" type="continuous">...
  </joint>
</robot>
```

The content of the XML tags has collapsed – which is inferred from the plus signs to the right of the line numbers – to show you that each block corresponds to one part of the robot:

- The top-level tag is `<robot>` and identifies the robot as a whole.
- The `<link>` tag refers to each mobile part, identified by the `name` property. All of the content inside specifies the characteristics of that part:
    - `name="base_link"` refers to the robot body and, in this case, the chassis and the parts attached to it: the Raspberry Pi, GoPiGo3 board, motors, and the battery package.

    - `name="caster"` refers to the caster freewheel, but it is within a `<visual>` subtag, meaning it is part of the robot body, not a separate mobile part. Although it is a rolling element, remember that a simulated model tries to catch the properties of its reality with a simple description. Since the caster is merely a support, it does not need to be driven by a motor. For this reason, we can keep it fixed with respect to the robot body, and only deal with three mobile parts (robot body, right wheel, and left wheel) instead of four. If you're wondering about the friction it could produce, then don't worry – later, we'll learn how to set a zero value to make sure it behaves like a freewheel. The `<visual>` tag refers to a rigid body representation of a part of the robot without needing to define it as a separate link.
    - `name="right_wheel"` refers to the right wheel.
    - `name="left_wheel"` refers to the left wheel.
- The `<joint>` tag represents a junction between two parts. From a mechanical point of view, these joint tags correspond to the bearings that the wheels are mounted on. There is one associated with each wheel link.

Next, we will explain the contents of each `<link>` and `<joint>` tag that's used in this model in detail.

URDF robot body

A `<link>` element, as defined in the URDF XML specification (`http://wiki.ros.org/urdf/XML/link`), defines a rigid body with inertia, visual features, and collision properties. In this chapter, we will introduce `<visual>`. We will leave `<inertia>` and `<collision>` for later in this book since these properties are only required when performing physics simulation with Gazebo (see `Chapter 5`, *Simulating Robot Behavior with Gazebo*).

The `<visual>` tag describes the visual appearance of the part. Don't confuse this with the `<collision>` tag, as that defines the volume to be considered for interference or crash calculation. Often, both may define different volumes, although it is very common that they are in agreement.

Why should they be different? For complex shapes, interference calculations can be heavy in terms of CPU load and time duration. Therefore, it is better to use simple shapes in `<collision>` tags, defining them as the envelope of the actual shapes of the parts. For example, for the manipulator in the following screenshot, you could define the `<visual>` elements of the arm as the actual shapes – the ones that are shown – and simplify the `<collision>` elements to make them the envelope cylinders of the arms to facilitate interference calculation:

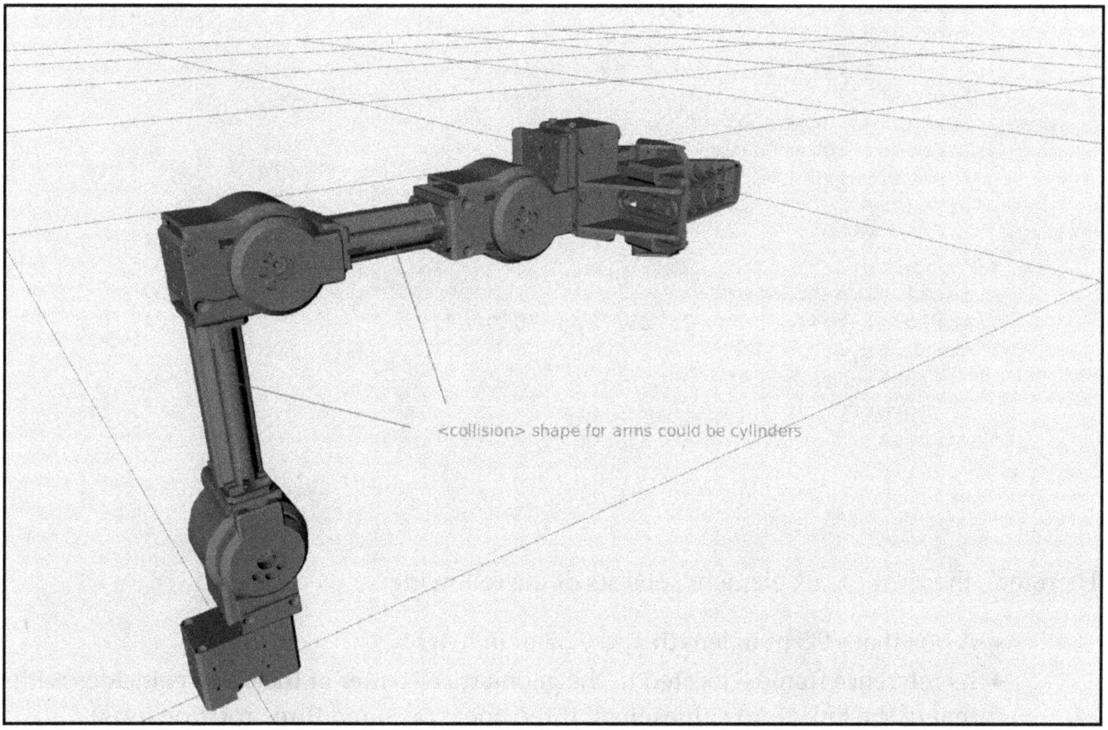

The `<origin>` tag specifies the reference frame of the `<visual>` element with respect to the reference frame of the link.

The `<geometry>` tag describes the visual shape (box, cylinder, sphere, or mesh) and its dimensions.

The `<material>` tag sets the appearance of the `<visual>` element with `<color>` and `<texture>`.

Given these tag descriptions, we can easily read about the `base_link` element, that is, the robot body, in the following code snippet:

```
<?xml version='1.0'?>
<robot name="gopigo3">

  <!-- Base Link -->
  <link name="base_link">
    <visual>
      <origin xyz="0 0 0" rpy="0 0 0" />
      <geometry>
          <box size="0.5 0.5 0.25"/>
      </geometry>
      <material name="blue">
        <color rgba="0 0.5 1 1"/>
      </material>
    </visual>

    <!-- Caster -->
    <visual name="caster">
      <origin xyz="0.2 0 -0.125" rpy="0 0 0" />
      <geometry>
        <sphere radius="0.05" />
      </geometry>
    </visual>

  </link>
...
```

Therefore, the `base_link` element consists of the following:

- A box that's 0.5 m in length and 0.25 m in height.
- Its reference frame – located in the geometrical center of the box – coincides with that of the link (zero values in all three linear axes and three rotation axes).
- The `<material>` tag specifies the blue color as RGBA indexes: Red = 0, Green = 0.5, Blue = 1. The fourth, A = 1, is the alpha channel, which refers to the degree of opacity. A value of 1 means an opaque object, while 0 means that it is transparent.

Rendering the link in RViz provides the following simple aspect of a box:

But wait – what is that semi-spherical shape attached to the lower face? That is the caster, the freewheel that we can model as an integral part of the robot body, as was explained previously.

Caster

The caster description is nested inside the `<link name="base_link">` element. This means that it's a rigid part that's fixed to the robot body. Let's go over what it is:

- It's a sphere that has a radius of 0.05 m, located at x=0.2 m, z=-0.125 m. Be aware that the *Z* coordinate is half of the box height (=0.25 m) and negative. This means that the top semi-sphere is embedded within the box and only the other semi-sphere stays visible on the bottom part of the box.
- By default, the same color is selected as what was defined for the box.

Inspect the following code carefully to ensure you understand it:

```
    <!-- Caster -->
<visual name="caster">
<origin xyz="0.2 0 -0.125" rpy="0 0 0" />
<geometry>
<sphere radius="0.05" />
</geometry>
</visual>
```

This is how the caster will appear in RViz, making the box semitransparent:

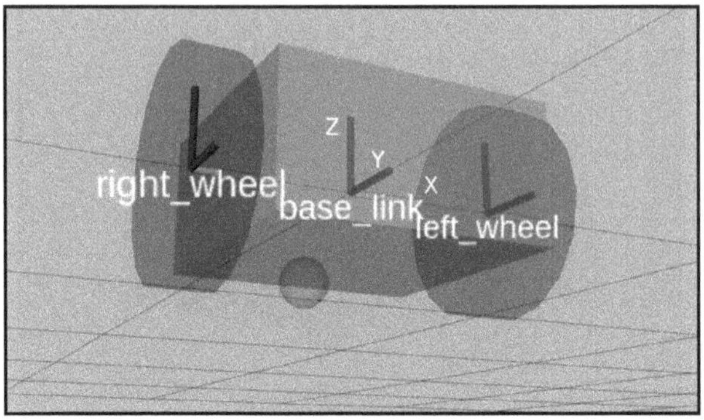

Take note of the position and direction of the **X**, **Y**, and **Z** axes, and pay attention to their directions. This fact is especially important when matching the axes of the IMU. The following photograph shows how you have to place such a sensor in a physical GoPiGo3 to make sure the IMU axes are parallel to the `base_link` frame and have the same directions (see the marked set of axes that are printed on the surface of the sensor):

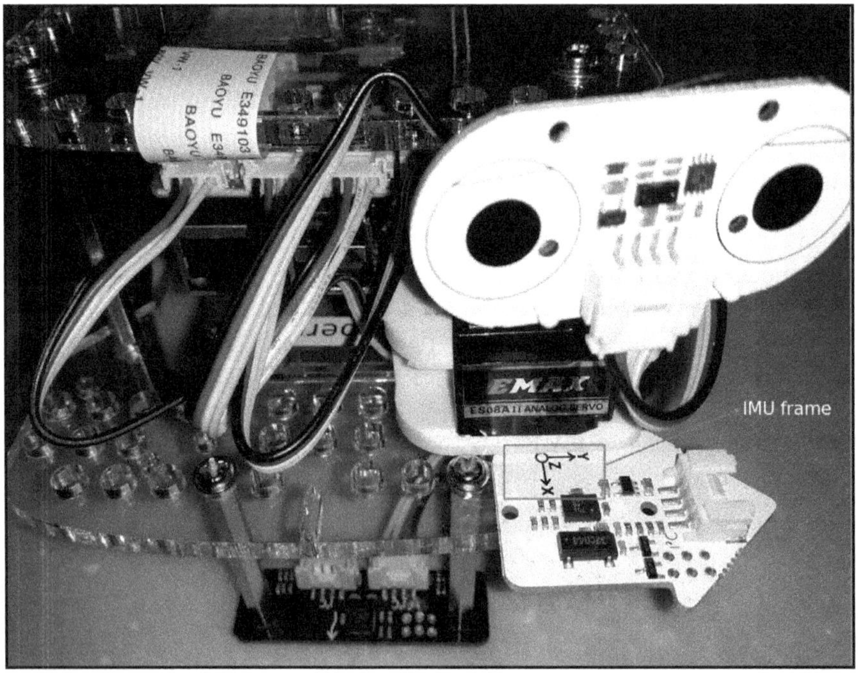

Finally, in the following photograph, you can see the whole robot. This will help you make sure that you know where the details in the preceding photograph are located:

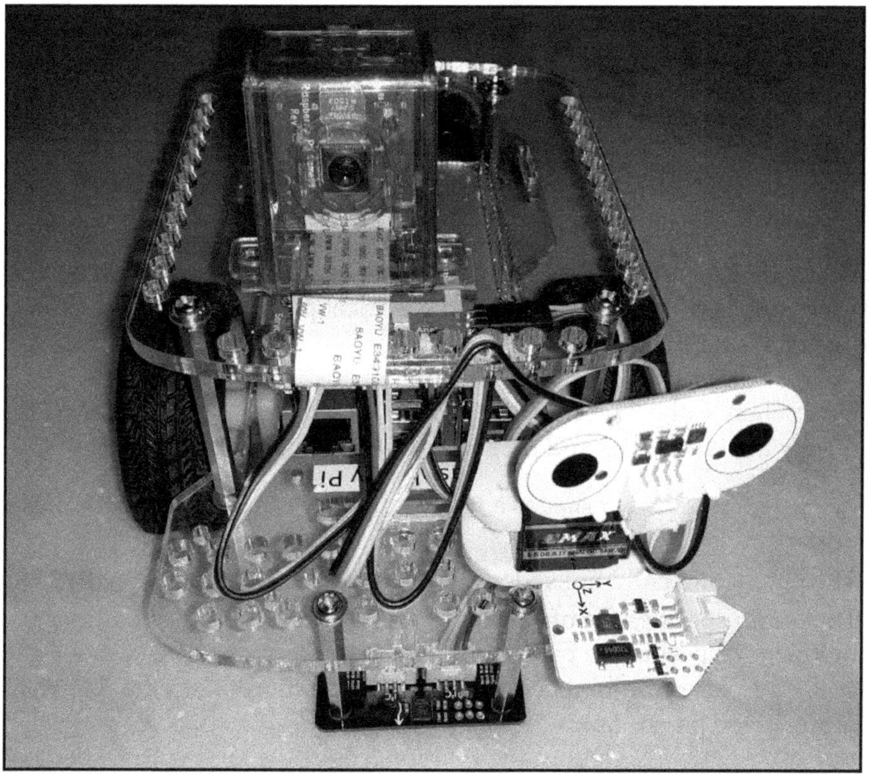

Next, let's have a look at the URDF model's left and right wheels.

The URDF model's left and right wheels

Given that you already know the basic URDF tags, it is straightforward to read the definition for the right wheel, as shown in the following code snippet:

```
<!-- Right Wheel -->
<link name="right_wheel">
  <visual>
    <origin xyz="0 0 0" rpy="1.570795 0 0" />
    <geometry>
        <cylinder length="0.1" radius="0.2" />
    </geometry>
    <material name="black">
```

```
        <color rgba="0.05 0.05 0.05 1"/>
      </material>
    </visual>
  </link>

  <joint name="joint_right_wheel" type="continuous">
    <parent link="base_link"/>
    <child link="right_wheel"/>
    <origin xyz="0 -0.30 0" rpy="0 0 0" />
    <axis xyz="0 1 0" />
  </joint>
```

Inside the `<origin>` tag, the first component of the `rpy` attribute (rotation around the *X* axis), 1.570795 = $\pi/2$, is what sets the wheel to a vertical position. The cylindrical wheel has a 0.2 m radius and is 0.1 m in length.

The new element here is the `<joint>` tag (`http://wiki.ros.org/urdf/XML/joint`), which is used to specify the kinematics and dynamics of the joint and its safety limits:

- `type="continuous"` means a hinge joint that rotates around the axis and has no upper and lower limits.
- The parent and child links identify what links are connected by this joint.
- The origin specifies the offsets in *X*, *Y*, and *Z* and the three rotations of the child link with respect to the parent link. Then, `<origin xyz="0 -0.30 0" rpy="0 0 0" />` places the joint at Y = -0.30 m. These coordinates are referred to the frame of the parent link:
    - `axis` defines the rotation axis of the joint with respect to the parent frame. Here, `<axis xyz="0 1 0" />` means that the rotation axis is Y (value 1 in the Y coordinate).

The XML description for the left wheel is almost identical. The only change is the position of the joint at Y = 0.30 m (`<origin xyz="0 0.30 0" ... />`), with an opposite sign to that of the right wheel, that is, `<origin xyz="0 -0.30 0" ... />`:

```
  <!-- Left Wheel -->
  <link name="left_wheel">
    <visual>
      <origin xyz="0 0 0" rpy="1.570795 0 0" />
      <geometry>
          <cylinder length="0.1" radius="0.2" />
      </geometry>
      <material name="black"/>
    </visual>
  </link>
```

```
<joint name="joint_left_wheel" type="continuous">
  <parent link="base_link"/>
  <child link="left_wheel"/>
  <origin xyz="0 0.30 0" rpy="0 0 0" />
  <axis xyz="0 1 0" />
</joint>
```

In the next section, you are going to learn how to visualize the URDF description in RViz, the ROS visualization tool.

Inspecting the GoPiGo3 model in ROS with RViz

Now, it's time to start working with ROS! You are going to discover `roslaunch`, the ROS command that allows us to launch several nodes in one shot, avoiding the need to open separate Terminals, as we did in the previous chapter.

Given that you already cloned the code repository of this book, the files that we will deal with are inside the `Chapter4_RViz_basics` folder of the repository, and all of them are part of the `rviz_basics` ROS package, as defined within `package.xml`. The file structure of this chapter can be seen in the following screenshot of the RoboWare Studio IDE:

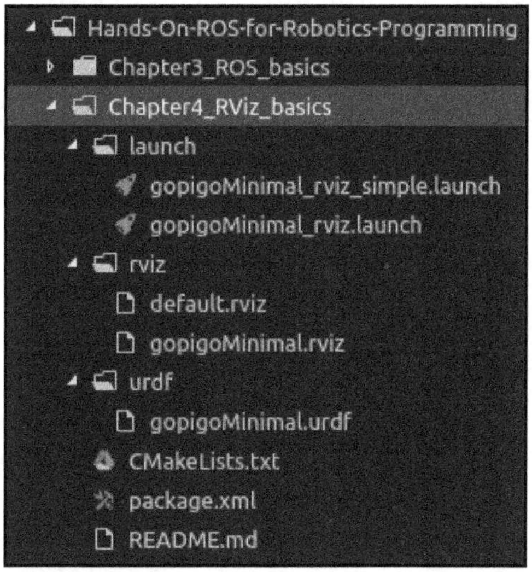

You can obtain this tree structure in the Terminal by using the `tree` bash command:

```
$ tree ~/catkin_ws/src/book/Chapter4_RViz_basics
```

Bear in mind that it does not come with Ubuntu by default and that you may need to install it:

```
$ sudo apt-get update
$ sudo apt-get install tree
```

This will result in the following output:

```
├── CMakeLists.txt
├── launch
│   ├── gopigoMinimal_rviz.launch
│   └── gopigoMinimal_rviz_simple.launch
├── package.xml
├── README.md
├── rviz
│   ├── default.rviz
│   └── gopigoMinimal.rviz
└── urdf
  └── gopigoMinimal.urdf
```

This tree organizes the files into a variety of folders, depending on the types of files:

- `./launch` groups the files with the `*.launch` extension, that is, the different robot configurations and packages that will be used in the runtime environment. Each launch file corresponds to a specific run's setup.
- `./rviz` stores the files of specific RViz configurations, one file for each possible configuration.
- `./urdf` contains the XML URDF file of the robot model we described previously.

Make sure this folder is in your workspace and build it with `catkin` so that ROS is aware of your new package:

```
$ cd ~/catkin_ws
$ catkin_make
```

> In `Chapter 3`, *Getting Started with ROS*, in the *Using Roboware – creating a workspace and building it* section, we explained how to do these operations in the Roboware IDE. Take a look at that chapter and section if you prefer to use a desktop application.

Finally, you can execute `roslaunch` from a Terminal with the following snippet:

```
$ roslaunch rviz_basics gopigoMinimal_rviz.launch model:=gopigoMinimal
```

The RViz window will launch and you will see a simplified GoPiGo3 model, as follows:

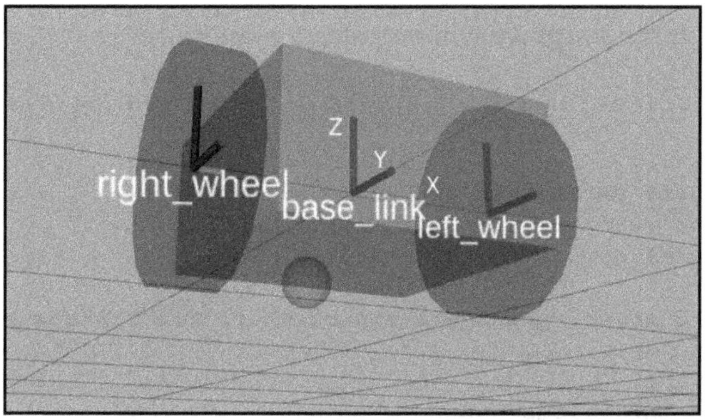

You can inspect the model by rotating it with the mouse while clicking the left button, and zoom in/zoom out by using the mouse wheel or, alternatively, clicking the right button and moving the mouse forward (zoom in) or backward (zoom out).

The left pane of RViz contains two items that are of interest to us. Expand them with a mouse click to inspect them:

- **RobotModel**: Where you can use the ticks to visualize what you need. The items under **Links** allow us to access individual parts of the GoPiGo URDF model: `base_link` (robot body), `left_wheel`, and `right_wheel`.
- **TF**: which provides access to the multiple coordinate frames. In our case, there is one frame for each of the parts of GoPiGo3 and one for each of the joints.

Next, we'll look at the `roslaunch` command.

Understanding the roslaunch command

Let's go one step back and use a minimal launch file to understand the syntax of these kinds of scripts:

```
$ roslaunch rviz_basics gopigoMinimal_rviz_simple.launch
```

As we saw with `rosrun`, the structure of the ROS command is very similar:

- First is the command name itself, `roslaunch`.
- Second is the package name, `rviz_basics`.
- The third is the script we will execute, `gopigoMinimal_rviz_simple.launch`.

The content of the `gopigoMinimal_rviz_simple.launch` file looks like this:

```
<launch>
   <!-- set these parameters on Parameter Server -->
   <param name="robot_description" textfile="$(find
rviz_basics)/urdf/gopigoMinimal.urdf" />

   <!-- Start 3 nodes: joint_state_publisher, robot_state_publisher and
rviz -->

   <!-- Send joint values -->
   <node pkg="joint_state_publisher" type="joint_state_publisher"
name="joint_state_publisher"/>

   <!-- Combine joint values to TF-->
   <node name="robot_state_publisher" pkg="robot_state_publisher"
type="state_publisher"/>

   <node name="rviz" pkg="rviz" type="rviz" args="-d $(find
rviz_basics)/rviz/gopigoMinimal.rviz" required="true" />
</launch>
```

The syntax, in XML format, should be familiar to you. In this file, there are three types of tags:

- `<launch> </launch>`: Delimits the block of lines that are part of the `roslaunch` description.

- `<node />`: This is the sentence that's used to execute a ROS node. It is equivalent to the `rosrun` command that we explained in the previous chapter. Due to this, the equivalent command to a `<node />` tagged line is as follows:

```
<node name="robot_state_publisher" pkg="robot_state_publisher"
type="state_publisher"/>

is equivalent to...

$ rosrun robot_joint_state_publisher state_publisher
```

  You can easily infer that the `pkg` attribute of the `<node>` tag is the package name and that the attribute type refers to the script that contains the code of this node.

- `<param />` stands for parameter and is a new ROS concept. It contains a value that is stored in the ROS parameter server that you can visualize as the place where the robot's characterization is stored. A whole set of parameters defines a specific robot configuration. The ROS parameter server, as explained in the ROS official documentation (`http://wiki.ros.org/Parameter%20Server`), is as follows:

"It is a shared, multi-variate dictionary that is accessible via network APIs. Nodes use this server to store and retrieve parameters at runtime. As it is not designed for high performance, it is best used for static, non-binary data such as configuration parameters."

In our particular case, we have the following declaration in the launch file:

```
<param name="robot_description" textfile="$(find
rviz_basics)/urdf/gopigoMinimal.urdf" />
```

The `robot_description` parameter is the path where the URDF file is stored. You will see that such a path contains an environment variable in the `$(find rviz_basics)` textfile attribute. This is a very nice feature that ROS provides out of the box so that you don't have to provide absolute or relative paths. The `find` command is applied to the `rviz_basics` package and returns the absolute path of the package, that is, `~/catkin_ws/src/book/Chapter4_RViz_basics`. The `$` sign means the value of, in the same way as you would do for system environment variables.

Using Roboware to execute a launch file

What you did using the `$ roslaunch` **`rviz_basics`** `gopigoMinimal_rviz_simple.launch` command can be done in the **Roboware** IDE by just placing it on top of the file, right-clicking the mouse to show the contextual menu, and selecting the first item, that is, **Run Launch File**:

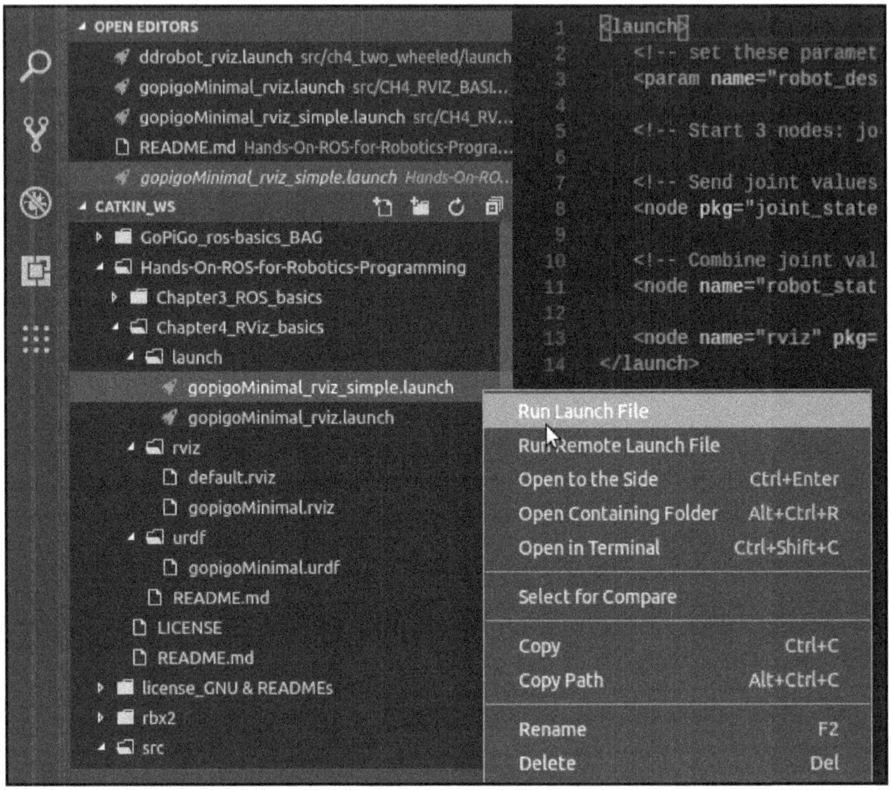

In the following section, we are going to execute the other launch file, `gopigoMinimal_rviz_simple.launch`, which introduces more advanced features. Prior to that, close any open RViz windows or hit *Ctrl* + *C* in the Terminal to shut down the running ROS processes.

Controlling the GoPiGo3 robot's wheels from RViz

The complete version of the robot can be launched with the following command:

```
$ roslaunch rviz_basics gopigoMinimal_rviz.launch model:=gopigoMinimal
```

What we are doing here is supplying an argument, `gopigoMinimal`, from the command line. If you pay attention to the content of the launch file, that is, `gopigoMinimal_rviz.launch`, you will find a new section at the beginning of the file tagged with `<arg />`:

```
<launch>
    <!-- values passed by command line input -->
    <arg name="model" default="gopigoMinimal" />
    <arg name="gui" default="False" />

    <!-- set these parameters on Parameter Server -->
    <param name="robot_description" textfile="$(find
rviz_basics)/urdf/$(arg model).urdf" />

    <!-- Start 3 nodes: joint_state_publisher, robot_state_publisher and
rviz -->

    <!-- Send joint values -->
    <node pkg="joint_state_publisher" type="joint_state_publisher"
name="joint_state_publisher">
      <param name="/use_gui" value="$(arg gui)"/>
    </node>
    <!-- Combine joint values to TF-->
    <node name="robot_state_publisher" pkg="robot_state_publisher"
type="state_publisher"/>

    <node name="rviz" pkg="rviz" type="rviz" args="-d $(find
rviz_basics)/rviz/$(arg model).rviz" required="true" />
    <!-- (required = "true") if rviz dies, entire roslaunch will be killed
-->
</launch>
```

The values that have been tagged as arguments can be passed from the command line by simply adding the argument name, the := sign, and its value after `<filename>.launch`:

```
<arg name="model" default="gopigoMinimal" />

is invoked with...

model:=gopigoMinimal
```

In the `<arg />` tag, you can provide a default value with a default attribute. In our specific case, we wouldn't have needed to add the argument value to the `roslaunch` command because the value is the default. Therefore, the result is exactly the same as if you had written the following:

```
$ roslaunch rviz_basics gopigoMinimal_rviz.launch
```

In the launch file, there is a second optional argument, `gui`:

```
<arg name="gui" default="False" />
```

It is a Boolean value and the default value is `False`, that is, nothing different happens. Now, let's say you execute the command while specifying it to be `True`:

```
$ roslaunch rviz_basics gopigoMinimal_rviz.launch model:=gopigoMinimal
gui:=True
```

If you do this, you will see an additional window to the side of RViz. The exposed GUI allows you to rotate each of the wheels independently with sliders:

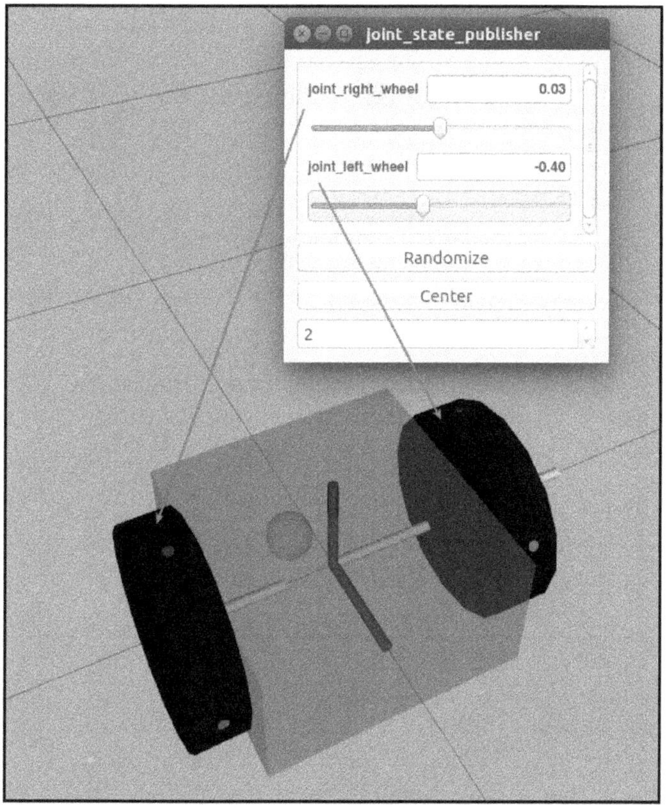

This interactive functionality is part of the `joint_state_publisher` package (`http://wiki.ros.org/joint_state_publisher`), whose `joint_state_publisher` node is invoked from the launch file with the `gui:=True` argument. We are going to explain this feature in the next section.

Using the joint_state_publisher package

The section of the launch file that allows us to interactively rotate the wheels using a GUI is as follows:

```
<node pkg="joint_state_publisher" type="joint_state_publisher"
name="joint_state_publisher">
  <param name="/use_gui" value="$(arg gui)"/>
</node>
```

The joint_state_publisher node exposes the /use_gui parameter to decide whether it should show the joint_state_publisher window. If it's set to True, the window is active. If it is, we pass the desired value as a parameter to the node via the gui argument that's defined in the launch file:

```
<arg name="gui" default="False" />
```

Remember the roslaunch command:

```
$ roslaunch rviz_basics gopigoMinimal_rviz.launch model:=gopigoMinimal
gui:=True
```

The gui argument is set to True. The /use_gui parameter value of joint_state_publisher is then set to the value of the gui argument, as expressed with the <param name="/use_gui" value="$(arg gui)"/> tag inside the gopigoMinimal_rviz.launch file.

The joint_state_publisher node launches the widget that allows to interactively rotate each wheel. Finally, issue rqt_graph from a Terminal to watch the ROS graph:

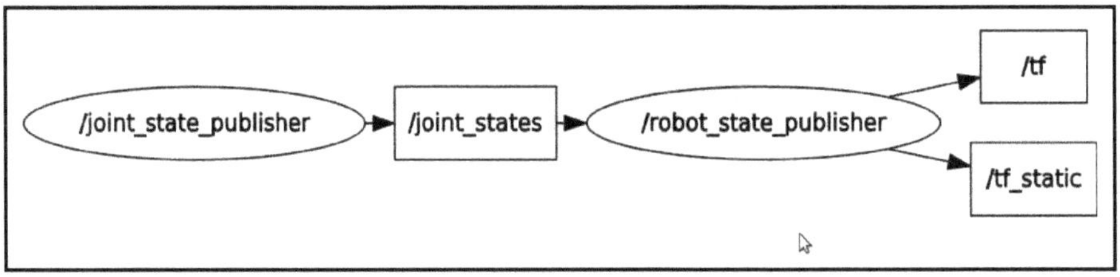

The /joint_states topic is the one that we modify when moving the sliders in the window.

Robot frames of reference in the URDF model

It is very important to understand how to place the different reference frames you will use for your robot. First, you have to decide where the <joint> elements are located in the space. In our case, we have two: one for the right wheel and one for the left wheel. Let's look at the one for the right wheel first:

```
<joint name="joint_right_wheel" type="continuous">
  <parent link="base_link"/>
```

```
    <child link="right_wheel"/>
    <origin xyz="0 -0.30 0" rpy="0 0 0" />
    <axis xyz="0 1 0" />
  </joint>
```

Now, let's look at the one for the left wheel:

```
<joint name="joint_left_wheel" type="continuous">
  <parent link="base_link"/>
  <child link="left_wheel"/>
  <origin xyz="0 0.30 0" rpy="0 0 0" />
  <axis xyz="0 1 0" />
</joint>
```

Here, you can see that the `<origin>` tags specify the locations:

- The right joint origin is -0.30 m along the *y* ground axis (green axis).
- The left joint origin is +0.30 m along the *y* ground axis.

As in both cases, regarding the `rpy="0 0 0"` attribute, there is no rotation and both coordinate frames are parallel to that of the coordinate frame of the ground. We know that both `<joint>` tags are relative to the ground because both have `base_link` as the parent link, and you know that the first link of our model, `base_link`, is the absolute reference for the robot's overall position and orientation.

In general, `<origin>` is the transform from the parent link to the child link. The joint is located at the origin of the child link. The tag `<axis xyz="0 1 0">` specifies the rotation axis. In this case it is `y` axis, since it has a value of `1`, while `x` and `z` have `0` values.

The frames you can see in the following screenshot are the respective ones for `base_link`, `right_wheel`, and `left_wheel`. They are specified inside the `<visual>` tag of each link. In these three cases, in the URDF file, you will see that they follow the following pattern:

```
<link name="base_link">
   <visual>
     <origin xyz="0 0 0" rpy=".. .. .." />
```

xyz="0 0 0" means that they coincide with the joint reference frame:

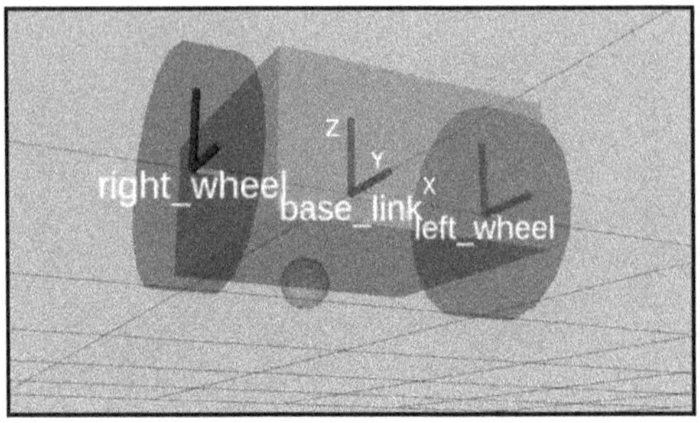

In the case of the wheels, we have the following:

```
<origin xyz="0 0 0" rpy="1.570795 0 0" />
```

1.570795 = pi/2 = 90° is the rotation around the x axis (red). This is what ensures that the cylinders shaping the wheels are oriented vertically.

Using RViz to check the model while building

Taking into account all the concepts we have introduced about URDF, we can use the RViz tool to assist us while building the robot model. Some checks that it can provide are as follows:

- The total size of the robot has to match the dimensions of the actual robot. As you build the model part by part, if you make a mistake regarding a part's dimension, an error will arise when you measure the total size (length, width, and height). You can check this by using the measure tool in the RViz toolbar.
- You can also visually check for possible interference between robot parts, especially between the ones that are adjacent and move relative to each other (in respect to one another).
- The orientation of the reference frames.
- You can visualize the parts that are hidden by others by unchecking the corresponding link in RViz or by changing the <color> tag in order to apply transparency effects.

In the following diagram, you can see that we have extracted a top view from RViz and used transparency to check that all the parts are aligned and relative to each other:

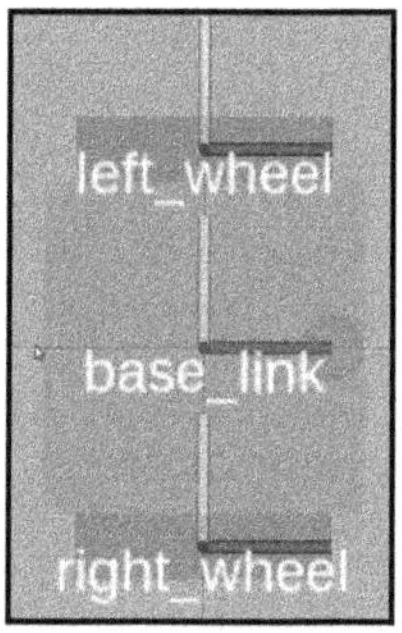

This transparency allows us to check that the caster position is right in the middle of `base_link`. Furthermore, the wheels do not interfere with `base_link`, and their rotation axes are coaxial.

Changing the aspect of the model in the RViz window

To control the visual aspect of your model in RViz, you can modify some of the parameters in the **Displays** window, as shown in the following screenshot:

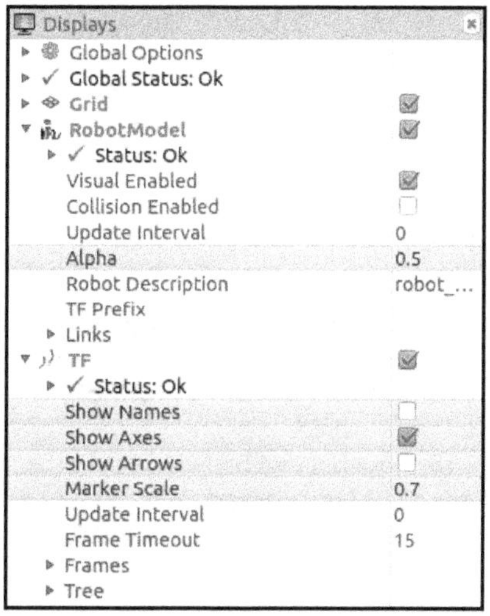

We have marked the basic changes we've made for this chapter in gray:

- **Alpha**: This parameter controls the level of opacity of the whole model. The value `1` corresponds to its opaque appearance, while `0` is fully transparent, that is, not visible. There is also an **Alpha** parameter for each link to control the individual opacity of a single part (under the **Links** subtree, expand to access it).
- **Show Names**: If ticked, the name of the links will be shown on the screen.
- **Show Axes**: If ticked, it will show the frame of reference of each link.
- **Show Arrows**: If ticked, it will show the direction of each joint.
- **Marker Scale**: The default is `1`. Reduce its value so that words are smaller on the screen.

To save this set of parameters, go to the **File** item in the top menu and select **Save Config As**. Here, you specify the name of the file with the `.rviz` extension, which is where your custom settings will be saved.

Be aware that within the same **File** menu, you have the **Save Image** option, which will produce a screenshot of the current RViz window.

Helpful ROS tools for checking purposes

Finally, you should know that there are two helpful ROS tools if you want to make some checks:

- `check_urdf` attempts to parse a URDF file in order to verify the kinematic chain:

  ```
  $ roscd rviz_basics
  $ check_urdf ./urdf/gopigoMinimal.urdf
  ```

  The `roscd` command changes the prompt to the path of the ROS package whose name you are indicating as an argument, that is, `rviz_basics`. The output is as follows, where the current folder is the `rviz_basics` path, as requested, that is, `~/catkin_ws/src/CH4_RVIZ_BASICS` before the `$` sign:

  ```
  ~/catkin_ws/src/CH4_RVIZ_BASICS$ check_urdf
  ./urdf/gopigoMinimal.urdf
  robot name is: gopigoMinimal
  ---------- Successfully Parsed XML ---------------
  root Link: base_link has 2 child(ren)
   child(1): left_wheel
   child(2): right_wheel
  ```

  Everything is fine!

- `rqt_tf_tree` allows us to visualize the `tf` information in the GUI environment, like so:

```
$ roslaunch rviz_basics gopigoMinimal_rviz.launch
model:=gopigoMinimal
$ rosrun rqt_tf_tree rqt_tf_tree
```

A window will open, showing this aspect graph:

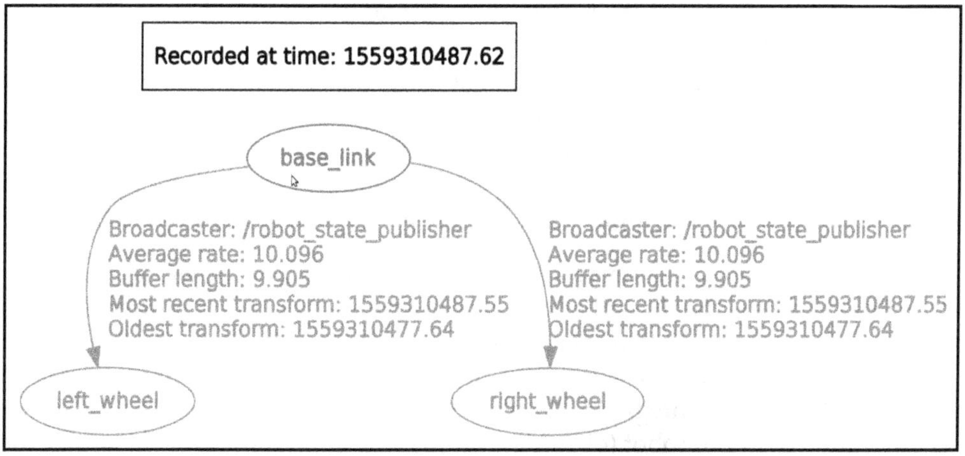

The preceding graph tells you that `base_link` (robot body part) and the wheels are well connected. The arrows represent the joint elements: `joint_right_wheel` and `joint_left_wheel`.

Alternatively, you can generate this same output as a PDF file:

```
$ rosrun tf view_frames
```

Then, you can open the created PDF, like so:

```
$ evince frames.pdf
```

This second way of doing things is more convenient if you want to share the output with colleagues.

Summary

In this chapter, we introduced two essential elements of ROS. One is the URDF format, which is the standard way of describing the virtual model of a robot. The other is RViz, the ROS visualization tool, which lets you inspect your model while building and check the final result.

You have learned about these essential elements by looking at GoPiGo3, where you created a simplified model that includes its chassis, motors, and wheels. We have shown you how to interactively rotate the wheels with a GUI by accessing the `joint_states` topic of the `joint_state_publisher` node, which belongs to the package with the same name. This package offers a tool for setting and publishing joint state values for a given URDF model. In the case of GoPiGo3, we have two joints: the left wheel and the right wheel. The caster is the third joint, but as it is a freewheel (not driven by a motor), so we don't need to define it as such in the virtual GoPiGo3. Rigidly attaching it to the robot body is sufficient.

In RViz, we can simulate the kinematics of the robot. In the next chapter, we will go one step further and simulate the dynamics. This is something that will require us to complete our URDF model with mass and inertia properties, as well as specify the rolling resistance in the wheels to reproduce all the forces that act on our robot. We will do that with Gazebo, a dynamics simulator that's integrated with ROS. With Gazebo, we can also reproduce the physical environment of the robot (obstacles, ramps, walls, and more).

Questions

1. What is the format of the URDF model?

   A) It is a text file.
   B) JSON.
   C) XML.

2. How many links and joints does the URDF model of GoPiGo3 have?

   A) Four links (robot body, caster, left, and right wheels) and two joints
   B) Three links (robot body, left, and right wheels) and two joints
   C) Three links (robot body, left, and right wheels) and three joints

3. Which tag in the URDF model can you use to specify the color of a link?

   A) `<visual>`
   B) `<geometry>`
   C) `<material>`

4. Is it mandatory to group file types by folders (SRC, URDF, RViz, launch) in an ROS package?

   A) No, the only mandatory condition is to put the package under `~/catkin_ws/src/`.
   B) It is only recommended to make a clean package structure.
   C) No, but if you do so, you have to declare the locations in the `package.xml` configuration file.

5. Do you always need to run `roscore` in a Terminal to launch a ROS process?

   A) Yes, because the master node launched by `roscore` is what keeps the communication between the nodes of the graph.
   B) You can launch the master node implicitly when using `roslaunch`.
   C) If you have installed the `roscore` package, it is mandatory to run the `roscore` process.

Further reading

- ROS URDF tutorials: `http://wiki.ros.org/urdf/Tutorials`.
- ROS visualization tutorials: `http://wiki.ros.org/visualization/Tutorials`.
- *ROS Robot Programming: A Handbook Written by TurtleBot3 Developers*, YoonSeok Pyo, HanCheol Cho, RyuWoon Jung, and TaeHoon Lim (2017), ROBOTIS Co. Ltd, first edition: `http://www.pishrobot.com/wp-content/uploads/2018/02/ROS-robot-programming-book-by-turtlebo3-developers-EN.pdf`. Chapter: *ROS Tools: RViz and rqt* and 10.8 *TurtleBot3 Simulation using RViz.*

5
Simulating Robot Behavior with Gazebo

This chapter deals with the dynamic simulation of a robot, which, conceptually, is a better approach to examining the actual behavior of the robot rather than just using software. Rigid body mechanics, including mass and inertia, friction, damping, motor controllers, sensor detection properties, noise signals, and every aspect of the robot and the environment that can be retained in a model with reasonable accuracy is much less expensive when replicated in a simulator than if you tried to do this with physical hardware.

By reading this chapter, you will learn how to plug the digital definition of your robot (the URDF file) into the simulation environment of **Gazebo**, which is powered with a physics engine that's able to emulate realistic behaviors. You will also extend your training by checking and testing the digital robot so that its behavior represents what should happen in the physical world.

To achieve ROS integration with Gazebo, a set of ROS packages grouped under `gazebo_ros_pkgs` (`http://wiki.ros.org/gazebo_ros_pkgs`) provides the required wrappers. These packages provide the interfaces that are used to simulate a robot in Gazebo using ROS messages, services, and reconfigurable ROS parameters.

By following a guided path, you will become familiar with the ROS simulation environment of Gazebo. Specifically, you will learn how to prepare the model of a robot in order to simulate realistic behavior with the Gazebo physics engine. Finally, you will simulate the maximum weight that GoPiGo3 can carry and compare this with the real world.

In this chapter, we will cover the following topics:

- Getting started with the Gazebo simulator
- Making modifications to the robot URDF
- Verifying a Gazebo model and viewing the URDF
- Moving your model around

Technical requirements

The code files for this chapter can be found at `https://github.com/PacktPublishing/Hands-On-ROS-for-Robotics-Programming/tree/master/Chapter5_Gazebo_basics`.

By completing the previous chapter, you should have cloned this book's code repository into the home folder of your laptop. In case you didn't, we'll go over this now. From a Terminal on your laptop, clone the repository into your home folder, like so:

```
$ cd ~
$ git clone
https://github.com/PacktPublishing/Hands-On-ROS-for-Robotics-Programming
```

Next, we copy the code for this chapter to the ROS workspace. This way, you will have a cleaner ROS environment:

```
$ cp -R ~/Hands-On-ROS-for-Robotics-Programming/Chapter5_Gazebo_basics
~/catkin_ws/src
```

This chapter contains a new ROS package called `gazebo_basics`, so rebuild the workspace so that it is known to your ROS environment:

```
$ cd ~/catkin_ws
$ catkin_make
$ source ~/catkin_ws/devel/setup.bash
```

Check that the package is correctly installed by selecting it and listing its files:

```
$ roscd gazebo_basics
$ pwd
  ~/catkin_ws/src/Chapter5_Gazebo_basics
```

The output of the `pwd` command shows the location, as expected. Now, you are ready to complete this chapter.

Getting started with the Gazebo simulator

Let's go through a quick tour so that you have a clear understanding of what you can expect when implementing a dynamic simulation for GoPiGo3. Gazebo is an open source 3D robotics simulator and includes an ODE physics engine and OpenGL rendering, and supports code integration for closed-loop control in robot drives—that is, sensor simulation and actuator control. There are two new concepts within this definition. Let's explain each one:

- **Open Dynamics Engine** (**ODE**), a physics engine written in C/C++ that includes two main components: rigid-body dynamics simulation and collision detection (`https://www.ode.org/`).
- **Open Graphics Library** (**OpenGL**), which is both a cross-language and cross-platform API for rendering 2D and 3D vector graphics. This API is typically used to interact with a GPU in order to achieve hardware-accelerated rendering. It is a specification that sets a standard for how the GPU of a PC has to display graphics on the screen by rendering 2D and 3D vector graphics. Being a specification, it is cross-platform by nature, and every manufacturer can make a different implementation with it (GPU driver). The point of this is that the functionality it provides has to be as it's specified in the standard so that we can say that the driver is OpenGL compliant.

Follow these steps to get started with Gazebo:

1. Test the Gazebo installation by launching it with a premade environment:

```
$ roslaunch gazebo_ros empty_world.launch
```

The `gazebo_ros` package is a ROS package that resides in the `/opt/ros/kinetic/share/` system folder. It comes with the installation of `ros-kinetic-desktop-full` (or `ros-melodic-desktop-full`, if you are in Ubuntu 18.04) that was detailed in `Chapter 3`, *Getting Started with ROS*.

> TIP: If you don't want to run a full installation of ROS, you can install the packages individually. In the case of Gazebo, the installation command is `$ sudo apt-get install ros-kinetic-gazebo-ros-pkgs ros-kinetic-gazebo-ros-control` if you're on Ubuntu 16.04 or `$ sudo apt-get install ros-melodic-gazebo-ros-pkgs ros-melodic-gazebo-ros-control` if you're on Ubuntu 18.04.

Apart from `empty_world.launch`, you have additional world launch files available whose names can be found by using the following command, which lists the files inside the launch folder of the `gazebo_ros` package:

```
$ roscd gazebo_ros/launch && ls -la
```

The `&&` symbol is commonly used in bash to run two commands in the same line. They are executed in the same order that they're written in. The output is as follows:

```
-rw-r--r-- 1 root root 2013 Jan 23 16:58 elevator_world.launch
-rw-r--r-- 1 root root 2300 Jan 23 16:58 empty_world.launch
-rw-r--r-- 1 root root 637 Jan 23 16:58 mud_world.launch
-rw-r--r-- 1 root root 850 Jan 23 16:58 range_world.launch
-rw-r--r-- 1 root root 640 Jan 23 16:58 rubble_world.launch
-rw-r--r-- 1 root root 640 Jan 23 16:58 shapes_world.launch
-rw-r--r-- 1 root root 646 Jan 23 16:58 willowgarage_world.launch
```

2. Launch `mud_world.launch` and be patient; it will take a few seconds to render since it contains mobile parts:

```
$ roslaunch gazebo_ros mud_world.launch
```

The following screenshot shows the output of the preceding commands:

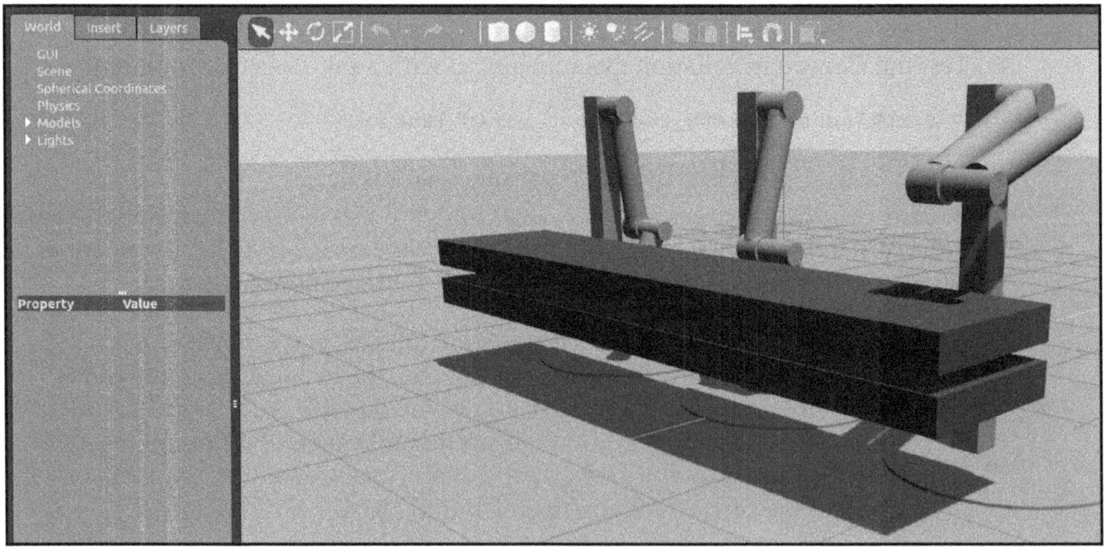

Using the mouse, you can move and rotate the world to change the perspective:

- Hold down the left button of the mouse when the Gazebo window is active. Moving the mouse will cause the world to move on the screen.
- Hold down the central wheel button and move the mouse to turn the world. The point of rotation will be the one that the mouse pointer was in when you first pressed the wheel.
- Hold down the right button of the mouse. By moving the mouse forward and backward, you will get to zoom in and zoom out, respectively.

TIP

To stop Gazebo, you have to press *Ctrl* + *C* in the Terminal where you executed the command. It can take several seconds to stop this process. Be aware that closing the Gazebo window is not enough to end the simulation process.

A more complex version is `willowgarage_world`:

```
$ roslaunch gazebo_ros willowgarage_world.launch
```

This looks as follows:

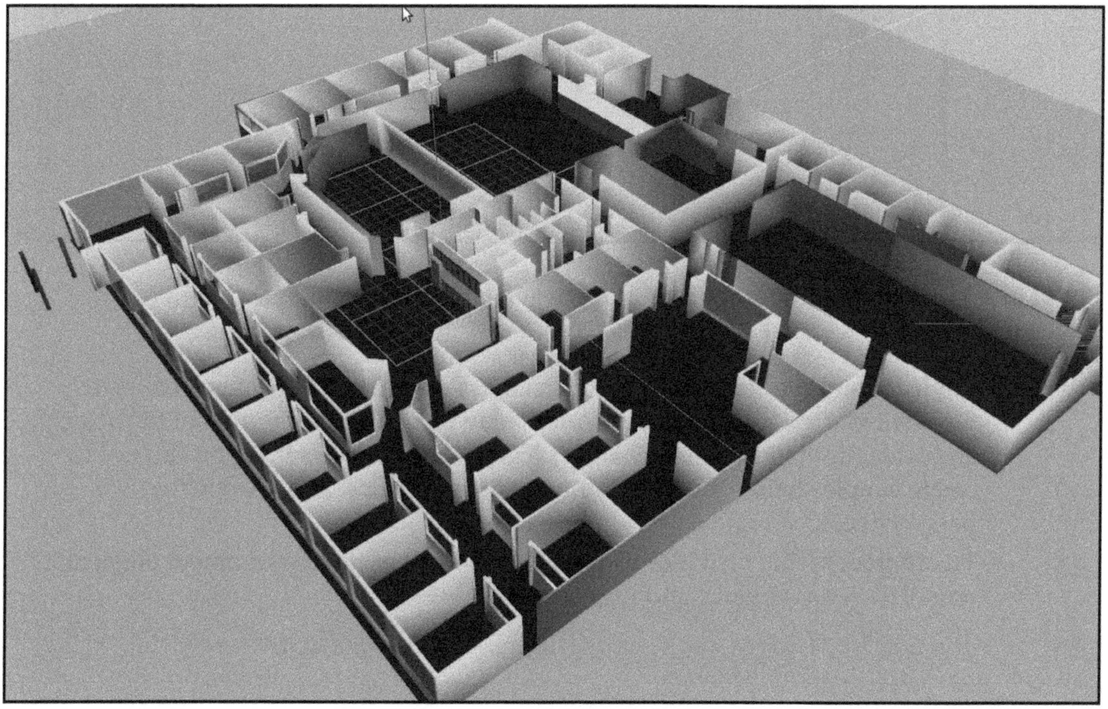

As a brief insight into Gazebo, we are going to identify the panels in the user GUI—as depicted in the following screenshot—that you can reproduce with this command:

```
$ roslaunch gazebo_basics gopigo_gazebo.launch
```

For this to work, you need to have copied the files in this chapter's repository, as we explained in the *Technical requirements* section:

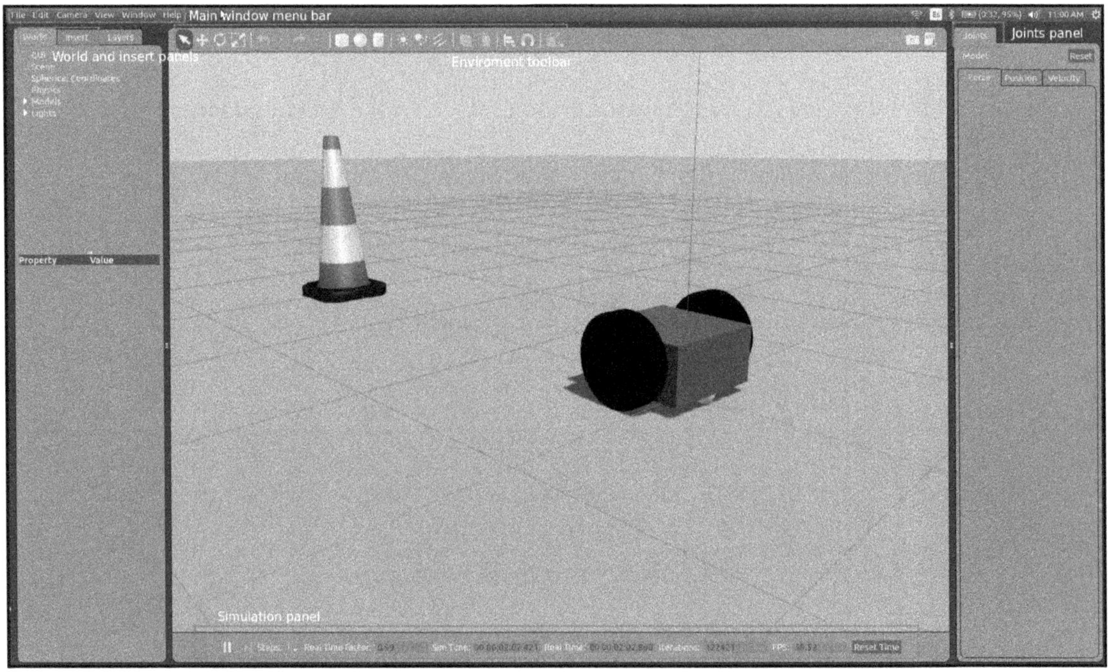

Let's have a look at the different fields that are available on the panel in the preceding screenshot in detail:

- **Environment toolbar**: There are icons that you can use to change between different modes: selection, translation of an object/robot, rotation of the object, and scale (limited to simple shapes). There are also icons that you can use to create simple shapes, provide lighting characteristics, and change the perspective.
- **World panel**: This provides us with access to all of the environment elements: Scene, Physics, Models, and Lights.

- **Joints panel**: This provides us with access to the locations that you can pick models up from. The first is `/home/<username>/.gazebo/models`, which is the user's repository of Gazebo models that have been selected from the main Gazebo repository. This repository is the second option and is available at `http://models.gazebosim.org`.
- **Main window menu bar**: This provides options under the basic **File**, **Edit**, **View**, **Window**, and **Help** headings.
- **Simulation panel**: Located at the bottom of the environment display, it is a handy tool that's used to run simulation scripts and provide real-time information when recording or playing back a simulation.

Now that we have understood how the Gazebo simulator works, let's make some modifications to the robot URDF.

Making modifications to the robot URDF

URDF, as we explained in the previous chapter, stands for Unified Robot Description Format and has an XML-compliant syntax to simulate the visual properties of a robot. This format, fitting the scope it was conceived for, does not model some of the characteristics that are needed for a dynamic simulation. More precisely, it cannot specify the following:

- The pose of the robot itself within a world.
- Joint loops (parallel linkages).
- Friction and other properties.
- Things that are not robots, such as lights, height maps, and so on.

For such reasons, an evolved XML format called **Simulation Description Format** (**SDF**) started its development as part of the Gazebo robot simulator. SDF allows us to describe objects to the environments for robot simulators, visualization, and control. Over the years, SDF has become a stable, robust, and extensible format that's capable of describing all aspects of robots.

Extending URDF to produce an SDF robot definition

The way to arrive at an SDF specification for your robot is quite straightforward if you start from the URDF definition we saw in the previous chapter.

Always have the SDF format specification at hand (`http://sdformat.org/spec`) since it offers an interactive tree so that you can navigate through all the tags, allowing you to understand the purpose of each one and how it relates to others. The open source code repository is located at `https://bitbucket.org/osrf/sdformat`.

To show that SDF extends and does not break URDF specification, here are some simple guidelines that allow you to convert your URDF model into a Gazebo-ready SDF description:

- The minimum required adaptation is to include an `<inertia>` element within each `<link>` element. The goal of this new element is to include the mass and moment of inertia properties of all of the robot links, which is essential to carrying out a dynamic simulation. The rest of the adaptations that we'll list here are optional.
- Adding a `<gazebo>` element for every `<link>` provides the functionality of converting visual colors into Gazebo format and translating STL files into DAE files for better textures. Sensor plugins are placed inside this tag.
- Adding a `<gazebo>` element for every `<joint>` allows us to specify damping, friction, and spring stiffness, and also allows us to add actuator control plugins.
- Add a `<gazebo>` element for the `<robot>` element.
- Add a `<link name="world"/>` link if the robot should be rigidly attached to the `world/base_link`.

You can find out more about this conversion by following the tutorial *Using a URDF in Gazebo* (`http://gazebosim.org/tutorials?tut=ros_urdf`), along with the applied examples.

The `<gazebo>` tag sets some default values that will be automatically included with your SDF description. This tag allows us to identify any elements that are found in SDF format that can't be found in URDF format. If a `<gazebo>` tag is used without a `reference=" "` property, it is assumed that the description inside refers to the whole robot model. The reference parameter usually refers to a specific robot link—that is, it defines its material.

Collisions and physical properties

Collision tags specify the volumes that need to be taken into account by the physics engine to detect interference/clearance between bodies. The visual tag from URDF is ignored for the purpose of this computation since it's only used for visualization purposes. This means that, in general, you can decouple visible aspects of the robot (more detailed) from the envelope shapes that are used for computing interference (simpler shapes).

The **inertia** tag of a part specifies its mass and tensor of inertia (3 x 3), along with all of its components (only six components are needed since the matrix is symmetrical).

In the `gopigo.urdf` file under the `urdf` folder, you can find the blocks of XML for the `base_link` and caster (remember that the latter has been modeled as part of `base_link` as an acceptable simplification of the model). This first snippet corresponds to the `base_link` itself and specifies the collision and mass properties:

```
<link name="base_link">
...
    <!-- Base collision, mass and inertia -->
    <collision>
        <origin xyz="0 0 0" rpy="0 0 0" />
        <geometry>
            <box size="0.5 0.5 0.25"/>
        </geometry>
    </collision>
    <inertial>
      <mass value="5"/>
      <inertia ixx="0.13" ixy="0.0" ixz="0.0" iyy="0.21" iyz="0.0"
izz="0.13"/>
    </inertial>
```

This includes the frame origin and orientation (`<origin>` tag), the geometry of the element (`<geometry>`), the mass (`<mass>`), and the inertia tensor (`<inertia>`). The second part models the caster and closes the block with the `</link>` tag:

```
    <!-- Caster collision, mass and inertia -->
    <collision>
      <origin xyz="0.2 0 -0.125" rpy="0 0 0" />
      <geometry>
        <sphere radius="0.05" />
      </geometry>
    </collision>
    <inertial>
      <mass value="0.5"/>
 <inertia ixx="0.0001" ixy="0.0" ixz="0.0" iyy="0.0001" iyz="0.0"
izz="0.0001"/>
```

```
    </inertial>
</link>
```

These properties use the same tags we explained previously. For the right wheel, the following is the corresponding piece of code:

```
<!-- Right Wheel -->
<link name="right_wheel">
...
    <!-- Right Wheel collision, mass and inertia -->
    <collision>
      <origin xyz="0 0 0" rpy="1.570795 0 0" />
      <geometry>
          <cylinder length="0.1" radius="0.2" />
      </geometry>
    </collision>
    <inertial>
 <mass value="0.5"/>
 <inertia ixx="0.01" ixy="0.0" ixz="0.0" iyy="0.005" iyz="0.0"
izz="0.005"/>
 </inertial>
</link>
```

For the left wheel, the specification is exactly the same.

Gazebo tags

As we mentioned previously, `<gazebo>` tags are used to specify the additional elements to URDF that are needed within the native Gazebo format, SDF. In the `gopigo.gazebo` file under the `URDF` folder, you can find the following blocks of code, which specify the material for each link:

- The first is the robot body (`base_link`). This block specifies the color of the part, as well as its initial pose:

  ```
  <gazebo reference="base_link">
    <material>Gazebo/Blue</material>
    <pose>0 0 3 0 0 0</pose>
  </gazebo>
  ```

- Next is the wheels. These blocks are only needed to specify the colors since the pose was defined in `base_link`:

  ```
  <gazebo reference="right_wheel">
    <material>Gazebo/Black</material>
  ```

```
  </gazebo>
...
  <gazebo reference="left_wheel">
    <material>Gazebo/Black</material>
  </gazebo>
```

If you plan to reuse this code or share it, it is recommended that you add the dependency to your `package.xml` file for the `gazebo_basics` package. The following statement should be added under the dependencies section of such a file:

```
<exec_depend>gazebo_ros</exec_depend>
```

This way, when building the ROS workspace, the requested dependencies will be taken into account, providing an output that permits the package to be executed when called from the runtime.

Verifying a Gazebo model and viewing the URDF

Once the SDF definition has been completed in the `gopigo.urdf` file, you should perform some checks to ensure that the file can be read by Gazebo. To do so, navigate to the folder where the model resides:

```
$ roscd gazebo_basics/urdf
```

The `roscd` command is a very useful ROS command that's equivalent to the Linux `cd` command, but specifies the paths that are relative to a given package. It's also easier to use because all you have to do is provide the name of the package that you want to move to the Terminal. The first part, `gazebo_basics`, retrieves the absolute path of the package, as well as the second part of the folder or subfolder path you want to show. This ROS command, as well as other useful ones, will be covered in detail in the next chapter, under the *Shell commands* subsection.

Use the following two commands to print and check the model, respectively:

```
$ gz sdf --print gopigo.gazebo
$ gz sdf --check gopigo.gazebo
```

The first command prints the XML file in the Terminal window so that you can inspect it. The second checks the syntax of such a file. Alternatively, you can do this with a single command, respectively (without needing the initial roscd):

```
$ gz sdf --print $(rospack find gazebo_basics)/urdf/gopigo.gazebo
$ gz sdf --check $(rospack find gazebo_basics)/urdf/gopigo.gazebo
```

In this case, we are using another ROS command, rospack find, to write the path of the model.

> The $ symbol before the opening bracket in bash is telling us this: return me the path of the gazebo_basics package.

After the closing bracket, there is the route inside the package—that is, /urdf—which is where gopigo.gazebo is located.

If everything goes well in the checking process, you will obtain a successful message:

```
Check complete
```

If you intentionally remove the closing > of a tag or a complete <tag>, the check command will throw the following error:

```
Error [parser.cc:293] Error parsing XML in file
[~/catkin_ws/src/CH5_GAZEBO_BASICS/urdf/gopigo.gazebo]: Error reading end
tag.
Error: SDF parsing the xml failed
```

If you remove the opening <link> and closing </link>, you'll obtain the following error:

```
Error [parser_urdf.cc:3474] Unable to call parseURDF on robot model
Error [parser.cc:310] parse as old deprecated model file failed.
Error: SDF parsing the xml failed
```

Remove any incorrect syntax from the file and make sure it passes the check procedure. When you're ready, proceed to the next section, where we will see the model in action.

Launching the GoPiGo model in Gazebo

The single-launch file of this chapter can be found under the launch folder of the package and is called `gopigo_gazebo.launch`. We've divided its code into the following two snippets for explanation purposes:

```
<launch>
  <include file="$(find gazebo_ros)/launch/empty_world.launch">
    <arg name="world_name" value="$(find
gazebo_basics)/worlds/gopigo.world"/>
    <arg name="paused" default="false"/>
    <arg name="use_sim_time" default="true"/>
    <arg name="gui" default="true"/>
    <arg name="headless" default="false"/>
    <arg name="debug" default="false"/>
  </include>
```

Here, you can see two new tags, `<include>` and `<arg>`. The former allows us to include launch files from other ROS packages, while the latter allows us to make the launch file configurable using local arguments. The `<arg>` tag will be explained in the *Explaining configurable launch files using the <arg> tag* section.

The `<include>` block calls external files and defines the default values for the parameters. Its syntax can be clearly understood if we bear its equivalent command in mind when using the Terminal:

```
$ roslaunch gazebo_ros empty_world.launch
```

As you might have guessed, the `<include>` tag specifies the `empty_world.launch` file belonging to the `gazebo_ros` ROS package (which ships with the ROS installation, and is, therefore, a system package).

Regarding the file path, it is worth mentioning the mechanism that ROS uses to abstract the physical location of any package in the disk by using the `find` keyword:

```
$(find gazebo_basics)
```

Similar to the purpose of the `$` symbol in bash—that is, accessing the value of an environment variable—the preceding snippet provides us with a message stating `return me the path of the gazebo_basics package`. After the closing bracket, we can see the route inside the package—that is, `/launch`—which is where `empty_world.launch` is located.

You can explore its contents by listing the file, as usual:

```
$ roscd gazebo_ros/launch
$ cat empty_world.launch
```

This is where the available worlds (that the line in bold letters refers to) are loaded from the Gazebo installation directory—`/usr/share/gazebo-7/worlds` if you are in Ubuntu 16.04 or `/usr/share/gazebo-9/worlds` if you are in Ubuntu 18.04. In the case of our launch file, we are using `worlds/empty.world`. It's marked in bold in the following code:

```
<launch>
  <!-- these are the arguments you can pass this launch file, for example
paused:=true -->
  ...
  <arg name="physics" default="ode"/>
  <arg name="verbose" default="false"/>
  <arg name="world_name" default="worlds/empty.world"/>
  ...

  <!-- start gazebo server-->
  ...
  <!-- start gazebo client -->
  ...
</launch>
```

The `<include>` tag is followed by the second snippet, which describes the Gazebo node to be launched:

```
  ...
  <node name="spawn_urdf" pkg="gazebo_ros" type="spawn_model"
output="screen"
     args="-file $(find gazebo_basics)/urdf/gopigo.gazebo -urdf -model
gopigo" />
</launch>
```

This node spawns the GoPiGo3 model into Gazebo using the `spawn_model` script of the `gazebo_ros` package. So why aren't we using the `<include>` tag here? Because we are including an external single node. We reserve `<include>` for launch files, where there are more nodes and configuration options.

Finally, issue the `roslaunch` command to start the simulation:

```
$ roslaunch gazebo_basics gopigo_gazebo.launch
```

This will result in the following output (be patient; depending on your graphics card, the 3D scene can take several seconds to be launched in a Gazebo window):

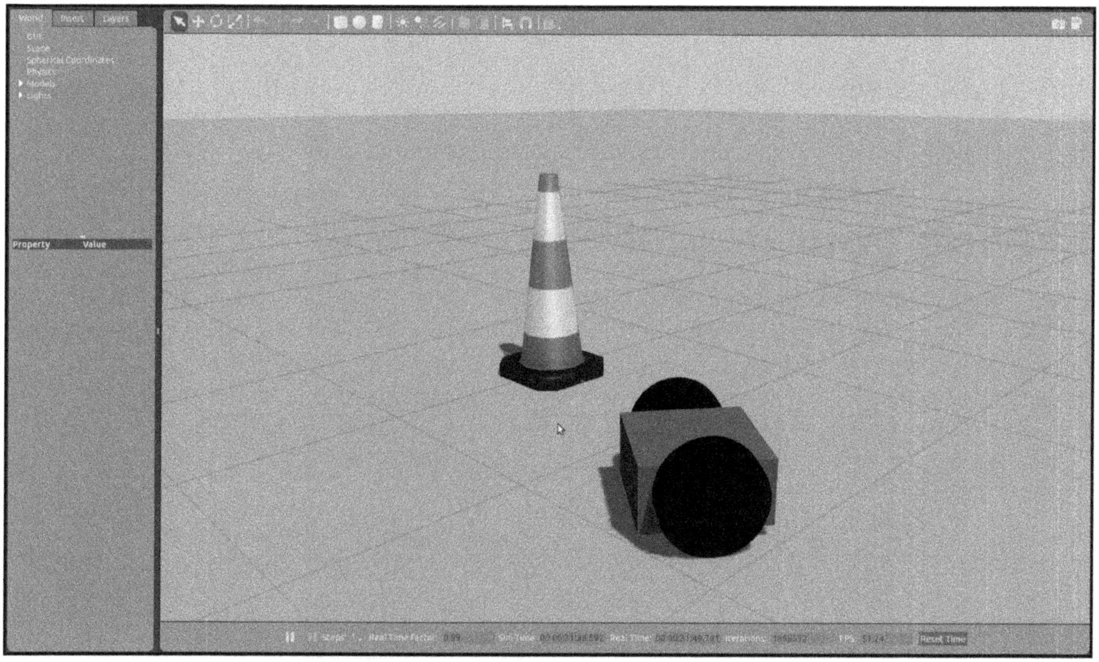

We will conclude this section by explaining the `<arg>` tag that we skipped previously.

Explaining configurable launch files using the <arg> tag

Arguments are a way to use variables in the scope of a launch file. Let's take the example of the `world_name` argument inside the `include` tag:

```
<include file="$(find gazebo_ros)/launch/empty_world.launch">
    <arg name="world_name" value="$(find
gazebo_basics)/worlds/gopigo.world"/>
```

This tag tells us which Gazebo world to use—referenced by the `name` attribute—and specifies the path where the file for the world can be found—that is, `value="$(find gazebo_basics)/worlds/gopigo.world"`. Be aware that how you specify the file path is done in exactly the same way in which we tell it the launch file to include.

The syntax for the `<arg>` tag is neatly explained in the official documentation at `http://wiki.ros.org/roslaunch/XML/arg`. Remember that, in the *Controlling GoPiGo3 wheels from RViz* section of the previous chapter, we explained how to specify the argument values when issuing the `roslaunch` command while providing default values in the launch file.

At this point, you are ready to understand how the model simulates the dynamics of your robot.

Moving your model around

Once the simulation has been launched, you can use the interaction icons in the Gazebo window. For example, you can play with the rotation tool of the environment toolbar to see how gravity affects the cone when you move it from its point of equilibrium:

Also, you can access the **Joints** panel (drag from the right border of the Gazebo window if it is not visible), select the GoPiGo model from the left pane, and under the **Force** tab in the **Joints** panel, apply 1 N.m torque to the left wheel. You will see how the robot starts to rotate around the right wheel, where no external force is acting:

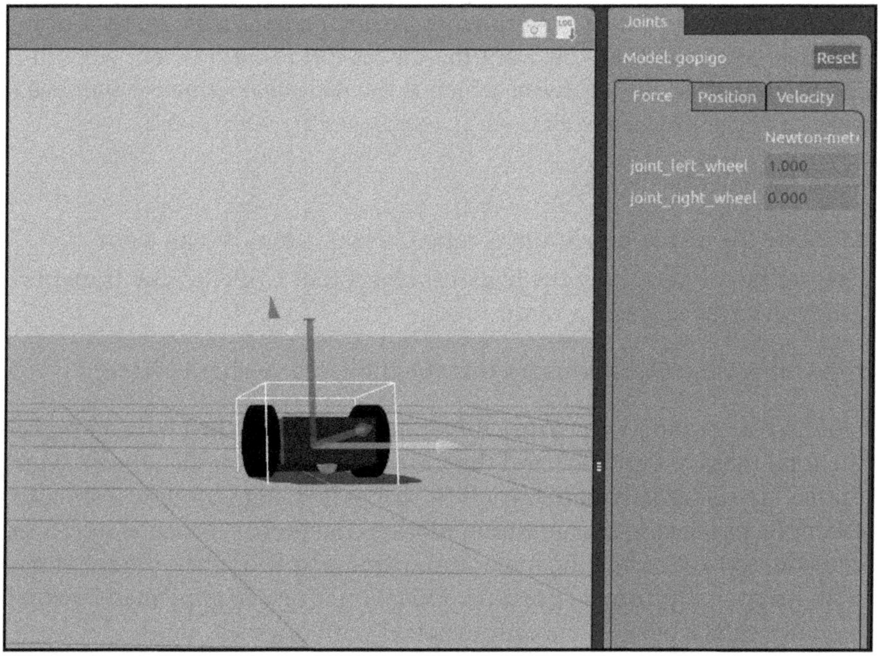

These interactions are quite simple, and at this point, they should give you a good taste of what simulation can support your work as a robotics engineer.

Guidelines for tuning the Gazebo model

The general goal in simulation is to reproduce reality to some extent with minimal effort, and this approximation should serve to be your concrete goal of designing a robot or evaluating the performance of existing ones.

Digital models are an abstraction of reality. You don't need to reproduce every detail of the physical robot in its Gazebo model. If you tried to do so, the required workload would be so high that the benefits of simulation would not compensate for the effort. Instead, what you do is reproduce those characteristics to verify the robot. You should start by defining the concrete goals and then build the simplest model that will allow us to comply with them.

Let's go through an example to understand these concepts. In this chapter, you've seen that the GoPiGo3 model is just a box (robot body), a semisphere (caster), and two cylinders (left and right wheels). The real GoPiGo3 contains many more parts, including bolts, washers, and nuts, as you know from experience when you put the hardware together in `Chapter 1`, *Assembling the Robot*. If you try to reproduce all these elements in URDF, we are sure you would be discouraged from continuing to work on such a hard task. Instead of following that dead end, ask yourself what you want the model for. From now on, we will refer to the simulated model as the **digital twin**, which is the technical name we will use to refer to the digital replica of the physical robot.

Here are two of the possible goals:

- Measure the actual maximum torque that servomotors can exert
- Determine the weight of the heaviest object that GoPiGo3 can transport as a function of the slope of a ramp

Now, let's think about the characteristics that the digital twin should have:

- Since we are trying to measure dynamic features, we just have to reproduce the total mass of GoPiGo3 and the torque actuating on the wheels. Moments of inertia are not strictly necessary if the robot is going to follow a smooth path. For example, in the case of a spinning motion, the inertia tensor would need to be considered to simulate the maximum turning speed when the robot goes around without moving from its position. This would be accomplished by rotating the left and right wheels at maximum speed with opposite signs.
- We will need `<visual>` tagged elements to see the digital model on the screen, but will not need `<collision>` elements since there is no need to include obstacles for our purposes.

With just those characteristics, you will have the minimum digital twin. The procedure to achieve these goals would be as follows:

1. In the real world, take a ramp that you can manually change the slope of. Then, get GoPiGo3 to climb the ramp and determine the maximum slope it can deal with. You will reach a point where the robot stays almost still, without climbing or going backward. Let's say that this angle is a.
2. The force that the two motors are exerting is given by the formula $F = m \cdot g \cdot sin(a)$, where m is the robot's mass and g is the acceleration of gravity (9.8 m/s^2).
3. The torque that's applied by each motor to produce such traction is given by the formula $T = (F \cdot r)/2$, where r is the radius of the wheels and the factor 2 means that we produce this force using two motors (one per wheel).

4. Once you've determined the maximum torque, *T*, you can go to the simulation environment, apply it to each of the motors, and see the robot rolling on a ramp of a slope, $\alpha < a$. By progressively increasing the mass of the robot body (concentrated in the `base_link` URDF element), you will find the total weight that makes the robot stop moving forward.

> Bear in mind that if the ramp had slope *a*, the force that the wheels have to exert to make the robot climb will correspond to the maximum motor torque, so it won't have the capacity to transport more weight. Therefore, you should always consider a slope, α, lower than *a*.

By doing this, you will obtain a good estimation of the maximum weight that GoPiGo3 can carry for a given maximum ramp slope, α. You can introduce this modification in Gazebo very easily by modifying the mass value of the `base_link` in the URDF file, as follows:

```
<link name="base_link">
...
    <inertial>
         <mass value="m+dm"/>
    </inertial>
...
```

Here, `m + dm` represents the sum of two terms:

- `m` is the mass of the unloaded robot.
- `dm` is the mass of the object to be transported. The value of `dm` (in kilograms) that makes sure the robot does not climb the ramp will be the maximum load for the slope, α. For a ramp slope equal to *a*, we have $dm = dm^* = 0$.

We'll cover how we can specify the maximum motor torque in Gazebo in `Chapter 7`, *Robot Control and Simulation*, in the *Simulating GoPiGo3 with Gazebo* section. Here, you will see that there is a plugin element that can be used to simulate the motor controller that mobile robots such as GoPiGo3 have.

With these modifications to the URDF file, as well as the check we made in Gazebo regarding $dm^* = 0$ for a ramp slope equal to *a*, you have tuned the digital twin so that it can simulate freight transport and has the transport capability of *dm* kilograms for a maximum slope of α.

Summary

In this chapter, we introduced the simulation environment of ROS called Gazebo, a standalone simulator that also provides full integration with ROS.

First, you learned about SDF, the standard XML format for robot simulation driven by Gazebo. SDF extends URDF and allows us to describe objects and environments for robot simulators, visualization, and control.

Following a parallel process to that of `Chapter 4`, *Creating the Virtual Two-Wheeled ROS Robot*, we produced a robot description within the `./urdf/gopigo.gazebo` file. The simulation was then started by running `./launch/gopigo_gazebo.launch`.

In this chapter, you were provided with an overview of how the Gazebo interface GUI is organized and performed some simple interactions with the GoPiGo3 model to see how it is affected by the gravity or the application of torque in the joint of one of its wheels.

By now, you should have started to develop a feeling of how to simulate realistic behavior with the robot with the physics engine of Gazebo. This will provide you with a powerful and cost-effective tool that you can use to troubleshoot the differences between the physical robot and its digital twin.

In the next chapter, we will look at the physical robot and explain how to interface with it. What you have done so far with the virtual robot will help you anticipate how the actual GoPiGo3 behaves when you run a ROS program in its CPU.

Questions

1. What is the format of the SDF?

   A) It is a text file
   B) JSON
   C) XML

2. Why can't the UDRF format be directly used by simulation for robots?

   A) Because URDF cannot specify the pose of the robot within a world
   B) Because it cannot specify the dynamic properties of joints, such as stiffness, damping, and/or friction
   C) All of the above

3. What is the `<collision>` tag used for?

   A) For defining the physical obstacles the robot has to avoid
   B) It is an optional tag for performing the interference checking of robot joints
   C) To define the volume to be considered for the interference checking of robot links

4. What is the ROS `find` command used for?

   A) It is used to refer to other ROS nodes with the same name
   B) It returns the absolute path of the ROS package that is specified as its argument
   C) It allows you to easily find any file within the ROS environment

5. What is a robot simulation in Gazebo used for?

   A) To find out more about a robot before purchasing it
   B) To develop functionality prior to applying it to the real robot
   C) To check the visual aspect of a robot before manufacturing it

Further reading

- Gazebo tutorials: `http://gazebosim.org/tutorials`
- Simulator Gazebo tutorials (ROS-specific): `http://wiki.ros.org/simulator_gazebo/Tutorials`
- *ROS Robot Programming: A handbook Written by TurtleBot3 Developers*, YoonSeok Pyo, HanCheol Cho, RyuWoon Jung, TaeHoon Lim (2017), ROBOTIS Co. Ltd, first edition: `http://www.pishrobot.com/wp-content/uploads/2018/02/ROS-robot-programming-book-by-turtlebo3-developers-EN.pdf`, Chapter: *ROS Tools: RViz and rqt* and 10.9 *TurtleBot3 Simulation using Gazebo*

3
Section 3: Autonomous Navigation Using SLAM

This section is purely about ROS and robotics engineering. You will acquire the skills to enforce ROS applications in order to execute navigational tasks. You will learn that path planning is essential for success and how this feature is built on top of the map of the covered area that's generated with **Simultaneous Localization and Mapping** (**SLAM**) techniques.

This section comprises the following chapters:

- `Chapter 6`, *Programming in ROS – Commands and Tools*
- `Chapter 7`, *Robot Control and Simulation*
- `Chapter 8`, *Virtual SLAM and Navigation Using Gazebo*
- `Chapter 9`, *SLAM for Robot Navigation*

6 Programming in ROS - Commands and Tools

This chapter focuses on running ROS within GoPiGo3. In the previous chapter, we did the same for a remote laptop, and in the next chapter, we will teach you how to make both a robot and your laptop work together as a single ROS environment.

In this chapter, you will finally learn how to use ROS in the depth required for the advanced chapters later on, which deal with robot navigation and machine learning. ROS can be hard to use at the beginning due to the following factors:

- It is command-line-based.
- It handles asynchronous events.
- It is a distributed computing environment.

Paradoxically, these are the three features that make it really powerful for programming robots. The effort you've invested will be worth it, as you will soon discover.

By working through this chapter, you will become familiar with ROS's command-line interaction and understand the scope of several types of ROS command. You will get used to working with the most frequently used communication pattern in ROS: publish-subscribe. To access real-time robot data while ROS is running, you will be introduced to the *rqt* GUI tools, which ease the work of developing and debugging an application. Additionally, ROS parameters will be introduced to give you an overview of their power to manage robot configuration at a high level.

We will be covering the following topics in this chapter:

- Setting up the physical robot
- A quick introduction to ROS programming
- How to write a ROS package (**case study 1**)
- An overview of ROS commands

- Creating and running publisher and subscriber nodes
- Automating the execution of nodes with roslaunch
- ROS GUI development tools (**case study 2**)
- How to use ROS parameters

We will provide explanations of these concepts based on two practical case studies:

- **Case study 1**: Publishing and reading distance sensors
- **Case study 2**: Acquiring and visualizing images from the Pi camera

There is a third case study dealing with robot control and simulation – **case study 3**: robot drives (motors and encoders) – which as a practical example will support the concepts that will be covered in `Chapter 7`, *Robot Control and Simulation.*

So, we have three case studies and, as a result of both this chapter and the next chapter, we will have our first complete version of the ROS package for GoPiGo3. This will be the foundation on which smart robot behaviors will be built in the remaining chapters of the book.

Technical requirements

The code files for this chapter are available at `https://github.com/PacktPublishing/Hands-On-ROS-for-Robotics-Programming/tree/master/Chapter6_ROS_programming`.

When you have completed the Raspberry Pi setup, as explained in the *Setting up a physical robot* section, clone the book repository (`https://github.com/PacktPublishing/Hands-On-ROS-for-Robotics-Programming`) in your home folder:

```
$ cd ~
$ git clone
https://github.com/PacktPublishing/Hands-On-ROS-for-Robotics-Programming
```

Remember this location in order to keep a check of your work because, in this chapter, our intention is that you create all the code by yourself. Alternatively, if you decide to use the provided code, you will just need to copy the `Chapter6_ROS_programming` folder to the ROS workspace as usual:

```
$ cp -R ~/Hands-On-ROS-for-Robotics-Programming/Chapter6_ROS_programming
~/catkin_ws/src
```

The ROS workspace in the robot is initialized in the next section.

Setting up a physical robot

As mentioned in `Chapter 3`, *Getting Started with ROS*, we will now start working with a physical robot. Therefore, the first thing to do is to prepare the software you need to be running in the Raspberry Pi. This section will guide you through the process step by step.

Downloading and setting up Ubuntu Mate 18.04

Mate is, at the time of writing, the recommended Ubuntu desktop to run under Raspberry Pi. It is a complete Ubuntu distribution with a nice desktop interface. Follow these steps to make it run in your GoPiGo3:

1. Download the image from `https://ubuntu-mate.org/download/`, selecting the Raspberry Pi version (recommended): AArch32 (ARMv7). Burn the image onto a micro SD card. Afterward, place it in the slot in the Raspberry Pi, plug in a mouse and keyboard, connect to an HDMI screen, and then power on the board.
2. The first time you initiate it, a setup assistant will guide you through the process of configuring the operating system. In this book, we assume that the Ubuntu user is named `pi`. Change the code as necessary if you use another username.
3. Make sure that you connect to the local WiFi by selecting a network from the list that is deployed when clicking on the wireless icon in the upper-right corner of the screen. It is strongly recommended that you add a second mobile WiFi network preferably like the one that your smartphone provides. This will avoid the need to connect to the HDMI screen, keyboard, and mouse when you move the robot away from home in the future.

The following instructions are optional and are believed to provide a friendlier way to access the Raspberry Pi.

Access customization

For more friendly access to your system, it is recommended that you allow your Ubuntu user to access `sudo` without a password:

1. In a terminal, type the following:

```
$ sudo visudo
```

2. Then, add this line at the end of the file:

```
pi ALL=(ALL) NOPASSWD: ALL
```

3. Save your changes and exit so that they take effect.

Updating your system and installing basic utilities

By running the following command, first you will update the Ubuntu repositories in your system; afterward, the system packages will be upgraded:

```
$ sudo apt update && sudo apt upgrade -y
```

You will need a `git` package in order to clone the repositories of code. If this is not on your system, then you can install it using the following command:

```
$ sudo apt install git
```

We will also add another useful package, `tree`, in order to get information from the filesystem:

```
$ sudo apt install tree
```

The `tree` package is a utility that enables you to view the content of a folder and its subfolders at the same time, representing it visually via a tree structure.

Enabling SSH access

It is common to have issues with the SSH server that comes preinstalled with Ubuntu:

1. To avoid any problems, remove the OpenSSH package and install it again:

```
$ sudo apt remove openssh-server
$ sudo apt install openssh-server
```

2. Enable the service so that it starts on boot:

```
$ sudo systemctl enable ssh
$ sudo systemctl start ssh
```

3. Confirm that the SSH server is up and running:

```
$ sudo systemctl status ssh
```

At this stage, you should be able to log in from this host to any other SSH-enabled Ubuntu server, such as your laptop.

Setting up a VNC server (x11vnc)

OpenSSH allows us to log in remotely to our Raspberry Pi using a terminal. We will also equip our robot with another remote way of connection, that is, by accessing its desktop. In order to do this, we will use `x11vnc`, a package that implements a remote desktop using **Virtual Network Computing** (VNC):

1. Update the Ubuntu repositories and install:

```
$ sudo apt-get update
$ sudo apt-get install x11vnc
```

2. Now create a password to connect with a client:

```
$ x11vnc -storepasswd
```

3. Type in a password and remember it. The password is stored in `/home/pi/.vnc` assuming that the current user is `pi`. Then, start the `x11vnc` server:

```
$ sudo x11vnc -auth guess -forever -loop -noxdamage -repeat \
              -rfbauth /home/pi/.vnc/passwd -rfbport 5900 -shared
```

4. If you want to start the server without needing a password, just remove the option from the command:

```
$ sudo x11vnc -auth guess -forever -loop -noxdamage -repeat \
                                          -rfbport 5900 -shared
```

Now you are ready to connect with a client using a VNC client such as RealVNC (`https://www.realvnc.com/download/viewer/`).

Setting up autostart on boot

We want `x11vnc` to start automatically when we reboot or power on the Pi. Hence, create a script named `x11vnc.service` at location `/lib/systemd/system/`, perform the following:

```
$ sudo nano /lib/systemd/system/x11vnc.service
```

While editing, add the following lines:

```
[Unit]
Description=Start x11vnc at startup.
After=multi-user.target

[Service]
Type=simple
# If  using a password
ExecStart=/usr/bin/x11vnc -auth guess -forever -loop -noxdamage -repeat -
rfbauth /home/pi/.vnc/passwd -rfbport 5900 -shared

[Install]
WantedBy=multi-user.target
```

Then, enable and start the newly created service:

```
$ sudo systemctl daemon-reload
$ sudo systemctl enable x11vnc.service
$ sudo systemctl start x11vnc.service
```

To connect with the RealVNC viewer from a remote PC, enter the IP address of the Raspberry Pi followed by the display number, that is, `<IP address>:<display number>`. If no display is specified, then it takes `0` as default. Hence, the `0` value will be assigned to the first server you launch (which is your unique server).

As you are running VNC with the default port, `5900`, you do not need to specify it for the connection. If this is not the case, you should specify the custom port in the connection string.

Forcing the HDMI output and screen layout

For debugging purposes, it is useful to make sure that you can always access the Ubuntu Mate desktop from a screen, even though the system does not start with it. In order to achieve this, you have to modify the configuration options of the Raspberry Pi:

```
$ sudo nano /boot/config.txt
```

The content of the file will be accessible on the screen. Uncomment the following lines, setting the shown values:

```
hdmi_force_hotplug=1

hdmi_group=2
hdmi_mode=47
```

The last two lines enforce the following display: at 1440 x 900 at 60 Hz. If you want to increase this to full HD resolution (1080 px), then you can do so as follows, depending on the refresh rate:

- For a 50 Hz monitor, use the following:

```
hdmi_group=1
hdmi_mode=31
```

- For a 60 Hz monitor, use the following:

```
hdmi_group=2
hdmi_mode=82
```

These commands make it easy to get 1080 px.

The Geany IDE

Ubuntu Mate comes with a lightweight editor called **Pluma**. While it is good for editing, it does not include a terminal window or other common characteristics that are found in a typical development environment. For this reason, we will install **Geany**, a lightweight IDE suitable for running on a Raspberry Pi that supports common programming languages:

```
$ sudo apt-get update
$ sudo apt-get install -y geany
```

We will be mainly using Python, so Geany is perfect for us.

Installing drivers for the GoPiGo3 and DI Sensors

Now we will prepare the system to work with GoPiGo3. Dexter Industries supplies automated scripts to accomplish all the installations tasks:

- The GoPiGo3 library, with the following script `https://dexterindustries.com/update_gopigo3`
- The DI Sensors library, with the following script `https://dexterindustries.com/update_sensors`

The relevant steps are provided in the official documentation at `https://dexterindustries.com/update_gopigo3`. In short, you only have to open a terminal and execute following two commands, one after another:

```
$ curl -kL dexterindustries.com/update_gopigo3 | bash
$ curl -kL dexterindustries.com/update_sensors | bash
```

The installation process takes several minutes, so be patient. When finished, you will see the following new icons on your desktop:

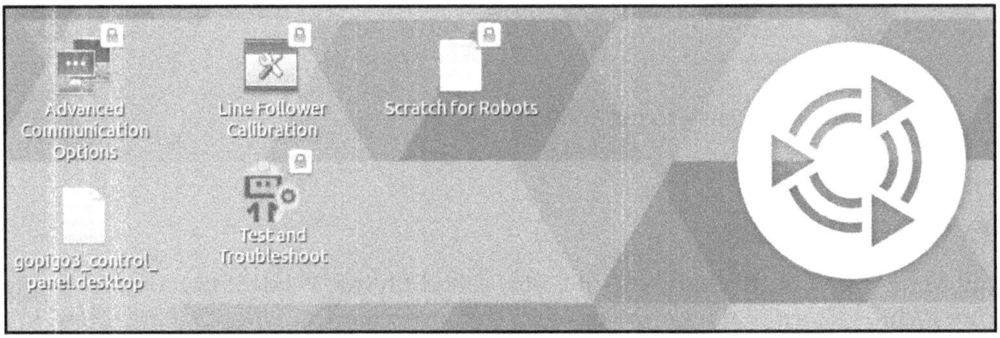

These additional utilities are as follows:

- **Advanced Communication Options**: This icon is used to enable Bluetooth and/or infrared receivers.
- **Line Follower Calibration**: This icon is used to adjust sensor sensibility to the current illumination conditions.
- **gopigo3_control_panel**: This icon is used to drive the robot with a simple panel shown on the screen.
- **Test and Troubleshoot**: This utility generates a log file for your robot that can be sent to the manufacturer so that it can provide technical support.

As an example, double-click on the **Test and Troubleshoot** icon. It will generate a log file of your robot that should look like the following globally:

```
GoPiGo3 Troubleshooting Script log

Checking for hardware, and checking hardware and firmware version.
==================================================================
Manufacturer : Dexter Industries
Board : GoPiGo3
Serial Number : F92DD433514E343732202020FF112535
Hardware version: 3.x.x
Firmware version: 1.0.0
```

```
Battery voltage : 9.414
5v voltage : 4.889
```

At this point, your operating system is ready to run any GoPiGo3 code, that is, the Python scripts that we used in `Chapter 2`, *Unit Testing of GoPiGo3*.

Setting up the Pi Camera

The setup is done in steps 1-2. First, we will enable access to the camera hardware from the Raspberry Pi, and second, we will install the Python module to handle the camera:

1. First, we need to edit the `/boot/config.txt` file:

   ```
   $ sudo nano /boot/config.txt
   ```

2. Then, we add these two lines at the end:

   ```
   start_x=1
   gpu_mem=128
   ```

3. Alternatively, you can get the same result by adding these lines from the command line:

   ```
   $ sudo bash -c "echo 'start_x=1' >> /boot/config.txt"
   $ sudo bash -c "echo 'gpu_mem=128' >> /boot/config.txt"
   ```

4. Next, install the Python module as follows:

   ```
   $ sudo pip install picamera
   ```

5. To check that the camera works properly, create this Python script and name it `captureFile.py` (you can find it inside the `piCamera` folder in the code for this chapter):

   ```
   from time import sleep
   from picamera import PiCamera

   camera = PiCamera()
   camera.resolution = (1024, 768)

   camera.start_preview()

   # Camera warm-up time
   sleep(2)

   camera.capture('test.jpg')
   ```

6. Give execution permissions and run the Python module:

```
$ chmod +x captureFile.py
$ ./captureFile.py
```

The camera will be active for 2 seconds. Check that the red LED on the camera board is on. This is a visual sign that it is acquiring images. After this period, the LED will switch off and you should find – in the same path as the script – a new file called `test.jpg`. If you open it, you should see what the camera was viewing at the end of those 2 seconds; this is performed by: `camera.capture(test.jpg)`.

The last step in getting ready with the Raspberry Pi is to install ROS.

Installing ROS Melodic

The instructions on the ROS Melodic installation page (`http://wiki.ros.org/melodic/Installation/Ubuntu`) are pretty clear and straightforward. We include them here for the sake of completeness:

1. First, add the ROS source repositories:

```
$ sudo sh -c 'echo "deb http://packages.ros.org/ros/ubuntu
$(lsb_release -sc) main" > /etc/apt/sources.list.d/ros-latest.list'
```

2. Then, set up your keys:

```
$ sudo apt-key adv --keyserver 'hkp://keyserver.ubuntu.com:80' --
recv-key C1CF6E31E6BADE8868B172B4F42ED6FBAB17C654
```

If you don't get a validated key, then it might have been changed (for security reasons). If that's the case, then go to the official installation page (`http://wiki.ros.org/melodic/Installation/Ubuntu`), search for the line, and then replace it with the new one.

3. Next, update your sources:

```
$ sudo apt-get update
```

4. Install the desktop version of ROS so that you can take advantage of the Mate desktop environment. This will allow you to use ROS GUI tools (such as rqt or RViz):

```
$ sudo apt-get install ros-melodic-desktop
```

5. Initialize `rosdep`. This is the component that enables you to easily install system dependencies for your source code to compile. It also requires you to run some core components in ROS:

```
$ sudo rosdep init
$ rosdep update
```

6. Set up the ROS environment for your interactive shell session:

```
$ source /opt/ros/melodic/setup.bash
```

To avoid having to run this command each time, you can open a new terminal and include it in your `.bashrc` file:

```
$ echo "source /opt/ros/melodic/setup.bash" >> ~/.bashrc
$ source ~/.bashrc
```

Now all that remains is to configure the Pi Camera. Let's do that next.

Installing a Pi Camera ROS package

As part of the ROS installation, we should include software that will allow you to access the Pi Camera from ROS. The most used package is that from Ubiquity Robotics, and it is hosted on GitHub at `https://github.com/UbiquityRobotics/raspicam_node`.

To install the package, we first need to have a ROS workspace and to have mastered some practical concepts for cloning and creating ROS packages. This installation will be accomplished later on in the chapter; you will find it in the *Case study 2 – ROS GUI development tools – the Pi Camera globally*.

Hence, let's proceed now to create a workspace and add the first package inside it.

A quick introduction to ROS programming

This section is devoted to explaining an easy ROS example with GoPiGo3. By doing this, we can put our robot to work quickly so that, in later sections, we can deal with ROS commands and tools in a practical way, applying such commands and understanding what they do.

This very simple example is based on the distance sensor in GoPiGo3. It consists of publishing sensor readings and accessing them from other ROS nodes.

Setting up the workspace

To start using contributed ROS packages or to create your own, you will need to have a workspace in which to put the code. The step-by-step procedure to accomplish such a task is as follows:

1. From a bash terminal, create a folder and initialize the workspace:

   ```
   $ mkdir -p ~/catkin_ws/src
   $ cd ~/catkin_ws/src
   $ catkin_init_workspace
   ```

   The initialization is as simple as creating a symlink to a file definition located in the ROS installation folder. If you list files in the `src` folder, then you will see the new `CMakeLists.txt` file pointing to `/opt/ros/melodic/share/catkin/cmake/toplevel.cmake`:

   ```
   $ ls -la

   ... CMakeLists.txt ->
   /opt/ros/melodic/share/catkin/cmake/toplevel.cmake
   ```

2. Next, build the workspace:

   ```
   $ cd ~/catkin_ws
   $ catkin_make
   ```

3. Then, add it to your ROS environment:

   ```
   $ source ~/catkin_ws/devel/setup.bash
   ```

4. Alternatively, you can automate the execution of this command by including it at the end of your `.bashrc` file. To do so, execute the following command, and, afterward, run the file so that its contents take effect in the system:

   ```
   $ echo "source ~/catkin_ws/devel/setup.bash" >> ~/.bashrc
   $ source ~/.bashrc
   ```

At this point, you should have the following two lines at the end of the file (the first one is for the ROS global environment, while the second is for your private workspace):

```
source /opt/ros/kinetic/setup.bash
source ~/catkin_ws/devel/setup.bash
```

Everything is now ready to include the ROS packages we need. In the following section, we will add two of them: one cloning an existing repository and another one creating a package from scratch.

Cloning a ROS package

For the cloning option, we are going to use a basic GoPiGo3 ROS package that is publicly available in GitHub from `https://github.com/ros-gopigo/gopigo3_node`. Change to the `src` folder, which is the location where we will place all ROS packages, and then clone the source code:

```
$ cd ~/catkin_ws/src
$ git clone https://github.com/ros-gopigo/gopigo3_node
```

Every time you add a new package, you have to rebuild the workspace so that ROS is aware of its existence and can add it to the execution environment. Hence, run the following commands:

```
$ cd ~/catkin_ws
$ catkin_make
```

Now, you will see a number of lines indicating the progress in % and what the current building step is doing. If everything is okay, the last line displays 100% complete and returns the control to the command line. This means that you have just successfully installed the `gopigo3_node` package.

Our first execution of a ROS node

Since ROS will be running on the Raspberry Pi, you will have to remotely connect to it. In order to do so, open a VNC connection to GoPiGo. Then, open a terminal in its desktop and install Terminator (the same utility we used in `Chapter 3`, *Getting Started with ROS*) to have as many terminals as you need in the same window:

```
$ sudo apt-get update
$ sudo apt-get install terminator
```

Move to the location of the newly added ROS package and list the files inside:

```
$ cd ~/catkin_ws/src/gopigo3_node/src
$ ls
```

You will see several Python files for controlling GoPiGo3 sensors and drives. Assuming that you have installed the GoPiGo3 and DI Sensors libraries, as explained in the *Setting up a physical robot* section, open Terminator and divide the window into at least three terminals. We are going to execute the `distance_sensor.py` file under ROS. For that, we will need to issue three commands as follows:

```
T1 $ roscore
T2 $ rosrun gopigo3_node distance_sensor.py
T3 $ rostopic echo /distance_sensor/distance
```

The following is globally what each command performs:

- `T1` launches the roscore process. This is necessary for all subsequent processes that can communicate in ROS.
- `T2` executes the `distance_sensor` node, which takes the readings and publishes them under the `/distance_sensor/distance` topic.
- `T3` listens to published data in real time and prints a new message each time a reading is acquired.

In the following screenshot, you can see what each terminal shows. Each reading of the sensor delivers a message that has several fields. Later on, in the *Case study 1 – writing a ROS package – distance sensor* section, we will explain how this message is created. For now, it is enough that you know that the `range` field, boxed in red, is the sensor measurement in a meters:

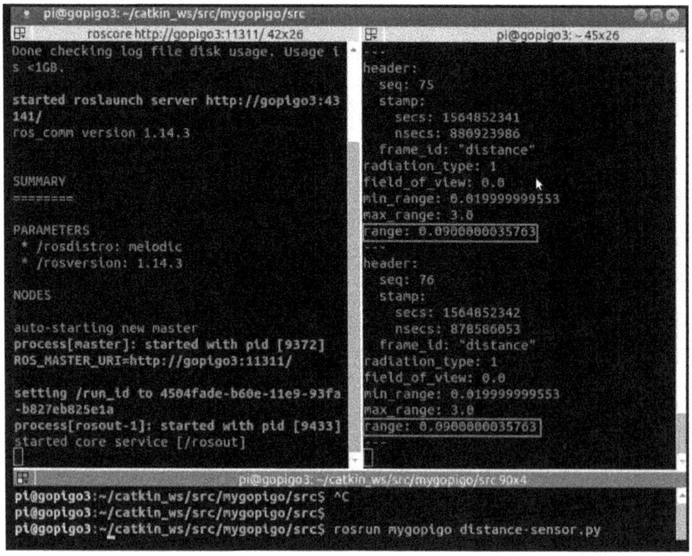

To take just the last measurement, simply run the following command, where the number after *-n* indicates how many messages you want to print, which, in our case, is 1:

```
T4 $ rostopic echo /distance_sensor/distance -n 1
```

The next step will be to create your own ROS package. The code we are going to write makes the same package as the `distance_sensor.py` script but uses the `EasyDistanceSensor` class (from the `di_sensors.easy_distance_sensor` library) instead of the full `DistanceSensor` version (from the `di_sensors.distance_sensor` library), which was used by the script in the package that we cloned previously.

Case study 1 – writing a ROS distance-sensor package

In this section, you will create a ROS package from scratch and produce the code to provide minimal ROS functionality with GoPiGo3, that is, reading its distance sensor. Be aware that the code you previously cloned at this location is the working solution for what your code is expected to do:

```
~/Hands-On-ROS-for-Robotics-
Programming/Chapter6_ROS_programming/pkg_mygopigo
```

We encourage you to try to build the ROS package by yourself, following the explanations that are provided next in this chapter.

Creating a new package

First, let's set up a folder in the workspace where we will place the package files:

1. Move to the `src` location in the `catkin_ws worspace` folder:

    ```
    $ cd ~/catkin_ws/src
    ```

2. Create a package called `mygopigo`:

    ```
    $ catkin_create_pkg mygopigo
    ```

This command creates two files of the package definition `CMakeLists.txt` and `package.xml`, which were already introduced in the previous chapter. As there is a new package, you should rebuild the workspace:

```
$ cd ~/catkin_ws
$ catkin_make
```

If, at some point, you wish to change the project name, then you need to complete these three steps:

1. Edit in the `<name>mygopigo</name>` tag in package.xml.
2. Edit the line project (`mygopigo`) in CMakeLists.txt, where the project has to be the same as the `package.xml` <name> tag.
3. Rebuild the workspace.

The folder under which the files of the package are stored can be named however you like – it does not have to be the same as the package name.

Producing your source code

The `mygopigo` folder is ready so that we can create the package structure and place the files:

1. Create the `src` folder inside the package – note that this is a convention we use to standardize where the code is placed in repositories:

   ```
   $ roscd mygopigo
   $ mkdir src
   $ cd src
   ```

   The `roscd` ROS command is equivalent to the Linux bash `cd` command. Its advantage is that you only have to specify the package name in order to move to the package's folder, which is `~/catkin_ws/src/mygopigo/`. Then, create a Python file to acquire data from the distance sensor:

   ```
   $ nano distance-sensor.py
   ```

2. Copy and paste the following lines globally inside the file:

   ```
   #!/usr/bin/env python

   # import the modules
   from di_sensors.easy_distance_sensor import EasyDistanceSensor
   from time import sleep
   ```

```
# instantiate the distance object
my_sensor = EasyDistanceSensor()

# and read the sensor iteratively
while True:
  read_distance = my_sensor.read()
  print("distance from object: {} cm".format(read_distance))
  sleep(0.1)
```

This is the unit test file for the distance sensor that we reviewed in the previous chapter. We will explain how to convert it into a ROS-integrated script.

> ROS requires that source code be in files with the following execution permission: `$ chmod +x distance-sensor.py`.

3. To run, just invoke it from the command line:

```
$ ./distance-sensor.py
```

This will print the measured distance in centimeters every 0.1 seconds. At this point, the code is still pure Python.

We will now explain what changes need to be carried out so that it can be integrated into ROS:

1. First, import the modules required by ROS:

```
import rospy
from sensor_msgs.msg import Range
```

The `rospy` library is the Python client and `sensor_msgs.msg` defines message types for handling data from sensors within ROS. In our particular case, we only need the `Range` type message, which is what we will need for the distance sensor.

2. Python's `time` library is no longer required since `rospy` provides methods to handle time features in ROS. Hence, you may remove the line:

```
from time import sleep
```

3. Next, we put the code under the `main()` function definition:

```
def main():
    my_sensor = EasyDistanceSensor()
    rospy.init_node("distance_sensor")
    pub_distance = rospy.Publisher("~distance", Range,
```

```
queue_size=10)
    msg_range = Range()
    msg_range.header.frame_id = "distance"
    msg_range.radiation_type = Range.INFRARED
    msg_range.min_range = 0.02
    msg_range.max_range = 3.0
    rate = rospy.Rate(rospy.get_param('~hz', 1))
```

4. We launch a ROS node called `distance_sensor`, define a publisher called `pub_distance`, set the characteristics of the sensor in the `msg_range message`, and specify the rate we want to read the sensor at, which is 1 Hz. We complete the code of the main function by running an infinite loop that takes a reading of the sensor in each iteration:

```
while not rospy.is_shutdown():
    read_distance = my_sensor.read()/100.0
    msg_range.range = read_distance
    msg_range.header.stamp = rospy.Time.now()

    print msg_range.range*1000," mm"
    pub_distance.publish(msg_range)

    rate.sleep()
```

In each iteration, this code saves the sensor data in the `msg_range` instance, publishes the message to the `/distance_sensor/distance` topic, and runtime-delays the next reading to respect the specified rate. Finally, we tell Python to run the `main()` function:

```
comment ...
if __name__ == '__main__':
    main()
```

In the following subsections, we will cover more information about these pieces of code in detail.

Including the required libraries – rospy and msgs.msg

The following two lines import the required ROS libraries:

```
import rospy
from sensor_msgs.msg import Range
```

These libraries are explained as follows:

- rospy (http://wiki.ros.org/rospy): This is the official Python client for ROS. It implements API methods so that you can integrate ROS nodes coded in Python.
- sensor_msgs (http://wiki.ros.org/sensor_msgs): This is the ROS package that lets you handle different types of ROS message depending on the sensors and drives of your robot; for example, BatteryState, FluidPressure, and LaserScan. In the case of the distance sensor, we use the Range type.

Assigning a node name to the script

This task is accomplished using the init_node method of the rospy library:

```
rospy.init_node("distance_sensor")
```

Using the distance_sensor name, we will reference the distance sensor node anywhere in ROS.

Defining the publisher

The publisher is a function – again, a rospy method that permits you to assign to the pub_distance variable the result of the measurement, which, in our case, is of the Range type:

```
pub_distance = rospy.Publisher("~distance", Range, queue_size=10)
```

The value between the quotation marks is the topic name, ~distance. The prepended symbol, ~, is equivalent to <name of node>/, which, in our case, is distance_sensor. Following this, the namespace topic will be as follows:

```
/distance_sensor/distance
```

The queue_size parameter specifies how many messages ROS keeps in memory to ensure that the subscriber nodes read them. A value of 10 is a good default.

Setting up the msg_range object

The distance sensor uses the message type defined in the `Range` class of the `sensor_msgs.msg` library, whose structure is as follows:

```
uint8 ULTRASOUND=0
uint8 INFRARED=1

std_msgs/Header header
uint8 radiation_type
float32 field_of_view
float32 min_range
float32 max_range
float32 range
```

These are the fields that will be part of any message involving the data flow from the sensor, and its syntax is explained in detail in the documentation (`http://docs.ros.org/api/sensor_msgs/html/msg/Range.html`). All the fields are specific characteristics of the sensor except for the measurement itself, `range`. Hence, the following snippet gives a particular definition for our distance sensor:

```
msg_range = Range()

msg_range.header.frame_id = "distance"
msg_range.radiation_type = Range.INFRARED
msg_range.min_range = 0.02
msg_range.max_range = 3.0
```

Here, the first line initiates the `msg_range` variable to be of the `Range()` type. In the `header.frame_id` field, we indicate the physical magnitude we are going to measure, which is `distance`.

The `radiation` type is set to `INFRARED` (there is no option to set this to `LASER`, but specifying it as `INFRARED` is more adequate than the other option, `ULTRASOUND`, for which you would have a wide field of view instead of a straight ray). `LASER` is directional, as is `INFRARED`, so it is better to use this type.

The last two lines specify the maximum (3 meters) and minimum (2 centimeters) distances the sensor can measure.

Changing units to the International System of Units

Adopting the **International System of Units** (**SI**) is the ROS convention stated in its specification (`https://www.ros.org/reps/rep-0103.html`). Since the `read()` method provides measurements in centimeters, we only have to divide by 100 to obtain the distance in meters and feed this to the system according to the ROS standard:

```
read_distance = my_sensor.read()/100.0
```

This value will be inserted afterward into the `msg_range` object, which we will cover next.

Adding a measured distance and timestamp to the msg_range object

In the `msg_range.range` field, we allocate the measured distance, and in the other field – `msg_range.header.stamp` – we allocate the current timestamp:

```
msg_range.range = read_distance
msg_range.header.stamp = rospy.Time.now()
```

The timestamp is obtained from the `Time.now()` method of the `rospy` library. In this way, we have a full record of the measurement.

Setting the reading frequency

Using the `Rate` method, we can set the reading frequency to 1 Hz (this is equal to 1 sample per second; in SI units) as follows:

```
rate = rospy.Rate(rospy.get_param('~hz', 1))
```

We do this by defining a ROS parameter at the same time whose name is as follows (remember the meaning of the ~ symbol):

```
distance_sensor/hz
```

With this setup, the sensor will be read once per second.

Running an infinite loop

We run the infinite loop using a specific ROS method from `rospy`:

```
while not rospy.is_shutdown():
```

Its syntax is self-explanatory, that is, it will run unless ROS is shutdown.

Publishing each new event

We publish a new `msg_range` message each time a measure is available by using the `pub_distance` publisher defined previously:

```
pub_distance.publish(msg_range)
```

Waiting until the next reading

To ensure we respect the acquisition rate of 1 Hz, we apply the `sleep` method to the `rate` object that we defined above (for which we set a frequency of 1 Hz, that is, one cycle per second):

```
rate.sleep()
```

Bear in mind that this does not block ROS execution (it just blocks the script of this node), that is, just the code of this `distance_sensor` node. If there were other nodes in the environment, then they would have their own independent execution threads. If you were using a native asynchronous language such as JavaScript, then you could also run asynchronous code within the node and also avoid the blockage in the execution of the script, that is, your node could be executing other lines while waiting for the next sensor reading

If you are curious about this, you can investigate the ROS client library, `rosnodejs` (`https://www.npmjs.com/package/rosnodejs`), which allows you to write nodes in the JavaScript language. At this point, remember that one of the cool characteristics of ROS is that you can mix the same ROS graph nodes written in Python with nodes written in JavaScript or in any of the other ROS client libraries (`http://wiki.ros.org/Client%20Libraries`).

Launching the ROS execution environment

Now that we have understood how the Python script integrates with ROS, we will execute it in one terminal as part of the ROS runtime environment using the following steps:

1. Prepare your divided Terminator window again for better visibility, and then run each of the following commands in independent terminals:

```
T1 $ roscore
T2 $ rosrun mygopigo distance-sensor.py
T3 $ rostopic echo /distance_sensor/distance
```

The first one launches the ROS master node. The second one is the script we have just explained, while the third allows us to watch messages published under the `/distance_sensor/distance` topic in real time. This is what you should see:

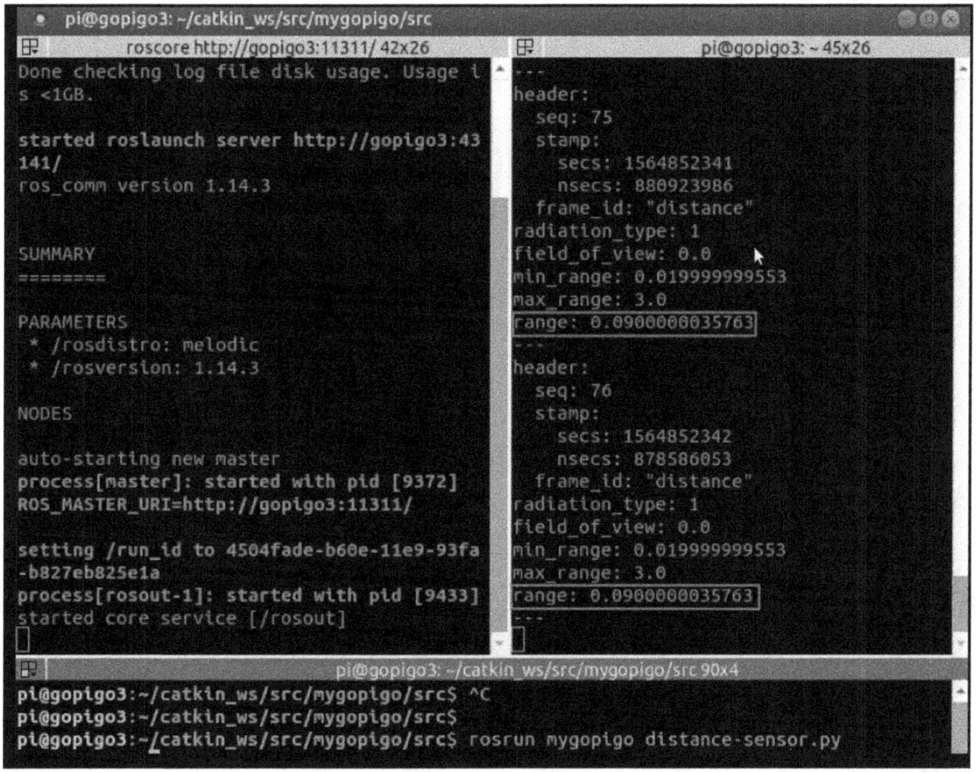

2. Then, draw the ROS graph to get a visual insight into how nodes and topics are wired:

```
T4 $ rqt_graph
```

A new window pops up showing the current ROS graph:

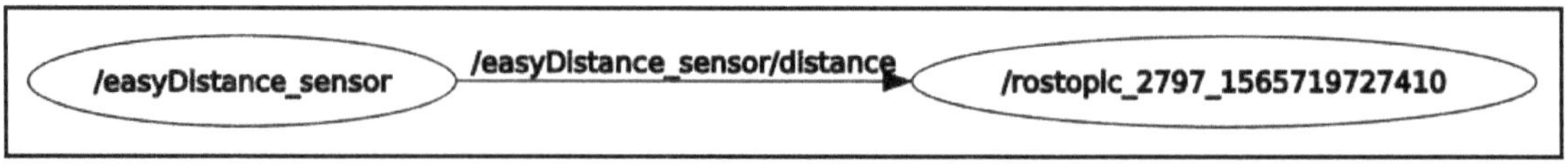

Here, you can see that it reproduces what we are doing in the three terminals: we execute the `/easyDistance_sensor` node, which is publishing sensor data at the `/easyDistance_sensor/distance` topic, and then we show the readings with a topic subscription node, `/rostopic_2797_156571927410`.

After going through this example, we will use it to illustrate the various ROS commands and tools that you have available.

Working with ROS commands

In the first part of this section, we will cover three categories: commands to be used inside bash (shell), ROS execution commands, and information commands.

Shell commands

Shell commands are bundled into a ROS core package, `rosbash` (`http://wiki.ros.org/rosbash`). Let's move on to see what each one provides.

Changing the current location

First, we will cover `roscd`, which is equivalent to the Linux bash `cd` command. Its advantage is that you only have to specify the package name in order to move to the location of the package:

```
$ roscd mygopigo
```

This will take you to the `~/catkin_ws/src/mygopigo/` folder. You can also navigate through the package folder structure by appending the relative path of the desired location. For example, to move to the `src` folder of the `mygopigo` package, use the following command:

```
$ roscd mygopigo/src
```

`roscd` is equivalent to the Linux `cd` command. It will change the prompt to the directory of any ROS package in your system by referencing its path with the package name. No matter what the actual path is, ROS will automatically drive you there.

Listing files and folders inside a package

Next, we have `rosls`, which is the equivalent of Linux `ls`. To list the source code of your package wherever you are, simply write the following:

```
$ rosls mygopigo/src
```

`rosls` allows you to easily list files and folders inside any ROS package in your system by referencing its path with the package name. No matter what the actual path is, ROS will automatically take you there.

Editing any file inside a package

Finally, we have `rosed`, which opens a terminal editor, such as `nano`, so that you can modify any file in the package:

```
$ rosed mygopigo distance-sensor.py
```

For `rosed` to work properly, you have to specify an editor:

```
export EDITOR=nano
```

To make it part of your configuration, add the preceding line to the end of your `.bashrc` file:

```
echo 'export EDITOR=nano' >> ~/.bashrc
```

rosed is equivalent to launching the Linux terminal editor, which is nano. It will allow you to edit any file inside a ROS package by simply telling it the package name, no matter which subfolder the file is actually in.

This command is a convenient way to modify a file when you are connected remotely to the robot and you only have a terminal to interact with. If you are on a desktop session, you can even use a desktop IDE if you wish:

```
EDITOR=geany rosed mygopigo distance-sensor.py
```

In this case, you are calling the editor on the fly and superseding the default set in .bashrc.

Execution commands

In Chapter 3, *Getting Started with ROS*, we already introduced the roscore and rosrun commands for running our first project.

The central process of the ROS environment

roscore is the first process you have to launch so that the ROS environment works.roscore allows nodes to communicate between themselves. It has no parameters, so write this line in a terminal:

```
$ roscore
```

roscore launches the master node, which is the central process of your ROS environment and keeps all nodes that are actually running connected.

Executing a single node

rosrun allows you to manually launch a node from a package. The syntax is quite simple:

```
$ rosrun <name_of_package> <name_of_script>
```

The script includes a declaration of a node. In the case of our `distance-sensor.py` example, this is accomplished in the following line:

```
rospy.init_node("distance_sensor")
```

Then, to launch the node, write this command in another terminal:

```
$ rosrun mygopigo distance-sensor.py
```

After these two commands, you already have a ROS functional environment that provides sensor readings. The node also prints the current measure in the terminal process, transformed into millimeters (there is no need to open another terminal to listen to the topic). The usage of millimeters is just for visualization purposes. The ROS message keeps its distance units as meters, which you can check by subscribing to the topic in another terminal:

```
print msg_range.range*1000," mm"
```

`rosrun` allows you to launch a single node from a package. It is a command for performing manual node execution within your ROS environment.

Finally, we have `roslaunch`. This is the most relevant execution command since it allows you to describe a robot with an XML file. You can declare its nodes and link each one with the scripts that execute it. We will view this command in more detail in the *Automating the execution of a node using roslaunch* section.

Information commands

This category groups several commands that allow you to extract information from ROS environment as well as interactively modify some values. All of the commands are prepended with `ros-`. Simply writing the command in the terminal, supplies help with the different options regarding how to use each of them. A brief description and an example for each command are provided next.

Exploring topics

`rostopic` provides information about published topics:

```
$ rostopic list
```

This lists all the topics that are currently alive. From the list, you can access the real-time feed of any of them:

```
$ rostopic echo distance_sensor/distance
```

Exploring nodes

`rosnode` provides information about nodes that are alive:

```
$ rosnode list
```

This lists all the nodes of the current ROS graph. From the list, you can access information about any of them:

```
$ rosnode info distance_sensor
```

Here, `info` will provide you with useful information about the `distance_sensor` node. Do not confuse this with the name of the Python script where the node is declared, `distance-sensor.py`. The `rosnode` command always refers to the name of the node.

The rosmsg command

`rosmsg` provides information about the types of message used by topics during runtime. To give you a practical example, we select the `distance_sensor/distance` topic and get the following information about it:

```
$ rostopic info distance_sensor/distance
```

This command tells us that the topic has a message type of `sensor_msgs/Range`. Then, `rosmsg` informs us of the message structure:

```
$ rosmsg info sensor_msgs/Range
```

The output of this command is what we showed and explained in the *Setting up the msg_range object* subsection of the *Case study 1 – writing a ROS package – distance sensor* section. In the next chapter, we will provide extended explanations about the new message types we will be using in the GoPiGo3 ROS package.

The rosbag command

This command allows you to save a session and play it back on demand. Let's look at how to do that:

```
T1 $ roslaunch mygopigo easyDistance.launch
T2 $ rosbag record /distance_sensor/distance
```

Press *Ctrl* + *C* in the T2 terminal when you want to end the recording. Type `rosbag info <bag filename>` into `T2` to get information about the recorded file (the default name for the file is composed by the sequence `date-time-topic_name`, and it is given the `.bag` extension):

```
T2 $ rosbag info 2019-08-15-20-36-36_distanceSensor.bag

path: 2019-08-15-20-36-36.bag
version: 2.0
duration: 46.0s
start: Aug 15 2019 20:36:37.48 (1565894197.48)
end: Aug 15 2019 20:37:23.50 (1565894243.50)
size: 14.5 KB
messages: 47
compression: none [1/1 chunks]
types: sensor_msgs/Range [c005c34273dc426c67a020a87bc24148]
topics: /distance_sensor/distance 47 msgs : sensor_msgs/Range
```

Bear in mind that the bag file is placed in the location from which you launched the recording session in the `T2` terminal.

The recorded bag file allows to reproduce the topic history whenever we want, just as we do when we play a recorded song. One example of a typical situation where you would use this is to replay the robot behavior without the robot itself, using ROS on your laptop. This method eases debugging of the application and enables you to drastically reduce the number of times you need to run the software in the actual robot.

First, let's play it back in the Raspberry Pi by running the following set of commands, which include the visualization of the ROS graph (the `rqt_graph` command) and the measured distance over time (the `rqt_plot` command):

```
T1 $ roscore
T2 $ rosbag play 2019-08-15-20-36-36_distanceSensor.bag

T3 $ rostopic echo /distance_sensor/distance
T4 $ rqt_graph
T5 $ rqt_plot
```

In this snippet, we have introduced a new command, `rqt_plot`, that will be explained later in the *Case study 2– ROS GUI development tools – the Pi camera* section. Briefly, it plots a selected ROS topic over time.

Now you can playback the session on the laptop by launching the same set of commands. You will get the following result for `rqt_plot`:

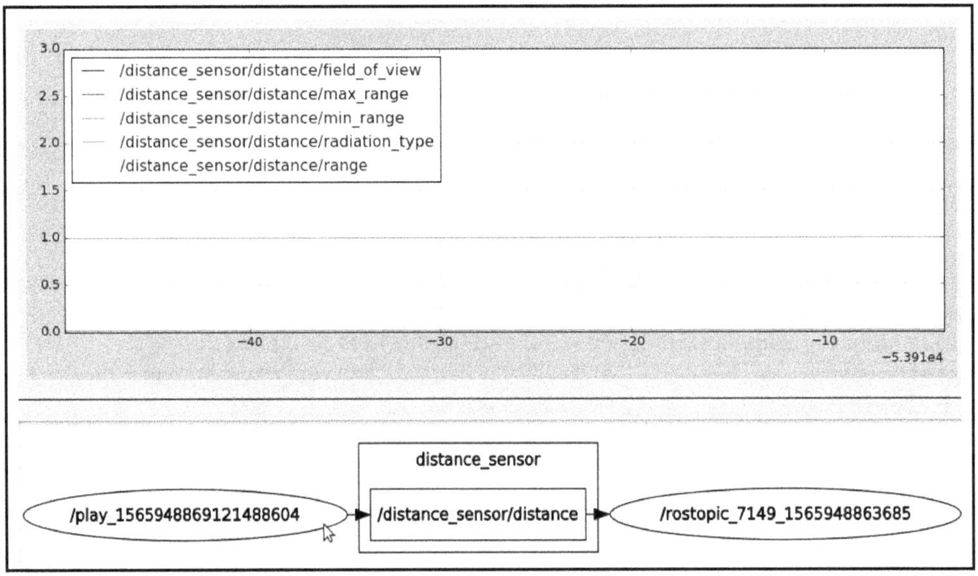

From the point of view of ROS, the result is exactly the same as if you were running the actual launch file in GoPiGo3. The difference, with respect to the figures, is due to the fact that you have ROS Kinetic on your laptop, while the robot has the Melodic version (which is more recent).

Packages and the catkin workspace

Some commands in this section have already been used when configuring your ROS environment. Let's briefly review them now:

- catkin_init_workspace initializes a new workspace, as you did at the beginning of this chapter.
- catkin_create_pkg creates a new package.
- catkin_make builds a workspace and should be invoked each time you add a package or remove one.

These are the essential commands. Nevertheless, there are some additional commands that are worth mentioning:

- catkin_find lists the working folders of your ROS environment.
- rospack provides information about a ROS package, be it from the core, contributed, or made by yourself. If you want to know which ROS packages are installed when dealing with GoPiGo, you can do so with this command:

```
$ rospack list | grep gopigo
    gopigo3_node /home/pi/catkin_ws/src/gopigo3_node
    mygopigo /home/pi/catkin_ws/src/mygopigo
```

The only caution you should have is that all of them should have the letters gopigo within their name so that grep can filter them without missing any.

In this section, we have provided an overview of the most frequent commands. Take all the time that you need to feel comfortable using them as you will be continuously using them when working with ROS. In the next section, we will extend our knowledge of the publish-subscribe pattern by explaining the syntax of the subscriber node, which is the node that will read messages from the selected topic.

Creating and running publisher and subscriber nodes

If you have understood how the requirement, distance-sensor.py, publisher script works, then the following subscriber script should be pretty straightforward to follow:

```
#!/usr/bin/env python

import rospy
```

```
from sensor_msgs.msg import Range

def callback(msg):
    print msg.data
    rospy.loginfo(rospy.get_caller_id() + 'GoPiGo3 measures distance %s
mm', msg.data*1000)

rospy.init_node('distance_sensor_subscriber')

sub = rospy.Subscriber('distance_sensor/distance', Range, callback)

rospy.spin()
```

This snippet corresponds to the `distance-sensor_subscriber.py` file in the `./pkg_mygopigo/src` folder of the code for this chapter. The main difference in the subscriber script is that, since we are listening to a topic, we do not need to specify a rate of execution. We simply loop forever with the following line:

```
rospy.spin()
```

Whenever a message is received in the topic, a callback function will be executed:

```
sub = rospy.Subscriber('distance_sensor/distance', Range, callback)
```

In this case, this callback function is defined to print the measured distance in millimeters:

```
def callback(msg):
    print msg.data
    rospy.loginfo(rospy.get_caller_id() + 'GoPiGo3 measures distance %s
mm', msg.data*1000)
```

Execute the script within ROS by using several terminals in the Terminator window:

```
T1 $ roscore
T2 $ rosrun mygopigo distance-sensor.py
T3 $ rostopic echo distance_sensor/distance
T4 $ rosrun mygopigo distance-sensor_subscriber.py
T5 $ rqt_graph
```

Take a look at the terminal window, as follows:

The following is globally the ROS graph:

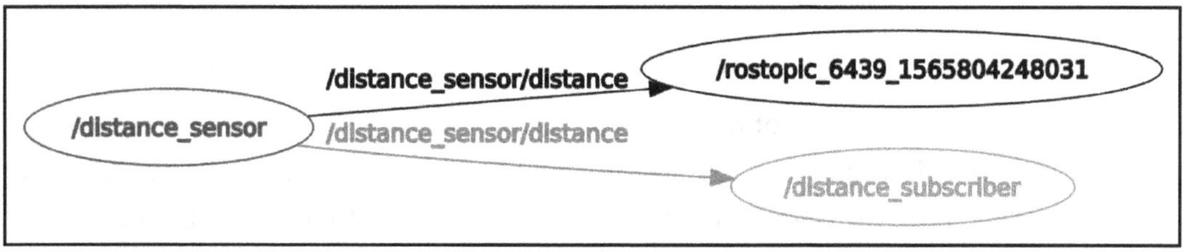

There are two nodes listening to the same topic. One is the subscriber script we have explained with the `/distance_subscriber` node, and the other is the node created by the `rostopic echo` command.

So far, you have manually launched each ROS node. In the next section, you will learn how to do it programmatically to run the robot software as an automated task.

Automating the execution of nodes using roslaunch

Once you have decided which nodes you want to run as part of your robot, you can automate the launch process for all scripts by using the `roslaunch` command. Its syntax is as follows:

```
$ roslaunch <name_of_package> <name_of_launch_file>
```

For our example, this is pretty simple as there is only one node. The launch file is in the repository at `./pkg_mygopigo/launch/easyDistance.launch` and its syntax is based on XML:

```
<launch>
   <node name="easyDistance_sensor" pkg="mygopigo" type="distance-
sensor.py" output="screen" />
   node name="distance_subscriber" pkg="mygopigo" type="distance-
sensor_subscriber.py" output="screen" />
</launch>
```

The `<launch>` tag delineates the robot description. Then, you include one `<node>` tag for each node you want to launch. In our case, there is only one: the `distance_sensor` node. The description of its attributes is as follows:

- `name`: The designation to identify the node. This supersedes the given name in the line of the script:

  ```
  rospy.init_node("distance_sensor")
  ```

  We set a different name in this launch file, `easyDistance_sensor`:

- `pkg`: This is the name of the package, which is `mygopigo`.
- `type`: This is a reference to the script that launches the node, `easyDistance.py`.
- `output`: We specify the screen (the default is the log that directs the output to `$ROS_HOME/log`).

Once you understand the XML launch file, repeat the process of raising up the robot, but, this time, use the automated way:

```
T1 $ roslaunch mygopigo easyDistance.launch
T2 $ rostopic echo /easyDistance_sensor/distance
```

`roslaunch` implicitly initiates `roscore`. You should see the same output as when you run it manually with `rosrun`. Obviously, `roslaunch` is really useful when you have to launch many nodes at the same time. We will see examples of this later.

Execute the script within ROS by using several terminals under the Terminator window:

```
T1 $ roslaunch mygopigo easyDistance.launch
T2 $ rostopic echo distance_sensor/distance
T3 $ rqt_graph
```

Take a look at the following terminal window:

Here is the ROS graph:

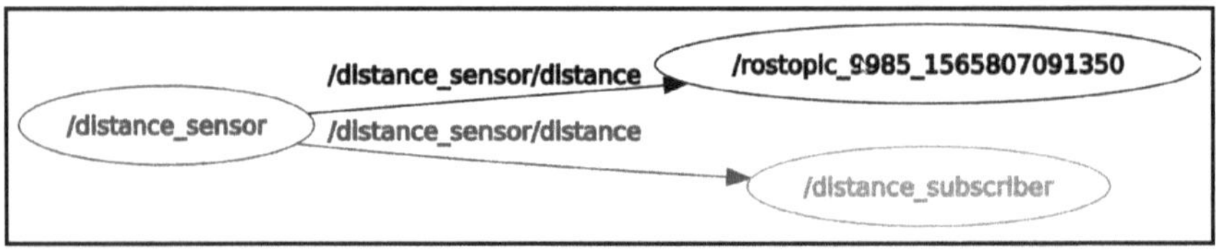

You will find exactly the same result as in the previous section. Let's now look at the ROS visual tools that ease our life as a software robotics developer.

Case study 2 – ROS GUI development tools – the Pi Camera

As we mentioned at the end of the *Installing ROS Melodic* section, in order to be able to use the camera, we first need to install its ROS package. Since the binaries are not available for ROS Melodic (only for Kinetic), we need to build the package from the source, and this is a perfect example in that you will know how to do it with any other package. Let's do this with the following steps:

1. Go to your `catkin` workspace and download the source code:

```
$ cd ~/catkin_ws/src
$ git clone https://github.com/UbiquityRobotics/raspicam_node.git
```

2. There are some dependencies to be installed for ROS. To carry out this task, we are going to create the `30-ubiquity.list` file:

```
$ sudo -s
$ echo "yaml
https://raw.githubusercontent.com/UbiquityRobotics/rosdep/master/ra
spberry-pi.yaml" > /etc/ros/rosdep/sources.list.d/30-ubiquity.list
$ exit
```

3. Afterward, run the ROS dependencies update as follows:

```
$ rosdep update
```

4. Now install the ROS dependencies:

```
$ cd ~/catkin_ws
$ rosdep install --from-paths src --ignore-src --rosdistro=melodic
-y
```

5. Compile the new package as follows:

```
$ catkin_make --only-pkg-with-deps raspicam_node
$ catkin_make -DCATKIN_WHITELIST_PACKAGES=""
```

   If you were using `catkin_make` without any option, the build process would traverse all the packages in the workspace. So, this snippet shows you how to compile a single package while ignoring the rest. The second line allows you to switch back to enable building all the packages the next item you need to compile the workspace.

6. To run the Pi Camera node, simply launch the following command:

```
T1 $ roslaunch raspicam_node camerav2_1280x960.launch
```

7. If you own the previous Pi Camera version, `V1`, use the following instead:

```
T1 $ roslaunch raspicam_node camerav1_1280x720.launch
```

8. Then, in another terminal, run the image viewer utility that comes with the package to check that the camera is working properly:

```
T2 $ rosrun raspicam_node imv_view.py
```

   You should see a new window similar to the following:

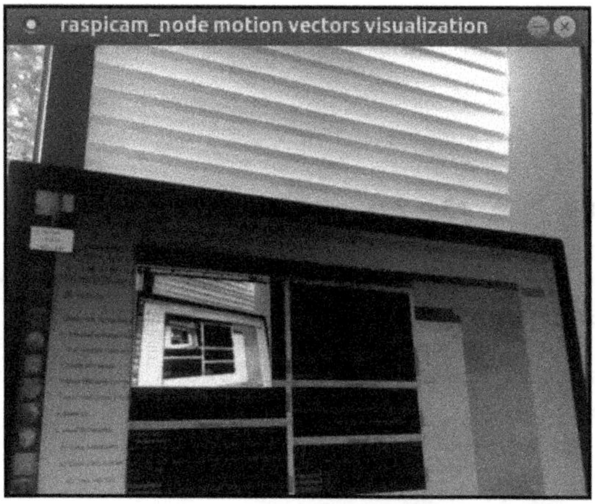

If you move the robot, you will find that the image also changes, so you are watching a live camera stream. Now we are ready to proceed with practical explanations for the ROS GUI development tools, which is the scope of this section.

Analyzing the ROS graph using rqt_graph

By issuing this command, you can visualize the current ROS graph:

```
T3 $ rqt_graph
```

It will show the following diagram:

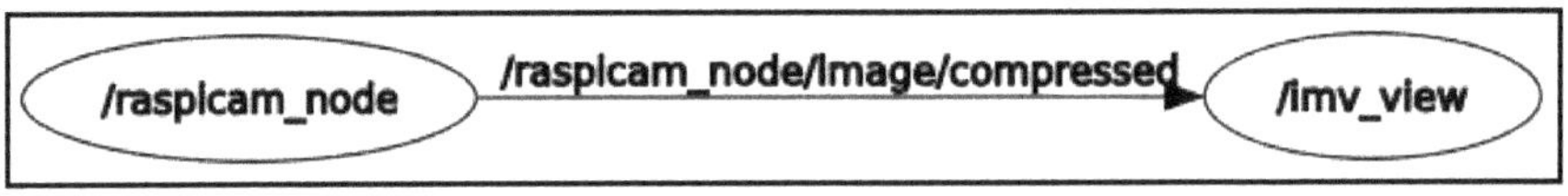

`raspicam_node` is the root node of the package that interfaces with the physical Pi Camera. It publishes images in the `/raspicam_node/image/compressed` topic. The other node, `imv_view`, from the process in the `T2` terminal, launches a window where you can watch the live stream (as shown in the preceding section).

Finally, inspecting the topic's `raspicam_node` provides the following:

```
T4 $ rostopic list | grep raspicam_node

/raspicam_node/camera_info
/raspicam_node/image/compressed
/raspicam_node/parameter_descriptions
/raspicam_node/parameter_updates
```

You can find in the list the node that the `imv_view` node is subscribed to, which is `/raspicam_node/image/compressed`.

Displaying image data using rqt_image_view

This plugin allows you to visualize image data that is published in a ROS topic. Kill the previous two terminals and launch the following new ones:

```
T1 $ roslaunch raspicam_node camerav2_410x308_30fps.launch
T2 $ rqt_image_view
```

In the upper-left drop-down list, select the topic of the image that you want to visualize. It needs to be in compressed format as it is published by `raspicam_node`. The following screenshot shows the result:

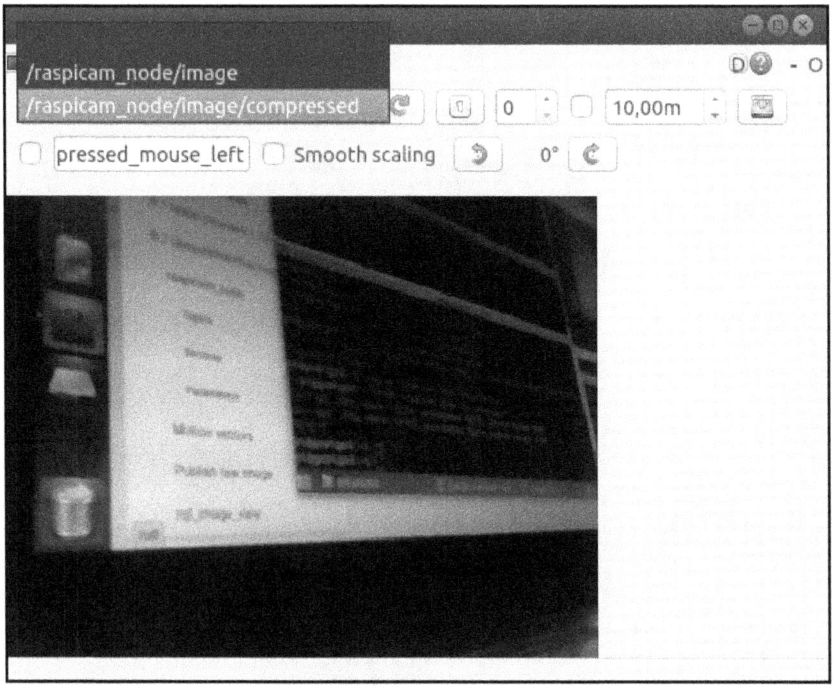

In the event you have several topics with image data, the plugin allows you to interactively select what feed to watch and also change between them on demand.

Graphing time series of sensor data with rqt_plot

This is a plugin to visualize two-dimensional data. As we want to see two-dimensional data, let's briefly switch to the distance sensor case study so that we can view the measured distance over time. The process is straightforward: launch the robot, list the topics, and then launch the plugin:

```
T1 $ roslaunch mygopigo easyDistance.launch
T2 $ rostopic list | grep distance_sensor
T3 $ rqt_plot
```

In the upper-left box, write the name of the topic you want to visualize, that is, `/distance_sensor/distance` as per `T2`. A window will pop up showing the distance to the obstacle over time:

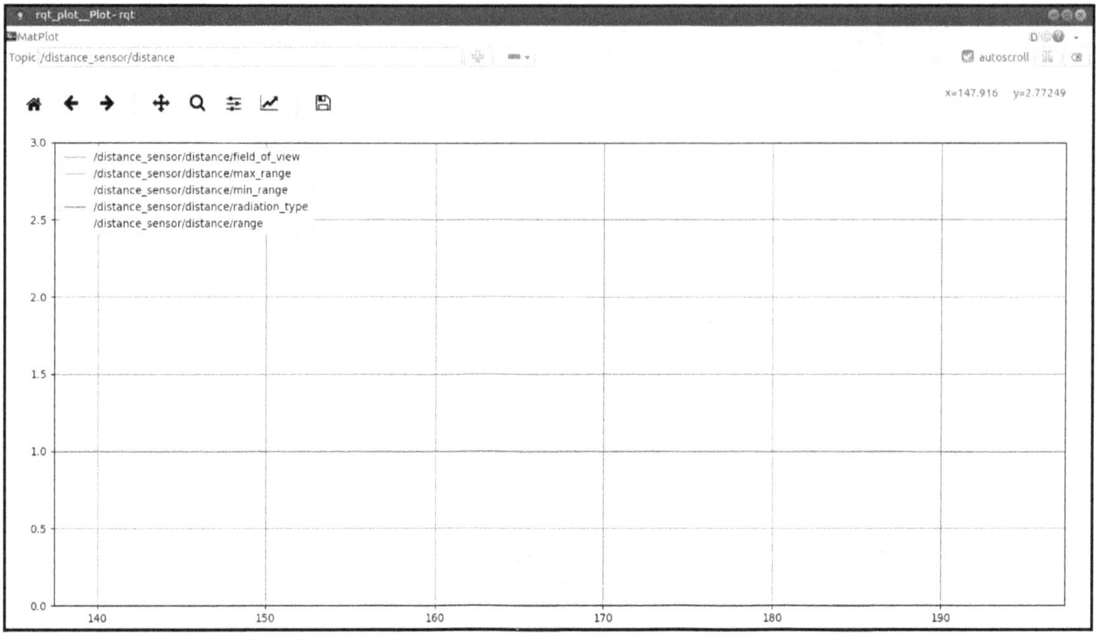

The green line, `msg_range.range`, is the actual measurement. The other fields of the `msg_range` object (this is the content of `topic/distance_sensor/distance`) display the maximum and minimum values of all the measurements: `msg_range.max_range` and `msg_range.min_range`, respectively.

Playing a recorded ROS session with rqt_bag

The `rqt_bag` plugin plays a bag file, which is the same as the `rosbag` command explained in the *ROS commands* section. Here, the advantage is that you have interactive control of the playback: you can jump to any instant, play single time steps, rewind to the beginning, and so on. Let's examine this with the distance sensor case study first, and then with the Pi Camera.

Distance sensor

You can perform the playback wherever you want, using the robot or the laptop. As with `rosbag`, you will need prior access to a `roscore` process, then you can issue `rqt_bag`:

```
T1 $ roscore
T2 $ rqt_bag
```

A new window pops up. Select the bag file to play, that is, `2019-08-15-20-36-36_distanceSensor.bag`, right-click on the windows, and then mark the `/distance_sensor/distance` topic to be published. Run the same set of commands as when you used `rosbag`:

```
T3 $ rostopic echo /distance_sensor/distance
T4 $ rqt_graph
T5 $ rqt_plot
```

In the following screenshot, you can check that the result is the same:

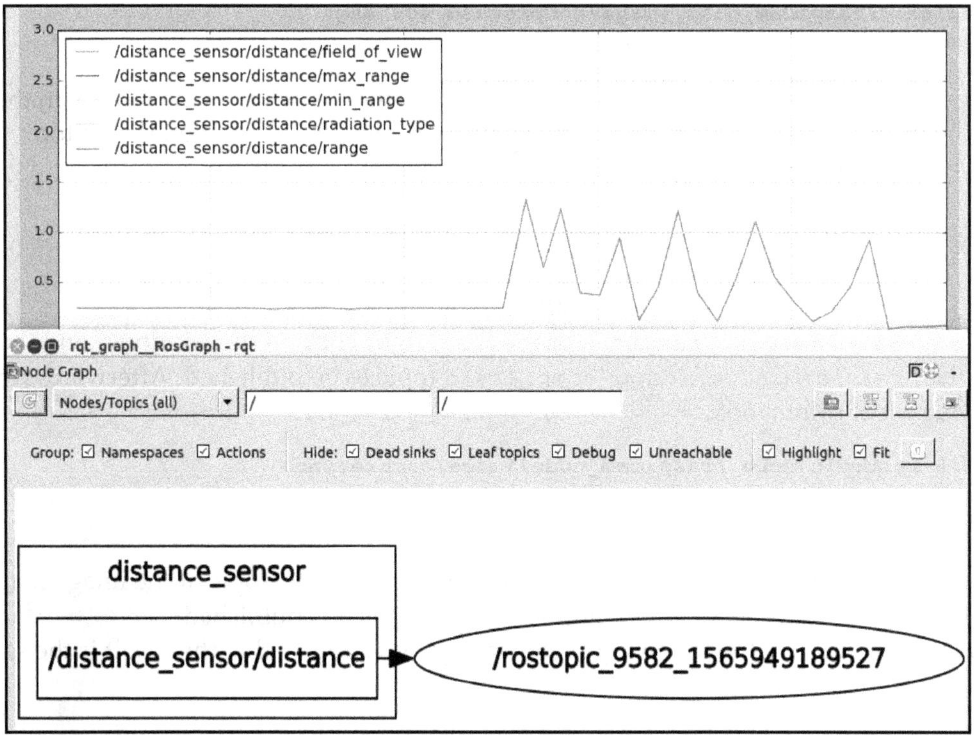

Now we will play the image stream from the Pi Camera case study.

The Pi Camera

First, we need to record a session with the robot:

```
T1 $ roslaunch raspicam_node camerav2_410x308_30fps.launch
T2 $ rosbag record /raspicam_node/image/compressed
```

Check the information about the recorded file:

```
$ rosbag info 2019-08-15-20-44-53_raspicamImage.bag

path: 2019-08-15-20-44-53_raspicamImage.bag
version: 2.0
duration: 13.3s
start: Aug 15 2019 20:44:54.09 (1565894694.09)
end: Aug 15 2019 20:45:07.38 (1565894707.38)
size: 37.5 MB
messages: 400
compression: none [47/47 chunks]
types: sensor_msgs/CompressedImage [8f7a12909da2c9d3332d540a0977563f]
topics: /raspicam_node/image/compressed 400 msgs :
sensor_msgs/CompressedImage
```

You can perform the playback wherever you want, using the robot or the laptop. In this case, the image data is bulkier. So, it is much better to play the session on the laptop. Launch the processes as before:

```
T1 $ roscore
T2 $ rqt_bag
```

In the launched `rqt_bag` plugin, select the bag file to play, which is `2019-08-15-20-44-53_raspicamImage.bag`, right-click on the windows, and then mark the `/raspicam_node/image/compressed` topic to be published. Afterward, run the following set of commands:

```
T3 $ rostopic echo /raspicam_node/image/compressed
T4 $ rqt_graph
T5 $ rqt_image_view
```

In the upper-left drop-down list of `rqt_image_view`, select the topic of the image that you want to visualize. It needs to be in compressed format as it is published by `raspicam_node`. In the following screenshot, you can check that the result is the same:

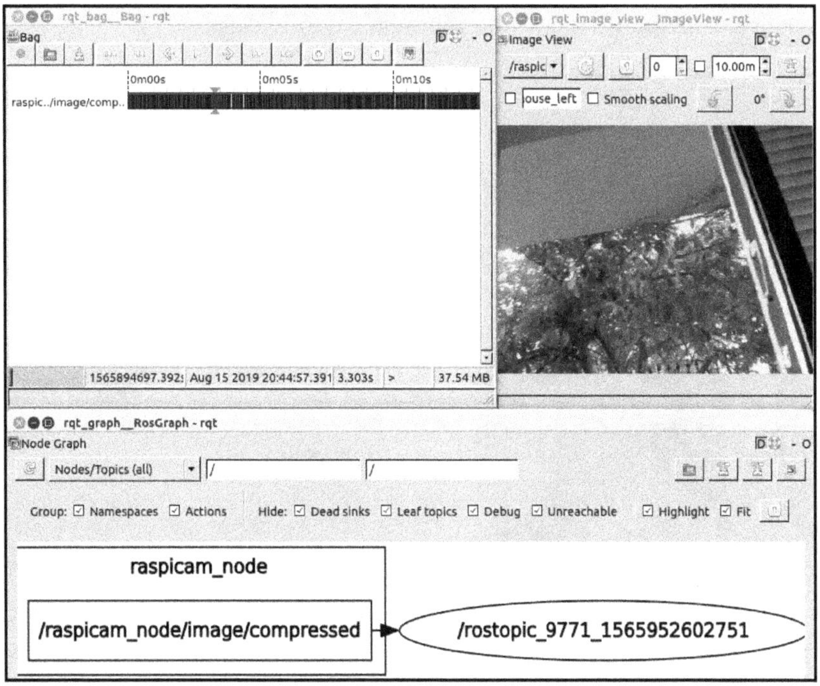

While playing the *bag* file, you can check that the image stream is very fluent thanks to the fact that your laptop has a powerful GPU compared to what the Raspberry Pi provides. So, it is clear that, when you are dealing with computer vision tasks, you will take advantage of this visualization capability of robot sessions within your laptop.

Customizing robot features using ROS parameters

ROS parameters store the global configuration of the robot. This is a convenient way in which to define your application so that you can abstract the functionality to a high level and make it available for the end user. We are going to illustrate how ROS parameters work by using a `rqt` plugin that allows for dynamically reconfiguring of some of them. It is as it sounds; you can modify robot characteristics on the fly:

1. Launch `raspicam_node` and then the `rqt` plugins:

```
T1 $ roslaunch raspicam_node camerav2_410x308_30fps.launch
T2 $ rqt_image_view
T3 $ rosrun rqt_reconfigure rqt_reconfigure
```

Your desktop should show the following two windows:

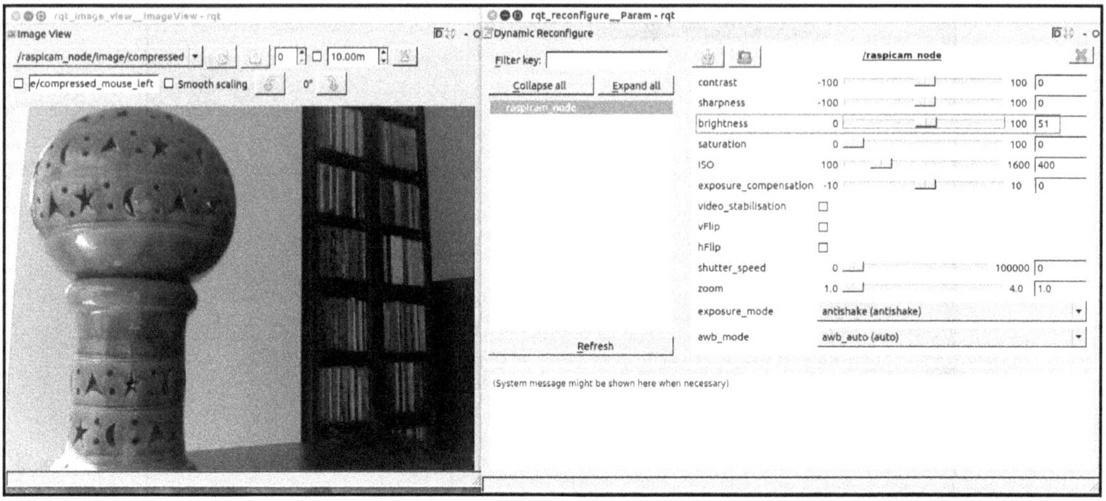

2. Check the parameters on the right-hand side and focus on the brightness (the box marked in red). Modify its value from `51` to `81` and then check the result:

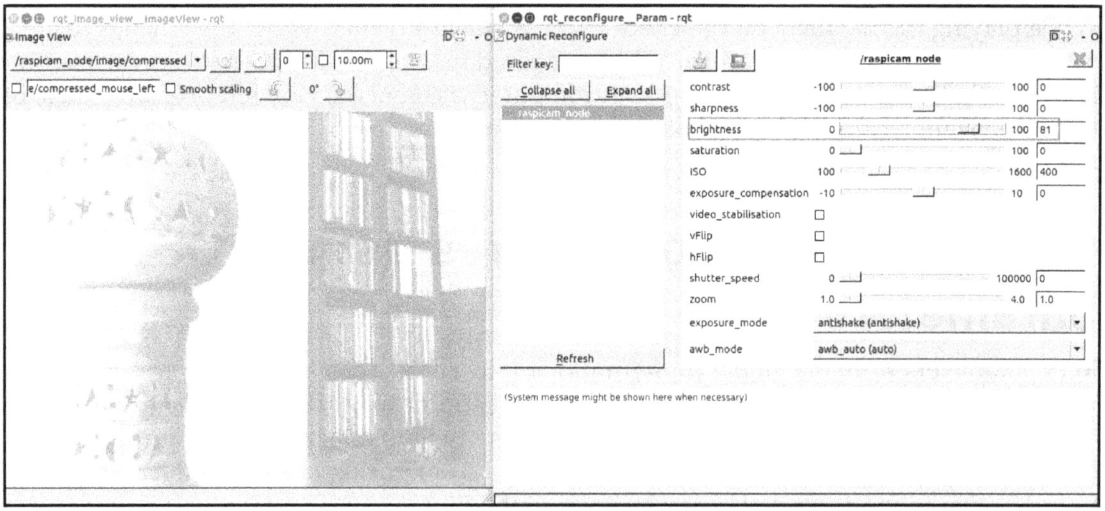

Wow! You can dynamically modify the configuration of the robot without needing to restart it.

3. You also have the `rosbash` command, which allows you to inspect the parameters. List them with the following line:

```
T4 $ rosparam list | grep raspicam_node

/raspicam_node/ISO
/raspicam_node/awb_mode
/raspicam_node/brightness
/raspicam_node/camera_frame_id
/raspicam_node/camera_id
/raspicam_node/camera_info_url
/raspicam_node/camera_name
/raspicam_node/contrast
/raspicam_node/enable_imv
/raspicam_node/enable_raw
/raspicam_node/exposure_compensation
...
/raspicam_node/zoom
```

Additionally, get the state of the one we have dynamically modified:

```
T4 $ rosparam get /raspicam_node/brightness
      81
```

If you have arrived at this point and understand the concepts in the practical exercises, you now know almost everything that you need to work with ROS from now on.

Summary

In this chapter, we have established the basis for programming in ROS. You have built your own package with a simple GoPiGo3 functionality: reading a distance sensor in order to work on programming concepts. You have also learned how to read Pi Camera images and make them available to ROS for further processing, which is the starting point for performing computer vision tasks.

In the next chapter, you will put the two ROS worlds together: the robot and your laptop. This way, once you have the GoPiGo3 package running in the robot, you will have the power to undertake all computing and processing tasks from your powerful laptop.

Questions

1. What is the difference between ROS topics and ROS messages?

   A) Both stand for the data transmitted from one node to the other.
   B) A topic is how you identify a transmission channel and a message is one sample of the content that flows through that channel.
   C) Any topic name has to be unique, while several topics can transmit the same message.

2. Which command would use to record a ROS session?

   A) `rosbag`
   B) `rosrecord`
   C) `roswrite`

3. Can a ROS node have a publisher and a subscriber at the same time?

   A) Yes, if the topic subscriber is the same as the topic publisher.
   B) No, because it would imply a programming conflict: a node with a publisher loops at a constant rate, that is, `rate.sleep()`, while a node with a subscriber only runs an iteration if it receives a message, that is, `rospy.spin()`.
   C) Yes, and the node is driven by the subscriber, that is, the node broadcasts a new message each time it receives a message from the topic it is subscribed to.

4. How many `roslaunch` commands can you run in the same ROS session?

   A) As many as you need; `roslaunch` is a description file that tells ROS what nodes to launch when the command is called.
   B) Just one, because `roslaunch` implicitly runs a `roscore` process, and you can only have one ROS master node in the session.
   C) If you need two sets of nodes, it is recommended that you launch each of them manually when you need to add each to the execution environment. Then, start a `roscore` process and later execute a `rosrun` for every new node you need.

5. Is there a programmatic way to visualize an image that is published in a ROS topic?

   A) Yes, using `rqt_plot`
   B) Yes, using `rqt_image_view`
   C) Yes, using `rqt_image_view`, but it is necessary that the image is in a compressed format

Further reading

To go deeper into the concepts we have explained in this chapter, you can follow the following references and tutorials:

- ROS technical overview: http://wiki.ros.org/ROS/Technical%20Overview
- ROS cheatsheet: https://kapeli.com/cheat_sheets/ROS.docset/Contents/Resources/Documents/index
- ROS command line – the rosbash commands: http://wiki.ros.org/rosbash
- Master node – the roscore command and process: http://wiki.ros.org/roscore
- ROS topics – the rostopic command description: http://wiki.ros.org/rostopic
- ROS nodes – the rosnode command description: http://wiki.ros.org/rosnode
- Messages – the rosmsg command description: http://wiki.ros.org/rosmsg
- ROS parameters – the rosparam command description: http://wiki.ros.org/rosparam
- Record sessions – the rosbag command description: http://wiki.ros.org/rosbag
- Recording and playing back data with rosbag: http://wiki.ros.org/rosbag/Tutorials/Recording%20and%20playing%20back%20data
- Catkin command-line tools: https://catkin-tools.readthedocs.io
- The Pi Camera official documentation: https://picamera.readthedocs.io
- ROS rqt GUI tools: http://wiki.ros.org/rqt
- The rqt_graph plugin: http://wiki.ros.org/rqt_graph
- The rqt_image_view plugin: http://wiki.ros.org/rqt_image_view
- The rqt_plot plugin: http://wiki.ros.org/rqt_plot
- The rqt_bag plugin: http://wiki.ros.org/rqt_bag
- Using rqt tools for analysis – rqt_console, rqt_graph, and urdf_to_graphviz: https://industrial-training-master.readthedocs.io/en/melodic/_source/session6/Using-rqt-tools-for-analysis.html

7 Robot Control and Simulation

In this chapter, you will set up your ROS development environment specifically for programming GoPiGo3. This understanding is going to be built by going from using the keys of your laptop keyboard to the more technical way of using ROS topics. Finally, you will guess what topics will allow you to wire manual keyboard/topic-based control to internal programming logic (that is, smart behavior) that will make the robot capable of executing autonomous tasks. In this sense, 3D simulation in Gazebo is an essential tool for testing behavior during development before pushing the app to the physical robot, saving time and effort when it comes to field-based work.

By the end of this chapter, you will have learned how to set up the ROS environment for a real robot. Remote control and autonomous control establish a qualitative difference in terms of robot software development. By experimenting with remote control by yourself, you will be ready to cross the frontier of what makes a robot really autonomous.

Finally, you will understand the usefulness of using simulation during the development of robotic applications by establishing a comparison with how the physical robot behaves. These observed differences will allow you to adjust the parameters of the virtual robot's simulation in Gazebo. The main advantage of this approach is that you can keep on developing and testing the software with the virtual model and then only test with the real hardware in the final development stage.

The following topics will be covered in this chapter:

- Setting up the GoPiGo3 development environment and making it capable of networking with ROS on a laptop
- Case study 3 – remotely controlling the physical robot using the keyboard
- Remotely controlling robots using ROS topics from the command line
- Comparing the behavior of both of the physical robot and the virtual model in Gazebo under manual remote control

We will provide explanations of these concepts based on our third case study regarding robot drives (motors and encoders). Remember that the first two case studies were covered in `Chapter 6`, *Programming in ROS – Commands and Tools*, and were as follows:

- **Case study 1**: Publishing and reading the distance sensor
- **Case study 2**: Acquiring and visualizing images from the Pi camera

By the end of this chapter, we will have our first complete version of the ROS package of GoPiGo3. This will be the basis that our smart robot behaviors will be built upon in the rest of this book.

Technical requirements

For this chapter, no additional hardware or software configuration will be needed. Just make sure that you have the following:

- GoPiGo3, as per the *Technical requirements* section of `Chapter 6`, *Programming in ROS – Commands and Tools*
- A laptop, as per the *Configure your ROS Development Environment* section of `Chapter 3`, *Getting Started with ROS*

In the next section, we will prepare the ROS environment so that your laptop and the robot can communicate with each other under a unique ROS graph. Let's go over the code we'll need:

- **Code for this chapter (laptop)**: In this chapter, we will make use of the code located in the `Chapter7_Robot_control_simulation` folder (`https://github.com/PacktPublishing/Hands-On-ROS-for-Robotics-Programming/tree/master/Chapter7_Robot_control_simulation`). Copy its files to the ROS workspace so that they're available to you and leave the rest outside the `src` folder. This way, you will have a cleaner ROS environment:

```
$ cp -R ~/Hands-On-ROS-for-Robotics-
Programming/Chapter7_Robot_control_simulation ~/catkin_ws/src
```

  The code contains a new ROS package named `gazebo_control`. Rebuild the workspace so that it is known to your ROS installation:

```
$ cd ~/catkin_ws
$ catkin_make
$ source ~/catkin_ws/devel/setup.bash
```

Check that the package has been correctly installed by selecting it and listing the files:

```
$ roscd gazebo_control
$ ls -la
```

- **Code for this chapter (GoPiGo3)**: You will be using the same code that we developed in `Chapter 6`, *Programming in ROS – Commands and Tools*. Remember that it corresponds to the ROS package called `mygopigo` that's located in the Raspberry Pi.

Now, you are ready to follow the explanations in this chapter and understand them in a practical way.

Setting up the GoPiGo3 development environment

In the previous chapter, you tried the ROS desktop version in the Raspberry Pi of GoPiGo3. For a serious development strategy, you should launch the minimum configuration of the application in the robot and launch all the accompanying development tasks within the laptop.

Remember that in `Chapter 3`, *Getting Started with ROS*, you run ROS on your laptop. Hence, the robot application itself was executed in such an environment, with no possibility to move a physical robot since we didn't establish a connection outside of the computer.

In this section, you will learn how to work simultaneously with the laptop and Raspberry Pi ROS environments when they're linked, that is, the Raspberry Pi controlling the GoPiGo3 robot and the laptop for CPU-intensive computing/visualization tasks.

ROS networking between the robot and the remote computer

To make two ROS environments, there are two prior conditions we need to meet:

- The robot and computer ROS environments need to know how to communicate with each other.
- The master node (`roscore` process) should be unique and run in either.

Let's learn how to accomplish both conditions.

Communication between ROS environments

The way that a computer is identified in a network is by means of its IP address, normally using the IPv4 protocol. In general, you can find the IP that's been assigned to your machine with the `ifconfig` command:

```
$ ifconfig

eth0: ...
lo:   ...
wlan0: flags=4163<UP,BROADCAST,RUNNING,MULTICAST> mtu 1500
        inet addr: 192.168.1.58 netmask 255.255.255.0 broadcast
192.168.1.255
        inet6 addr: fe80::7d9d:84a9:ec7:20cd prefixlen 64 scopeid
0x20<link>

        RX packets 212 bytes 46561 (46.5 KB)
        RX errors 0 dropped 0 overruns 0 frame 0
        TX packets 202 bytes 43986 (43.9 KB)
        TX errors 0 dropped 0 overruns 0 carrier 0 collisions 0
```

You should focus on the wireless interface, typically named `wlan0`, since you configured your robot for Wi-Fi access. The IP address is the 4 x 4 bytes field following the word `inet`. So, for the Raspberry Pi in GoPiGo3, this field is `192.168.1.58`.

Do the same for the laptop, opening in it a Terminal. If you are using a wired connection, you should look at `eth0` instead of `wlan0`. For our example case, the computer's IP is `192.168.1.54`. If there were too many network interfaces, the output could be too verbose. To focus on what you are looking for, you can filter the output, like this:

```
$ ifconfig | grep 'inet'
```

Once you have both IP addresses, you just have to indicate them using ROS environment variables. In the following subsections, we will show you how to configure each of the computers.

Robot network configuration

Next, you have to follow three steps to set up the Raspberry Pi:

1. Execute the following two commands in a Terminal to define the environment variables needed by ROS:

   ```
   $ export ROS_HOSTNAME=192.168.1.58
   $ export ROS_MASTER_URI=http://${ROS_HOSTNAME}:11311
   ```

   The first command sets the variable that allows ROS to know the IP of the host where it is currently running. The second line is the URL of the master node. Since it is set to `ROS_HOSTNAME`, we are saying that it will run on the robot computer. Port `11311` is the default that's set by ROS to communicate with the master node. Each subsequently launched node will be automatically assigned a new available port.

2. There is a way to abstract the IP number itself because, in Ubuntu systems, `avahi-daemon` (`http://manpages.ubuntu.com/manpages/bionic/man8/avahi-daemon.8.html`) allows you to point to a machine in the local network by simply appending `.local` to its hostname. For this, the configuration command will be as follows:

   ```
   $ export ROS_HOSTNAME=gopigo3.local
   ```

   The hostname can be found in the prompt of the Terminal and is usually in the format `user@hostname :~$`. If you have any doubts, you can ask for it in the Terminal by using `hostname` command:

   ```
   pi@gopigo3 :~$ hostname
        gopigo3
   ```

3. Each new Terminal you launch will need this configuration. So, if we include it as additional lines in the `.bashrc` file, you won't have to care about doing this by hand:

   ```
   $ echo export ROS_HOSTNAME=gopigo3.local >> ~/.bashrc
   $ echo export ROS_MASTER_URI=http://${ROS_HOSTNAME}:11311 >>
   ~/.bashrc
   ```

Check the result by listing the end of the file:

```
$ tail ~/.bashrc
```

You should see the cited two configuration lines.

Now that the Raspberry Pi has been configured, we will do something similar for the laptop.

Laptop network configuration

For the remote computer, these are the equivalent steps:

1. Execute the following two commands in a Terminal to set the environment variables:

```
$ export ROS_HOSTNAME=192.168.1.54
$ export ROS_MASTER_URI=http://gopigo3.local:11311
```

   You specify its IP address as `192.168.1.54` in the first line, while in the second, we are stating that the ROS master is located in the robot, that is, `gopigo3.local`. This way, your system won't need to be reconfigured if the network is restarted and a different IP address is assigned to the Raspberry Pi.

2. As for the robot, add the following two lines to the `.bashrc` file to automate the configuration each time a new Terminal is launched:

```
$ echo export ROS_HOSTNAME=rosbot.local >> ~/.bashrc
$ echo export ROS_MASTER_URI=http://gopigo3.local:11311 >>
~/.bashrc
```

We are also showing the alternative for setting `ROS_HOSTNAME`, that is, using `rosbot.local` instead of the numeric IP address.

Launching the master node and connecting

The following procedure allows us to establish a connection between the laptop and the Raspberry Pi:

1. Launch the ROS master node in the robot by using the already familiar `roscore` command:

```
pi@gopigo3 :~$ roscore
```

2. Then, perform a basic check in the laptop to find out if it is aware of the master node's existence:

```
bronquillo@rosbot:~$ rostopic list
 /rosout
 /rosout_agg
```

`/rosout_agg` and `/rosout_agg` are the topics that are published by the master node.

If everything has gone well, you can remotely control your GoPiGo3. Close the Terminal before moving on to the next section to make sure `roscore` is off.

Case study 3 – remote control using the keyboard

This case study will help you complete the first version of the GoPiGo3 ROS package. In the previous chapter, you were dealing with the distance sensor and the Pi camera, and we devoted one case study to each of them.

By including the motion functionality with the present robot drives, you will have a robot that is able to perform basic interactions with its environment:

- **Perception capabilities** include detecting obstacles with the distance sensor and visual recognition of the surroundings with the Pi camera.
- **Actuation capability**, where the robot is able to move on the floor while being aware of the possible obstacles with the distance sensor and recognizing shapes and people with the image feed from its camera.

Case study 3 focuses on actuation capability. In this section, you will learn how to remotely move the robot using a keyboard and a mouse.

Running the gopigo3 node in the robot

In this section, we are going to run a node in the Raspberry Pi that will provide the control capability:

1. Launch the GoPiGo3 ROS package in the robot:

```
$ roslaunch mygopigo gopigo3.launch
```

This is the only command you need to run directly in the Raspberry Pi. Since you configured ROS so that the laptop can talk to the robot, the following commands can be run on the laptop.

When preceding a bash command with `T1`, `T2`, `T3`, or `T4`, we will always be referring to consecutive Terminals on the laptop.

2. Then, on your laptop, ensure that you have a single node, that is, `gopigo3`:

```
T1 $ rosnode list
 /gopigo3
 /rosout
```

Remember that the `/rosout` topic corresponds to the master node.

3. Next, list all the available ROS topics to find out what their names are:

```
T1 $ rostopic list
/battery_voltage
/cmd_vel
...
/motor/encoder/left
/motor/encoder/right
...
/motor/status
/odom
/rosout
/rosout_agg
/servo/position/1
/servo/position/2
...
/tf
```

Bear in mind that the three topics of interest are called /battery_voltage, /cmd_vel, and /motor/status. We will provide details about them later in this section.

4. To get additional information about these topics, you can use the info option of the rosnode command. This will tell you what the gopigo3 node can do:

```
T1 $ rosnode info gopigo3
Node [/gopigo3]
Publications:
 * /battery_voltage [std_msgs/Float64]
 * /joint_state [sensor_msgs/JointState]
 * /motor/encoder/left [std_msgs/Float64]
 * /motor/encoder/right [std_msgs/Float64]
 * /motor/status [gopigo3_node/MotorStatusLR]
...
Subscriptions:
 * /cmd_vel
 ...
 * /motor/dps/left
 * /motor/dps/right
 ...
```

Here, you can see that /battery_voltage and /motor/status are publishers (objects in the code of the node that stream data to such topics), while /cmd_vel is a subscriber (as well as an object that's declared in the node that allows us to consume data from an existing topic):

- The publishers allow you to get status information from the battery level and the motors, respectively.
- The /cmd_vel subscriber allows the robot to accept motion commands for remote control.

In the next subsection, we will inspect the publishers in order to understand the structure of the messages they stream.

Inspecting published topics and messages

Now that we've identified the three topics, let's take a look at them and get some robot-specific information:

1. To find the last five values of the battery, run the following command in a Terminal. This will allow you to inspect the `/battery_voltage` topic:

```
T1 $ rostopic echo battery_voltage -n 5

data: 9.568
---
data: 9.551
---
data: 9.594
---
data: 9.568
---
data: 9.586
```

   You can infer that the voltage is about 9.6V on average, which means the batteries are charged.

2. Let's investigate how this topic is built:

```
T1 $ rostopic info battery_voltage
      Type: std_msgs/Float64
```

   It uses the `std_msgs/Float64` message type, which corresponds to a floating-point number that's 64 bits size. This message type is part of the ROS standard message library (`http://wiki.ros.org/std_msgs`). To find out what a ROS message is made up of, you can use the `rosmsg` command:

```
T1 $ rosmsg info std_msgs/Float64
       float64 data
```

3. There is another topic in this node, `/motor/status`, that makes use of a custom and more complex message:

```
T1 $ rostopic info motor/status
      Type: mygopigo/MotorStatusLR
```

4. Let's find the structure of the message. Note that the definition of the message is declared within the `mygopigo` package under the `msg` folder:

```
T1 $ rosmsg info mygopigo/MotorStatusLR

  std_msgs/Header header
  uint32 seq
  time stamp
  string frame_id

mygopigo/MotorStatus left
  bool low_voltage
  bool overloaded
  int8 power
  float32 encoder
  float32 speed

mygopigo/MotorStatus right
  bool low_voltage
  bool overloaded
  int8 power
  float32 encoder
  float32 speed
```

There are three parts to this:

- A header with the sequence number and the timestamp
- Data from the left motor
- Data from the right motor

If we take the content of the last published message, we can visualize this structure in practice:

```
T1 $ rostopic echo motor/status -n 1
header:
  seq: 177
  stamp:
    secs: 1566220531
    nsecs: 946445941
  frame_id: ''
left:
  low_voltage: False
  overloaded: False
  power: -128
  encoder: 0.0
  speed: 0.0
right:
```

```
low_voltage: False
overloaded: False
power: -128
encoder: 0.0
speed: 0.0
```

Here, you can see that the topic reports the `low_voltage` level warning, the motor `overload` warning, `power`, `encoder` data, and the current `speed`.

Now, let's proceed to the practical part of moving the robot.

Teleoperation package

`key_teleop` (`http://wiki.ros.org/key_teleop`) is a ROS-contributed package that provides a very simple mechanism for controlling a robot using the arrow keys of the keyboard. Clone the source code and install the package on your laptop as usual:

```
$ cd ~/catkin_ws/src
$ git clone https://github.com/ros-teleop/teleop_tools
$ cd .. && catkin_make
```

Another two packages are available here that are also part of the `teleop_tools` bundle:

- `joy_teleop`, a generic joystick interface for topics and actions
- `mouse_teleop`, a pointing device (for example, mouse, touchpad, and so on) teleoperation utility

Since you have built the whole repository, both of these are available to you.

Running teleoperation on a laptop

Since you've completed the *Running gopigo3 node in the robot* subsection, you should have the `gopigo3` node running as a result of the `$ roslaunch mygopigo gopigo3.launch` command. Let's learn how to achieve remote control of it:

1. Launch the teleoperation node on your laptop:

```
T1 $ rosrun key_teleop key_teleop.py /key_vel:=/cmd_vel
```

The preceding command launches the `key_teleop` node, and the Terminal's prompt is substituted by an interface that looks similar to the one shown in the following screenshot:

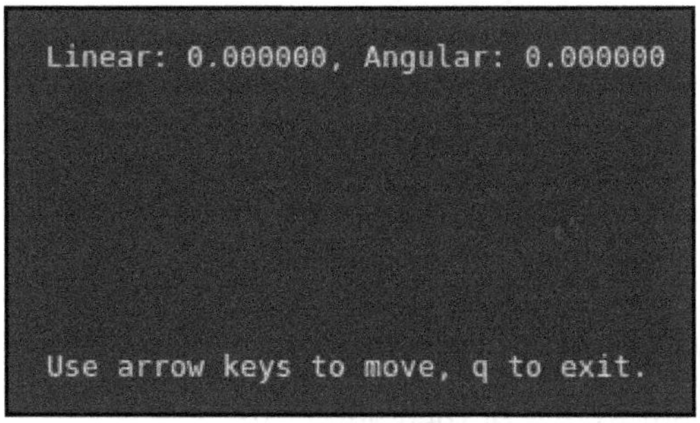

This gray window tells you how to move the robot using the arrow keys of the keyboard:

- The up arrow key moves the robot forward at 0.8 m/s. You can see the commanded speed in the interface.
- The down arrow key moves the robot backward at -0.5 m/s (the minus sign means backward).
- The left arrow key rotates the robot counter-clockwise (left) at 1 rad/s.
- The right arrow key rotates the robot clockwise at -1 rad/s (the minus sign means rotation to the right).

> So that you can effectively move it, be aware that the Terminal that you launched the `key_teleop` node from has to be the active window. If that's not the case, just click anywhere on it to make it the active one.

2. With the `T2` command, we can visualize the ROS graph as usual:

```
T2 $ rqt_graph
```

It should look as follows:

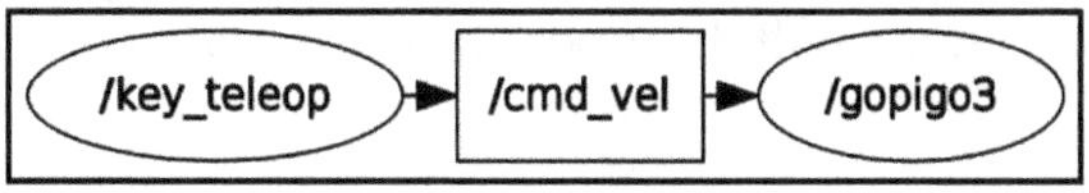

The T1 command that was appended after the executable script of the node with the /key_vel:=/cmd_vel assignment is what we call remapping. This technique allows two nodes to communicate, where the literal of the subscriber of the listener node, /cmd_vel, does not match the literal of the publisher node, /key_vel. Hence, remapping consists of wiring the published topic of one node to the subscribed topic of another node. This way, we know that the output from the key_teleop node is going to be the input of the gopigo3 node.

Now, let's learn how to teleoperate the robot with the mouse instead of the keyboard.

Teleoperation with the mouse

This procedure is equivalent to that of the keyboard:

1. Write the following command in a third Terminal to apply the mouse_teleop package from the teleop_tools bundle:

```
T3 $ rosrun mouse_teleop mouse_teleop.py /mouse_vel:=/cmd_vel
```

   In this case, the remapping topic is /mouse_vel:=/cmd_vel.

2. Refresh the rqt_graph window; you will see the following:

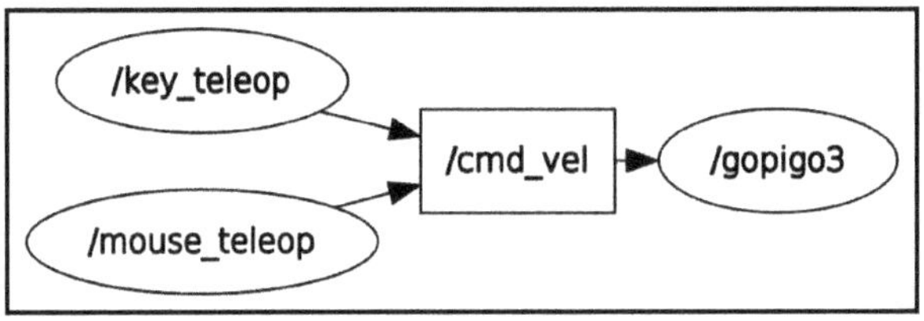

   The preceding graph suggests that the robot simultaneously accepts commands from the mouse and the keyboard without any trouble. This happens if we don't kill the keyboard control in the T1 Terminal before launching the mouse control command.

   On the other hand, if you kill the T1 terminal, the robot will keep on working, but then you will only control it with the mouse since the process in T3 keeps it live (the key_teleop node will disappear from rqt_graph if we refresh the window).

3. Finally, check if the mouse control works (restart the `T1` command if you killed it previously):

    - Select the window of `T1`. You will move GoPiGo3 with the arrow keys.
    - Select the new window that appeared by implementing the `T3` command. Now, you can move GoPiGo3 with the mouse (while the left button is being held down).

The following is the new window that appears for controlling the mouse:

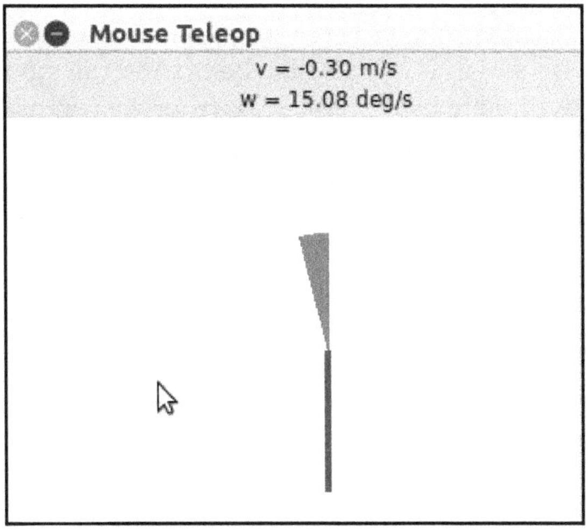

The blue line represents the forward (positive speed)-backward directions. In this case, it moves at -0.3 m/s (backward). The longer the line, the greater the speed. The red circular sector represents the same but for the rotation. It is positive when rotating left (counter-clockwise), at 15.08 degrees/second in this case.

This example illustrates two important concepts of ROS:

- **The concurrency of messages**: If there two or more nodes that publish to a topic that is mapped to the subscriber of another node, this node will accept the messages from both and will try to execute all of them. This is a nice feature that you will exploit when working with ROS at an advanced level.
- **The resilience of the runtime enviroment**: The robot can work with partial functionality. It will only lose the functionality provided by the ROS nodes that die.

At this point, it is important that you think of how ROS provides a high-level layer for programming robots compared to the usage of procedural languages such as C or Python. Furthermore, this also means that you will focus more on the robot's functionality and less on programming the code: you will integrate existing packages that provide the low-level layer (control commands from a keyboard or mouse, for example) and relate them via ROS topics to build the high-level layer (motion control of the robot with the keyboard and/or mouse).

Remote control using ROS topics

In the previous section, you controlled the robot's publishing messages in the `/cmd_vel` topic using a human interface, the keyboard and the mouse. In this section, you will publish the messages directly using `rostopic` from the command line. This way, you will become familiar with this relevant topic and the structure of its messages. It is crucial to understand how `/cmd_vel` works under the hood since you will be using it in many of the advanced examples we'll be covering in the remaining chapters of this book.

The motion control topic – /cmd_vel

Now that we've enjoyed playing with the robot, let's understand how this form of control works. The `/cmd_vel` topic that the gopigo3 node is subscribed to is the key to producing translations and rotations of the robot. Run the `rostopic` command while having the `gopigo3` node running in the robot to retrieve the information from the topic:

```
T1 $ rostopic info /cmd_vel

      Type: geometry_msgs/Twist

      Publishers: None
      Subscribers:
       * /gopigo3 (http://gopigo3.local:40605/)
```

The topic `/cmd_vel` uses the `geometry_msgs/Twist` type (64 bits) of the `geometry_msgs` message library (`http://wiki.ros.org/geometry_msgs`). This library provides messages for working with geometric primitives: points, vectors, and poses. The command is also telling you which nodes are subscribed to the topic, which is only `gopigo3` in our case. Now, let's retrieve the structure of the message type:

```
T1 $ rosmsg info geometry_msgs/Twist
      geometry_msgs/Vector3 linear
        float64 x
```

```
    float64 y
    float64 z
  geometry_msgs/Vector3 angular
    float64 x
    float64 y
    float64 z
```

Here, we can see that it is composed of six 64-bit float numbers that will allow you to treat it as two vectors of three components each. The first three components form the linear vector and refer to the speed along the *X*, *Y*, and *Z* axes, while the remaining three form the rotation vector, expressing the angular speed about each of those axes. Let's see how this works in practice.

Using /cmd_vel to directly drive GoPiGo3

Previously, we focused on the end user's perspective of controlling the robot, that is, keyboard strokes or mouse clicks and displacement. Now, we are going to discover how to achieve the same kind of control from the developer's perspective, which is the one you need to build new applications in ROS. Let's get started:

1. Rotate the robot at a 1 rad/s rate by publishing a message from the command line. Remember that the `gopigo3` node must be running in the robot:

```
T1 $ rostopic pub /cmd_vel geometry_msgs/Twist  'angular: {z: 1}'
     publishing and latching message. Press ctrl-C to terminate
```

2. As soon as you enter the command, apart from seeing GoPiGo3 rotating left (counter-clockwise), you will receive the accompanying information message about the command.
3. Since you did not specify a publishing frequency, ROS assumes that you want to keep that message latched, that is, running forever. Check this by using `rostopic` in another Terminal:

```
T2 $ rostopic echo /cmd_vel
     linear:
       x: 0.0
       y: 0.0
       z: 0.0
     angular:
       x: 0.0
       y: 0.0
       z: 1.0
     ---
```

4. How can we stop the robot? Easy – send a new message with the rotation set to zero:

```
T3 $ rostopic pub /cmd_vel geometry_msgs/Twist  'angular: {z: 0}'
```

   You will see that GoPiGo3 stops and that `T2` throws a new set of six values, informing us that angular `z` is now equal to `0`.

5. The next step is to introduce a message update at a given rate. Stop the process in `T1` and write the following command:

```
T1 $ rostopic pub -r 0.5 /cmd_vel geometry_msgs/Twist  'angular:
{z: 1}'
```

   In `T2`, you should see a new message every 2 seconds (= 0.5 Hz frequency). The `-r` option (initial of rate) is the one you use to specify how often you want the message to be sent. Since you are keeping the same rotation speed, you won't appreciate any changes in the robot motion.

6. Go to another Terminal and publish a double speed (2 rad/s) in the `/cmd_vel` topic at the same frequency of 0.5 Hz:

```
T3 $ rostopic pub -r 0.5 /cmd_vel geometry_msgs/Twist  'angular:
{z: 2}'
```

   You will see GoPiGo3 alternating between angular speeds of 1 and 2 rad/s at the specified rate.

7. Go to `T4` and send a stop rotation command:

```
T4 $ rostopic pub -r 0.5 /cmd_vel geometry_msgs/Twist 'angular: {z:
0}'
```

   Observe how the robot stops for a while every 2 seconds.

8. What if you want the robot to stop more often? Stop the process in `T4` and relaunch the command with a higher rate of 1 Hz:

```
T4 $ rostopic pub -r 1 /cmd_vel geometry_msgs/Twist  'angular: {z:
0}'
```

9. How do we make it stop for longer? Easy – specify a higher frequency, that is, 10 Hz. When using such a value, you will find that GoPiGo3 rotates very little, since 10 times every second, it receives a stop command, superseding the most recent effect of the speeds set in `T1` (1 rad/s) and `T3` (2 rad/s).

10. Finally, how do we stop everything? Follow these steps:
    1. Stop Terminal `T1`. This avoids new messages from being sent by setting the speed at 1 rad/s.
    2. Stop Terminal `T3`. This cancels the speed commands of 2 rad/s. At this point, the robot only receives zero speed commands from the last Terminal. The robot has stopped, but ROS is still running some processes, although they're not visible as robot motions.
    3. Stop Terminal `T4`. This makes sure that the gopigo3 node is now idle from any message that's published in the `/cmd_vel` topic.
    4. You should check how `T2` (using the`$ rostopic echo /cmd_vel` command) stops providing updates. You can also kill this Terminal.

Try to think about what would happen if the first action you had made were to stop `T4`. Check this by applying the sequence to the physical robot and see what result you get.

In the next section, you will publish `geometry_msgs/Twist` messages in the `/cmd_vel` topic to find about what the actual *X*, *Y*, and *Z* axes of your robot are.

Checking the X, Y, and Z axes of GoPiGo3

Now, you will apply what you have learned to practically find the *X*, *Y*, and *Z* axes of your robot and their positive and negative direction. Apply the following command in `T1` and make sure you're ready with `T2` to stop it afterward to avoid the robot crashing into any obstacles:

```
T1 $ rostopic pub /cmd_vel geometry_msgs/Twist 'linear: {x: 0.1}'
T2 $ rostopic pub /cmd_vel geometry_msgs/Twist  'linear: {x: 0}'
```

You should see GoPiGo3 advancing forward, that is, the distance sensor facing forward while the caster wheel is facing back. For the negative *X* axis, change the sign of the linear speed:

```
T1 $ rostopic pub /cmd_vel geometry_msgs/Twist 'linear: {x: -0.1}'
T2 $ rostopic pub /cmd_vel geometry_msgs/Twist  'linear: {x: 0}'
```

You should find that GoPiGo is now advancing backward, that is, the distance sensor is facing backward. To guess the direction of the remaining axis, *Y*, remember that, in the previous subsection, you checked that the rotation around the *Z* axis is positive when the robot rotates left (counter-clockwise). This means that the *Z* axis points up, to the ceiling. Since you have empirically found the orientation of the *X* and *Z* axes, you can easily infer that the Y axis points left.

Why haven't we checked the *Z* axis with **rostopic pub**? You have a robot moving on a plane, that is, the floor. If you tried to apply a linear speed command for the *Z* axis, you will see nothing, because... well, GoPiGo3 cannot fly!

It is left to you to deduce why a similar linear speed command for the *Y* axis will have no visible effect on GoPiGo3's motion.

Composing motions

We have already learned how to find the actual X, Y, and Z axes of the robot. Go back to `Chapter 4`, *Creating the Virtual Two-Wheeled ROS Robot*, the *Building a differential drive robot with URDF* section, if you need to remember how.

Keeping their orientations in mind, let's design a more complex trajectory by combining both translation (linear *X*) and rotation (angular *Z*). The goal is to get GoPiGo3 to follow a circumferential path that has a 0.25 m radius at a speed of 45º/s:

- The angular *Z* speed is 45º/s = 0.785 rad/s. We just need to change units from sexagesimal degrees to radians.
- The linear *X* speed can be obtained by multiplying the requested radius by the angular speed; that is, *0.25 m * 0.785 rad/s = 0.196 m*.

Follows these steps to do so:

1. Apply these two values in a single `/cmd_vel` message:

```
T1 $ rostopic pub /cmd_vel geometry_msgs/Twist '{linear: {x:
0.196}, angular: {z: 0.785}}'
```

2. To stop this process, you can send a message where all six components are equal to zero:

```
T2 $ rostopic pub -r 10 /cmd_vel geometry_msgs/Twist  '[0, 0, 0]'
'[0, 0, 0]'
```

This is an alternative `geometry_msgs/Twist` message syntax, in which you specify a three-component vector for linear speed (following the order *X*, *Y*, *Z*) and another vector with the three components of the angular speed (also in the order *X*, *Y*, *Z*).

3. Finally, check how the superposition principle applies to motion composition by sending separate commands for the translation and rotation:

```
T1 $ rostopic pub /cmd_vel geometry_msgs/Twist 'linear: {x: 0.196}'
T2 $ rostopic pub /cmd_vel geometry_msgs/Twist 'angular: {z:
0.785}'
```

The command in `T1` makes GoPiGo3 move forward at 0.196 m/s. Then, the command in `T2` adds an angular motion of 0.785 rad/s, thereby producing the trajectory for GoPiGo3 to evolve from a straight line to a circumference of 0.25 m radius, as expected.

Stop the robot and shut down the Raspberry Pi. In the next section, we'll switch to the Gazebo simulation environment, so we will only need the laptop. We will return to the virtual model of GoPiGo3 at the point we left it in `Chapter 5`, *Simulating the Robot Behavior with Gazebo*.

Remotely controlling both physical and virtual robots

Up to this point, you have dealt with a piece of configuration where the ROS master node ran in the robot. For the rest of this chapter, you will only be working with the laptop. Due to this, you need to revert your configuration so that the master node can be located again on the desktop computer. Otherwise, you will receive an error and won't be able to launch any ROS environment.

Reverting the ROS master to the local computer

The solution to this is pretty simple; just follow these steps:

1. Open your local `.bashrc` file and comment the line at the end that specifies what URL to point to in order to find the ROS master:

```
$ nano ~./bashrc
   ...
```

```
    export ROS_HOSTNAME=rosbot.local
  # THIS LINE IS NOW A COMMENT # export
ROS_MASTER_URI=http://gopigo3.local:11311
```

TIP: Be aware that, in place of `rosbot.local`, you should have your current hostname, `<your-hostname>.local`. Simply run `$ hostname` in a Terminal to recall it if you are in doubt and it hasn't been set correctly in your configuration file.

2. Close all the Terminals, open a new one, and check the `ROS_MASTER_URI` variable:

```
$ echo $ROS_MASTER_URI
    http://localhost:11311
```

You should find that the environment variable has reverted to the default server (localhost) and default port (`11311`). Now, we are ready to switch to the virtual robot.

Simulating GoPiGo3 with Gazebo

Recall the Gazebo simulation we performed in `Chapter 5`, *Simulating the Robot Behavior with Gazebo*, in the *Launching the GoPiGo model in Gazebo* section. Its files have been included in the sample code for this chapter so that we can use them as a starting point. Now, follow these steps:

1. Launch the Gazebo environment with the GoPiGo3 model:

```
T1 $ roslaunch gazebo_control spawn.launch
```

Although you may find that the launch filename is different from what it was in the code of `Chapter 5`, *Simulating the Robot Behavior with Gazebo*, its content is exactly the same, that is, `gopigo_gazebo.launch`.

2. Then, in another Terminal, list the relevant topics:

```
T2 $ rostopic list
    /clock
    /gazebo/link_states
    /gazebo/model_states
    /gazebo/parameter_descriptions
    /gazebo/parameter_updates
    /gazebo/set_link_state
    /gazebo/set_model_state
    /gazebo_gui/parameter_descriptions
    /gazebo_gui/parameter_updates
```

```
/rosout
/rosout_agg
```

All the new ones correspond to Gazebo nodes.

3. In particular, the /clock topic is where Gazebo publishes timestamps, thus allowing for a system with simulation-synchronized time. The parameter definition within the spawn.launch file for /clock is as follows:

```
<launch>
      ...
      <arg name="use_sim_time" default="true"/>
      ...
</launch>
```

4. The use_sim_time parameter asks ROS to simulate a clock whose timestamps are published on /clock. You can inspect the topic and its message type as usual:

```
T2 $ rostopic info /clock
 Type: rosgraph_msgs/Clock

 Publishers:
 * /gazebo (http://rosbot.local:37865/)

 Subscribers:
 * /rosout (http://rosbot.local:34729/)
 * /gazebo (http://rosbot.local:37865/)
 * /gazebo_gui (http://rosbot.local:38297/)

T2 $ rosmsg info rosgraph_msgs/Clock
 time clock
```

The clock message type belongs to the rosgraph_msgs package. Take a look at the following link to find out more about this package: http://wiki.ros.org/rosgraph_msgs.

Now that we've set up the environment, we can add a virtual controller that will allow us to control GoPiGo3 inside Gazebo in the same way we did before with the physical robot.

Adding the controller to the Gazebo model of the robot

Here, we are going to use a mechanism called **controller** to transform speed /cmd_vel messages into motions for the left and right wheels of the robot. For the case of a two-wheeled robot, this is known as a **differential drive controller**. This name is due to the fact that straight paths are achieved by rotating the wheels at the same speed. Any difference between the left and right angular speeds will make the robot describe a circumferential path. The larger the difference, the lower the radius of such a circumference (a straight path corresponds to describing a sector of a circumference of infinite radius, that is, the infinitesimal speed difference between wheels).

Let's get to the practical part:

1. To include the differential drive controller in your model of the robot, add the following snippet inside the <robot> tag of the urdf/gopigo.gazebo file:

```
<gazebo>
    <plugin filename="libgazebo_ros_diff_drive.so"
name="differential_drive_controller">
        <alwaysOn>true</alwaysOn>
        <updateRate>20</updateRate>
        <leftJoint>joint_left_wheel</leftJoint>
        <rightJoint>joint_right_wheel</rightJoint>
        <wheelSeparation>0.4</wheelSeparation>
        <wheelDiameter>0.2</wheelDiameter>
        <torque>0.1</torque>
        <commandTopic>cmd_vel</commandTopic>
        <odometryTopic>odom</odometryTopic>
        <odometryFrame>odom</odometryFrame>
        <robotBaseFrame>base_link</robotBaseFrame>
    </plugin>
 </gazebo>
```

You must set these correspondences, as defined in the URDF model of your robot:

- <robotBaseFrame> to base_link
- <leftJoint> to joint_left_wheel
- <rightJoint> to joint_right_wheel

The <torque> tag is where you specify the maximum torque each can exert. This is all you need to know to carry out the experiment we suggested in Chapter 5, *Simulating the Robot Behavior with Gazebo,* in the last section, entitled *Guidelines for tuning the Gazebo model.*

2. Notice how you tell the controller what topics it will receive the motion commands in by setting the `<commandTopic>` tag to the ROS `/cmd_vel` topic:

```
...
<commandTopic>cmd_vel</commandTopic>
...
```

3. Then, stop and relaunch Gazebo to find the new features that the differential drive provides to the simulation:

```
T1 $ roslaunch gazebo_control spawn.launch
```

4. There are two new topics, `/cmd_vel` and `/tf`:

```
T2 $ rostopic list
    ...
    /cmd_vel
    ...
    /tf
```

5. Remember from the previous section that we controlled the physical GoPiGo3 with the `/cmd_vel` topic. Following the same steps, you can teleoperate the virtual robot with the keyboard (arrow keys):

```
T2 $ rosrun key_teleop key_teleop.py /key_vel:=/cmd_vel
```

   Make sure you are on the window where you launched `T2` so that any keystrokes are caught and you can see the effect they have on the robot in Gazebo.

6. Visualize the ROS graph with `T3 $ rqt_graph`. You should obtain the result shown in the following diagram:

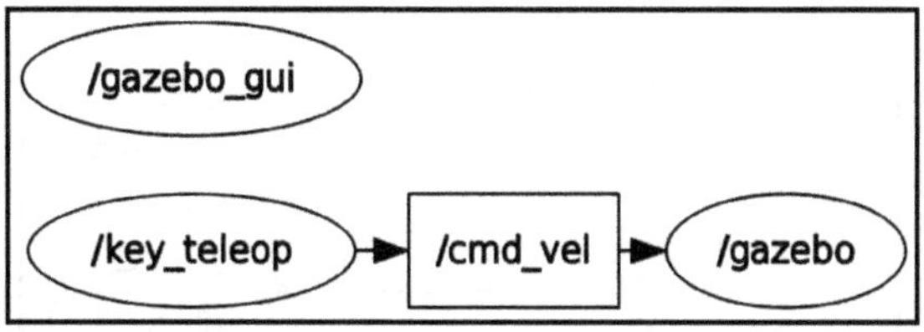

   As before, the topic that's remapping `/key_vel:=/cmd_vel` in the `T2` Terminal allows the virtual robot to be controlled with the arrow keys.

Finally, we are going to join the physical and the virtual robot in the same ROS environment.

Real-world and simulation at once

Since we will be working with the robot, we need to specify the ROS master in the laptop so that it's pointing to GoPiGo3. To do so, uncomment the following line in your local `.bashrc` file to switch back to that configuration:

```
export ROS_MASTER_URI=http://gopigo3.local:11311
```

Instead of killing the rest of the bash Terminals, you can reload the updated `.bashrc` in each of them:

```
$ source ~/.bashrc
```

Now, you are ready to execute ROS with both versions of GoPiGo3:

1. First, launch the robot:

   ```
   $ roslaunch mygopigo gopigo3.launch
   ```

2. Then, launch the rest of the ROS environment on the laptop. First, launch the keyboard control:

   ```
   T1 $ rosrun key_teleop key_teleop.py /key_vel:=/cmd_vel
   ```

3. Next, launch the virtual model:

   ```
   T2 $ roslaunch gazebo_control spawn.launch
   ```

4. Finally, check the ROS graph:

   ```
   T3 $ rqt_graph
   ```

   If everything went well, you should see the following familiar graph:

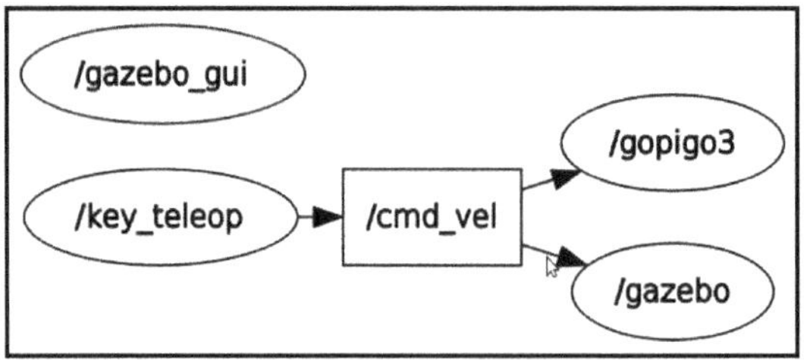

   This states that you should be able to simultaneously control the physical robot (the `gopigo3` node) and the virtual robot (the `gazebo` node) with the same keystrokes (the `key_teleop` node).

5. Check teleoperation by clicking the left or right arrow key of the laptop keyboard. Both the physical and virtual GoPiGo3 will rotate at the same time. A similar result will be obtained if you press the *up* or *down* arrow keys.

> TIP: For the keystrokes to be effective, you need to have selected the Terminal window where you launched the `key_teleop.py` node, that is, `T2`.

Congratulations – you have successfully completed a whole tour of how to control a robot in ROS!

Summary

In this chapter, you have achieved correspondence between the physical GoPiGo3 and its virtual model in Gazebo. You have checked how it doesn't matter whether you're controlling the actual robot or a virtual robot from the point of view of ROS. Since both are moved using the same topic, `/cmd_vel`, ROS does not care about which type of robot you're dealing with.

This fact explains how, from the point of view of ROS, you have the choice to test your code with a virtual robot and then safely apply it to the physical robot. We just need to launch the ROS node of the physical robot. This is useful in three situations. First, when you are developing a new application for an existing robot, you can debug the code with a virtual model in Gazebo. Second, when you do not have available the hardware of the robot – because you are still deciding which one to buy – you can virtually play and test the robot prior to the buy decision. And third, when you are designing a new robot, you have the choice of launching its mechanical design and software development in parallel. When you do this, the developed code will send feedback to your mechanical design before carrying out any manufacturing activities. This iterative loop should benefit the final product by cutting its development costs.

In the next chapter, you will tackle the first autonomous task of the robot: to make it aware of its environment and be able to navigate to reach a predefined destination. These tasks will introduce you to the **Simultaneous Localization and Mapping** (**SLAM**) technique, an algorithm that's intensively used in all kinds of autonomous vehicles, especially in self-driving cars.

Questions

1. If you need to have two different computers communicating over ROS, where should you locate the ROS master node?

   A) In the one that has the more recent version of ROS.
   B) The ROS master node will run in the first one where you launch the `roscore` process.
   C) You can place the master wherever you want. In one of the computers, you run `roscore`, and in the other one, you tell ROS that the master node is located in the other machine.

2. You have a physical robot named `mazinger_zeta` that accepts `geometry_msgs/Twist` messages in the `/walk` topic. What is the correct topic remapping command for remotely controlling the robot with the keyboard?

   A) `rosrun key_teleop key_teleop.py /walk:=/cmd_vel`
   B) `rosrun key_teleop key_teleop.py /key_vel:=/walk`
   C) `rosrun key_teleop key_teleop.py /walk:=/key_vel`

3. If you apply a speed command of 1 m/s to the *Y* axis, how will it move GoPiGo3?

   A) The robot will move left at 1 m/s
   B) Nothing will happen
   C) You need to specify a publishing frequency so that the command takes effect

4. What visible effect does this command have on the physical robot?

```
T1 $ rostopic pub /cmd_vel geometry_msgs/Twist 'angular: {z: 90}'
```

   A) It will rotate at the maximum possible speed since this is lower than 90 radians/seconds.
   B) GoPiGo3 cannot move at such a large angular speed.
   C) Since it exceeds the maximum speed that GoPiGo3 can handle, the robot will stay still.

5. If you're controlling GoPiGo3 and the virtual robot with the keyboard simultaneously, what difference will you appreciate if you tell both of them to rotate at π rad/s every 2 seconds?

A) Both will do a complete turn of 360º.
B) The virtual robot will rotate 360º but the physical robot will not complete the turn since there is the opposing force of the friction of the wheels against the floor.
C) The virtual robot will do exactly 360º, but the physical robot won't because of the wheel encoder's limited precision.

Further reading

- ROS networking and time synchronization: `http://wiki.ros.org/ROS/NetworkSetup`
- *ROS Robot Programming: A handbook Written by TurtleBot3 Developers*, YoonSeok Pyo, HanCheol Cho, RyuWoon Jung, TaeHoon Lim (2017), ROBOTIS Co. Ltd, 1st edition: `http://www.pishrobot.com/wp-content/uploads/2018/02/ROS-robot-programming-book-by-turtlebo3-developers-EN.pdf`, Chapter: *Mobile Robots*
- Integrating sonar and IR sensor plugins into the robot model in Gazebo with ROS: `https://medium.com/teamarimac/integrating-sonar-and-ir-sensor-plugin-to-robot-model-in-gazebo-with-ros-656fd9452607`

8
Virtual SLAM and Navigation Using Gazebo

In this chapter, you will be introduced to the concepts and components of robot navigation. Using **SLAM** (short for **Simultaneous Localization and Mapping**) techniques, you will be able to execute autonomous navigation with GoPiGo3. This chapter deals with advanced topics in simulation. Hence, it is essential that you have understood the concepts of the previous chapter, where we gave you the basics to interact with a virtual robot in Gazebo.

SLAM is a technique used in robotics to explore and map an unknown environment while estimating the pose of the robot itself. As it moves all around, it will be acquiring structured information of the surroundings by processing the raw data coming from its sensors.

You will explore this concept with a practical approach using the digital twin of GoPiGo3, neatly understanding why a SLAM implementation is required for proper navigation. The simulation will be run in Gazebo, the ROS native simulation tool with a physics engine that offers realistic results.

The following topics will be covered in this chapter:

- Dynamic simulation using Gazebo
- Components in navigation
- Robot perception and SLAM
- Practicing SLAM and navigation with GoPiGo3

By covering these topics, you will get more familiar with the Gazebo environment. You will understand the concepts of navigation and SLAM and how they relate to each other. With a very practical approach, you will learn to run SLAM and navigation tasks in Gazebo with a virtual model of a robot.

Technical requirements

To summarize and clarify the purposes of the steps that we'll take in this chapter dealing with the virtual robot, and in the next chapter regarding the physical GoPiGo3, the following list shows all these sensors and actuators we are going to work with, as well as the sections of the previous chapters that have dealt with each one:

- **Distance sensor**: In `Chapter 6`, *Programming in ROS – Commands and Tools,* the *Case study 1: publishing and reading the distance sensor* section taught you how to use the distance sensor under ROS with the physical robot.
- **Line follower**. See the following list for assembly and unit-testing instructions.
- **IMU sensor**. See the following list for assembly and unit-testing instructions.
- **Pi camera**: In `Chapter 6`, *Programming in ROS – Commands and Tools,* the *Case Study 1: Publishing and reading the distance sensor* section taught you how to use the Pi camera under ROS with the physical robot.
- **Drive motors and encoders**: In the previous chapter, the *Case study 3: Remote control using the keyboard* section taught you first how to use these items in ROS with the physical robot, and then how to implement a differential drive controller under the Gazebo simulator in ROS.

For all of these, you have the following:

- Assembly instructions, which can be found in the *Deep dive into the electromechanics* section of `Chapter 1`, *Assembling the Robot*
- Unit testing instructions, which can found in the *Unit testing of sensors and drives* section of `Chapter 2`, *Unit Testing of GoPiGo3,* where the provided software taught you how to deal with unit tests using Python

For optimal and easy-to-understand coverage of the topic of SLAM, we will implement a 360º-coverage **Laser Distance Sensor** (**LDS**) in the virtual robot. There are low-cost versions of this sensor technology, such as **EAI YDLIDAR X4** (available at `https://www.aliexpress.com/item/32908156152.html`), which is the one we will make use of in the next chapter.

In this chapter, we will make use of the code located in the `Chapter8_Virtual_SLAM` folder at `https://github.com/PacktPublishing/Hands-On-ROS-for-Robotics-Programming/tree/master/Chapter8_Virtual_SLAM`. Copy its files to the ROS workspace to have them available, and leave the rest outside of the `src` folder. This way, you will have a cleaner ROS environment:

```
$ cp -R ~/Hands-On-ROS-for-Robotics-Programming/Chapter8_Virtual_SLAM
~/catkin_ws/src/
```

The code contains two new ROS packages as follows:

- `gopigo3_description`, which contains the URDF model plus the SDF (Gazebo tags) for a complete, dynamic simulation. This package provides the `gopigo3_rviz.launch` launch file to interactively visualize the model in RViz.
- `virtual_slam` contains the virtual robot simulation itself, plus the launch files needed to run SLAM in Gazebo.

Then, rebuild the workspace so that it is known to your ROS installation:

```
$ cd ~/catkin_ws
$ catkin_make
```

Check that the packages have been correctly installed by selecting them and listing the files:

```
$ rospack list | grep gopigo3
```

Then you need to make some installation and configuration to run the exercises, as follows.

ROS navigation packages

The following steps provide the installation instructions for ROS Kinetic, the version running in Ubuntu 16.04:

1. First, let's prepare your machine with the required ROS packages needed for the navigation stack:

```
$ sudo apt install ros-kinetic-navigation ros-kinetic-amcl ros-
kinetic-map-server ros-kinetic-move-base ros-kinetic-urdf ros-
kinetic-xacro ros-kinetic-compressed-image-transport ros-kinetic-
rqt-image-view
```

2. In **ROS Kinetic**, you can install `slam_gmapping` from binaries:

```
$ sudo apt-get install ros-kinetic-slam-gmapping
```

This installs the `gmapping` and `openslam_gmapping` packages. If working with ROS Melodic (that is, you are in Ubuntu 18.04):

- Install the corresponding versions for Melodic:

```
$ sudo apt install ros-melodic-navigation ros-melodic-amcl ros-melodic-map-server ros-melodic-move-base ros-melodic-urdf ros-melodic-xacro ros-melodic-compressed-image-transport ros-melodic-rqt-image-view
```

- And finally the `slam_gmapping` package, that the time of writing is already available in its binary version:

```
sudo apt-get install ros-melodic-slam-gmapping
```

ROS master running on the local computer

Since, in this chapter, you will only be using your local machine, you need to reconfigure the ROS master URI so that it does not point to the robot but to your local computer. Then, open your local `.bashrc` file and comment out the line at the end that specifies the URL where the ROS master can be found:

```
$ nano ~./bashrc
   ...
   export ROS_HOSTNAME=rosbot.local
  # THIS LINE IS NOW A COMMENT # export
ROS_MASTER_URI=http://gopigo3.local:11311
```

Close all Terminals, open a new one, and check the `ROS_MASTER_URI` variable:

```
$ echo $ROS_MASTER_URI
    http://localhost:11311
```

You should find that the environment variable has reverted to the default server (`localhost`) and default port (`11311`). Now, we are ready to switch to the virtual robot.

Dynamic simulation using Gazebo

In the previous chapter, you performed a very basic version of navigation, where the feedback to the robot about its environment always came from you as a human operator. For example, you saw that GoPiGo3 is advancing to an obstacle, so you made it turn left or right to avoid it.

This section takes you one step forward in remote control by providing feedback not only from your human vision, but also from robotic sensors. More precisely, GoPiGo3 will provide data from the Pi camera and from its distance sensor. The goal is that you can teleoperate it more precisely by getting as high-quality sensor data as possible. You may be able to guess at least two common scenarios in the real world where this kind of manual teleoperation is key for the execution of a planned task:

- **Surgical robot teleoperation**: Where an expert surgeon can carry out a surgical operation without being present in the operating room where the patient is being attended to.
- **Teleoperated rescue robots**: This used in accidents where human cannot access the location on their own, such as a ravine between mountains in the occurrence of a flood, or disasters where direct human presence is to be avoided, for example in a nuclear disaster where the level of radioactivity is so high that an exposed human could absorb a dose of deadly radiation in a few minutes.

Having these keys in mind, you should understand this section not only as a prior learning step before entering into autonomous navigation, but also as a motivational introduction to a common way of working with teleoperated robots in the real world.

Adding sensors to the GoPiGo3 model

Up to now, you should have equipped your virtual robot with a differential drive controller that provides the capability to convert velocity commands into rotations of the left and right wheels. We need to complete the model with some sort of perception of the environment. For this, we will add controllers for two common sensors, a two-dimensional camera and an LDS. The first corresponds to the Pi camera of your physical robot, while the second is the unidirectional distance sensor of the GoPiGo3 kit.

Camera model

You can add the solid of the camera as usual with `<visual>` tags, but since it is a commercial device, you can a get better look by using a realistic three-dimensional CAD model supplied by the manufacturer or made by someone else in the open source community. The URDF definition is as follows:

```
<link name="camera">
  <visual>
    <origin xyz="0.25 0 0.05" rpy="0 1.570795 0" />
    <geometry>
      <mesh filename="package://virtual_slam/meshes/piCamera.stl"
```

```
scale="0.5 0.5 0.5"/>
    </geometry>
  </visual>
  ...
</link>

<joint name="joint_camera" type="fixed">
    <parent link="base_link"/>
    <child link="camera"/>
    <origin xyz="0 0 0" rpy="0 0 0" />
    <axis xyz="1 0 0" />
</joint>
```

We can see two blocks in the preceding snippet: the `<link>` element to specify the solid, and the `<joint>` block to attach the camera to the robot chassis. Since the camera is rigidly attach to the body, we specify the `type="fixed">` to model such a characteristic.

Regarding the `<link>` element, we introduce the `<mesh>` tag to import the geometry from a CAD DAE filetype, marked in bold in the preceding snippet. The following screenshot shows the CAD model of the camera:

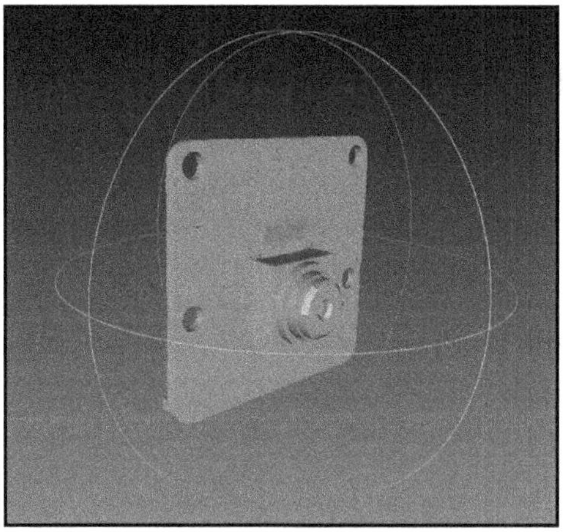

Then we add the camera technical features using a `<gazebo>` tag:

```
<gazebo reference="camera">
  <sensor type="camera" name="camera1">
    <update_rate>30.0</update_rate>
    <camera name="front">
      <horizontal_fov>1.3962634</horizontal_fov>
      <image>
        <width>800</width>
```

```
        <height>800</height>
        <format>R8G8B8</format>
      </image>
    <clip>
      <near>0.02</near>
      <far>300</far>
    </clip>
    </camera>
    <!-- plugin "camera_controller" filename="libgazebo_ros_camera.so" -->
  </sensor>
</gazebo>
```

The <update_rate> tag specifies that the sensor is read at a frequency of 30 Hz, that is, it takes 30 images per second. Finally, we add the Gazebo plugin that emulates the behavior of the camera. The following snippet is what substitutes the commented line that referred to `plugin "camera_controller"` in the preceding code block:

```
<plugin name="camera_controller" filename="libgazebo_ros_camera.so">
  <alwaysOn>true</alwaysOn>
  <updateRate>0.0</updateRate>
  <cameraName>gopigo/camera1</cameraName>
  <imageTopicName>image_raw</imageTopicName>
  <cameraInfoTopicName>camera_info</cameraInfoTopicName>
  <frameName>camera</frameName>
  <hackBaseline>0.07</hackBaseline>
  <distortionK1>0.0</distortionK1>
  <distortionK2>0.0</distortionK2>
  <distortionK3>0.0</distortionK3>
  <distortionT1>0.0</distortionT1>
  <distortionT2>0.0</distortionT2>
</plugin>
```

The controller for the camera is in the `libgazebo_ros_camera.so` file, so what you provide within this block are the technical specifications of the camera you are using. Setting <updateRate> to `0.0` means that Gazebo should take the refreshment rate from the preceding <sensor> tag, that is, 30 Hz. As specified (see fields in bold letters), camera images will be published in the `/gopigo/camera1/image_raw` topic.

Launch the ROS visualization tool to check that the model is properly built. Since **RViz** only represents its visual features—it does not include any physical simulation engine—it is a much lighter environment than Gazebo and you have available all the options to check every aspect of the appearance of the model:

```
$ roslaunch gopigo3_description gopigo3_basic_rviz.launch
```

This launch file is very similar to the one you used in `Chapter 4`, *Creating the Virtual Two-Wheeled ROS Robot*. The following screenshot shows the result you should see:

In the next section, you will do a practical exercise to see how the camera works with Gazebo.

Simulating the camera

Follow these steps for the simulation:

1. Let's first place the robot in Gazebo the same way we did in the previous chapter and enable remote control with the keyboard:

```
T1 $ roslaunch virtual_slam gopigo3_basic_world.launch
T2 $ rosrun key_teleop key_teleop.py /key_vel:=/cmd_vel
```

   `key_teleop` allows you to remotely control the GoPiGo3 with the arrow keys of your keyboard.

2. Now, launch a node from the `image_view` package that comes preinstalled with ROS:

```
T3 $ rosrun image_view image_view image:=/gopigo/camera1/image_raw
```

We are remapping the `image` topic so that the node takes its data from the camera node topic, `/gopigo/camera1/image_raw`. This topic is defined in the preceding snippet of the camera controller plugin with the combination of the `<imageTopicName>` and `<cameraInfoTopicName>` tags. Teleoperate the robot with the arrow keys and you will see the subjective view in the image window:

The background window corresponds to Gazebo (launched from Terminal `T1`) and there you can see the virtual robot looking at the traffic cones. The subjective view is shown in the left window (`T2`), provided by the Pi camera image live feed using the `image_view` package. Finally, the left-bottom window (`T3`) is the one you need to select to be able to move the robot with the arrow keys of the keyboard. We have used them to place the robot in front of the traffic cones, as shown in the preceding screenshot.

At this point, let's obtain the ROS graph with the well-known command, `rqt_graph`, and have a look at how the topic remapping for the image is handled:

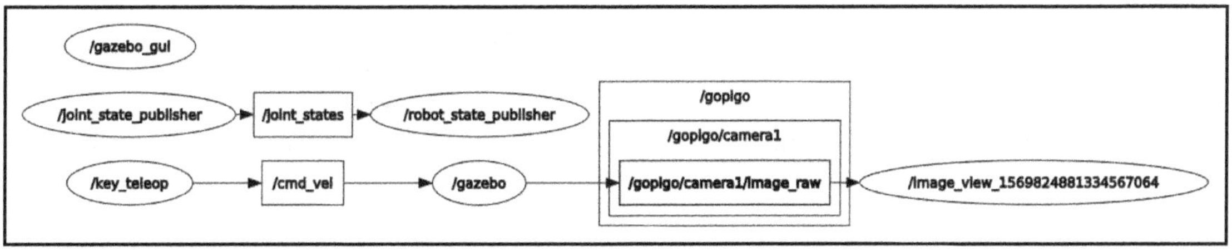

Thanks to the mapping argument, `image:=/gopigo/camera1/image_raw`, the `image` topic of the `image_view` package remains implicit and just the `/gopigo/camera1/image_raw` is visible.

Are you aware how quick and easy it is to deliver a robot behavior when you are using prebuilt ROS modules and your custom robot definition? In the next section, we will cover these same steps for the second sensor.

Distance sensor

We add the solid model of this sensor under the `<visual>` tag by following the same procedure we covered for the camera. The URDF definition is as follows:

```
<joint name="distance_sensor_solid_joint" type="fixed">
    <axis xyz="0 1 0" />
    <origin rpy="0 0 0" xyz="0 0 0" />
    <parent link="base_link"/>
    <child link="distance_sensor_solid"/>
  </joint>

  <link name="distance_sensor_solid">
    <visual>
      <origin xyz="0.2 0 0.155" rpy="1.570795 0 1.570795" />
      <geometry>
        <mesh
filename="package://gopigo3_description/meshes/IR_Sensor_Sharp_GP2Y_solid.s
tl" scale="0.005 0.005 0.005"/>
      </geometry>
      <material name="red"/>
    </visual>
    ...
  </link>
```

We can see two blocks in the preceding snippet: the `<link>` element to specify the solid, and the `<joint>` block to attach the sensor body to the robot chassis. Since the distance sensor is rigidly attach to the robot chassis, we specify the `type="fixed">` to model this characteristic. The solid model that we are using is shown in the following screenshot. In this case, we use a CAD model in STL format and reference it from the `<mesh>` tag:

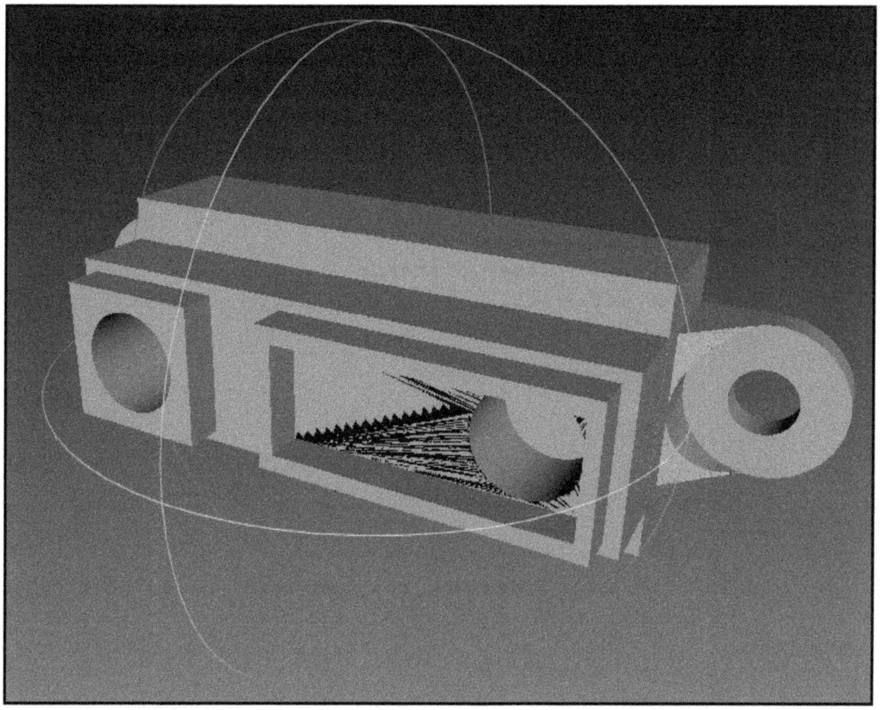

We will base the sensor itself in another solid, since, if you do this with the solid in the preceding screenshot, you will see in Gazebo that the distance rays are blocked by the solid, and so the sensor will always produce a zero value for distance. So, we are going to explain to you a trick with which you can separate the solid model of the sensor from the sensing point, located at the origin of the link frame:

```
<joint name="distance_sensor_joint" type="fixed">
    <axis xyz="0 1 0" />
    <origin rpy="0 0 0" xyz="0.245 0 0.13" />
    <parent link="base_link"/>
    <child link="distance_sensor"/>
</joint>
<link name="distance_sensor">
    <visual>
        <origin xyz="0 0 0" rpy="0 0 0"/>
        <geometry>
            <box size="0.01 0.01 0.01"/>
        </geometry>
        <material name="red"/>
    </visual>
</link>
```

This snippet creates a box of 10 cm x 10 cm and place it in the coordinates specified by the <joint> tag.

Then we add the sensor technical features using a <gazebo> tag, which you can see refers to the distance_sensor link defined in the preceding snippet (not distance_sensor_solid):

```
<gazebo reference="distance_sensor">
   <sensor type="ray" name="laser_distance">
      <visualize>true</visualize>
      <update_rate>10</update_rate>
      <ray>
         ...
         <range>
            <min>0.01</min>
            <max>3</max>
            <resolution>0.01</resolution>
         </range>
      </ray>
      <!-- plugin filename="libgazebo_ros_range.so" name="gazebo_ros_ir" -
->
    </sensor>
   </gazebo>
```

The <update_rate> tag specifies that the sensor is read at a frequency of 10 Hz, and the <range> tag sets measured distance values between 10 cm and 3 m at 1 cm resolution.

> The <visualize>**true**</visualize> tag block allows you to see in Gazebo the laser ray of the distance sensor covering the <range> limits explained here; that is, its detection coverage reaches up to 3 meters.

Finally, we add the Gazebo plugin that emulates the behavior of the distance sensor. The following snippet is what substitutes the commented line referring to plugin "gazebo_ros_ir" in the preceding code block:

```
<plugin filename="libgazebo_ros_range.so" name="gazebo_ros_ir">
  <gaussianNoise>0.005</gaussianNoise>
  <alwaysOn>true</alwaysOn>
  <updateRate>0.0</updateRate>
      <topicName>gopigo/distance_sensor</topicName>
      <frameName>distance_sensor</frameName>
  <radiation>INFRARED</radiation>
  <fov>0.02</fov>
</plugin>
```

The controller for the distance sensor is in the `libgazebo_ros_range.so` file, so what you provide within this block are the technical specifications of the sensor you are using. Setting the `<updateRate>` tag to `0.0` means that Gazebo should take the refreshment rate from the preceding `<sensor>` tag, that is, 10 Hz. As specified (see fields in bold letters), range values will be published in the `/sensor/ir_front` topic.

Launch the ROS visualization tool to check that the model is properly built. Since **RViz** only represents its visual features, it is a much lighter environment than Gazebo and you have available all the options to check every aspect of the appearance of the model:

```
$ roslaunch gopigo3_description gopigo3_basic_rviz.launch
```

In the following screenshot, you can see the result together with the camera that we included earlier:

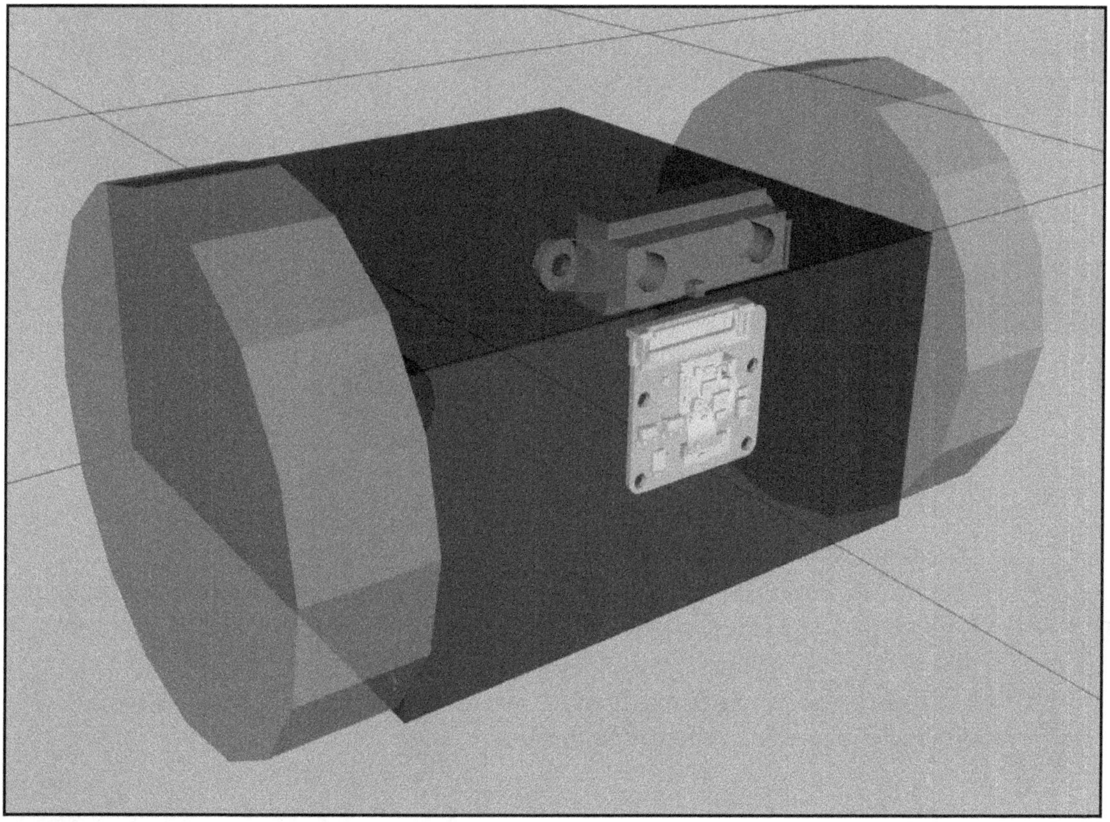

In the next section, you will do a practical exercise to see how it works with the distance sensor under Gazebo.

Simulating the distance sensor

This test includes both the distance sensor and the two-dimensional camera. Run the example by using four Terminals, as indicated in the following code:

```
T1 $ roslaunch virtual_slam gopigo3_basic_world.launch
T2 $ rosrun key_teleop key_teleop.py /key_vel:=/cmd_vel
T3 $ rostopic echo /gopigo/distance_sensor
T4 $ rosrun image_view image_view image:=/gopigo/camera1/image_raw
```

The following screenshot is a composed view of the result you should obtain:

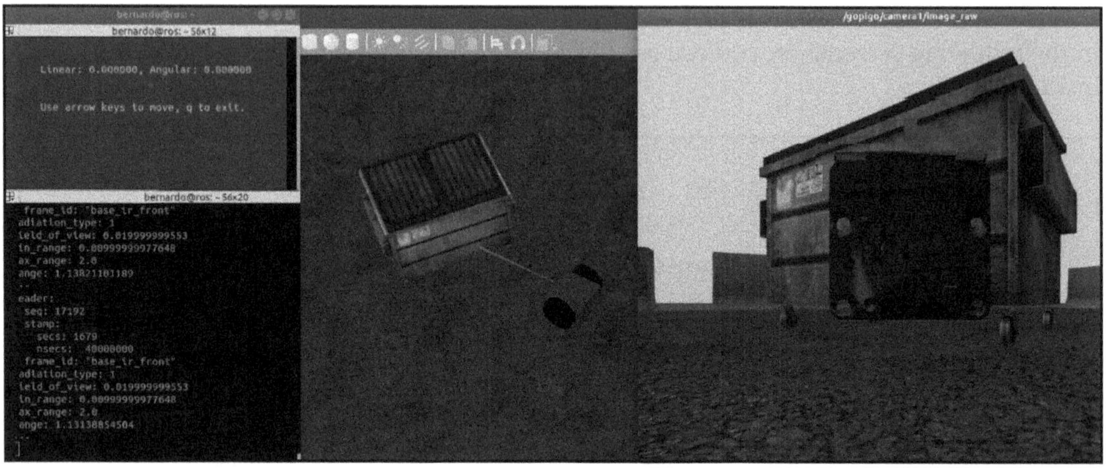

In the preceding screenshot, you can find the following components:

- The central window is the Gazebo one, where you can see GoPiGo3, an obstacle, and the rays of the distance sensor.
- The top-left gray window is the one we need to have selected so that arrow-key pushes are received as `/cmd_vel` topic messages for remote control.
- The bottom-left black window shows in real time the messages transmitted to the topic of the distance sensor, that is, `/gopigo/distance_sensor`. The current distance to the obstacle is found in the `range` field, with a value of **1.13** m.
- The right window shows the live view seen by the robot thanks to its two-dimensional camera, received in the`/gopigo/camera1/image_raw` topic.

You can manually drive from one side of the scene to the other without crashing into any of the furniture. You plan—as a human—the optimal trajectory, and execute it to bring the robot to the destination goal while avoiding the obstacles. What you have done yourself previously is what the robot now has to do itself, performing as well as possible. This task is known as **navigation** and is what we are going to cover in the next section.

Components in navigation

Navigation is the movement of a robot from the current position to a target location following a planned trajectory. This ability in a robot means that it is capable of determining its position at any point along the trajectory, as well as to setting up a plan of action given a representation of the environment, such as a map. We should also add the ability to avoid dynamic obstacles or others that were not present when the map was built for the first time.

There are four components to consider when building the navigation ability:

- A map of the environment, preexisting and given to the robot as an input, or built by its own means using the sensory data that it collects with its sensors. This whole process, that is, data acquisition plus interpretation, constitutes what we call the capability of robot perception. One well-known technique that takes advantage of robot perception is known as SLAM, as discussed earlier.
- Real-time pose, understood as the ability of a robot to locate itself in terms of position and rotation (together referred to as pose) with respect to a fixed frame of reference in the environment. The typical technique in robotics for obtaining pose is known as dead reckoning, in which the current pose is estimated relative to the previous one plus internal odometry data—coming from the rotary encoders of the motors—and IMU sensor data to reduce the error of these calculations. Both of them are present in the GoPiGo3.
- Robot perception, which arises from the combination of sensor data plus its interpretation, making the robot aware of the objects and obstacles that are around. In the GoPiGo3, the sensors that contribute to perception are the distance sensor, the Pi camera, and the LDS.

- Path planning and execution, which includes the calculation of the optimal path and its execution so that the robot can achieve the target location. Since the map does not include all the details of the environment and there can be dynamic obstacles, the path planning should also be dynamic. Its algorithm will be better as it will be able to adapt to the varying conditions in the environment.

Next, we will cover the costmap, a key concept on top of which navigation is based.

Costmaps for safe navigation

The costmap for robot navigation arises from the combination of the robot's pose, estimated from the odometry data (encoders) and the IMU sensor, the perception of objects and obstacles in the environment using the distance sensor and LDS, and the **occupancy grid map** (**OGM**) obtained from the SLAM technique.

These sources of information provide as output a joint measurement of obstacle areas, probable collisions, and the movable area for the robot. There is a global costmap and a local one. The global one accounts for the navigation path using the fixed map obtained through SLAM, while the local version allows the robot to deal with the fine-grained details of its immediate environment to move around obstacles and avoid collisions.

The costmap, be it local or global, is measured in a range of 8 bits, that is, a value from 0 to 255 in each cell of the grid occupancy map. A zero value means a free area, and 255 is an occupied area. Values near 255 account for collision areas, while intermediate values range from low collision probabilities (0-127) to high (128-252).

In the next section, we will finally deal with SLAM, the technique that is at the core of robot navigation. As a starting point, we will complete the setup of the GoPiGo3 perception capability with the integration of an LDS.

Robot perception and SLAM

The most straightforward way to implement robot navigation in ROS is by using an LDS that provides 360° coverage, allowing the robot to be aware of all the objects and obstacles around it.

In the introduction to this chapter, we identified the **EAI YDLIDAR X4** as a low-cost option that can be integrated with our physical robot. That will be covered in the next chapter, while in the present one we will develop its virtual model to be integrated in Gazebo.

The next subsection extends the virtual GoPiGo3 that we've worked on in this chapter to include this very model of LDS. Afterward, we will deploy a quick SLAM example to get an overview of what this functionality can provide to robot navigation.

Adding a Laser Distance Sensor (LDS)

The process to add the sensor is similar to what we did for the distance sensor in the previous section. Follow these steps to do it:

1. We add the solid model of this sensor under the `<visual>` tag by following the same procedure we covered for the previous sensors. The URDF definition is as follows:

```
<link name="base_scan">
  <visual name="sensor_body">
    <origin xyz="0 0 0" rpy="0 0 0" />
    <geometry>
      <mesh
filename="package://gopigo3_description/meshes/TB3_lds-01.stl"
scale="0.003 0.003 0.003"/>
    </geometry>
    <material name="yellow"/>
  </visual>
  <visual name="support">
    <origin xyz="0 0 -0.0625" rpy="0 0 0" />
    <geometry>
      <cylinder length="0.12" radius="0.1" />
    </geometry>
  </visual>
</link>
```

We can see two `<visual>` blocks within the `<link>` element in the preceding snippet: `sensor_body` is the LDS itself, and `support` creates the physical interface between the sensor and the robot chassis. The solid model that we are using for the sensor body is the one shown in the following screenshot, which consists of a CAD model in STL format referenced from the `<mesh>` tag:

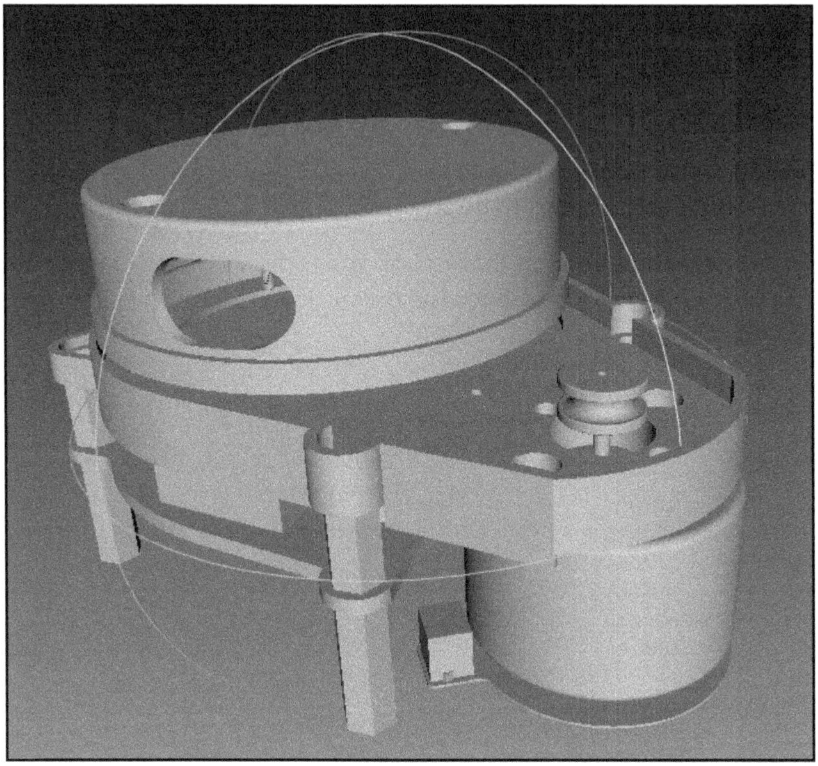

2. Next, we add a `<joint>` element of `<type="fixed">` to attach the sensor assembly to the robot chassis:

```
<joint name="scan_joint" type="fixed">
  <parent link="base_link"/>
  <child link="base_scan"/>
  <origin xyz="-0.1 0 0.25" rpy="0 0 0"/>
</joint>
```

3. Then we add the sensor technical features using a <gazebo> tag that you can see refers to the distance_sensor link defined in the preceding snippet (not distance_sensor_solid):

```
<gazebo reference="base_scan">
  <sensor type="ray" name="lds_lfcd_sensor">
    <visualize>true</visualize>
    <update_rate>5</update_rate>
    <ray>
      <scan>
        <horizontal> <samples>721</samples> ... </horizontal>
      </scan>
      <range>
        <min>0.12</min>
        <max>10</max>
        <resolution>0.015</resolution>
      </range>
    </ray>
      <!-- plugin name="gazebo_ros_lds_lfcd_controller"
filename="libgazebo_ros_laser.so" -->
  </sensor>
</gazebo>
```

The <range> tag sets measured distance values between 12 cm and 10 m, as can be found in the technical specification of the EAI YDLIDAR X4. Pay special attention to the <visualize>true</visualize> tag, since, with a sensor like this, with 360º vision, the screen will be filled with rays to show the angle range that it covers. It is recommended to set this to false once you have visually checked that the sensor is working properly.

> The <visualize>true</visualize> tag block has the same meaning and effect for the distance sensor, as explained in the previous section when we built its model, in the *Distance sensor* subsection. The only difference is that the LDS covers all angles with 360º coverage, tracing as many rays as the number of samples specified inside the <samples> tag.

The <update_rate> tag specifies that the sensor is read at a frequency of 5 Hz, but the specification of the LDS is 5,000 Hz. Why don't we put the actual value? This is for CPU usage reasons:

Bear in mind that, if we set the reading frequency at its actual physical capability, it will take 5,000 samples per second, and each sample is a vector of 720 points.

> Since LDS covers all possible directions, to get 720 rays evenly spaced at 0.5º, you have put one more sample, that is, 721, since 0º and 360º are actually the same angle.

Each point will be characterized by two float values (64 bits), so each sample needs 720 x 2 x 64 = 92160 bits = 11 Kb. Since there would be 5,000 samples, we would need a bandwidth of 53 Mb/s. That's a huge value to be managed by a Raspberry Pi CPU.

Since the robot will move at low speed, there is no need to have such a high-frequency reading, so we can limit it to only 5 Hz, which will have no impact on the robot behavior. This will require only 55 Kb/s of bandwidth, 1,000 times lower than what the sensor can provide.

This is a clear example of why you should not directly introduce the specifications of sensors within Gazebo, since it can impact the performance of the simulation. You need to critically analyze each sensor and decide what parameters to set in its virtual controller so that it reproduces the actual behavior well, while not unnecessarily overloading the CPU.

4. The next step is to add the Gazebo plugin that emulates the behavior of the distance sensor. The following snippet is what substitutes the commented line referring to `plugin "gazebo_ros_lds_lfcd_controller"` in the preceding code block:

```
      <plugin name="gazebo_ros_lds_lfcd_controller"
filename="libgazebo_ros_laser.so">
         <topicName>/gopigo/scan</topicName>
         <frameName>base_scan</frameName>
      </plugin>
```

The controller for the distance sensor is in the `libgazebo_ros_laser_range.so` file, so what you provide within this block are the technical specifications of the sensor for which you want to override the values provided in the `<sensor>` tag in the preceding snippet. As specified (see fields in bold letters), the range values will be published in the `/gopigo/scan` topic.

5. Finally, launch the ROS visualization tool to check that the model is properly built. Since RViz only represents its visual features, it is a much lighter environment than Gazebo and you have available all the options to check every aspect of the appearance of the model:

   ```
   $ roslaunch gopigo3_description gopigo3_rviz.launch
   ```

   In the following screenshot, you can see the result together with the camera that we included earlier:

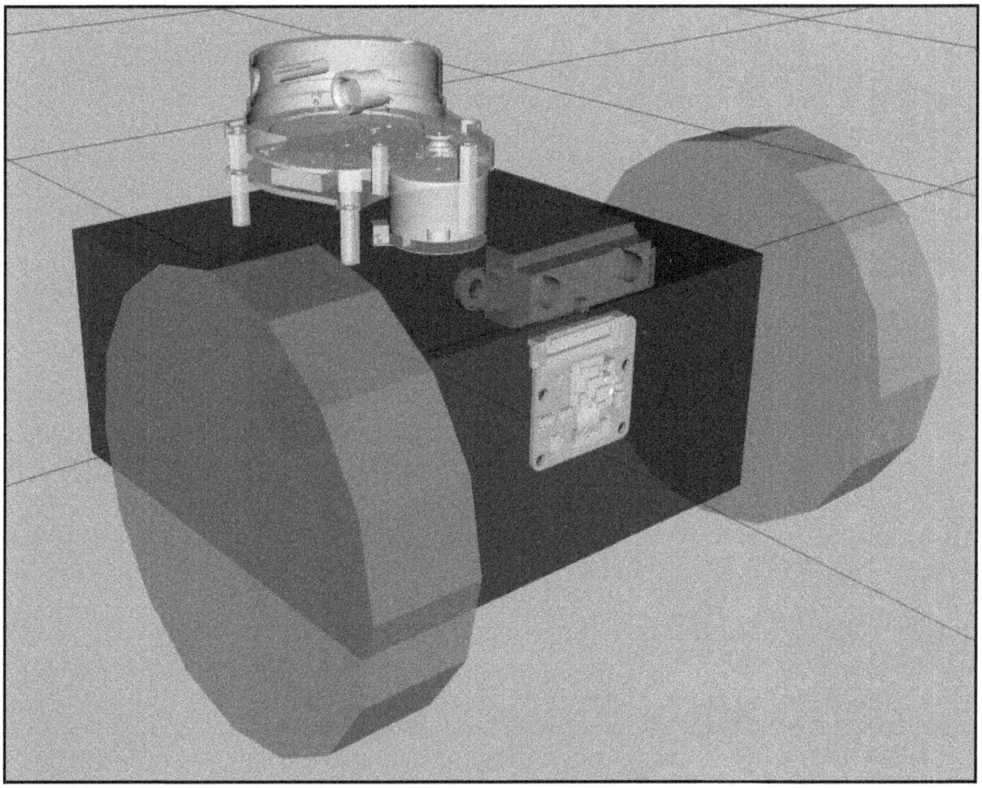

In the next subsection, you will do a practical exercise to see how it works the laser distance sensor under Gazebo.

Simulating the LDS

After including the LDS model in the virtual robot, we can proceed to see how it works by running the simulation in Gazebo:

1. Execute the following commands in separate Terminals to see the sensor in action:

```
T1 $ roslaunch virtual_slam gopigo3_world.launch
T2 $ rosrun key_teleop key_teleop.py /key_vel:=/cmd_vel
T3 $ rostopic echo /gopigo/scan
```

   In `T3`, you will see a large feed of data, since each `LaserScan` message contains 720 points to cover the 360° view around the sensor.

2. To test this sensor, it is better to use a Python script that makes the robot wander in the environment while avoiding the obstacles. To do this, we have implemented the following rules in our script:

    - If there is no obstacle, move forward at a reference speed of 0.8 m/s.
    - If the range provided by the distance sensor is lower than 2 meters, go back and rotate counter-clockwise until avoiding the obstacle.
    - Since the distance sensor throws unidirectional measurements, we should check the measurements from the LDS to find if there are obstacles to the sides, and the threshold should be lower than 1.6 meters. If obstacles are detected, go back and rotate counter-clockwise faster to avoid the obstacle and not get stuck on it.

   This simple algorithm is implemented in the `wanderAround.py` script, and can be found under the `./virtual_slam/scripts/wanderAround.py` folder.

3. Now, give it a try, and enjoy watching how the GoPiGo3 goes from one side of the world to the other while avoiding obstacles. The sequence to run is the following:

```
T1 $ roslaunch virtual_slam gopigo3_world.launch
T2 $ rosrun virtual_slam wanderAround.py
```

The following screenshot shows the robot wandering around:

To finish this section, we will briefly cover the key concepts of the SLAM theory so that you know what's under the hood when we proceed in the last section of the chapter, covering the practical part of this implementation of robot navigation.

SLAM concepts

SLAM allows the robot to build a map of the environment using the following two sources of information:

- Robot pose estimation, coming from the internal odometry (rotary encoders) and IMU sensor data
- Distance to objects, obstacles and walls, coming from distance sensors, the LDS in particular

In its most basic version, a map includes two-dimensional information, while in more advanced applications using industrial-grade LIDAR sensors, a richer map is built using three-dimensional information from LIDAR and/or from three-dimensional cameras. For the purpose of our learning path, we will deal with the two-dimensional OGM, also very common in ROS projects.

Occupancy Grid Map (OGM)

Take the example of a square room with four static obstacles inside. The following diagram shows the map generated using SLAM in ROS (you will later learn how to generate it yourself):

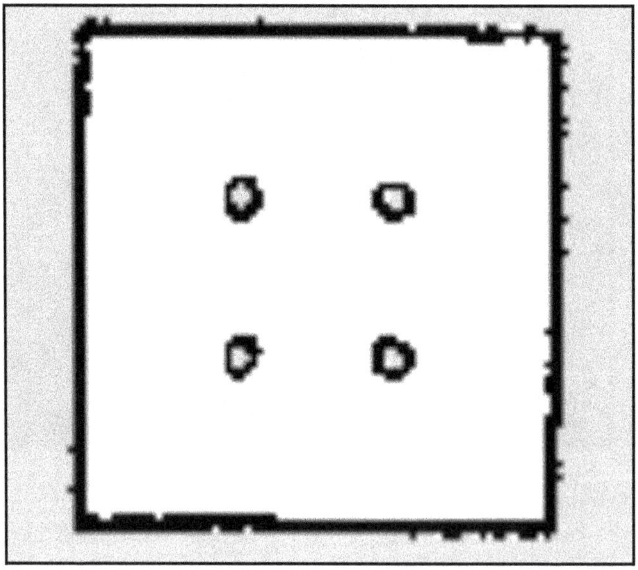

In such a two-dimensional map, the free areas and occupied areas are drawn in different intensities of gray in 8-bit format (0-255 range, as was already mentioned earlier when describing the costmaps). Then, the occupancy probability for each cell is obtained as the difference between 255 and the intensity value, divided by 255. This means the following:

- White areas (255 value) give a 0% probability; that is, there is no obstacle in them.
- Black areas (0 value) give a 100% probability; that is, they are occupied.

This probability distribution allows a costmap to be built that helps the robot to determine which trajectory to select to achieve the target location. When published to ROS, the occupancy probabilities translate into integer values between 0 (0% probability, that is, free space) and 100 (100%, that is, occupied space). A value of -1 is assigned to unknown areas. Map information is stored using two files:

- A `.pgm` format file, known as portable graymap format.
- A `.yaml` file containing the configuration of the map. See the following example of its content:

```
image: ./test_map.pgm
resolution: 0.010000
origin: [-20.000000, -20.000000, 0.000000]
negate: 0
occupied_thresh: 0.65
free_thresh: 0.196
```

The most interesting parameters are the last two:

- `occupied_thresh = 0.65` means that a cell is considered as occupied if its probability is above 65%.
- `free_thresh = 0.196` establishes the threshold value below which the cell is considered free, that is, 19.6%.

Given the size in pixels of the image, it is straightforward to infer the physical dimension of the cells in the map. This value is indicated by the `resolution` parameter, that is, 0.01 meter/pixel.

The SLAM process

Building the map using a Gazebo simulation involves employing the following workflow:

1. Launch the robot model within a modeled environment.
2. Launch the mapping ROS package.
3. Launch a special visualization in RViz that lets us see the areas the robot is scanning as it moves.
4. Teleoperate the robot to make it cover as much as possible of the surface of the virtual environment.
5. Once the exploration is finished, save the map, generating the two files in the formats indicated in the preceding section, that is, `.pgm` and `.yaml`.

Having finished this information acquisition phase, we are ready for the robot to try and successfully complete a navigation task.

The navigation process

Once your robot has generated a map, it will use it to plan a path to a given target destination. The process of executing such a plan is called navigation, and involves the following steps:

1. Launch the robot model within the modeled environment. This step is the same as the first step in the SLAM process described earlier.
2. Provide the costmap that the robot built before. Bear in mind that the map is a characteristic of the environment, not of the robot. Hence, you can build the map with one robot and use the same map in navigation for any other robot you put in the same environment.
3. Set up the navigation algorithm. We will use the **Adaptive Monte Carlo Localization** (**AMCL**) algorithm, the most common choice for effective navigation. It is out of the scope of the book to describe such algorithms, but useful references are provided in the further reading section at the end of the chapter.
4. Launch a RViz visualization that will let you visualize the robot in the environment and easily mark the target pose (position and orientation) that it should achieve.
5. Let the robot navigate autonomously to the target location. At this point, you can relax and enjoy watching how the GoPiGo3 drives to the indicated position while avoiding the obstacles and minimizing the distance it has to cover.

Should you want the robot to navigate to another location, you just have to indicate it in RViz once it has reached the previous target. Now it is time to see the preceding two processes—SLAM and navigation—in action. That is the scope of the last section of this chapter.

Practising SLAM and navigation with the GoPiGo3

Like it was mentioned at the end of the previous section, we are going to run an end-to-end example of SLAM and navigation with GoPiGo3. The first process deals with building a map of the environment using SLAM. Let's retrace the steps listed in the preceding section and see how to execute each of them in ROS.

Exploring the environment to build a map using SLAM

Let's follow these steps to build the map of a simple Gazebo world called `stage_2.world`:

1. Launch the robot model within a modeled environment by running the following line of code:

   ```
   T1 $ roslaunch virtual_slam gopigo3_world.launch
   world:=stage_2.world
   ```

   This command launches Gazebo and places the GoPiGo3 model in the middle of it, as shown in the following screenshot:

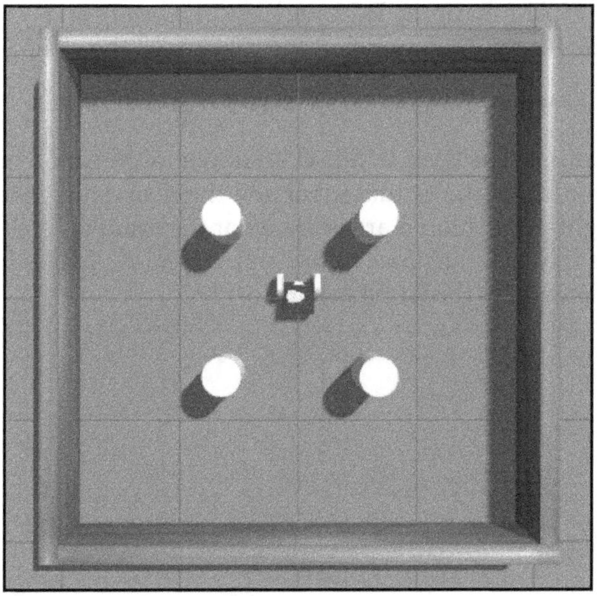

The environment consists of a square space with four static obstacles. The two-dimensional map we used in the *Occupancy Grid Map (OGM)* subsection of the previous section corresponds to this Gazebo world, whose filename is `stage_2.world`.

> You can see that this world is by far simpler than the one we used in the first part of the chapter (there is an even simpler environment without the obstacles, named `stage_1.world`). We use this to illustrate the navigation concepts with a minimal setup for better understanding.
>
> It is left as an exercise for the reader to repeat this process with the Gazebo world from the first *Dynamic simulation using Gazebo* section. To do so, just omit the `world` argument so that it takes the default specified within the launch file. The command to execute this simulation is `$ roslaunch virtual_slam gopigo3_world.launch`

Finally, take into account that we can specify any other environment we want to use in Gazebo by setting the `world` parameter to the filename of the one selected (available worlds are located inside the `./virtual_slam/worlds` folder of the code of this chapter):

```
T1 $ roslaunch virtual_slam gopigo3_world.launch world:=
<OTHER_WORLD.world>
```

2. Launch the SLAM mapping ROS package, including an RViz visualization that superimposes the virtual model of the robot with the actual scan data:

```
T2 $ roslaunch virtual_slam gopigo3_slam.launch
```

The appearance of the RViz window is shown in the following screenshot, where you can see together the virtual robot and the scan data (green points) in real time. The light-gray-colored areas are what the robot is actually perceiving with its LDS sensor, while the non colored areas (shadow spaces behind the obstacles) are not yet known by the GoPiGo3:

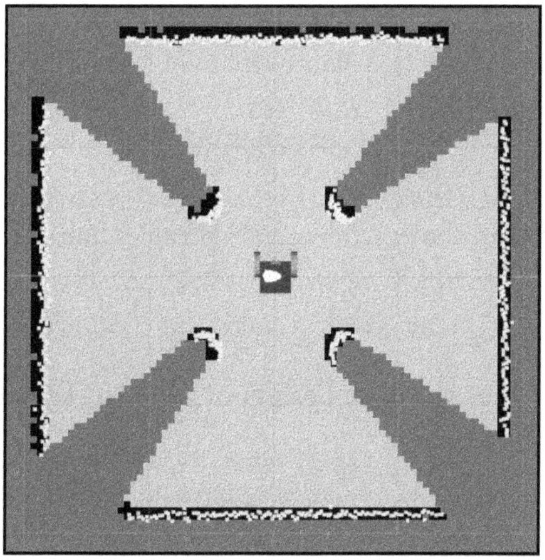

In the next step, we will explore the full environment to build the map.

3. Teleoperate the robot to make it cover as much as possible of the surface of the current Gazebo world. Let's do this as usual with the teleoperation package:

```
T3 $ rosrun key_teleop key_teleop.py /key_vel:=/cmd_vel
```

As you move the robot, the LDS sensor will acquire scan data from the unknown areas, and you will receive feedback in the RViz window:

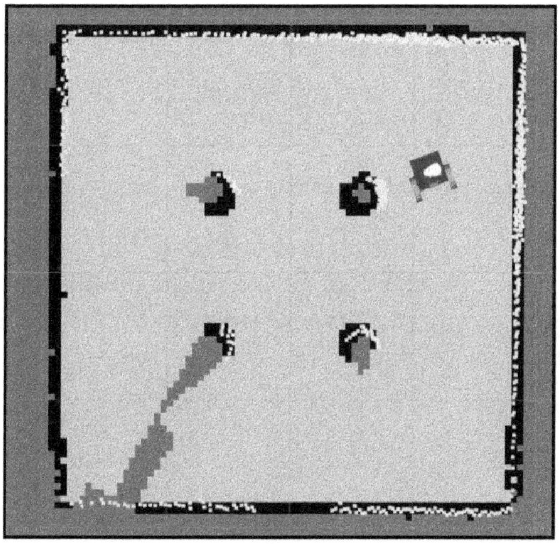

In the preceding screenshot, you can see that, after wandering in the environment, only the bottom-left part is not scanned. Then move the robot to that location, and, as soon as you have all the space filled with a homogeneous color (light gray), proceed to step 4 in order to save the map.

4. Once you've finished the exploration, save the map, generating two files of the formats indicated in the preceding *SLAM process* subsection, that is, `.pgm` and `.yaml`:

```
T4 $ rosrun map_server map_saver -f ~/catkin_ws/map_stage_2
```

You will get two files in the root folder of your workspace: `map_stage_2.pgm` and `map_stage_2.yaml`.

The appearance of the generated map is shown in the preceding *Occupancy Grid Map (OGM)* subsection.

Provided with the map, we are ready to perform robot navigation with the GoPiGo3.

Driving along a planned trajectory using navigation

First, close all open Terminals. Then, as in the SLAM process, let's proceed step by step to perform some navigation:

1. Launch the robot model within the modeled environment. This step is the same as the first step in the SLAM process:

```
T1 $ roslaunch virtual_slam gopigo3_world.launch
```

2. Set up the navigation algorithm and launch RViz. We will use AMCL, the most common choice for effective navigation. It is out of the scope of the book to describe such algorithm, but you are provided with useful references in the *Further reading* section at the end of the chapter.

In this step, we also provide the costmap that the robot built before. To do this, you just have to reference the `.yaml` map file you created before. Make sure that the corresponding `.pgm` file has the same name and is placed in the same location. This point is specified in the `roslaunch` command through the `map_file` argument:

```
T2 $ roslaunch virtual_slam gopigo3_navigation.launch
map_file:=$HOME/catkin_ws/map_stage_2.yaml
```

3. The RViz window, shown in the following screenshot, lets you visualize the robot in the environment and mark the target pose (position and orientation) that it should achieve:

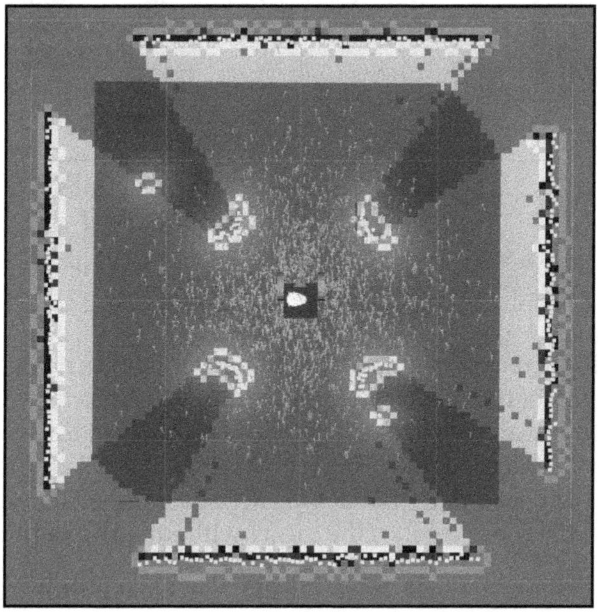

Find the 2D Nav Goal button at the top-right of the RViz window. You will use it to mark the target location to which the robot should navigate.

First of all, you have to tell the robot that this is the initial pose by pressing the **2D Pose Estimate** button. Then, mark it on screen (in this particular case, it isn't necessary, since the initial pose is the same as the one the robot had when it started to build the map in the preceding subsection).

Afterward, you can press **2D Nav Goal** button and set the target to the *bottom-left corner* by clicking the left mouse button. Release the mouse when the arrow has the desired orientation. After releasing, the robot will compute the path to follow and start navigating autonomously:

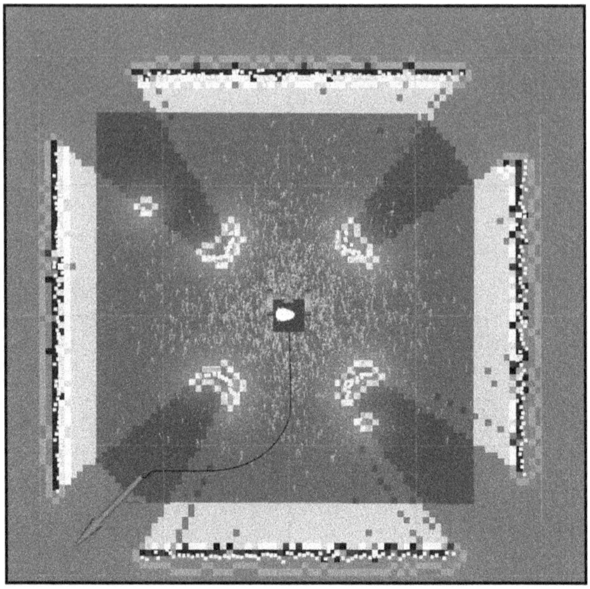

The preceding screenshot shows the first instant of the navigation plan execution. The orientation of the red arrow tells the GoPiGo3 in what direction it should stay facing once it has arrived at the target, and the curved line going from the robot to the target is the planned path. Since it has a map of the environment available, the robot is able to plan a path that avoids the obstacles. Wait a few seconds and you will see how the robot reaches the target without any external help.

4. Once the robot has arrived, press the **2D Nav Goal** button again and then mark the top-right corner. The following screenshot shows the first instant of the execution of the next navigation plan:

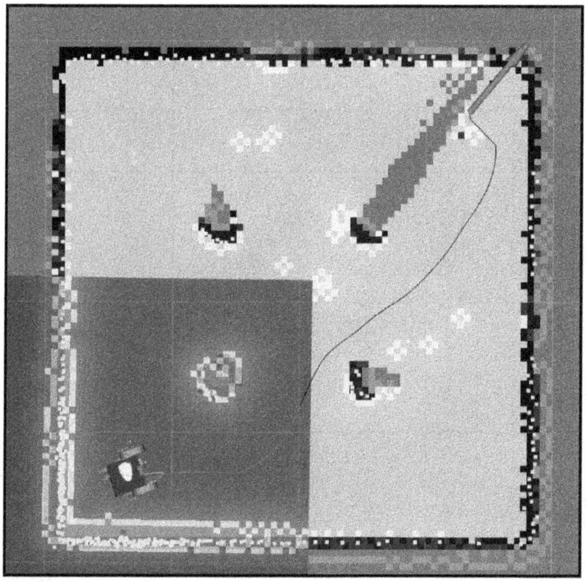

You can see the new planned path and how this takes into account the presence of obstacles along the way to avoid collisions. The blue square around the robot represents the local window for obstacle avoidance planning. This is used by the **Dynamic Window Approach** (**DWA**) method, which generates a local path that efficiently evades the obstacles. The DWA method performs the calculations taking into account the robot's dynamics, in particular, its limited velocity and acceleration.

The AMCL algorithm for robot navigation generates the global path to reach the target based on the provided map, while the DWA method calculates the local path that accounts for the local conditions the robot may find near it. The latter provides the capability to deal both with obstacles present in the map, and also dynamic ones, such as people crossing the robot's path, for example. The *global path* and *local path* combine together to produce *highly autonomous robot navigation*.

The following screenshot shows the GoPiGo3 in the final instant before reaching the goal. Appreciate how, at this point, the DWA window also includes the target:

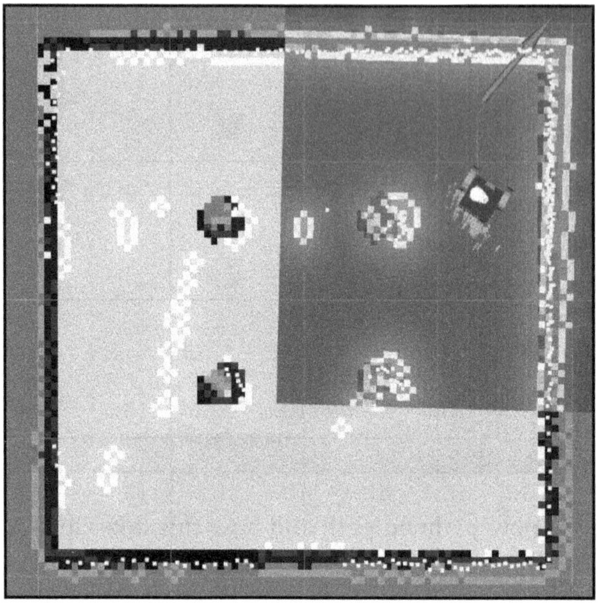

5. Finally, you should frame robot navigation within a sequence of tasks that the robot has to complete, one after the other, in order to achieve the goal that has been set by the user. Taking the examples of the navigation paths that we have used already in this chapter for explanation purposes, imagine a scenario in which the GoPiGo3 has to pick up an object in location *A* (the left-bottom corner) and deliver it to location *B* (the upper-right corner). In this case, the sequence of tasks would be as follows:
    1. Navigate to location *A*.
    2. Pick up the piece at location *A*.
    3. Navigate to location *B*.
    4. Drop off the piece at location *B*.

Conceptually, it is easy, right? But in this chapter, we have only covered the basics to accomplish tasks 1 and 3. Later, in `Chapter 10`, *Applying Machine Learning in Robotics*, you will be given the technical background on **object recognition** so that you can also program tasks 2 and 4. More precisely, it will be in the *A methodology to programmatically apply ML in Robotics* section where we will provide you with this insight.

Summary

This chapter has introduced you to the master task of robot navigation. SLAM and navigation are complex matters and active research topics in robotics. So, this chapter has given you a taste of how to implement it so that you can quickly understand its mechanics without entering into details of the algorithms and the mathematics behind.

We expect to have aroused your curiosity on this topic. Now you are prepared to carry out the same task in the real world with the physical GoPiGo3. In the next chapter, you will perform the navigation and SLAM tasks with the physical robot.

Questions

1. Where are the sensor specifications included within a Gazebo SDF file?

   A) Outside of a `<gazebo>` tag
   B) Within a `<joint>` tag
   C) Within a `<sensor>` tag

2. Regarding the controller specification of a sensor in Gazebo, what is the most relevant parameter in terms of CPU usage while running the simulation?

   A) The scan distance, because the larger the sensor range is, the more bandwidth consumption the CPU performs.
   B) The angular scan, since the greater the angular resolution, the more bandwidth consumption is required to store the readings in the RAM.
   C) The maximum sensor frequency, because they are so high in real sensors that they easily can overload the CPU.

3. Where are the sensor mechanical properties included within a Gazebo description of the robot?

   A) Outside of a `<gazebo>` tag
   B) Within a `<joint>` tag
   C) Within a `<sensor>` tag

4. What does the SLAM technique provide to a robot?

   A) A method to avoid moving obstacles in the environment
   B) A method to build a map of the environment
   C) A method to avoid static and moving obstacles in the environment

5. How do you operationally specify a navigation goal to a robot?

   A) Tell it the target location and orientation
   B) Set a target location in a two-dimensional map of the environment
   C) Mark the borders of the area where the robot is expected to navigate to

Further reading

To delve deeper into the concepts explained in this chapter, you can check out the following references:

- Adaptive Monte Carlo Localization (AMCL), at `http://roboticsknowledgebase.com/wiki/state-estimation/adaptive-monte-carlo-localization/`
- *Particle Filters in Robotics*, Proceedings of Uncertainty in AI (UAI), Thrun S. (2002), at `http://robots.stanford.edu/papers/thrun.pf-in-robotics-uai02.pdf`
- *SLAM for Dummies*, A Tutorial Approach to Simultaneous Localization and Mapping, Riisgaard S, at `http://zyzx.haust.edu.cn/moocresource/data/081503/U/802/pdfs/soren_project.pdf`
- *Robot Perception for Indoor Navigation*, Endres, F. (2015), Albert-Ludwigs-Universitat Freiburg, at `https://d-nb.info/1119716993/34`

9
SLAM for Robot Navigation

In this chapter, you will deep dive into robot navigation, a ubiquitous task in robotics engineering. Typical use cases include self-driving cars and transporting materials in a factory. You will find that the map we generated previously by applying **SLAM (Simultaneous localization and mapping)** is used for path planning along the way. Given an initial pose, the robot will travel along the optimal path and should be capable of reacting to dynamic events, that is, it should be able to avoid the obstacles (static or dynamic) that appeared after the map was built.

This chapter is a natural extension of the previous one. In the previous chapter, you gained a practical understanding of SLAM and navigation, and you did that inside the Gazebo simulator using a virtual model of GoPiGo3. Now, you are ready to complete the exercise again with a physical robot. By doing so, you will discover how many details and practical questions arise when you complete a robotic task in a real environment. Simulation is a good start, but the real proof that your robot performs as expected is by executing the task in an actual scenario.

In this chapter, we will be covering the following topics:

- Preparing **Laser Distance Sensor** (**LDS**) for your robot
- Creating a navigation application in ROS, including explanations about common algorithms that are used in navigation
- Practicing navigation with GoPiGo3

The main sensor for the navigation task will be the low-cost LDS by EAI model YDLIDAR X4 (`https://www.aliexpress.com/item/32908156152.html`), which we've simulated already within Gazebo. We will dedicate a large portion of this chapter to learning how to set up the LDS, understand how it works, and what practical information it provides to the robot.

Technical requirements

In this chapter, we will make use of the code located in the `Chapter9_GoPiGo_SLAM` folder (`https://github.com/PacktPublishing/Hands-On-ROS-for-Robotics-Programming/tree/master/Chapter9_GoPiGo_SLAM`). Copy its files to the ROS workspace so that they're available and leave the rest outside the `src` folder. This way, you will have a cleaner ROS environment:

```
$ cp -R ~/Hands-On-ROS-for-Robotics-Programming/Chapter9_GoPiGo_SLAM
~/catkin_ws/src/
```

The code in the aforementioned folder contains two new ROS packages, each one located within a folder that has the same name:

- `ydlidar`, the officially supported ROS package for the selected LDS.
- `gopigo3_navigation`, the top-level package for performing navigation with GoPiGo3.

You will use both on the laptop environment, but in the robot – that is, the Raspberry Pi – you will only need `ydlidar` since the computationally expensive task of navigation is recommended to be run on the laptop. This way, GoPiGo3 will receive the drive command through the familiar `cmd_vel` topic and publish a 360° range scan from the LDS through the `/scan` topic.

As usual, you need to rebuild the workspace separately, both for the robot and the laptop:

```
$ cd ~/catkin_ws
$ catkin_make
```

Check that the packages have been installed correctly by selecting them and listing the files:

```
$ rospack list | grep gopigo3
$ rospack list | grep ydlidar
```

Next, we have to point the ROS master to the robot.

Setting the ROS master to be in the robot

Since you'll be working with the physical robot once more, you need to reconfigure the ROS master URI so that it points to GoPiGo3. So that your laptop reflects such a configuration, open your local `.bashrc` file and uncomment the line at the end that specifies what URL to point to in order to find the ROS master:

```
$ nano ~./bashrc
   ...
   export ROS_HOSTNAME=rosbot.local
   export ROS_MASTER_URI=http://gopigo3.local:11311
```

Close any open Terminals, open a new one, and check the `ROS_MASTER_URI` variable:

```
$ echo $ROS_MASTER_URI
    http://gopigo3.local:11311
```

You should find that the environment variable has reverted to the default server (localhost) and default port (`11311`). Now, we are ready to switch to the virtual robot. If, for some reason, `gopigo3.local` does not resolve the robot IP, set up its IPv4 address directly. You can get it from the robot OS like so:

```
$ ip addr # or 'ifconfig' instead
    192.168.1.51
```

Then, in the `.bashrc` file, modify the following line accordingly:

```
export ROS_MASTER_URI=http://192.168.1.51:11311
```

Close the Terminal on your laptop and open a new one so that the configuration takes effect. Then, check for the following:

```
$ echo $ROS_MASTER_URI
   http://192.168.1.51:11311
```

Now, we can get familiar with our new sensor.

Preparing an LDS for your robot

Before you begin, you should take some time to review all the documentation provided by the manufacturer EAI. You can find all the resources at `http://www.ydlidar.com/download`. Pay special attention to the following items:

- The YDLIDAR X4 user manual, to get familiar with the hardware and install it safely with your robot.
- The YDLIDAR X4 ROS manual, located within the compressed `ROS.zip` file. The `ros` folder inside corresponds to the ROS package, but you should clone it from GitHub to make sure you get the latest version and stay updated. Follow the instructions at `https://github.com/EAIBOT/ydlidar` to get the most recent version of the code.

EAI has removed **CAD** (short for **Computer-Aided Design)** models from the download page.

- The YDLIDAR X4 development manual, which describes the communication protocol so that you can build your own driver to control the device.

Now, you are ready to get started with the hardware.

Setting up YDLIDAR

Follow the instructions provided in the user manual to physically connect the device to your laptop or to the robot. The following screenshot shows what it looks like once the sensor itself has been wired to the control board via the set of five colored cables:

Although the software instructions are also provided in the manual, we will list all the steps here since they refer to the core integration with ROS. First, we will integrate with the laptop, and then with the Raspberry Pi of the robot.

Integrating with the remote PC

As with any other hardware we integrate with ROS, we follow the standard procedure of cloning the package supplied by the manufacturer and building it with our workspace:

```
$ cd catkin_ws/src
$ git clone https://github.com/EAIBOT/ydlidar
$ cd ..
$ catkin_make
```

By running `catkin_make`, the `ydlidar_client` and `ydlidar_node` nodes will be available.

> This code is also bundled with the rest of the YDLIDAR models at `https://github.com/YDLIDAR/ydlidar_ros`. For a specific model, you just have to select the corresponding branch, X4. In our case, this is `git clone https://github.com/YDLIDAR/ydlidar_ros -b X4 --single-branch`.

After connecting X4 to a USB port of the laptop, change the permissions in order to access the new LDS:

```
$ sudo chown ubuntu:dialout /dev/ttyUSB0
```

The preceding command assumes that your user is `ubuntu`. If it isn't, replace it with your actual user. Then, initiate the device:

```
$ roscd ydlidar/startup
$ sudo chmod 777 ./*
$ sudo sh initenv.sh
```

This script creates a symbolic link to the `/dev/ydlidar--> /dev/ttyUSB0` device. The next step is to run a test inside ROS to check everything works as expected.

Running the YDLIDAR ROS package

Now, we are going to launch the laser scan node and visualize the results with a console client, before doing the same with RViz.

Follow these steps to do so:

1. Launch the YDLIDAR node with the following command:

```
T1 $ roslaunch ydlidar lidar.launch
```

For this part of this chapter, you should temporarily point the ROS master to the laptop, not the robot. Remember that you can do this for single Terminals by specifying `$ export ROS_MASTER_URI=http://localhost:11311` in each. Once you close any of these, the temporal definition will be thrown away.

2. From another Terminal, list the scan data using a client node:

```
T2 $ rosrun ydlidar ydlidar_client
```

You should see the YDLIDAR node's scan result in the console, as well as the ROS graph (obtained by running `rqt_graph` in a separate Terminal, `T3`):

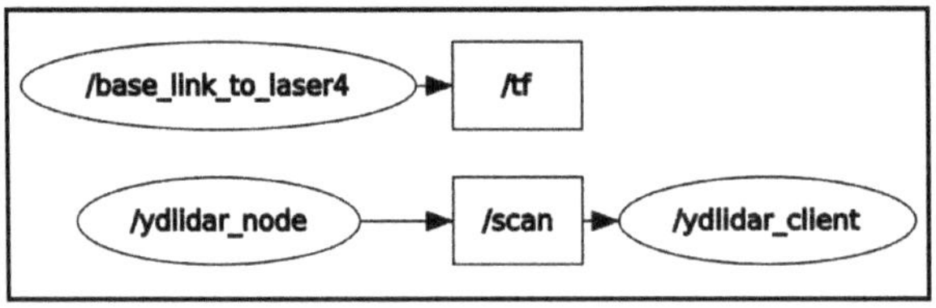

Note that `base_link_to_laser4` provides the coordinate frame transformation in the `/tf` topic, while `ydlidar_node` provides the sensor data feed in the `/scan` topic, which is visualized in the Terminal thanks to the `ydlidar_client` node.

3. Finally, launch RViz to see the distribution of red points at the positions where obstacles were found:

```
T3 $ roslaunch ydlidar display_scan.launch
```

Now, we will repeat this exercise with the LDS connected to the robot.

Integrating with Raspberry Pi

We will repeat the process we described in the preceding section, *Setting up YDLIDAR*, in order to connect the LDS to the Raspberry Pi. After attaching the sensor to a USB port of the Raspberry Pi, open a Terminal in the robot and follow these steps:

1. Clone the repository and rebuild the workspace:

```
$ cd catkin_ws/src
$ git clone https://github.com/EAIBOT/ydlidar
$ cd ..
$ catkin_make
```

2. When you've connected YDLIDAR to a USB port, check that the connection has been established properly:

```
$ ls -la /dev | grep USB
    crw-rw----  1 root dialout 188,   0 ene 28  2018 ttyUSB0
```

3. Then, change the permissions so that your normal user, `pi`, has access to the new device:

```
$ sudo chown pi:dialout /dev/ttyUSB0
```

4. Now, initiate the device:

```
$ roscd ydlidar/startup
$ sudo chmod 777 ./*
$ sudo sh initenv.sh
```

This script creates a symbolic link to the `/dev/ydlidar-->` `/dev/ttyUSB0` device. If this is not the case, you can do this by hand, like so:

```
$ cd /dev
$ sudo ln -s ttyUSB0 ydlidar
```

This way, you make sure that the `ydlidar_node` node finds the device.

Checking that YDLIDAR works with GoPiGo3

Just like we did with the laptop, use the `ydlidar_client` script to check that you have received data from the sensor:

```
r1 $ roslaunch ydlidar lidar.launch
r2 $ rosrun ydlidar ydlidar_client
```

The letter `r` in the preceding code snippet stands for the Terminals in the Raspberry Pi. If you receive data in `r2`, then this will be proof that the sensor is sending its readings to ROS.

Visualizing scan data in the Raspberry Pi desktop

Now, let's check the RViz visualization in the Raspberry Pi, just like we did for the laptop. For this, you need to use **VNC (Virtual Network Computing)**, as we explained in `Chapter 6`, *Programming in ROS – Commands and Tools*, in the *Setting up the physical robot* section. Set up a VNC server (`x11vnc`). Once connected from the remote laptop, launch the following four Terminals in the Raspberry Pi desktop:

```
r1 $ roslaunch ydlidar lidar_view.launch
r2 $ roslaunch mygopigo gopigo3.launch
r3 $ rosrun key_teleop key_teleop.py /key_vel:=/cmd_vel
r4 $ rqt_graph
```

This is the whole screen:

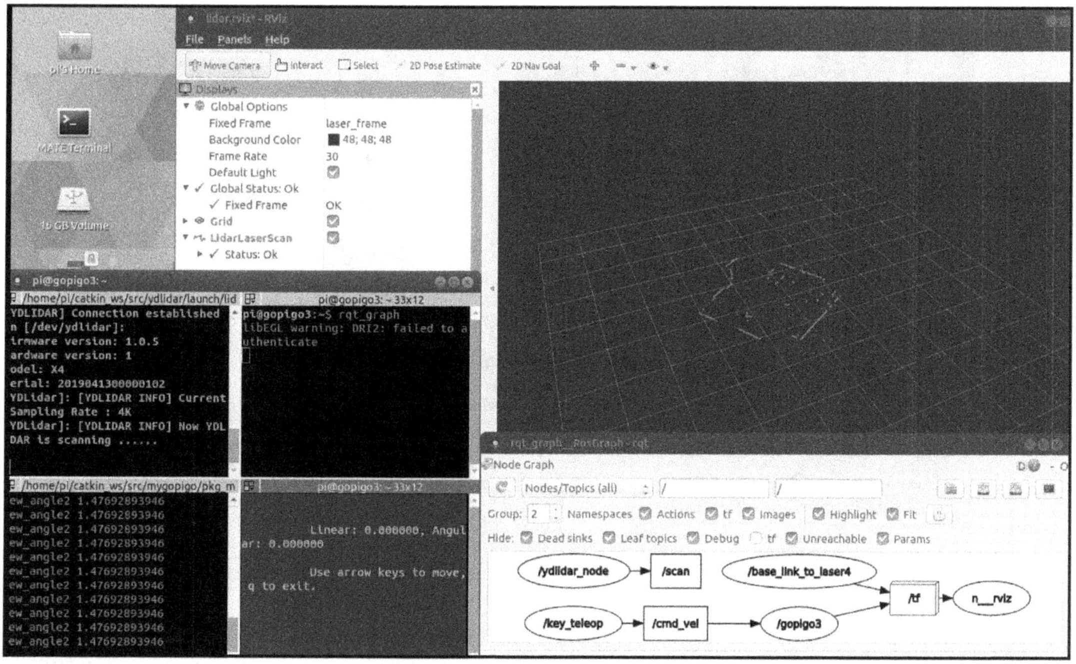

The laser scan view in RViz (top-right window in the preceding screenshot) is provided by `lidar_view.launch`. The ROS graph (bottom-right window) shows that the `key_teleop` node allows you to teleoperate the robot with the arrow keys by publishing messages in the `/cmd_vel` topic:

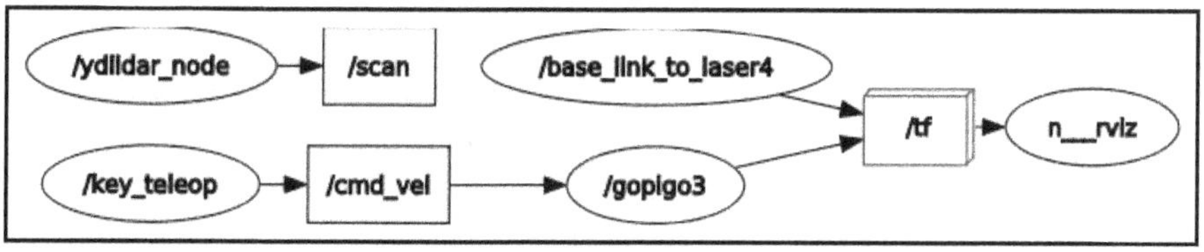

Let's take a look at what the RViz window is showing:

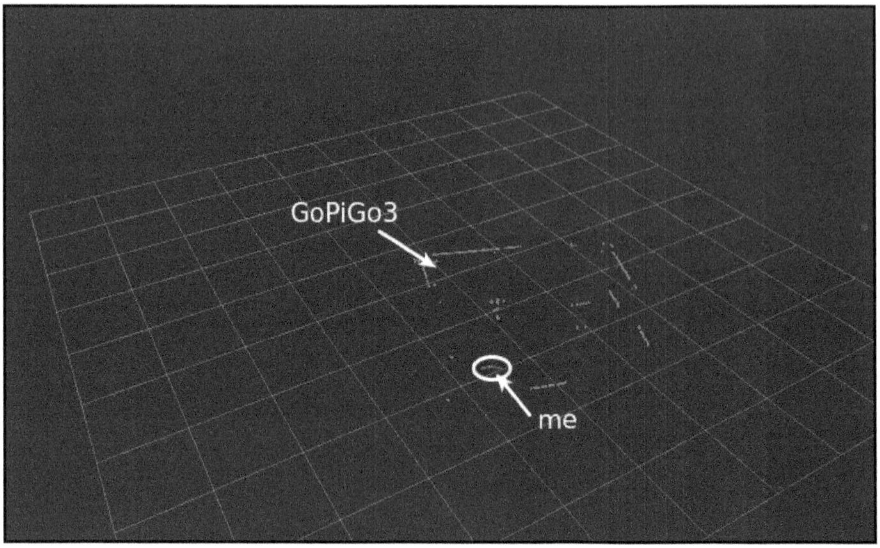

The arrow marked as **GoPiGo3** shows the location of the robot in a corner of the room. The external straight red lines stand for the walls, while the arrow pointing to **me** shows the contour of myself as I am leaving the room through the access door (the free space – no red points – in front of me).

Grouping launch files

For efficiency, we should offload the Raspberry Pi from visualization tasks and move them to the remote laptop. In order to so, we need to rework the launch files so that GoPiGo3 strictly runs the code that's necessary for the robot to work, that is, the `gopigo3_driver.py` part of the `mygopipo` package we described in `Chapter 6`, *Programming in ROS – Commands and Tools*, plus the `lidar.launch` part of the `ydlidar` package. These two components can be launched with the following commands:

```
r1 $ roslaunch mygopigo gopigo3.launch
r2 $ roslaunch ydlidar ydlidar.launch
```

The launch files in `r1` and `r2` can be grouped into one, like so. We will call this script `gopigo3_ydlidar.launch`:

```
<launch>
  <include file="$(find mygopigo)/launch/gopigo3.launch" />
  <node name="ydlidar_node" pkg="ydlidar" type="ydlidar_node"
output="screen" respawn="false" >
     <param name="port" type="string" value="/dev/ydlidar"/>
     <param name="baudrate" type="int" value="115200"/>
     <param name="frame_id" type="string" value="laser_frame"/>
      ...
     <param name="angle_min" type="double" value="-180" />
     <param name="angle_max" type="double" value="180" />
     <param name="range_min" type="double" value="0.1" />
     <param name="range_max" type="double" value="16.0" />
  </node>
  <node pkg="tf" type="static_transform_publisher"
name="base_link_to_laser4"
   args="0.2245 0.0 0.2 0.0 0.0 0.0 /base_footprint /laser_frame 40" />
</launch>
```

Thanks to this grouping, all the code of GoPiGo3 can be run with the following command:

```
r1 $ roslaunch ydlidar gopigo3_ydlidar.launch
```

This launches the `ydlidar` and `gopigo3` nodes, which provide a software interface so that we can talk to the robot sensors and actuators. This also creates the following ROS graph:

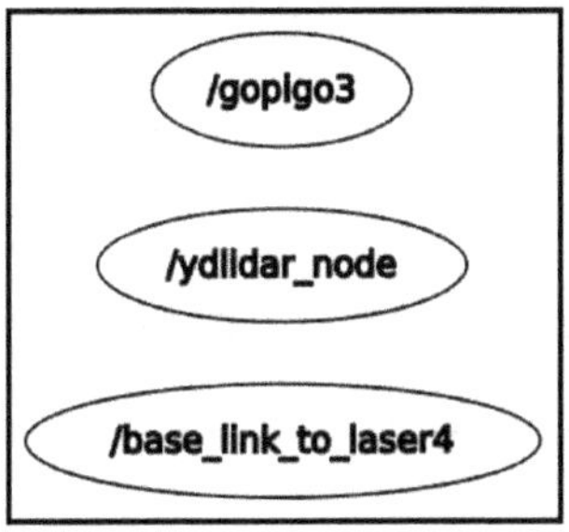

Next, to listen for the scan data, you need to execute the YDLIDAR client in the robot:

```
r2 $ rosrun ydlidar ydlidar_client
```

This results in the following output:

```
[YDLIDAR INFO]: I heard a laser scan laser_frame[720]:
[YDLIDAR INFO]: angle_range : [-180.000005, 180.000005]
[YDLIDAR INFO]: angle-distance : [-4.500002, 0.000000, 351]
```

```
[YDLIDAR INFO]: angle-distance : [-4.000005, 0.750000, 352]
[YDLIDAR INFO]: angle-distance : [-3.500007, 0.765000, 353]
[YDLIDAR INFO]: angle-distance : [-3.000010, 0.782000, 354]
[YDLIDAR INFO]: angle-distance : [-2.500013, 0.000000, 355]
[YDLIDAR INFO]: angle-distance : [-2.000002, 0.799000, 356]
[YDLIDAR INFO]: angle-distance : [-1.500005, 0.816000, 357]
[YDLIDAR INFO]: angle-distance : [-1.000008, 0.834000, 358]
[YDLIDAR INFO]: angle-distance : [-0.500011, 0.000000, 359]
[YDLIDAR INFO]: angle-distance : [0.000000, 0.853000, 360]
```

The ROS graph looks like this:

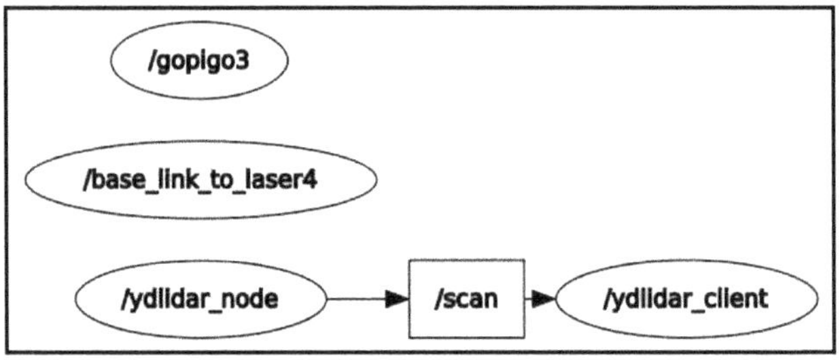

The `rqt_graph` command that throws the preceding graph can be executed either from the Raspberry Pi or a remote laptop. Since our goal is to offload the Raspberry Pi, you should run it from the laptop. In such cases, you won't need the desktop interface of the Raspberry Pi anymore.

The preceding graph shows that `ydlidar_node` publishes laser scan data in the `/scan` topic, which it is read by the `ydlidar_client` node and is printed in the Terminal where the node was launched from, that is, `r2`.

Visualizing scan data from the remote laptop

The final step is to get the RViz laser scan data on the desktop of the laptop. This is what we will accomplish in this section.

In the following paragraphs, the letter `r` in the code snippets stands for the Terminals in the robot, while `T` refers to the Terminals in the laptop.

Follow these steps to build the ROS environment:

1. First, launch the processes in the robot using the unified launch file that we built in the previous section:

```
r1 $ roslaunch ydlidar gopigo3_ydlidar.launch
```

2. From the laptop, find the content of the last message that was published in the `/scan` topic:

```
T1 $ rostopic echo /scan -n1
    header:
    seq: 2118
    stamp:
      secs: 1570384635
      nsecs: 691668000
      frame_id: "laser_frame"
    angle_min: -3.14159274101
    angle_max: 3.14159274101
    angle_increment: 0.00872664619237
    time_increment: 154166.671875
    scan_time: 111000000.0
    range_min: 0.10000000149
    range_max: 16.0
    ranges: [array of 720 items]
    intensities: [array of 720 items]
```

3. Ranges are provided in the `ranges` array field for 720 orientations, corresponding to an angle resolution of 0.5° for a 360° coverage. Then, find which message type it is:

```
$ rostopic info scan
Type: sensor_msgs/LaserScan
```

4. Finally, inspect the message structure:

```
T1 $ rosmsg info sensor_msgs/LaserScan
    std_msgs/Header header
    uint32 seq
    time stamp
    string frame_id
    float32 angle_min
    float32 angle_max
    float32 angle_increment
    float32 time_increment
    float32 scan_time
    float32 range_min
```

```
float32 range_max
float32[] ranges
float32[] intensities
```

5. Next, run the ROS visualization node in the laptop:

```
T1 $ roslaunch ydlidar display.launch
T2 $ rosrun key_teleop key_teleop.py /key_vel:=/cmd_vel
```

The `T1` Terminal will launch the visualization in RViz, while `T2` will let you teleoperate the robot to check how its perception of the environment changes as it moves by modifying the ranges of the laser scan. The visualization provided by `display.launch` adds the URDF model of YDLIDAR to RViz. The black circle in the following diagram represents the sensor:

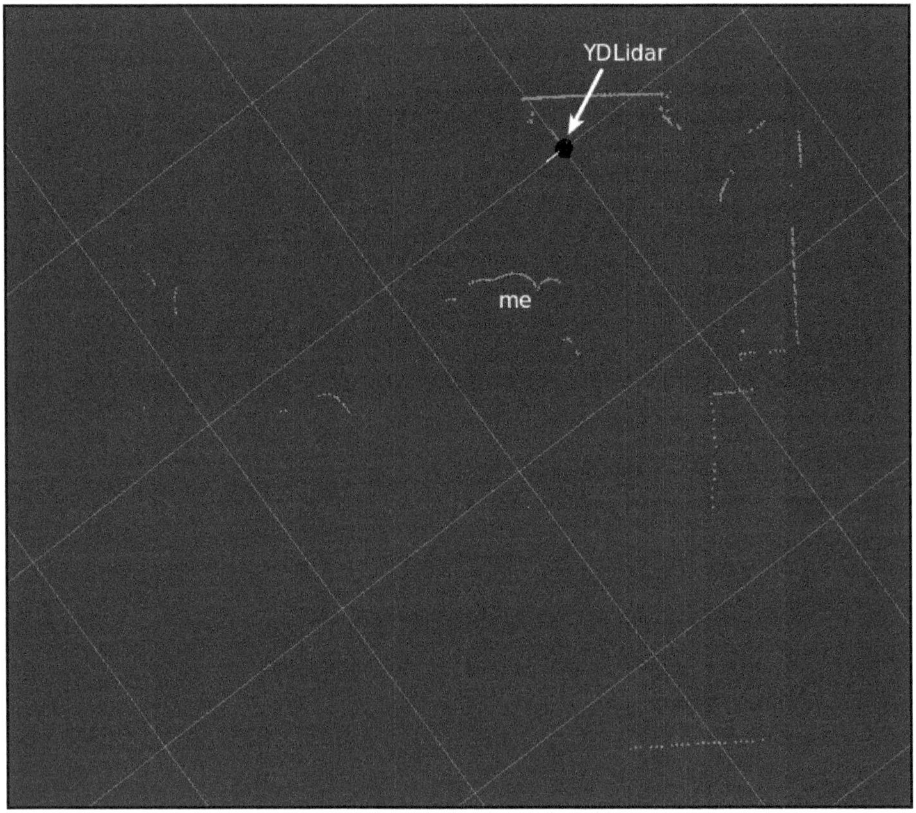

> Be aware that since the URDF model only includes the sensor, it doesn't move like the physical GoPiGo3 robot moves. The scan data – the red points – will change according to the robot's motion, but the virtual sensor will remain in the initial position, which is not its actual location anymore (unless you stop `T1` and launch it again). Hence, at this point, it is more coherent that you use `display_scan.launch` (which does not include a URDF model, just the scan data), instead of `display.launch`. In the *Practising navigation with GoPiGo3* section, you will link the URDF models of GoPiGo3 and the LDS sensor so that RViz shows the motion of the robot.

In the *Running the YDLIDAR ROS package* section, you will run a distributed system, where the Raspberry Pi collects sensor data and the remote laptop provides a visualization of it.

Processing YDLIDAR data from a remote laptop

Now, it's time to interpret the scan data. This can be accomplished with a simple snippet called `scan.py`, which is provided with the ROS package:

```
#! /usr/bin/env python
import rospy
from sensor_msgs.msg import LaserScan

def callback(msg):
 print "\nNumber of points =", len(msg.ranges)
 print "------------------"
 print "Range (m) at 0 deg = ", round(msg.ranges[360] , 1)
 print "Range (m) at 90 deg = ", round(msg.ranges[540] , 1)
 print "Range (m) at 180 deg = ", round(msg.ranges[719] , 1)
 print "Range (m) at -90 deg = ", round(msg.ranges[180] , 1), " or 270 deg"

rospy.init_node('scan_values')
sub = rospy.Subscriber('/scan', LaserScan, callback)
rospy.spin()
```

Type the following command into a Terminal on a laptop to see it in action:

```
T3 $ rosrun ydlidar scan.py
```

The preceding code lists the detected range along the main axes, *X* and *Y*, on the screen. Keep the following photograph in mind regarding the reference frame of the sensor, which was extracted from the X4 documentation. The angle is measured clockwise, taking the *X* axis as its origin. In the following photograph, you can see the LDS mounted on the GoPiGo3 and the *X* and *Y* axes directions drawn on top:

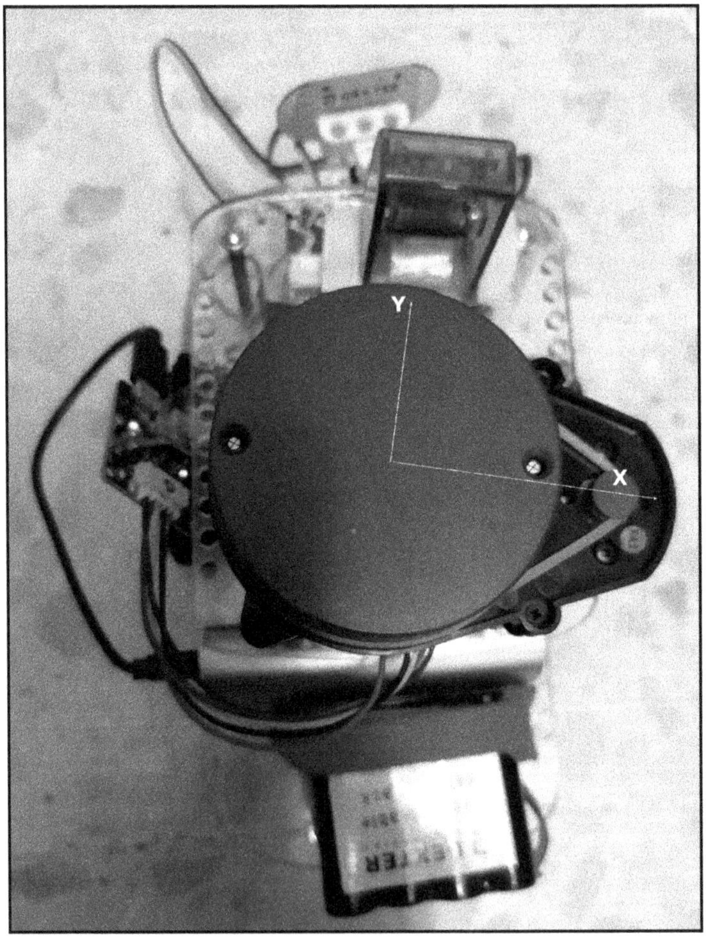

Going back to the screenshot in the *Visualizing data from the remote laptop* section, you can guess how the robot is oriented in the room. Take into account that the green axis corresponds to *X* and that the red lines corresponds to *Y*:

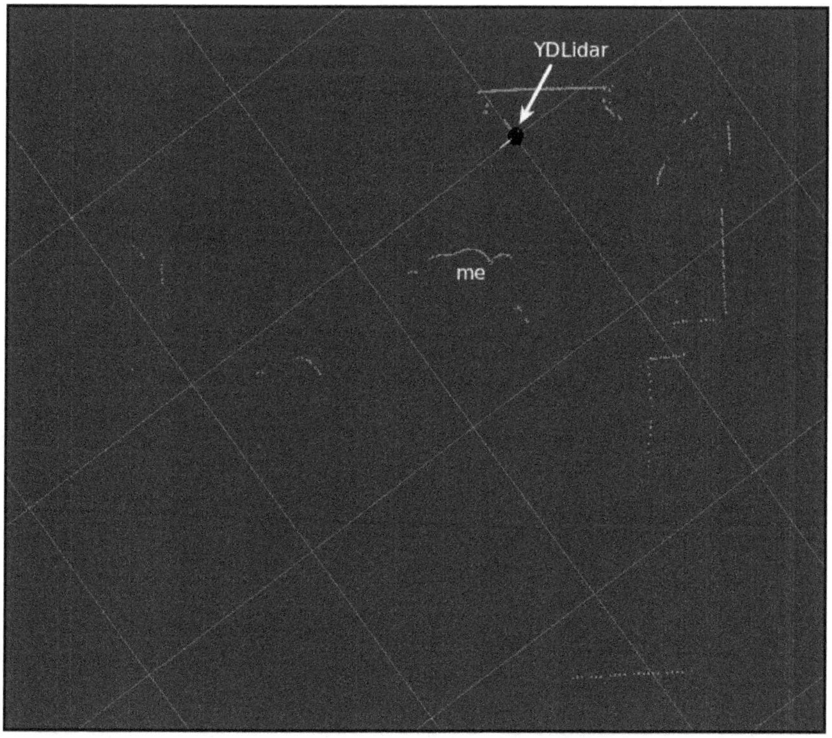

The callback function ranges along the main axes (+*X (0°)*, +*Y (-90°)*, -*X (180°)*, -*Y (90)°*), where you can detect obstacles for the right (+*X*), front (+*Y*), left (-*X*), or back (-*Y*), respectively.

Creating a navigation application in ROS

An application that provides a robot with navigation capabilities has to take into account the following points:

- **Sensing**: This provides us with the ability to acquire motion data so that the robot is able to estimate its position in real time. This kind of information is known as **robot odometry**. There are two main sources of sensor data: the encoders, which let us know the rotation of the robot wheels, and the IMU sensor, which provides acceleration and rotation information about the robot as a whole. Generally speaking, data from encoders is used the most, although it may be combined with IMU data to improve the accuracy of the pose estimation. This is an advanced topic called **fusion sensor**, which is out of the scope of this book.

- **Localization/pose estimation**: As a result of odometry and the current map of the environment, the **AMCL (Adaptive Monte Carlo localization)** algorithm allows us to update the robot pose estimation in real time, as we introduced in the previous chapter.
- **Path planning**: Given a target pose, such planning consists of creating a global optimum path of the whole map and a local path that covers a small area around the robot so that it is able to follow a precise path while avoiding obstacles. Local path planning is dynamic; that is, as the robot moves, the area around the robot changes accordingly.
- **Move/obstacle avoidance**: As we previously, there is a global optimum path that is combined with a local path, and this happens for every position of the robot as it moves to the target location. This is like making a zoom window of the surroundings. Hence, the local path is calculated by taking the global path and the close obstacles into account (for example, a person crossing in front of the robot). Local path planning is able to avoid such obstacles without losing the global path. This local zoom window is built using the real-time information provided by the LDS.

As a result of the aforementioned points, the following data has to be available to ROS so that navigation is possible:

- **Odometry**: It is published by the `gopigo3` node in the `/odom` topic.
- **Coordinate transformation**: The position of the sensors in the robot frame of reference is published in the `/tf` topic.
- **Scan data**: The distances from the robot to the obstacles around it are obtained from the LDS and made available in the `/scan` topic.
- **Map**: The occupancy grid that's built when executing SLAM is saved to a `map.pgm` file, with the configuration in the `map.yml` file.
- **Target pose**: This will be specified by the user in an RViz window once the ROS navigation's setup has been launched.
- **Velocity commands**: This is the final output of the algorithm. Commands are published in the `/cmd_vel` topic that the `gopigo3` node is subscribed to. Then, the robot moves accordingly to follow the planned path.

Given the preceding topics and concepts, the steps to create a navigation application in ROS are as follows:

1. Build a map of the environment. Taking the data from the LDS, the robot will create a map of the environment based on the range of data coming from the sensor. It will use the SLAM technique we discussed in the previous chapter to do so. This process of building the map follows a practical sequence:
    - Start ROS in the physical robot, meaning that the necessary nodes will be exposing the topics where sensor data is published, as well as the topic that will receive motion commands. The set of rules to publish the motion commands as a function of the acquired sensor data conforms to what we will call the **robot application logic**.
    - Establish the connection from the remote PC. If it's been configured properly, it should be automatic when launching ROS in the laptop. This topic was covered in the *Technical requirements* section at the beginning of this chapter.
    - Launch the SLAM process from the laptop. This will allow ROS to acquire real-time range data from the LDS so that it can start building a map of the environment.
    - Teleoperate the robot and check the zones that are mapped and the ones to be scanned in an RViz visualization. In this case, the robot application logic named in the first bullet is driven by you as a human, where you decide what motion GoPiGo3 has to perform at every instance. You may also automate teleoperation by letting the robot wander around randomly (remember the *Simulating the LDS* section of the previous chapter, where you let GoPiGo3 autonomously explore the environment while applying a set of rules to surround the obstacles it might encounter on its way). In this case, the robot application logic is implemented in a Python script and there is no human intervention.
2. Once the environment has been fully explored, you have to save the map so that it can be used in the next step for autonomous navigation.

3. Launch the navigation task by telling the robot the target location you want it to move to. This process of autonomous navigation follows the following sequence:
    - Start ROS in the physical robot. In this case, the robot application logic is part of the navigation task, which is intended to be performed autonomously by GoPiGo3, without any human intervention.
    - Load the map of the environment that was created in the first part of the navigation application.
    - Indicate a target pose to the robot, something you can directly perform on an RViz visualization, which shows the map of the environment.
    - Let the robot navigate by itself to the target location, checking that it is able to plan an optimum path while avoiding the obstacles it may encounter.

We will illustrate this process with a real-world example in the next section.

Practicing navigation with GoPiGo3

In this section, we'll cover the steps that we followed in the *Practising SLAM and navigation with GoPiGo3* section of the previous chapter by substituting the virtual robot and the Gazebo simulator with the actual GoPiGo3 and the physical environment, respectively.

Building a map of the environment

First, let's consider a physical environment that's simple enough for our learning purposes. This can be seen in the following photograph:

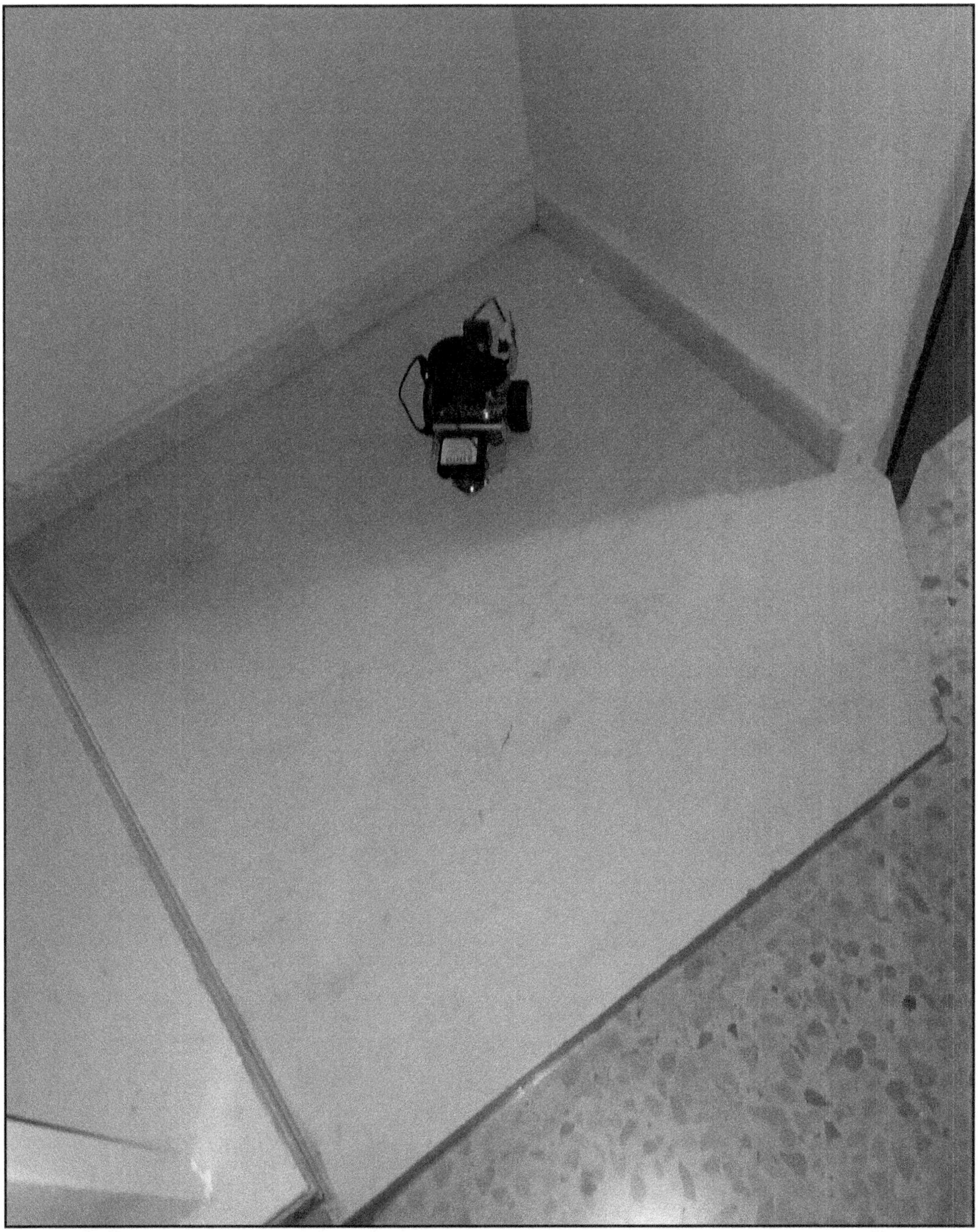

Be aware that this almost-square space has three limiting sides and one step that cannot be detected by the laser sensor because it is below the floor level of the robot.

Going to ROS, the first step consists of mapping the environment so that the robot can localize its surroundings and navigate around it. Follow these steps:

1. Launch all the ROS nodes in the robot. From a remote Terminal connected to the Raspberry Pi, this means running the ROS launch files that control the drives and the LDS:

   ```
   r1 $ roslaunch ydlidar gopigo3_ydlidar.launch
   ```

   Recall the *Integrating with Raspberry Pi* section: grouping launch files is how we built a unique launch file to run the robot configuration in one shot. This ensures that GoPiGo3 is ready to interact with ROS in the laptop, where all the processing related to the map of the environment and the navigation command will be done.

2. Launch the SLAM mapping ROS package, whose launch file includes a RViz visualization that overimposes the virtual model of the robot with the actual scan data:

   ```
   T1 $ roslaunch gopigo3_navigation gopigo3_slam.launch
   ```

3. Teleoperate the robot to make it cover as much of the surface of the virtual environment as possible. We can do this as follows:

   ```
   T3 $ rosrun key_teleop key_teleop.py /key_vel:=/cmd_vel
   ```

   As you explore the robot's surroundings, you should see something similar to the following in the RViz window:

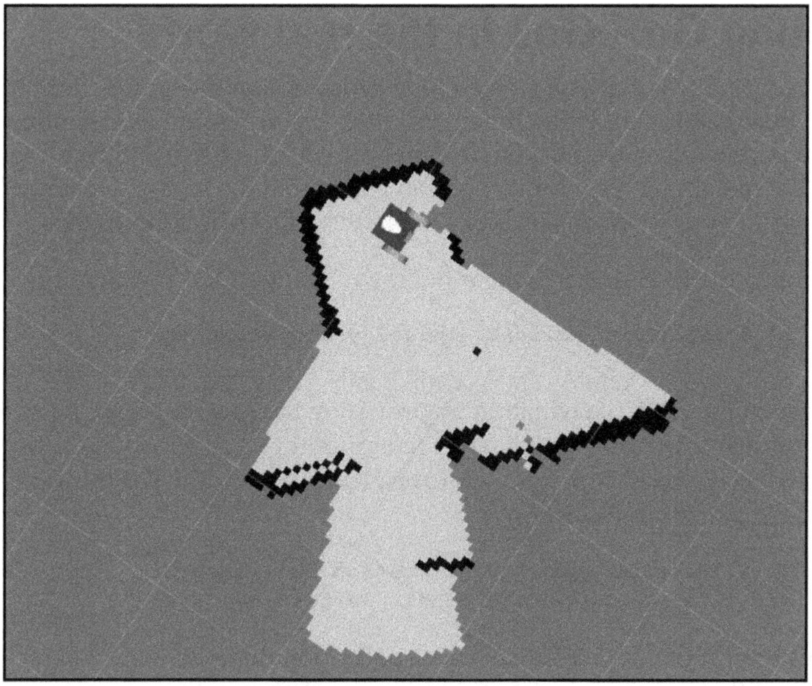

Here, you can see the three limiting walls of the square space. The rest of the map shows the first obstacles the laser finds in the remaining directions. Remember that the step in the fourth side cannot be detected because it is below the floor level of the robot.

4. Once you've finished exploring, save the map we generated into the two files we specified previously, that is, `.pgm` and `.yaml`:

```
T4 $ rosrun map_server map_saver -f ~/catkin_ws/test_map
```

Again, you will have the map files in the root folders of your workspace, that is, `test_map.pgm` and `test_map.yaml`. Now, we are ready to make GoPiGo3 navigate in the physical environment.

Navigating GoPiGo3 in the real world

This second part requires that you stop all ROS processes on the laptop, but not necessarily on GoPiGo3. Remember that, in the robot, you have the minimum ROS configuration so that the robot is able to perceive the environment (LDS X4 sensor) and move around (drives). All the remaining logic for navigation will run in the laptop. Hence, close any open Terminals in your PC and start the new phase by following these steps:

1. Launch the ROS nodes in the robot if you stopped the Terminal previously:

```
r1 $ roslaunch ydlidar gopigo3_ydlidar.launch
```

2. Launch the AMCL navigation by providing the cost map that the robot built previously. To do so, you have to reference the `.yaml` map file you created previously. Make sure that the corresponding `.pgm` file has the same name and is placed in the same location:

```
T1 $ roslaunch gopigo3_navigation amcl.launch
map_file:=/home/ubuntu/catkin_ws/test_map.yaml
```

This launch file includes an RViz visualization that will let us interact with the map so that we can set a target location, as shown in the following screenshot:

As in the case of the Gazebo simulation, the goal location is set by pressing the **2D Nav Goal** button at the top right of the RViz window and selecting the target pose, which is composed of both the position and orientation (a green arrow in RViz lets you define it graphically). As soon as you pick such a location, the AMCL algorithm starts path planning and sends motion commands via the `/cmd_vel` topic. Consequently, the robot moves to the specified location as the sequence of commands is executed.

Summary

In this chapter, you finally completed an autonomous task using GoPiGo3. This is only the entry point to the fascinating field of artificial intelligence applied to robotics. The most obvious functionality to be built on top of robot navigation is self-driving, which is the functionality that is currently being implemented by many vehicle manufacturers to make safer and more comfortable vehicles for the end users.

In the fourth and last part of this book, you will learn how machine learning techniques are applied nowadays to build smarter robots.

Questions

1. Which of these sensors is of the LDS type?

   A) LIDAR
   B) Ultrasonic distance sensor
   C) Capacitive sensors

2. Where does the ROS master node have to live to perform navigation?

   A) In the robot
   B) In the robot and the laptop
   C) In either the robot or the laptop

3. What will happen if an obstacle is placed in the environment after the map has been built?

   A) The robot will not detect it and may crash with it if it interferes with the planned path.
   B) The local path planning will be taken into account to provide a modified path that avoids the obstacle.
   C) You should rebuild the map with the new conditions before proceeding to the navigation task.

4. Can you perform navigation without previously running SLAM with the robot?

   A) No, because you have to build the map with the same robot that you will use for navigation.
   B) Yes, the only condition is that you provide a premade map of the environment.
   C) No, SLAM and navigation are two sides of the same coin.

5. What is the odometry of a robot?

   A) The total distance it has covered since the ROS application was started.
   B) The use of data from motion sensors to estimate the changes in the robot's pose over time.
   C) The use of data from motion sensors to estimate the current robot's pose.

Further reading

The main resource that you can read in order to deepen your knowledge of SLAM is the official documentation of the ROS Navigation Stack, which is located at `http://wiki.ros.org/navigation`. For those of you who are interested, here are some additional references:

- *ROS Navigation: Concepts and Tutorial, Federal University of Technology*, Longhi R., Schneider A., Fabro J., Becker T., and Amilgar V. (2018), Parana, Curitiba, Brazil.
- *Lidar design, use, and calibration concepts for correct environmental detection*, in IEEE Transactions on Robotics and Automation, M. D. Adams (2000) vol. 16, no. 6, pp. 753-761, Dec. 2000, doi: 10.1109/70.897786. URL: `http://ieeexplore.ieee.org/stamp/stamp.jsp?tp=arnumber=897786isnumber=19436`.
- *The LIDAR Odometry in the SLAM*, V. Kirnos, V. Antipov, A. Priorov, and V. Kokovkina, 23rd Conference of Open Innovations Association (FRUCT), Bologna, 2018, pp. 180-185. doi: 10.23919/FRUCT.2018.8588026, URL: `http://ieeexplore.ieee.org/stamp/stamp.jsp?tp=arnumber=8588026isnumber=8587913`.

4
Section 4: Adaptive Robot Behavior Using Machine Learning

This section is specifically devoted to artificial intelligence in robotics. Building on top of the robot navigation task we covered in the previous section, we will learn how to make that behavior adaptive so that the robot is capable of learning from the results of its actions in order to improve its performance, that is, so that it can achieve the desired goal faster.

This section comprises the following chapters:

- `Chapter 10`, *Applying Machine Learning in Robotics*
- `Chapter 11`, *Achieving a Goal through Reinforcement Learning*
- `Chapter 12`, *Machine Learning with OpenAI Gym*

10
Applying Machine Learning in Robotics

This chapter provides a hands-on introduction to **machine learning** (**ML**) in robotics. Although we assume that you have not yet worked in such a field, it will be helpful to have some background in statistics and data analytics. In any case, this chapter intends to be a gentle introduction to the topic, favoring intuition instead of complex mathematical formulations, and putting the focus on understanding the common concepts used in the field of ML.

Throughout this chapter, we will devote the discussion to such concepts by providing specific examples of robots. This is somewhat original because most references and books on ML give examples oriented to data science. Hence, as you become more familiar with robotics, it should be easier for you to understand the concepts this way.

With the explanations about deep learning, you will understand how crucial this technique is for the robot to acquire knowledge of its surroundings through the processing of raw data coming from the robot's camera (2D and/or 3D) and specific distance sensors. With the specific example of object recognition explained in this chapter, you will learn how raw image data is processed in order to build robot's knowledge in the robot, making it capable to take smart actions.

The following topics will be covered in this chapter:

- Setting up the system for TensorFlow
- How ML is being applied in Robotics
- The ML pipeline
- A methodology to programmatically apply ML in robotics
- Deep learning applied to robotics— computer vision

The concrete application we will do for GoPiGo3 deals with computer vision, the most common perception task in robotics. Equipped with this capability, the robot should be aware of the objects around itself, making it capable to interact with them. As a result of this chapter, we expect you to develop the basic insight of when and how to apply deep learning in robotics.

Technical requirements

For the examples in this chapter, we will use **TensorFlow** (`https://www.tensorflow.org/`), the ML framework open-sourced by Google in 2015, which has become the big brother in the data science community because of all of the people involved as active developers or end users.

The main TensorFlow API is developed in Python and is the one we are going to use. To install it, we need to have the well-known `pip` Python package manager in our system. Even though it comes bundled with the Ubuntu OS, we provide the instructions for installing it. Later, we will cover the TensorFlow installation process.

Let's first provide the path for the code of this chapter, and then describe the step-by-step procedure to configure your laptop with TensorFlow.

In this chapter, we will make use of the code located in the `Chapter10_Deep_Learning_` folder at `https://github.com/PacktPublishing/Hands-On-ROS-for-Robotics-Programming/tree/master/Chapter10_Deep_Learning_`.

Copy its files to the **ROS**(short for **Robot Operating System**) workspace to have them available and leave the rest outside the `src` folder:

```
$ cp -R ~/Hands-On-ROS-for-Robotics-Programming/Chapter10_Deep_Learning_
~/catkin_ws/src
```

This way, you will have a cleaner ROS environment. As usual, you need to rebuild the workspace on the laptop:

```
$ cd ~/catkin_ws
$ catkin_make
$ source ~/catkin_ws/devel/setup.bash
```

Then, let's start with the setup for TensorFlow.

Setting up the system for TensorFlow

First, we will set up `pip`, the Python package manager and afterward the framework for performing ML, that is, TensorFlow.

Installing pip

Ubuntu distributions typically ship with `pip` preinstalled. Unless a Python library requests you to upgrade, you can stay with the same version. In any case, we recommend working with the latest one, as explained in the following.

Installing the latest version

This section applies to the case in which you need to install `pip` or upgrade it:

1. First, remove the previous version if there is one:

```
$ sudo apt remove python-pip
```

   We do this because the Ubuntu repository may not have the latest version of `pip`. In the next step, you will access the original source to get all of the updates.

2. Download the installation script and execute it:

```
$ sudo apt update
$ curl "https://bootstrap.pypa.io/get-pip.py" -o "get-pip.py"
$ sudo python get-pip.py
```

3. Check which version is installed:

```
$ pip --version
    pip 19.3.1 from /usr/local/lib/python2.7/site-packages/pip
(python 2.7)
```

   If it was already present in your system, you can easily upgrade using `pip` itself:

```
$ sudo pip install --upgrade pip
```

Now, you are ready to proceed with the installation of the ML environment.

Installing TensorFlow and other dependencies

OpenCV, the well-known and open source computer vision library (https://opencv.org/), brings to ROS the capability of image processing. It is used by TensorFlow to deal with images that you will obtain from the robot camera. To install it in your system, you need the pip package manager that we explained earlier:

```
$ pip install opencv-python --user
```

The --user flag ensures that the package is installed locally to the user home folder at ~/.local/lib/python2.7/site-packages. Otherwise, it should be installed system-wide at the /usr/local/lib/python2.7/dist-packages path, as is the case of pip (in such cases, you should perform the installation with sudo).

The OpenCV ROS bridge (http://wiki.ros.org/cv_bridge) ships with the full-stack installation of ROS. If, for some reason, the package is missing in your environment, you can easily install it with this line:

```
$ sudo apt update && sudo apt install ros-<ROS_VERSION>-cv-bridge
```

For the <ROS_VERSION> tag, use the kinetic value or melodic depending on the ROS distribution you have.

Finally, install TensorFlow as follows:

```
$ pip install --upgrade tensorflow --user
```

The --upgrade flag gives you the advantage to update the package if it is already installed. If you are working in Ubuntu 16.04, TensorFlow V2 will throw compatibility issues. In such a case, install TensorFlow V1 as follows:

```
$ pip install --upgrade tensorflow==1.14 --user
```

In Ubuntu 18.04, you will be ready with the upgraded version of TensorFlow.

Achieving better performance using the GPU

Alternatively, you could use the GPU version of TensorFlow to take advantage of this hardware on your laptop. The **GPU** (short for **Graphical Processing Unit**) card of your laptop is primarily used to power the display output on the screen. Therefore, it is very good at image processing.

As the kinds of calculations we need to do in ML are very similar (that is, floating-point, vector, and matrix operations), you can speed up the training and usage of your ML models by using the GPU for calculations instead of the CPU.

By using the GPU, you may achieve at least a factor of 10 in speed calculation for using the CPU, even in the case of the cheapest GPU cards. Hence, the choice of GPU is worth it. The command to install the corresponding TensorFlow library in Ubuntu 18.04 is pretty simple:

```
$ pip install --upgrade tensorflow-gpu --user
```

As before, if you are working in Ubuntu 16.04, install TensorFlow V1 to avoid compatibility issues:

```
$ pip install --upgrade tensorflow-gpu==1.14 --user
```

With TensorFlow installed, being the normal version or the GPU-performant one, you are ready to use ML within ROS.

ML comes to robotics

ML has its roots in statistical science. Remember when you have a cloud of points on an x-y frame and try to find the straight line that best fits all of them at the same time? This is what we call a linear regression and can be solved with a simple analytical formula. **Regression** is the first algorithm that you typically study when getting started with ML.

To acquire perspective, be aware that, before 1980, artificial intelligence and ML were part of the same corpora of knowledge. Then, artificial intelligence researchers focused their efforts on using logical, knowledge-based approaches, and ML kept the algorithmic approach, *regression* being the most basic and having neural network-based algorithms as its main bundle. Hence, this fact favored that ML evolved as a separated discipline.

Following path of the traditional research in neural networks in the '60s and '70s, ML kept on developing in this field. Then, its first golden age came in the '90s.

However, 25 years ago, the computer resources that a neural network required were not within the reach of normal PCs, since a huge amount of data needed to be processed to obtain accurate results. It was more than one decade later that computing capacity was available to everyone, and then problem-solving based on neural network algorithms finally became a commodity.

This fact brings us to the present boom of ML, where functionalities such as content recommendation (shops, films, and music) and facial/ object recognition (camera-based apps) are used ubiquitously in most modern smartphones.

On the other side, robots started their path in the industry by 1950, being at the beginning just mechanical devices that performed repetitive motions. As artificial intelligence and its accompanying discipline, ML, developed in parallel, practical results in these fields could be transferred, since robots were also powered by similar CPUs to those with which ML problems were solved. Then, robots gradually acquired the capability to better accomplish actions by being aware of their effects in the environment. Data came from the robot's camera and sensors provides feedback to the *learning system* that allowed it to perform better every time. This learning system is just an ML pipeline.

And how different is robot learning from human learning? Well, our brain is far more efficient. To recognize for the first time whether an animal is a dog, a kid just needs four or five samples, while an ML algorithm needs hundreds to be accurate in its answers. This is the underlying reason why ML models used by robots need to be pretrained with lots of data so that the robot can respond—both **accurately** and in **real time**—with a smart action, that is, by picking an object from one location and moving it to another previously marked as the target (a typical problem in the logistics industry).

This task of identifying objects is what we will do in the practical example of this chapter. We will supply the robot with a trained model able to recognize different kinds of common objects (balls, mouses, keyboards, and so on) and will observe the response when putting it in front of several of these objects. Hence, let's keep on explaining the following concepts surrounding this practical example regarding the recognition of several kinds of objects.

Core concepts in ML

Before going into the use case of object recognition in images, let's take a much simpler example, the prediction of the price of a house as a function of several independent variables: area, number of rooms, distance to the center of the city, population density, and more.

First, to have a working ML algorithm, we need an underlying model that, when fed with input data, can produce a prediction. The data has to be supplied according to the features, that is, independent variables, that we have selected for our model. Then, establishing the correspondence with our simple example, we can explain the several concepts involved in an ML problem:

- The algorithm is the computation as a whole, specified as a sequence of instructions or steps that are to be followed to produce a result. All of the instructions have to be unambiguous and the actor that is running the algorithm does not have to make any additional decision; all of them are covered by the algorithm, which specifies what to do at a certain point if a condition needs to be evaluated. Then, you can easily infer that an algorithm is something that can be programmed in a computer, no matter which language is used. In the case of the example of the prediction of the price of a house, the algorithm consists of applying the sequence of instructions given sample data—that is, area, number of rooms, and so on—to obtain a prediction of its price.
- The model provides an assumption of the analytical function to apply to the input data to obtain a prediction. For example, we can say that the model for the price of the house is a linear function of the inputs, that is, given an increment in the percentage of the area of the house leads to the same percentual increment in its predicted price. For the rest of the independent variables, the same reasoning would apply because we have assumed a linear dependence. The model is applied in some steps of the algorithm.
- The features are the independent variables of our model, that is to say, the available data that you have to predict the price of a house. In our example, these are area, number of rooms, distance to the center of the city, and population density.
- The dataset is a structured data collection providing values for each of the selected features for a large number of items. In our example, the dataset should be a table in which each row contains the available data of a concrete house, and each column contains the values of each selected feature, that is, a surface column, number of rooms column, distance to the center of the city column, population density column, and so on.

When facing a new problem, the data scientist has to decide for all of these three elements: the algorithm, the model, and the features. The last topic, feature selection, is where there's the added value that a human provides to solving an ML problem; the rest of the tasks are automated and accomplished by a computer. The next subsection explains in detail what features are and emphasizes the importance of their selection to obtain accurate predictions.

Selecting features in ML

Features in ML constitute a set of characteristics that have to be selected by the user, and it is this selection upon which the dataset is built. The expertise for making a good feature selection is more a question of experience and insight than a structured process. Hence, a good data scientist is one who understands the problem and can decompose it in its essential parts to find what the relevant features are. These act as the independent variables from which accurate predictions can be made.

To solve an ML problem, it is crucial to perform the right feature selection. If you do not detect the relevant features, no matter how much data you put in the solver, you will never get a good prediction. As shown in the following diagram, we will feed the ML algorithm with a data collection to obtain a result, that is, a prediction:

Data collection has been built according to the selected features. For example, if you decide to build the model for price prediction of the houses in a given city based on three features—area, number of rooms, and distance to the center of the city—for every new house you want to predict the price of, you will have to feed the algorithm with the specific values of such features, for example, 85 square meters, 4 rooms, and 1.5 kilometers to the center of the city.

Next, it is crucial to understand how the values of these features are combined to obtain the prediction.

The ML pipeline

Problem-solving is split into two parts. The first is training the model according to the pipeline shown in this diagram:

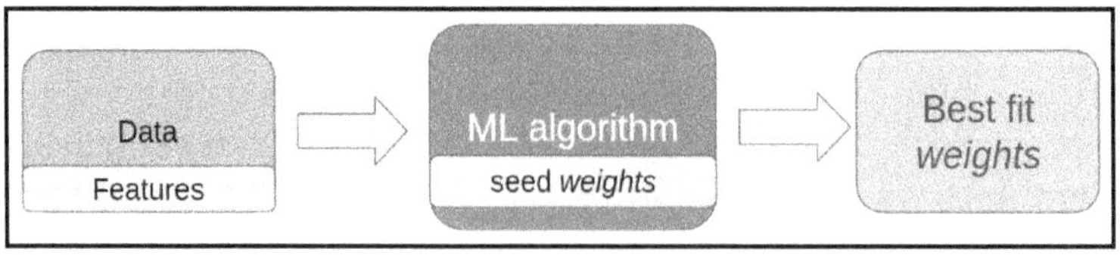

Since we are assuming a simple model where the output depends linearly on the values of the features, the goal of training consists of determining the weights to be applied to each of them to obtain the prediction. Let's explain it with this mathematical formulation:

$$Price = W1 * area + W2 * n^{\underline{o}}\ rooms + W3 * distance$$

As you may infer, the weights, *W1*, *W2*, and *W3*, are the coefficients that multiply each feature. After making the sum of the three products, we obtain the predicted price. So, the training phase consists of finding the set of weights that best fit the dataset we have available. In the training set, the data contains both the features and the actual prices. Hence, by applying the algorithm of least square regression (`https://www.statisticshowto.datasciencecentral.com/least-squares-regression-line/`), we determine the set of values for *W1*, *W2*, and *W3* that best fit all of the actual prices supplied. This algorithm guarantees that the resulting equation is the one that provides the minimum global error for all of the items used for the training.

But we do not want to best fit only the supplied data since we already know these prices. We wish that the resulting equation also be the best fit for any other house for which we do not know the price. So, the way to validate such an equation is by using a different dataset, called the test set, from the one we used for training. The programmatic way to do this is by splitting the available data before performing the training. The typical approach is to make two random sets: one containing 70%-90% of the data for training and another with the remaining 30-10% to perform the validation. This way, the training set provides us with the provisional best-fit weights, *W1*, *W2*, and *W3*, and the validation set is used to estimate how well our ML model is operationally defined as the least square error.

The second part corresponds to the prediction itself, that is, when our ML algorithm is put in production in a real application. In the prediction (production) phase, we have the following:

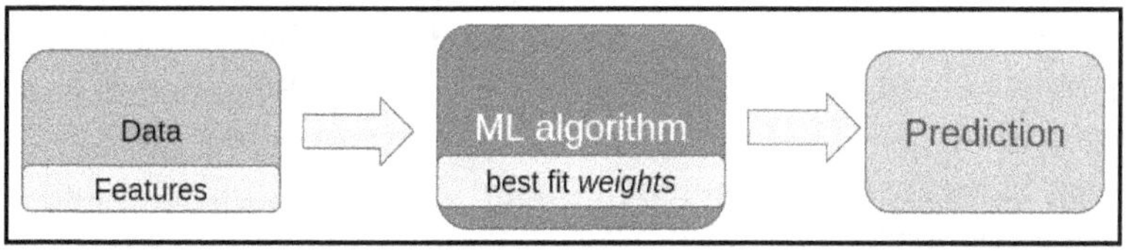

The process of ML, in reality, is more a circular one than a linear one because, as we get more data for training, we can improve the calculation of the weights, and then rewrite the equation with the new set of coefficients, *W1*, *W2*, and *W3*. This way, ML is an iterative process that can improve the accuracy of predictions as more data is available and the model is retrained again and again.

From ML to deep learning

In this section, you will understand what deep learning is and how it relates to ML. And the most straightforward way to get this insight is by giving a quick overview of the most commonly used algorithms. Then, from that perspective, you could appreciate why deep learning is the most active area of research nowadays.

ML algorithms

As pointed out in the preceding diagram and explanations, the algorithm is the central part of ML problem-solving. A data scientist has also to select which one to apply depending on the kind of problem they are facing. So, let's have a quick overview of the most commonly used algorithms.

Regression

Regression tries to find the curve that best fits a cloud of points, and it has been described in detail with the case of the prediction of house prices. In such a case, we have been talking about a linear dependency, but the algorithm can be generalized to any kind of curve that can be represented as a sum of dot products between coefficients (weights) and independent variables (features), that is, a polynomial. A common case is that of a term that is the square of a feature. In this case, the curve is a parabola and, mathematically, can be expressed as follows:

$$y = W1 * x + W2 * x^2 + W3 * 1$$

Let's review this with a real-life example. Given an independent variable, the years of experience of a candidate, we wish to predict what their salary will be when applying for a job opportunity. You can easily understand that the dependence of the salary, at least during the first years of experience, does not follow a linear dependence, that is, a candidate with 2 years will not get twice the salary with respect to when he/she had one year of experience. Percentual increments in salary will be gradually higher as he/she accumulates more experience. This kind of relationship can be modeled as a parabola. Then, from the independent variable, x, and the salary, we define two features: x and x^2.

Logistic regression

Logistic regression is used in classification problems, a very common type in ML. In this case, we try to predict a binary classification such as pass/fail, win/lose, alive/dead, or healthy/sick. This algorithm can be understood as a special case of regression, where the predicted variable is categorical, that is, it can only take a finite set of values (two if it is a binary classification). The underlying model is a probability function and, given a value of the independent variable, if the resulting probability is greater than 50%, we predict pass, win, alive, or healthy, and if lower, the prediction is the other category, that is, fail, lose, dead, or sick.

Product recommendation

Product recommendation is the most used functionality in the consumer sector, for example, shopping, watching films, and readings books, taking as input user characteristics and well-rated items by other users with similar characteristics. There are several algorithms to implement this functionality such as collaborative filtering or featurized matrix factorization. If you are interested in this field, we provide good introduction references in the *Further reading* section at the end of this chapter.

Clustering

Clustering is a scenario where we have many items and we want to group them by similarity. In this case, items are unlabeled and we ask the algorithm to do two things:

- Make a group of similar items.
- Label these groups so that new items are both classified and labeled by the algorithm.

As an example, think of a collection of texts about many topics and you wish the algorithm to group similar texts and identify the main topic of each group, that is, label them: history, science, literature, philosophy, and so on. One of the classical algorithms for this scenario is the nearest neighbor method, where you define a metric, calculate it for each pair of items, and group together those pairs that are close enough (based on the defined metric). It can be though as a distance-like function that is computed between each set of two points.

A **multiclassification scenario**, where there are more than two categories—let's say n—is addressed by solving n logistic regressions where each one performs a binary classification for each of the possible categories. For example, if we want to detect the dominant color in an image (of four possible categories: red, green, blue, or yellow), we can build a classifier consisting of four logistic regressions, as follows:

- Red/NOT red
- Green/NOT green
- Blue/NOT blue
- Yellow/NOT yellow

There could be a fifth category, which we can call *unknown*, for cases in which the image is not classified in any of the red, green, blue, or yellow colors. Finally, this type of multi-logistic regression applied to images is the entrance door to the last algorithm, deep learning, on which we will focus from now until the end of this chapter.

Deep learning

Deep learning is the most active research field in ML nowadays. The underlying model of this algorithm is a neural network whose way of working tries to mimic what the human brain does. Each neuron in the model performs a regression from its input with a special function, called **sigmoid**, that provides a sharp but continuous probability distribution of the output event. This function is the same as that of the probability function used in **logistic regression,** as described earlier. In this particular case of a neuron, if the resulting probability is greater than 50%, the neuron is activated and feeds another neuron or neurons downstream. If lower than 50%, the neuron is not active and hence it has negligible influence downstream.

Next, we are going to provide more details about how deep learning works so that when you perform the practical exercise with GoPiGo3, you know what it is going on under the hood in ROS.

Deep learning and neural networks

From now on, we will base our explanations on the practical example of the recognition of objects in images, which, in the case of the robot, will be supplied by the Raspberry Pi camera. In the following diagram, you can see a representation of a neural network that differentiates the three kinds of layers that there can be:

- The input layer is where we feed the dataset. Remember that such data has to be structured according to the selected features, that is, one neuron per feature. We will later discuss this particular and very common case of image datasets.
- The hidden layer(s)—one or more—are the intermediate steps in the deep learning pipeline that extract more features so that the algorithm is more capable of discriminating between objects. These hidden features are implicit, and the end user does not necessarily need to know about them because their extraction is intrinsic (automatic) to the network structure itself.
- The output layer provides the prediction. Each neuron provides a logical 1 if activated (a probability greater than 50%) or a 0 if not activated (lower than 50%). So, the resulting probability in the output layer will be the answer with a certain probability:

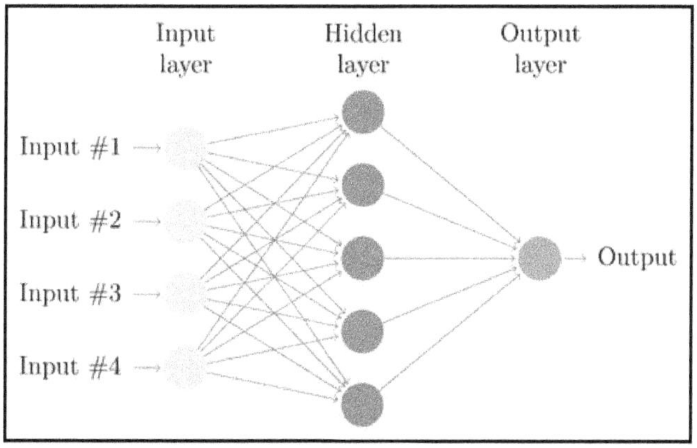

License CC-BY-SA-2.5 source: https://commons.wikimedia.org/wiki/File:Neural_Network.gif

Following a sequential approach, let's explain how a neural network works by covering what each layer makes on the supplied input data.

The input layer

This is the first step of the deep learning pipeline, and the most common structure of this layer is to have as many input neurons (features) as three times the number of pixels the image has:

- For images of a size of 256 x 256 pixels, this means 65.536 pixels.
- In general, we will deal with color images, so each pixel will have three channels: red, blue, and green; each value stands for the intensity ranging from 0 to 255 for 8 bits of color depth.
- Then, the number of features is *65.536 x 3 = 196.608* and the value of each feature will be a number between 0 and 255. Each feature is represented with one neuron in the input layer.

Afterwards, the neural network is asked to answer this question: is there a cat in the picture? And the goal of the next layers is to extract the essential aspects of the image to answer that question.

The hidden layer(s)

For understanding how this layer works, let's go back to the regression algorithm we explain earlier. There, we expressed the predicted variable as a linear combination of features—area, number of rooms, and distance to the center multiplied by weights, respectively, *W1*, *W2*, and *W3*. Establishing the analogy with our neural network, the features would apply to the neurons and the weights to the edges that connect each pair of neurons:

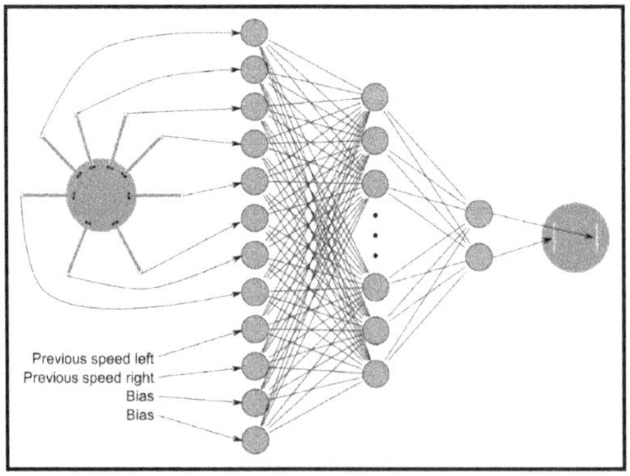

Source: https://commons.wikimedia.org/wiki/File:Artificial_neural_network_pso.png. Cyberbotics Ltd. CC BY-SA 3.0 https://creativecommons.org/licenses/by-sa/3.0

The value of each feature would be processed with the sigmoid function of its neuron (input layer; *j* neurons) to produce a probability value, *Sij*, which is then multiplied by the weight, *Wij*, of the edge that connects it to each neuron downstream (hidden layer ; *i* neurons). Hence, the feature input to this neuron, *i*, in the hidden layer is a sum of products, there being as many terms as neurons are connected to it upstream (input layer ; *j* neurons).

Such a result is the sum over *j* of all of the terms, *Sij*, with the index, *j*, which is an iterator that ranges over all of the neurons connected to *i* neurons in the input layer. The weights *Wij* of the edges connecting pairs of neurons are more properly called **hyperparameters**.

The neural structure of the hidden layers provides what we call intrinsic features, which are inherent properties of the network and do not have to be selected by the user (they are established by the designer of the neural network). What the user has to do is to train the network to obtain the best set of weights, *Wij*, that makes the network to as predictive as possible with the available dataset. Here is where the magic of deep learning resides because a well-designed architecture of layers can provide a very accurate predictive model. The downside is that you need a lot of data to get a well-trained network.

Recapping from the beginning, given an input image, you can calculate the feature input to the neurons of each layer, *Fi*, based on the probabilities from the previous layer, *Sij*, and the weights, *Wij*, of the edges connecting to neuron *i*:

$$Fi = (sum\ over\ j)\ [Sij * Wij]$$

Proceeding downstream layer by layer, you can finally obtain the probabilities of the neurons of the output layer and, therefore, answer with the prediction of what the analyzed image contains.

As was mentioned earlier, and given that complexity of the network structure, you may guess that, for training such a model, you would need much more data than for traditional ML algorithms such as regression. More specially, what you have to calculate are the values of how many hyperparameters as edges connecting pairs of neurons there are. Once you achieve this milestone, you get a trained network that can be applied to unlabeled images to predict its content.

The output layer

For the question of our example, that is, there is a cat in the picture? yes if the image shows a cat, or not if it doesn't. So we only need a neuron in the output layer, as shown in the diagram below. Then, if trained with many photos of cats, this network could classify an image to say whether it contains a cat (1) or not (0). An important point here is that the model should be able to identify the cat whatever position it occupies in the image, center, left, right, top, down, and so on:

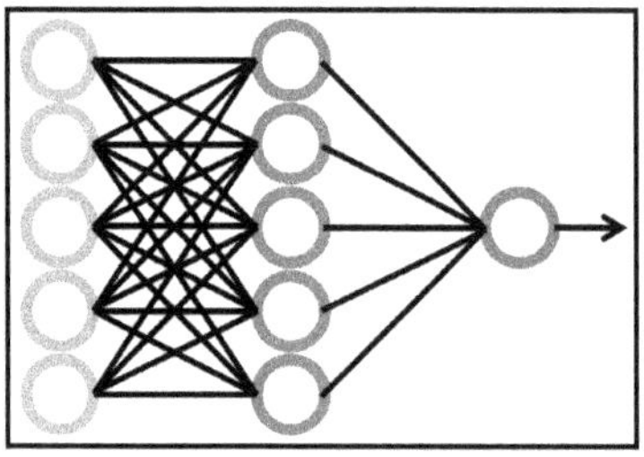

Source: https://commons.wikimedia.org/wiki/File:NeuralNetwork.png

If we need to classify 10 kinds of objects (several types of pets, for example), we would need an output layer with 10 neurons. The result of the computation of the network would be a vector with 10 probabilities—each one linked to each neuron, and the one that provides the largest value (the closest to 100%) would tell us what kind of pet there is in the input image with more probability.

Of course, you can make the network more complex and add more output neurons (and possibly more hidden layers) to obtain more details of the images. Consider the following:

- Identify whether there is one cat or two or more.
- Identify characteristics of the face, such as whether the eyes and/or mouth are open or closed:

Source: https://www.flickr.com/photos/55855622@N06/5173363938 by jeici1. License: CC BY 2.0

This is a quite complex topic and beyond of the scope of this introductory chapter, whose goal is just to provide a descriptive understanding of what deep learning is and how it works. Anyway, the reader is encouraged to delve deeper into the topic, and for that, two didactic references are included in the *Further reading* section at the end of this chapter: *Intuitive Deep Learning Parts 1 and 2*.

From this point, we move to the practical part and start by stating a general methodology to tackle ML problems in robotics.

A methodology to programmatically apply ML in robotics

A specific aspect of ML is that robot responses have to happen in real time, without delays, so that the actions taken are effective. For example, if it finds an obstacle crossing the path it is following, we expect that it avoids it. To do so, obstacle identification has to occur as it appears in the robot's field of view. Hence, the subsequent action of avoiding the obstacle has to be taken immediately to avoid a crash.

We will support our methodology description with an end-to-end example that covers all that GoPiGo3 can do up to this point. Then, with this example, we expect that GoPiGo3 can carry a load on top of its chassis from its current location to a target location (a common case in garbage collector robots).

A general approach to application programming

The steps involved in solving this challenge are as follows:

1. Determine what high-level tasks are involved.
2. List the atomic tasks that, put together, are capable of accomplishing the high-level tasks. This is the level at which we create our program in ROS, writing node scripts and launch files.
3. Program the robot application by adapting the algorithms of the high-level tasks to the specific situation we are trying to solve.

Next, we provide a breakdown of each of these steps so that we can implement the functionality in the real robot:

1. These are the high-level tasks to be carried out:
    - **SLAM**: This is **Simultaneous Localization and Mapping** (**SLAM**) to build a map of the actual environment.
    - **Navigation**: Setting a target pose, GoPiGo3 can move autonomously until achieving it.
    - **Visual recognition**: GoPiGo3 can identify where it has to be placed so that the garbage it carries can be collected.
2. List the atomic tasks that are involved in the example. Let's say that, to be successful, GoPiGo3 has to be able to do the following:
    1. Load a map of the environment.
    2. Calculate an optimum path to achieve the target location given the information from the map.
    3. Start navigating toward the goal.
    4. Avoid obstacles found along the path.
    5. Stop if unexpected conditions are found in the environment that do not let it advance anymore. Then, ask for help.
    6. After receiving help, resume the path to the target location.
    7. Recognize the garbage store entrance and stop at the exact position where a hoist will hook the loaded garbage.
3. Program the robot application. Each of the preceding atomic tasks will correspond to a ROS node script, which can be expressed as a launch file with just one `<node>` tag. Then, you have to put these seven nodes on a ROS graph and draw the edges that should connect pairs using topics:
    - For each published topic, you should determine which frequency the topic should be published with so that the robot can react quickly enough. For example, since the typical speed of GoPiGo3 is 1 m/s, we wish the scan distance to be updated 10 times every 1 m traveled. This means that the robot will receive a perception update every 10 cm(=0.1 m) traveled and will be able to detect the presence of obstacles outside of a circumference of 0.1 m radius. The minimum publishing rate so that the robot can react to avoid the obstacle is calculated with this simple formula: *(1 m/s) /0.1 m = 10 Hz*.

- For each topic a node is subscribed to the code should trigger a robot action that allows it to successfully adapt to such conditions in the environment. For example, given the topic providing distances around GoPiGo3, when its value is below a threshold, 20 cm, for example (you will see now where this number comes from), GoPiGo3 recalculates the local path to avoid the obstacle. We should select this threshold according to the 10 Hz rate of publishing we decided previously; remember that this rate came from the fact that the robot will receive a perception update every 10 cm traveling. Taking a safety factor of 2, the threshold is simply *10 cm * 2 = 20 cm*, providing room and time so that it avoids the obstacle.

There's no need for ML currently now for atomic tasks 1 through 6. But when it comes to aligning with the garbage stop entrance, GoPiGo3 needs to know not only its pose but also its relative position to the entrance, so that the hoist can successfully hook the loaded garbage.

Integrating an ML task

This node of step 7 formulates its functionality as *recognize the garbage store entrance and stop at the exact position where a hoist will hook the loaded garbage*. Hence, the Pi camera comes to the rescue and image recognition capability has to be included in the logic programming of this node. This logic can be briefly expressed as publishing the `cmd_vel` messages to robot differential drives that allow GoPiGo3 to be put right in place. So, it is a feedback mechanism between visual perception, that is, entrance shape alignment in the image or not, and a motion command to correct and center:

- If the entrance is shifted to the left in the image, the robot should rotate left.
- And if deviated to the right, it should rotate right an angle proportional to the distance from the entrance to the center of the image.

And your very first question should be: how can we integrate such an ML task with our robotic application? And the answer comes to enlighten how the ROS publish/subscribe mechanism is both powerful and simple at the same time. Its neutral nature allows us to integrate any kind of task that can be packaged into a black box by adhering to the following two rules:

- Input is supplied via a subscribed topic.
- Output is delivered using a published topic.

In the concrete case of ML applied to center the robot in the entrance door, we have the following:

- Input to the ML node (subscribed topic) is the image feed from the Pi camera.
- Output from the ML node (published topic) is the horizontal distance from the shape of the door to the center of the image.

Then, the GoPiGo3 drive node takes that output topic as the data to determine which `cmd_vel` command should be sent to the motors. This establishes a feedback loop with the ML node that makes it possible that the robot position converges to get finally centered in the entrance door:

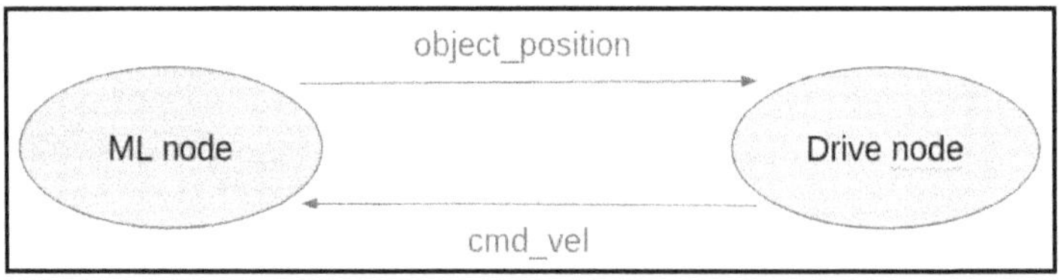

The ML published topic, `object_position`, is an integer that provides the distance in pixels from the centroid of the object (entrance door) to the center of the image frame.

Although it is out of the scope of this chapter, it is good to know at this point that ROS provides other interaction mechanisms between nodes, and the programmer's choice about which one to use depends on the specific functionality to be implemented:

- A ROS service is the classical implementation of the server/client architecture. The client node (*drive node*) makes a request to the server node (*ML node*) and this performs the calculation (the distance in pixels from the entrance door to the center of the image frame). Then, the response is sent back to the client. The key difference with the publish/ subscribe mechanism is that this is not expecting to receive requests; it publishes messages at the rate set within the code of the node, independently, whether other nodes are listening or not.
- A ROS action is similar to a ROS service, that is, it provides a response to a request from a node, with the difference that, in this case, the client node does not block the execution (until it receives the answer). That is to say, it keeps executing other code instructions and, when it receives the response, the client triggers the programmed action (rotates the robot for alignment). This behavior is called asynchronous, unlike a ROS service, which is synchronous in nature, that is, it blocks the node execution until the response is received.

So, let's dive into how to make GoPiGo3 aware of the objects it has around, and we will do this in the final section of this chapter where we will build a general ML node that is able to detect a wide range of object types.

Deep learning applied to robotics – computer vision

The practical part of this chapter consists of operationally implementing the ML node described earlier. What we represented there as a black box is developed now as a ROS package that you may integrate with the functionalities you discovered in previous chapters:

- The remote control in `Chapter 7`, *Robot Control and Simulation,* for both the virtual robot in Gazebo and the physical GoPiGo3
- Robot navigation for a virtual robot in `Chapter 8`, *Virtual SLAM and Navigation Using Gazebo,* and the physical GoPiGo3 in `Chapter 9`, *SLAM for Robot Navigation*

So, we divide this section into two parts:

- The first section, *Object recognition in Gazebo,* provides you with the tools to integrate the ML node for image recognition in Gazebo so that, after finishing the practice, you may let your creativity fly to combine object recognition with any of the drive nodes from **remote control** or **robot navigation** and make the virtual robot smarter.
- The second section, *Object recognition in the real world,* provides the same integration with the physical GoPiGo3 and you will discover the ML node black box is the same no matter where the images come from, that is, objects in Gazebo or the real world. The choice is made by you when linking the ML node subscription to images of any of those scenarios.

This procedure also gives an operational way to test a new robot application. Start with the validation in Gazebo, where you will mainly check that the developed code has no significant bugs and the robot works as expected; then, proceed with it to the real world—understand how all of the external variables that are not present in Gazebo act on the robot, see how it responds, and then decide which code refinements you need to make to get it to work.

Object recognition in Gazebo

To get the code, follow the instructions we provided at the beginning of this chapter under the section, *Technical requirements*. The exercise in Gazebo is going to be pretty simple and very effective at the same time. You will check how the virtual GoPiGo3 can recognize a common *tennis ball* from the image feed coming from the robot's camera:

1. Let's start by spawning a model of the ball in Gazebo:

```
T1 $ roslaunch tf_gopigo gopigo3_world.launch
```

2. Then, launch a `rqt_image_view` node to watch the subjective view as perceived from the robot's camera:

```
T2 $ rosrun rqt_image_view rqt_image_view
```

   Click on the top-left empty box, and select ;`/gopigo/camera1/image_raw` topic. Then, you will see the subjective view of the robot as acquired by its front camera.

3. Next, spawn a model of the ball in Gazebo:

```
T3 $ sudo -s
   $ roslaunch models_spawn_library spawn_tennisball.launch
```

   Bear in mind that the `models_spawn_library` package requires you to execute the launch file as superuser. As soon as the ball is spawned in Gazebo, the process finishes and `T3` is released.

4. Then, launch the remote control node so that you can control GoPiGo with the keyboard as usual:

```
T4 $ rosrun key_teleop key_teleop.py /key_vel:=/cmd_vel
```

> This package was installed in `Chapter 7`, *Robot Control and Simulation*. If you did not install it, do so now. The source of this ROS package is at `https://github.com/ros-teleop/teleop_tools`.

5. Finally, launch the image recognition node and watch the screen output. Use `T3` where you already have `sudo` enabled:

```
T3 $ sudo -s
   $ roslaunch tf_gopigo start_image_recognition.launch
```

   You can get a more condensed feed by subscribing to the `/result` topic, which provides just the name of the recognized objects:

```
T6 $ rostopic echo /result
```

See the composition of the following screenshots showing how the tennis ball is recognized in the Terminal window (bottom-left side):

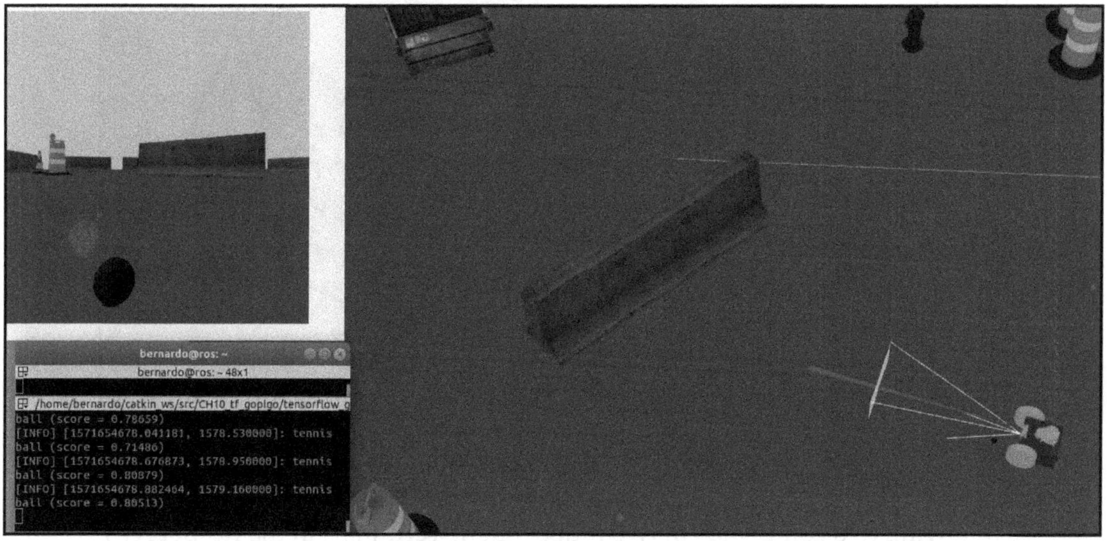

Is it easy to replicate? We expect so. Now,let's proceed to repeat the process with the physical robot.

Object recognition in the real world

First, remember to point the ROS master URI to the robot as usual:

```
$ export ROS_MASTER_URI=http://gopigo3.local:11311
```

Apply this for every new Terminal in the laptop, or include the line in the `.bashrc` file. The physical robot configuration is as shown here, with GoPiGo3 in front of a small yellow ball:

Run the following two commands in two independent Terminals in the Raspberry Pi:

```
r1 $ roslaunch mygopigo gopigo3.launch
r2 $ roslaunch raspicam_node camerav2_410x308_30fps.launch
```

The packages you are using in the preceding are the ones in `Chapter 6`, *Programming in ROS- Commands and Tools*. So make sure you did not delete them, and if so, get them back. In the laptop is where you run the new packages to perform image recognition:

```
T1 $ rosrun image_transport republish compressed in:=/raspicam_node/image
out:=/raspicam_node/image_raw
```

The image_transport- package (you can find its ROS wiki page at http://wiki.ros.org/image_transport) is commonly used in ROS to provide transparent support for transmitting images in low-bandwidth compressed formats.

Then, T1 makes raspicam_node/image—output from r2—available in raw format, that is, the /raspicam_node/image_raw topic, the output of T1. This facilitates the image feed, which can then be processed later by start_image_recognition.launch. At this point, it is very useful to look at the ROS graph:

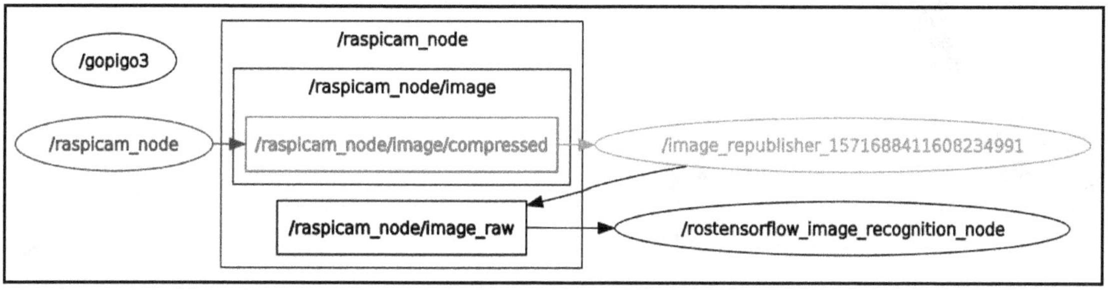

Remember that this visualization is launched with the rqt_graph command in another Terminal. Find that the transport operation is carried out by the image_republisher_157... node. Then, launch a rqt_image_view node to watch the subjective view as perceived through the Pi camera:

```
T2 $ rosrun rqt_image_view rqt_image_view
```

In the pop-up window, you have to select the /raspicam_node/image_raw topic to get the subjective view from the Pi camera.

Finally, as we did in simulation, launch the image recognition node and subscribe to the /result topic:

```
T3 $ sudo -s
   $ roslaunch tf_gopigo start_image_recognition.launch
rgb_image_topic:=/raspicam_node/image_raw
T4 $ rostopic echo /result
```

The only difference for the Gazebo scenario is that you have to remap the topic supplied by the Pi camera with raspicam_node, to the topic named rgb_image_topic, which is the one accepted by the image recognition node.

We have presented three different objects to the robot successively: the yellow ball, the mouse, and the monitor. Find out how the three of them are recognized by the robot in real time. Is it surprising?

The yellow ball can be seen here:

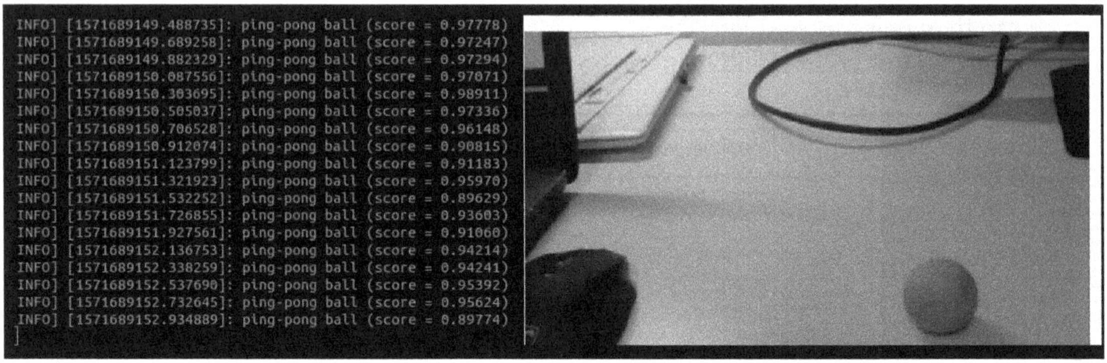

Then, the mouse can be seen here:

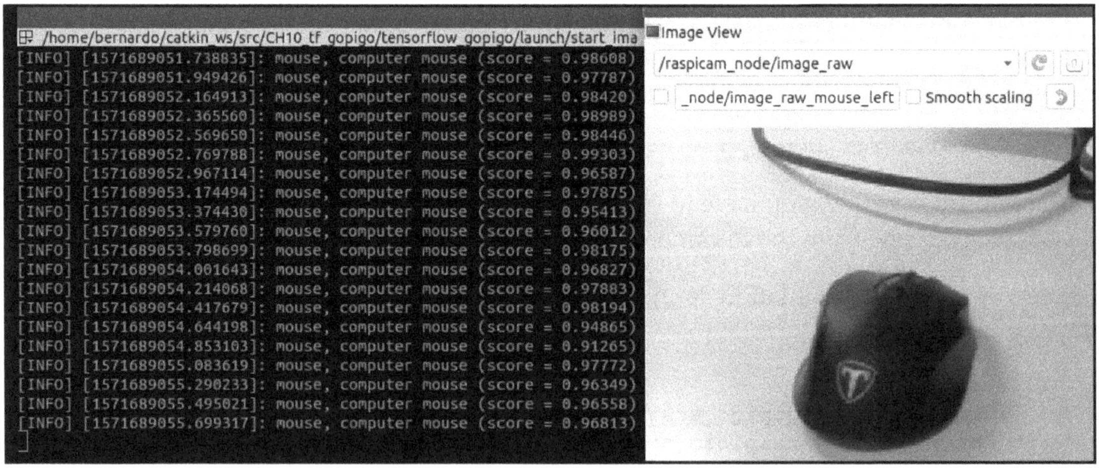

And, finally, the monitor can be seen here:

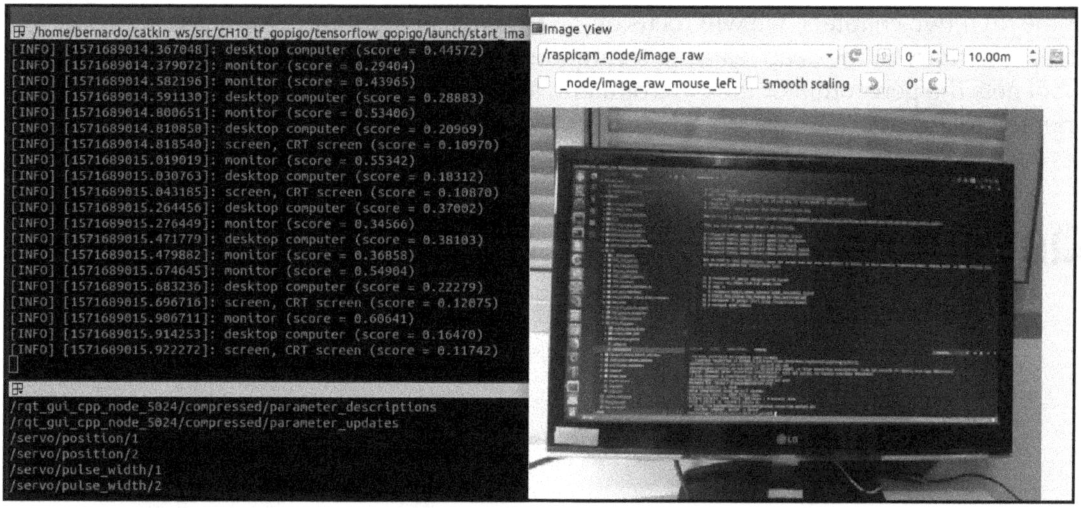

If you have arrived at this point, you are in a good position to start creating advanced applications in ROS that integrate object recognition as an ability that uses GoPiGo3 to execute smart actions.

Summary

This chapter provided a quick introduction to ML in robotics. We expect you to have acquired insight into what ML and deep learning are, qualitatively understood how a neural network processes images to recognize objects, and can operationally implement the algorithm in a simulated and/or physical robot.

ML is a very wide field and you should not expect nor really need to get an expert in the field. What you need to assimilate is the knowledge to integrate deep learning capabilities in your robots.

As you have seen in the practical case, we have used a pretrained model that covers common objects. Then, we have simply used this model and have not needed additional training. There are plenty of trained models on the web shared by data science companies and open source developers. You should spend time looking for these models, and only go to train your own models when the scenario that the robot is facing is so specific that general-purpose ML models do not cover it with decent accuracy.

In the final two chapters, we will focus on reinforcement learning, a task that is complementary to the deep learning technique described in this chapter. With the latter, the robot gets the perception of the environment, and with the former, it chains several actions oriented to a goal.

Questions

1. What is the task for solving ML that requires more experience and insight from the data scientist?

   A) The algorithm selection
   B) The feature selection
   C) The model

2. What is the relationship between ML and deep learning?

   A) ML covers many algorithms and deep learning only algorithms to find deep features.
   B) Deep learning is a subset of ML.
   C) Deep learning deals with all of the ML algorithms except neural networks.

3. How should you integrate an ML task with a ROS application?

   A) You should train the model outside and then provide ROS with a file of results.
   B) You have the choice of using publish/subscribe, a ROS service, or an action server.
   C) You have to use the specific communication protocol of the ML model.

4. What is the main difference between the publish/subscribe mechanism and the ROS service mechanism?

   A) ROS service is synchronous while publish/subscribe is asynchronous.
   B) ROS service is asynchronous while publish/subscribe is synchronous.
   C) Publish/subscribe does not need to receive requests from other nodes in order to publish messages.

5. If the practical example explained in the *Deep learning applied to robotics – computer vision* section was carried out with a red ball instead of a yellow one, will the prediction with the same model we are using?

A) Yes, the color is not a feature for object shape recognition.
B) Yes, and in addition to identifying a ball, it will also tell that it is red.
C) It depends on whether the model was trained with balls of different colors.

Further reading

To delve deeper into the concepts explained in this chapter, you can check out the following references:

- *A Brief History of ML:* `https://www.dataversity.net/a-brief-history-of-machine-learning`
- *A Brief History of Robotics Since 1950:* `https://www.encyclopedia.com/science/encyclopedias-almanacs-transcripts-and-maps/brief-history-robotics-1950`
- *ML for Recommender systems -Part 1 (algorithms, evaluation and cold start):* `https://medium.com/recombee-blog/machine-learning-for-recommender-systems-part-1-algorithms-evaluation-and-cold-start-6f696683d0ed`
- *ML for Recommender systems - Part 2 (Deep Recommendation, Sequence Prediction, AutoML, and Reinforcement Learning in Recommendation):* `https://medium.com/recombee-blog/machine-learning-for-recommender-systems-part-2-deep-recommendation-sequence-prediction-automl-f134bc79d66b`
- *Intuitive Deep Learning Part 1a: Introduction to Neural Networks:* `https://medium.com/intuitive-deep-learning/intuitive-deep-learning-part-1a-introduction-to-neural-networks-d7b16ebf6b99`
- *Intuitive Deep Learning Part 2: CNNs for Computer Vision:* `https://medium.com/intuitive-deep-learning/intuitive-deep-learning-part-2-cnns-for-computer-vision-24992d050a27`
- *Build your first Convolutional Neural Network to recognize images:* `https://medium.com/intuitive-deep-learning/build-your-first-convolutional-neural-network-to-recognize-images-84b9c78fe0ce`

11
Machine Learning with OpenAI Gym

In the previous chapter, we introduced you to the usage of deep learning in order to recognize objects based on a real-time image feed coming from the Raspberry Pi camera. Hence, this provides the robot the ability to take smart actions related to the recognized object. For example, if the object is a ball, the robot could collect it and put it apart so that nobody has an accident by stepping on the ball.

In this chapter, you will be introduced to **reinforcement learning** (**RL**), a field of machine learning that, nowadays, is a very active topic of research, having achieved the success of surpassing human performance in some scenarios, as shown in the recent case of the AlphaGo game (`https://deepmind.com/blog/article/alphago-zero-starting-scratch`).

You will learn in a practical manner using the Python framework **OpenAI Gym**, which is a toolkit for developing and comparing RL algorithms. We will provide a conceptual approach to RL that will allow us to handle various problems within a programmatic way using Gym environments. In order to do this, we will differentiate between three main components: *scenarios*, *tasks*, and *agents*. Here, the scenario is the physical environment where the robot evolves, the task is the action(s) the robot is expected to learn, and the agent is the software program that makes the decisions for the action(s) to execute.

This segregation will allow you to decouple these components and reuse them in a different scope. For example, you could have trained an agent so that a two-wheeled drive robot, such as our GoPiGo3, would be able to carry a load from one point to a target location and use the same agent with a different robot, for example, a four-wheel drive such as Summit XL (`https://www.robotnik.es/robots-moviles/summit-xl`). The code of the agent is the same because it abstracts the robot's concrete features.

Similarly, you could use different generated scenarios to test the same robot. This will show the ability of the trained agent to perform under different boundary conditions. With these ideas in mind, this chapter will teach you the basics of the OpenAI Gym API, how to integrate with an ROS environment, and how to follow the training process by representing the results graphically.

The following topics will be covered in this chapter:

- An introduction to OpenAI Gym
- Running an environment
- Configuring an environment file
- Running the simulation and plotting the results

In the first section, you will start using the base Gym API in its native Python environment. In the following ones, you will learn how to add the ROS wrappers to train robots in Gazebo.

Technical requirements

In this chapter, we will make use of the code in the `Chapter11_OpenAI_Gym` folder, located at `https://github.com/PacktPublishing/Hands-On-ROS-for-Robotics-Programming/tree/master/Chapter11_OpenAI_Gym`. Copy the files of this chapter to the ROS workspace, putting them inside the `src` folder:

```
$ cp -R ~/Hands-On-ROS-for-Robotics-Programming/Chapter11_OpenAI_Gym
~/catkin_ws/src/
```

Next, you will need to install Anaconda (`https://www.anaconda.com`). This is the Python distribution that has become the *de facto* open source standard for the Data Science community. It provides a complete Python environment for machine learning projects.

Visit the download section of the Anaconda website at `https://www.anaconda.com/distribution/#linux`, and select the Python 2.7 bundle. We select this package because the ROS Python client is focused on this version; however, you should be aware that it recently came to the end of life in December 2019.

Open Robotics intends to create a new ROS distribution in May 2020 targeting Python 3: `https://discourse.ros.org/t/planning-future-ros-1-distribution-s/6538`.

After downloading Anaconda, go to the download directory and enter the following command to execute the code for the installation:

```
$ bash Anaconda2-2019.10-Linux-x86_64.sh
```

The filename marked in bold letters should match the name of the one you have downloaded. If this is not the case, then run the `bash` command, replacing the filename with the actual one you have.

The `$ conda init` command is optionally executed from the installation script, and, if successful, it will provide the following output:

```
==> For changes to take effect, close and re-open your current shell. <==
If you'd prefer that conda's base environment not be activated on startup,
 set the auto_activate_base parameter to false:

 $ conda config --set auto_activate_base false
```

Conda is the package manager that ships with Anaconda. It allows you to easily install, remove, list, and inspect the Python packages in your Anaconda installation.

After installing Anaconda, you will see these lines added to your `~/.bashrc` file:

```
# >>> conda initialize >>>
# !! Contents within this block are managed by 'conda init' !!
__conda_setup="$('/home/${USER}/anaconda2/bin/conda' 'shell.bash' 'hook' 2>
/dev/n$
if [ $? -eq 0 ]; then
 eval "$__conda_setup"
else
 if [ -f "/home/${USER}/anaconda2/etc/profile.d/conda.sh" ]; then
 . "/home/${USER}/anaconda2/etc/profile.d/conda.sh"
 else
 export PATH="/home/${USER}/anaconda2/bin:$PATH"
 fi
fi
unset __conda_setup
# <<< conda initialize <<<
```

So that the added configuration takes effect, source it in the Terminal prompt:

```
$ source ~/.bashrc
```

The preceding `.bashrc` line should take you into the (base) default Anaconda environment. We recommend that you do not activate Conda's base environment on startup. To ensure this, set the `auto_activate_base` parameter to `false`:

```
$ conda config --set auto_activate_base false
```

If you wish to restore the default configuration, you can revert it by changing the value to `true`. Finally, you have the option to manually activate the default Anaconda environment, on demand, in a Terminal with this command:

```
$ conda activate
```

In this base environment, you are able to install Jupyter notebooks. You can use them to view, run, and modify Python notebooks:

```
(base) $ jupyter notebook
```

Remember that this is the user-friendly Python runtime you had preinstalled with DexterOS. It was used in `Chapter 2`, *Unit Testing of GoPiGo3*, to run most of the examples. To deactivate the virtual environment, just run the following:

```
(base) $ conda deactivate
```

TIP: You can find a useful cheatsheet for Conda Package Manager, which you should have at hand, at the following URL: `https://kapeli.com/cheat_sheets/Conda.docset/Contents/Resources/Documents/index`.

At this point, we are ready to proceed with OpenAI Gym and its installation; this will be explained in a dedicated section next.

An introduction to OpenAI Gym

In the previous chapter, we provided a practical overview of what you can expect in RL when applied to robotics. In this chapter, we will provide a general view in which you will discover how RL is used to train smart *agents*.

First, we will need to install OpenAI Gym and OpenAI ROS on our laptop in preparation for the practical examples. Then, we will explain its concepts.

Installing OpenAI Gym

As we did in the previous chapter, we are going to create a virtual environment for the Python setup of this chapter, which we will call `gym`. The following two commands allow for the creation and then the activation of `gym`:

```
$ conda create -n gym pip python=2.7
$ conda activate gym
```

Following this, install the specific Python packages that we are going to need for the examples:

- The Keras package (`https://keras.io/`), which is a high-level neural network API that it used within OpenAI Gym. Remember that it was also used in the previous chapter, but we need to install it again because this is a new `gym` environment. Keras will let us train an agent using the **DQN** (short for **Deep Q-Network**) algorithm, which is deep learning-based.
- You also need TensorFlow since it is used as the backend for Keras.
- Finally, you will need the Gym package (`https://github.com/openai/gym`), which is the implementation in Python of OpenAI Gym.

You can install three of the packages in a row, as follows:

```
(gym) $ pip install tensorflow keras gym box2d-py
```

Now check the version of `gym`:

```
(gym) $ pip show gym
```

The output should be as follows:

```
Name: gym
Version: 0.15.4
Summary: The OpenAI Gym: A toolkit for developing and comparing your
reinforcement learning agents.
Home-page: https://github.com/openai/gym
Author: OpenAI
Author-email: gym@openai.com
License: UNKNOWN
Location: ~/anaconda2/envs/gym/lib/python2.7/site-packages
Requires: pyglet, cloudpickle, six, scipy, numpy, opencv-python, enum34
```

In addition to this, install the Jupyter notebooks, since some of the Python examples are explained in this friendly format:

```
(gym) $ conda install jupyter
```

Finally, install an optional library called `pybox2d`. This is a 2D physics engine for games and simple simulations, used by some of the premade environments that ship with Gym:

```
(gym) $ conda install -c https://conda.anaconda.org/kne pybox2d
```

The technical requirements end here. The following subsections are optional and are intended to increase your background of different ways of managing Python and Anaconda. We will show you how to install OpenAI Gym from the source and host the package in your working folder, which is a typical way of using a Python package in development mode.

Without Anaconda (optional)

If you do not want to use Anaconda but instead keep working in the Python environment that ships with Ubuntu, you can install an in-home user directory by adding the `--user` flag:

```
$ pip install --user tensorflow keras tflearn gym
```

This places the necessary packages in the `~/.local/lib/python2.7/site-packages` folder.

Installing gym in development mode (optional)

This allows you to have the source code of OpenAI Gym in your working directory, change the files of the package, and see their effects instantly, without needing to reinstall the `gym` module:

```
(gym) $ conda deactivate
$ cd ~/catkin_ws
$ git clone https://github.com/openai/gym
$ cd gym
$ pip install --user -e .
```

The `-e` option allows this kind of installation, and it is suitable to be used as developer mode. The `--user` option performs the installation locally to the user at the `~/.local/lib/python2.7/site-packages` location.

To keep the environment clean, remove the package installation, keeping only the `gym` Python package in the Gym virtual environment:

```
$ rm -rf gym.egg-info
$ ls ~/.local/lib/python2.7/site-packages | grep gym | xargs rm
```

This snippet lets you know how to manually remove a Python package from the system.

To reproduce the examples in this chapter, we will be following the former approach, that is, installing Gym as a system package within the Conda environment.

Installing OpenAI ROS

So that the code can run inside ROS, you have to install OpenAI ROS, which is built on top of OpenAI Gym. Execute the following command to clone the contributed ROS package and start the setup for ROS:

```
$ cd ~/catkin_ws/src
$ git clone https://bitbucket.org/theconstructcore/openai_ros.git
$ cd ~/ros_ws
$ catkin_make
$ source devel/setup.bash
$ rosdep install openai_ros
```

Be aware that we had to install the ROS package from the source because the compiled binary is not available in Ubuntu. In particular, it is worth noting that the `rosdep install openai_ros` command does the equivalent of the general `sudo apt install <package>` command of Ubuntu; that is, every time you install a new component, it automatically includes the required dependencies. Remember that, for an ROS package, the dependencies are declared in the `package.xml` file located in the root folder of its source code.

Once the installation of OpenAI Gym is complete, we can go on to explain its concepts.

Agents, artificial intelligence, and machine learning

The concept of an agent comes from the artificial intelligence field and is used to designate anything that makes decisions. Well, that is, it is what a typical computer program does with the conditional instructions of the `if ... then ... else ...` type. Put simply, an *agent* is a program that can take more elaborated decisions rather than using pure conditionals. For example, consider a video game: when you play against a machine, your opponent observes your actions and decides what to do next to win the game. What powers the opponent's decisions is an agent. Generalizing this idea, an agent can be used to solve many kinds of problems; for example, when to stop and start a heater to keep a room warm at a set temperature point.

When instead of using analytical formulas—as in the case of using a **PID** controller (acronym of *Proportional–Integral–Derivative*) to address the problem of temperature regulation mentioned previously—you use empirical data to tell the *agent* what to do in *hundreds or thousands of particular situations* (the outside temperature, the room temperature, the number of people in the room, the time of the day, and so on), you are training it so that it is able to generalize and respond correctly when faced with a broad range of conditions. And this training process is what we call machine learning in general, and RL for the particular scope of these last two chapters of the book.

> TIP
>
> At this point, you should also be aware that an *agent* that uses machine learning can make good decisions when the input conditions are in the range for which it has been trained. You cannot expect good decisions if one or more relevant conditions are outside of the training range. Hence the importance of the preceding paragraph in providing the empirical data of *hundreds or thousands of particular situations* for the training process.

OpenAI Gym is a structured framework to train agents based on RL techniques. Once this agent is trained, it can be reused in similar problems to power the decision capability. To illustrate these concepts, we are going to use a simple mechanism, the cart pole, which is also known as the inverted pendulum.

The cart pole example

This is the classical control problem of the inverted pendulum that experiments with an unstable equilibrium (take a look at the following diagram). By applying lateral forces, *F*, you may compensate its tendency to fall down and get it to stay up (that is, when angle θ is close to zero):

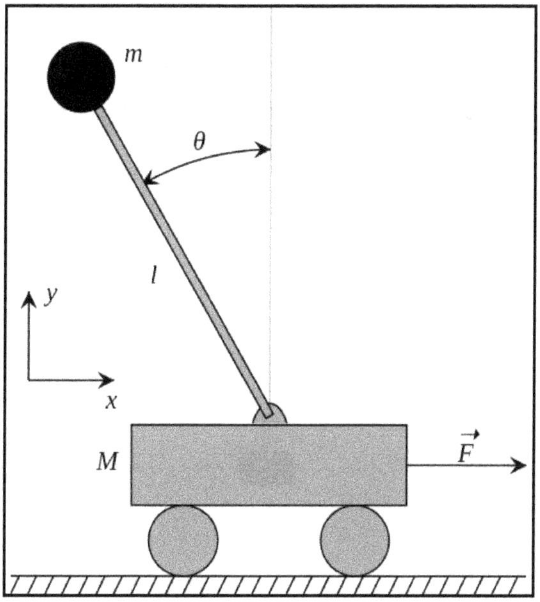

Source: https://de.wikipedia.org/wiki/Datei:Cart-pendulum.svg

We are going to solve this problem with OpenAI Gym, and the approach consists of starting with an *agent* that has no knowledge of the physics of the problem, that is, it does not have any idea of what lateral forces to apply so that the cart pole stays up. Following a trial-and-error strategy, the agent will learn which force directions and values are adequate for each angle of the pendulum. It is a quick problem to solve because you have only one degree of freedom—the angle θ—and one independent variable—the force, *F*.

This example is included with the code provided in the book repository, and we will take it as the base to explain the common concepts of the OpenAI Gym framework: environments, observations, and spaces.

Environments

An environment is a scenario that models a problem (such as keeping a cart pole standing up) with a minimal interface that an agent can interact with. You can see the cart pole environment in action by running this snippet of code:

```
$ cd ~/catkin_ws/src/Chapter12_OpenAI_Gym/cart-pole
$ conda activate gym
(gym) $ python cart-pole_env.py
```

You should see the cart pole moving and rotating randomly, as shown in the following screenshot:

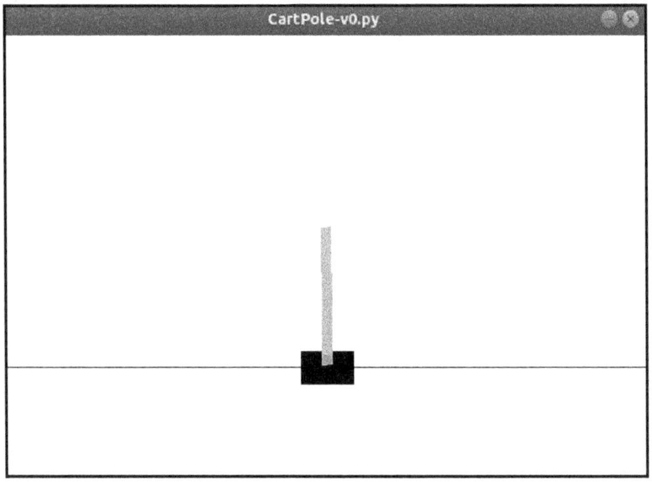

The content of the script is quite simple:

```
import gym

env = gym.make('CartPole-v0')
env.reset()

for _ in range(1000):
    env.render()
    env.step(env.action_space.sample())

env.close()
```

After importing the `gym` module, we set up the `env` variable to the predefined `CartPole-v0` environment. Then, in the next line, the `.reset()` method is applied to `env` so that the environment is initialized.

The body of the script is the `for` loop, which we set to 1,000 iterations. In each of these iterations, the script does two things:

- It renders the state of the cart pole with `env.render()`.
- It takes a random action to execute a step of the simulation, something that is done with the line `env.step(env.action_space.sample())`. The `.sample()` method provides a random force, *F*, to act on the base of the cart pole.

By chaining several steps together and letting the system evolve, the agent completes an episode, the end of which is defined by one of three possibilities:

- The pole angle is greater than ±12°.
- The position of the cart with respect to the center of the track is more than ±2.4 units.
- The episode length exceeds 200 steps.

This definition is part of the environment specification that can be found at `https://github.com/openai/gym/wiki/CartPole-v0`. Let's now review the definitions of observations and spaces.

Spaces

Spaces describe valid actions (*F* forces) and observations (cart pole angle θ). This concept of observations will be covered in detail in the next subsection. Every environment has two spaces attached:

- **Action space**: This is characterized by a set of state variables under the `env.action_space` *object*. This space defines the possible actions an agent is allowed to take. For the case of the cart pole, there is only one variable: to apply a lateral force, *F*.
- **Observation space**: This describes the physical state of the agent, that is, the angular position of the cart pole, θ. Operationally, it is a set of state variables under the `env.observation_space` object.

Let's now describe the concept of observations in order to get a full understanding of how they support the learning process.

Observations

Given an environment, an observation consists of a set of values that define a given state of the environment, the angle θ. It is like taking a snapshot of a scene. The environment's step function, `env.step`, returns the following:

- The current state; that is to say, it sets the current value of the state variable, **θ**. Operationally, it is an object type variable called `observation`.

- The reward that the agent has obtained from the last action, force *F*, as was previously mentioned when describing the action space. The reward is like points in a game—a quantitative value that accumulates all the rewards (points) obtained from the actions performed in the current episode from the beginning, that is, the current score in the game analogy. If the applied force contributes to getting the cart pole to stay up, the reward is positive; if not, a negative reward (or penalty) is given. This variable is of the float type and is called `reward`.
- Whether the current episode has finished, with a Boolean variable called `done`. When it finishes, the `env.reset` function is called to restart the environment, getting ready for the next episode.
- Diagnostic information under the form of a Python dictionary object called `info`.

Hence, the agent will try to maximize its score, which is calculated as the cumulative sum of rewards it receives for every force it applies. This maximization algorithm will make it learn to keep the cart pole up.

The preceding explanations should allow you to understand how the scripts work. Now we will run a training session of the cart pole so that you are able to see how the *good* actions are positively rewarded, encouraging the agent to build an effective strategy.

Running the full cart pole example

The first script that we ran, `cart-pole_env.py`, was intended to show a sequence of 1,000 random steps. The new script will provide feedback for every action that is taken by giving rewards for good actions:

```
$ cd ~/catkin_ws/src/Chapter12_OpenAI_Gym/cart-pole
$ conda activate
(gym) $ python CartPole-v0.py
```

The iterative block in the script includes the following lines:

```
env.render()

action = agent.act(state)
next_state, reward, done, _ = env.step(action)

score += reward

next_state = np.reshape(next_state, (1, 4))
agent.remember(state, action, reward, next_state, done)

state = next_state
```

Following the order of the lines, this is what is done in each step:

1. Render the environment. This is the window that shows you what is happening.
2. Choose the next action. This is where the accumulated experience is used to decide what to do, taking into account the current state.
3. Run the new step; that is to say, perform the selected action and observe what happens. The observation returns the new state of the agent, `next_state`, the reward the agent obtains, and the Boolean variable, `done`, telling you if the episode has finished.
4. The reward is added to the `score` variable, which accumulates all the rewards obtained from the beginning of the episode.
5. Next, the set (state, action, and reward) is stored in memory—`agent.remember`—so that the agent can take advantage of their past experience, promoting the actions in a given state that gave them more rewards.
6. Finally, we update the current `state` variable with the output of *step 3*, which is the value of `next_state`.

When the training finishes, a curve representing the evolution of the score as a function of the episode is depicted:

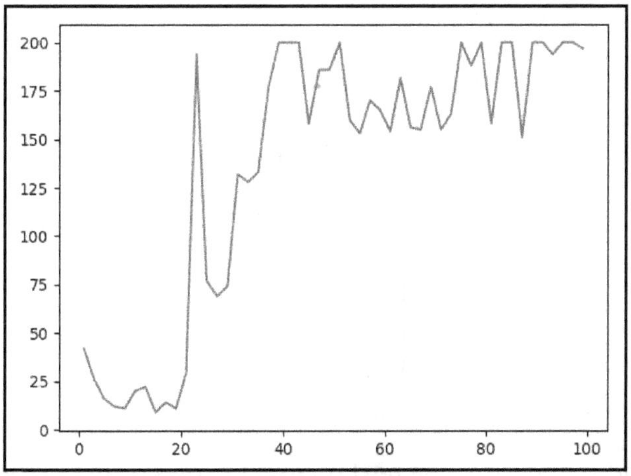

You can see how after 40 episodes the agent starts getting good scores of around 200. What this means is that the agent has learned to keep the pole in equilibrium by applying the force in the direction that prevents it from falling down. This simple example takes a few minutes to achieve the target of getting 200 points in every new episode, so let's quickly understand how RL works.

TIP: Be aware that the cart pole problem is not representative of real scenarios. In actual cases, the state is defined by a set of many variables, and the possible actions an agent may take are also many. Real RL problems are very CPU-intensive and they take thousands and even millions of episodes to get a reasonably good performance.

In the next section, we will describe a more realistic problem where there are 500 states and six possible actions. The goal of this second example is to understand the score maximization algorithm in its most basic version, that is, through the Q-learning algorithm.

Q-learning explained – the self-driving cab example

The problem we are going to solve consists of a self-driving cab that has to pick up passengers and drop them off to the right location. It must do so as quickly as possible while respecting the traffic rules. The graphics are based on ASCII characters and we are going to use real images to explain the goal. We will also follow a time-ordered sequence of frames:

- The first sequence represents the cab—the yellow square—in the start position. It can move up, down, left, or right except when it finds a vertical bar; that motion is not allowed. There are four possible taxi stands where the cab can pick up or drop off a passenger. They are marked with the letters **R**, **G**, **B**, and **Y**. The blue letter (**R**, in this case) is the pick-up location, and the purple letter (**G**) is the destination of where to transport the passenger to:

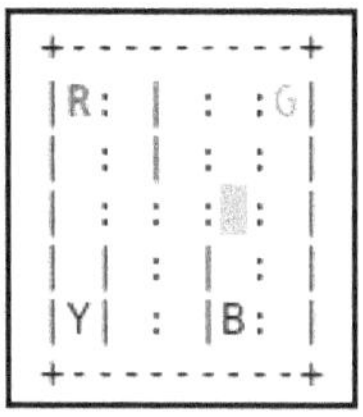

- This second sequence in the next diagram shows a step of the simulation where the passenger is inside the cab. They were picked up at location **R** and are being transported to the destination. This state is visually recognizable because the square representing the taxi is filled in green (when it does not carry any passenger, the color remains yellow):

```
+---------+
|R: | : :G|
| : | : : |
| : : : : |
| | : | : |
|Y| : |B: |
+---------+
```

- The final sequence corresponds to the scenario in which the taxi leaves the passenger at their destination; this is represented by the letter **G**, in this case. When this happens, the cab color changes to yellow again:

```
+---------+
|R: | : :G|
| : | : : |
| : : : : |
| | : | : |
|Y| : |B: |
+---------+
```

The goal of this problem is to train an RL agent to learn to drive the taxi following the shortest path for every trip. The shortest path is operationally implemented by a rewards policy, which gives the agent a predefined reward for every action it takes depending on its utility. Hence, the RL agent will try to maximize its total reward by associating states with *useful* actions. In this way, it will gradually discover a transport policy that will let it minimize (in global average) the time from traveling between pick-up locations to drop-off stands. The rewards policy will be detailed later in this section.

The advantage of using a simple example like this to explain Q-learning is that it allows you to apply a **model-free RL algorithm**. This is because it does not include any mathematical model to predict which will be the next state of the system based on the current state. To understand what the difference would be if there was a model, let's take the example of a robot at position x moving at the speed of v. After a time, t, the new position is expected to be as follows:

$$y' = f(v) = y + v \cdot t$$

Given that the state of the robot is represented by its position, y, the next state, y', shall be a function of the speed, v, that is, $f(v)$. If the applied speed is doubled—$2v$—the robot will reach a different state, x'', because it will travel double the distance for the same time step, t. In this case, the set of speed values constitutes the action space. Based on this prediction, the robot is able to anticipate what reward it will obtain before executing the action. On the other hand, for the model-free case, it is not possible to anticipate the reward. The only thing the robot can do is to execute the action and see what happens.

Having this perspective, you are aware of the didactic reason to explain Q-learning using a model-free RL algorithm. The agent simply learns to select the most rewarded action in every state—it does not need to make any prediction in advance. And after many attempts, it will learn an optimal transport strategy.

How to run the code for the self-driving cab

The code is a Python file located in the `Chapter12_OpenAI_Gym/taxi` folder of the repository. As for the cart pole, the program is written in Python and the filename is `Taxi-v3.ipynb`. The `.ipynb` extension is the known Jupyter notebook extension. We have chosen this way of coding in Python so that the example can be understood by just following the notebook, because you have the code and the explanations in one place.

> Jupyter notebooks were introduced in `Chapter 2`, *Unit Testing of GoPiGo3*. There, we have covered the practical explanations of the sensor and actuator using Python code in the notebook environment.

We suggest that you open the notebook, read it from the beginning until the end, and then come back here to complete your comprehension of the topic. To do so, follow these instructions:

1. Activate the `gym` environment:

```
$ conda activate gym
```

2. Move to the location of the example:

```
(gym) $ cd ~/catkin_ws/src/Chapter12_OpenAI_Gym/taxi
```

3. Launch the notebook server. This command will open a file explorer in a window of your default browser:

```
(gym) $ jupyter notebook
```

4. Click on the `Taxi-v3.ipynb` file and another window of the browser will open showing the notebook content.

After having read it, we are ready to return to the spaces (action and state) and reward concepts that we introduced in the previous section, covering them in detail for the current example.

Reward table

This table specifies what reward the agent gets for every action it takes. A well-designed policy incentivizes the most desired actions with greater rewards. For the case of the cab example, the reward table is as follows:

- The agent receives +20 points for a successful drop-off.
- It loses 1 point for every time step. This way, we encourage it to solve the environment as quickly as possible: all the time it is on the road it is consuming resources, such as fuel, so this negative reward can be understood as the fuel expense.
- It is given a 10-point penalty for every illegal action it performs (during the pick-up or drop-off actions).

Next, we proceed to describe the action and state spaces that the cab has to comply with to evolve in the environment.

Action space

The action space consists of the possible actions the agent can perform. For the case of the taxi example, these are as follows:

- The four possible moves: move (*S*) south, (*N*) north, (*E*) east, or (*W*) west
- Picking up a passenger (*P*)
- Dropoff (*D*)

Hence, there are six possible actions in total, and we will call them **action variables**.

State space

The state space is composed of all the possible combinations of values of the **state variables** that define our problem. For the case of the taxi example, these variables are as follows:

- The current position is defined on the basis of rows and column numbers. These account for 5 rows x 5 columns = 25 cells (positions).
- Four destinations: Marked with **R** (red; the color it shows in the accompanying Jupyter notebook), **B** (blue), **Y** (yellow) and **G** (green).
- Five possible passenger locations with regard to the taxi:
    - Pickup/drop-off in any of the four locations
    - Plus one for the passenger inside in any of the remaining cells (+1)

Hence, we have a total of 25 x 4 x 5 = 500 possible states. The following represents one of them:

```
+---------+
|R: | : :G|
| : | : : |
| : : : : |
| |o: | : |
|Y| : |B: |
+---------+
```

The movement of hitting a wall is known to the encoded environment thanks to the `|` character. If the wall is to be crossed, when the environment tries to update the state, the cab could not move and will remain in the same cell. This is accomplished by keeping the state unchanged. Otherwise, the `:` character lets the cab move to the new cell. Bear in mind that there is no additional penalty for hitting a wall, just the -1 of the time step.

TIP: If you introduce this new rule, the training should be somewhat faster since the agent will implicitly learn where there is a wall and will not insist on moving in that direction after hitting it several times.

Self-driving cab example using the RL algorithm

As stated previously, we will explain the learning process using Q-learning because of its simplicity and physical sense. Bear in mind that the Q-learning algorithm lets the agent keep track of its rewards to learn the best action for every single state:

- Each time an action is taken from a given state, a reward is obtained according to P.
- The reward associated with each pair (state, action) creates a q-table that is a 500 x 6 matrix.

The q-value for a concrete pair state-action stands for the *quality* of that action in that state. Hence, for a completely trained model, we will have a 500 x 6 matrix, that is, 3,000 q-values:

- Every row represents a state.
- The maximum q-value in each row lets the agent know what action is the best to take in that state.

In the first step, q-values are arbitrary. Then, when the agent receives rewards as it interacts with the environment, the q-value for every pair (**state, action**) is updated according to the following equation:

```
Q(state,action) ← (1-α)Q(state,action) + α(reward + γ maxQ(next state,all
actions))
```

The preceding equation is described as follows:

- α, or alpha, is the learning rate ($0<\alpha\leq 1$) and is applied to the new information the agent discovers, that is, the first part of the second term of the sum in the formula, α `* reward`.
- γ, or gamma, is the discount factor ($0\leq\gamma\leq 1$) and determines how much importance we want to give to future rewards. If this factor is 0, it makes the agent consider only the immediate reward, making it behave in a greedy manner. Hence, this parameter ponders the utility of future actions. It applies to the second part of the second term of the sum: γ `* maxQ[next_state, all actions]`.

Finally, we should also consider the trade-off between **exploration** and **exploitation**. Let's explain what these concepts mean:

- Exploration refers to the behavior where the robot executes an action from a given state for the first time. This will let it discover whether that state-action pair has a high reward or not. Operationally, it consists of taking a random action.
- On the other hand, exploitation refers to the behavior of executing an action from a given state that was the more rewarded in the past. Operationally, it consists of taking the action with the maximum q-value for that state.

We need to balance these two behaviors, and, for that, we introduce the ϵ (epsilon) parameter, which represents the percentage of actions that should be of the exploration type. This prevents the agent from following a single route, which may not necessarily be the best.

Evaluating the agent

The script runs 100,000 episodes in less than one minute. Then, we evaluate the agent with 100 episodes and obtain these average values:

- Steps per episode: 12
- Penalties per episode: 0

In front of the brute-force approach (which you can find in the Jupyter notebook), you obtain routes that vary from hundreds to thousands of steps and more than 1,000 penalties (remember that a penalty of 1 was given for each illegal action incurred).

Hyperparameters and optimization

So, how can you choose the values of alpha, gamma, and epsilon? Well, this strategy has to be based on both intuition and trial and error. In any case, the three of them should decrease over time as the agent learns the best actions:

- Decreasing the need for learning, alpha, as the agent knows more about the environment and may trust in the acquired experience
- Also decreasing the discount factor, gamma, as an agent develops an end-to-end strategy and not only focuses on the immediate reward
- And, finally, decreasing the exploitation rate, epsilon, because the exploration gains lose priority as the environment is well known

At this point, you should be ready to enter OpenAI ROS to train agents that power robots in Gazebo.

Running an environment

The goal of the rest of the chapter is to apply what you have learned about RL in general problems to a specific domain such as robotics. To easily transfer that knowledge, we will reproduce the simple cart pole example, modeling it as a robot in Gazebo. The code samples are in the `cart-pole_ROS` folder of the code repository of this chapter. Move to that location on your laptop:

```
$ cd ~/catkin_ws/src/Chapter12_OpenAI_Gym/cart-pole_ROS
```

Inside, you will find two ROS packages, each one giving its name to the folder:

- `cartpole_description` contains the Gazebo simulation framework for the cart pole using ROS. The structure of this package is very similar to the one described in `Chapter 5`, *Simulating Robot Behavior with Gazebo*. Hence, it is not necessary to dive into its details.
- `cartpole_dqn` contains the OpenAI Gym environment for the preceding Gazebo simulation. This is where the RL algorithm is introduced, and we will focus on this in the coming paragraphs.

The package is quite similar. Let's enter through the launch file, `start_training.launch`:

```
<launch>
    <rosparam command="load" file="$(find
cartpole_dqn)/config/cartpole_dqn_params.yaml" />
    <!-- Launch the training system -->
    <node pkg="cartpole_dqn" name="cartpole_dqn" type="cartpole_dqn.py"
output="screen"/>
</launch>
```

The line with the `<rosparam>` tag is the one that loads the configuration of the training process. We will explain this in the next section. This file is `cartpole_dqn_params.yaml` and it is hosted inside the `config` folder.

The other line, tagged with `<node>`, launches the single ROS `cartpole_dqn` node that implements the training process for the cart pole under the Python script, `cartpole_dqn.py`. What this code performs is briefly described in the following ordered points:

1. It creates the Gym environment for the cart pole.
2. It loads the configuration from the ROS parameter server (this point is detailed in the following subsection).
3. Then, it initializes the learning algorithm with the loaded parameters.
4. Finally, it loops over the predefined number of episodes, each one composed of a fixed number of steps (both values are also part of the configuration file).

5. For every episode, it performs the following:
    - Initialize the environment and get the first state of the robot.
    - For every step in the current episode, the agent chooses an action to run that will be one of random versus best action selection (depending on the epsilon exploration parameter):

    ```
    observation, reward, done, info = env.step(action)
    ```

    This is the key line of the loop, and you can see, it is the same that is used for the cart pole in pure Python and the taxi examples in the preceding section. Hence, the output of the steps are as follows:

    - `observation`: The new state of the environment resulting from applying the action
    - `reward`: The value that indicates how effective the action taken is
    - `done`: The Boolean variable telling you if the goal has been achieved

6. Finally, we let the algorithm learn from the result by following two subsequent steps:
    - Remember the running step: `self.remember(state, action, reward, next_state, done)`
    - Replay to optimize the action selection: `self.replay(self.batch_size)`

In this case, the algorithm that we use is somewhat different from the Q-learning we described in the *self-driving cab* example. It is called DQN and makes use of deep learning to select the best action for a given state. This is the algorithm that is more extensively used in RL problems, and if you want to deepen its formulation, you can do so by following the last reference in the *Further reading* section at the end of the chapter. In brief, this is what it performs:

- The remember process in every step of an episode saves what it is running and acts as the memory of the agent.
- Then, the replay process takes a mini-batch of the last steps of the episode and applies for the improvement of the neural network. Such a network provides the agent with the *best* action to be carried out at every given state.

Conceptually, what the agent does is to use its memory from previous experiences to guess which might be the most convenient action to maximize its total reward in the episode.

In the remaining sections, we will focus on the specific training and evaluation inside ROS with Gazebo.

Configuring the environment file

In *step 2* of the preceding algorithmic description of the `start_training.py` script, ROS parameters are loaded into the model. Their definitions come from this line of the `start_training.launch` file:

```
<rosparam command="load" file="$(find
cartpole_dqn)/config/cartpole_dqn_params.yaml" />
```

When executing this part, the parameters in the `cartpole_dqn_params.yaml` file are loaded into memory and are available to the `cartpole_dqn.py` script. The more relevant are the following:

```
alpha = rospy.get_param('/cartpole_v0/alpha')
gamma = rospy.get_param('/cartpole_v0/gamma')
epsilon = rospy.get_param('/cartpole_v0/epsilon')
```

`cartpole_v0` is the namespace that is declared before the definitions in the `yaml` file. The meaning of every parameter was covered in the *Self driving cab example using RL algorithm* subsection. Although the DQN algorithm is more sophisticated than Q-learning, the conceptual meaning of *alpha, gamma,* and *epsilon* is equivalent to both. You can remember them by reviewing the preceding Q-learning algorithm section.

Running the simulation and plotting the results

To run this simulation scenario, we follow the standard approach of first launching a Gazebo environment—part of the `cartpole_description` package with the model of the robot—and, afterward, we will start the training process:

```
T1 $ roslaunch cartpole_description main.launch
```

The result in the Gazebo window should be similar to the following screenshot. Although this is a 3D environment, the model itself behaves like a 2D model, since the cart pole can only slide along the direction of the guide:

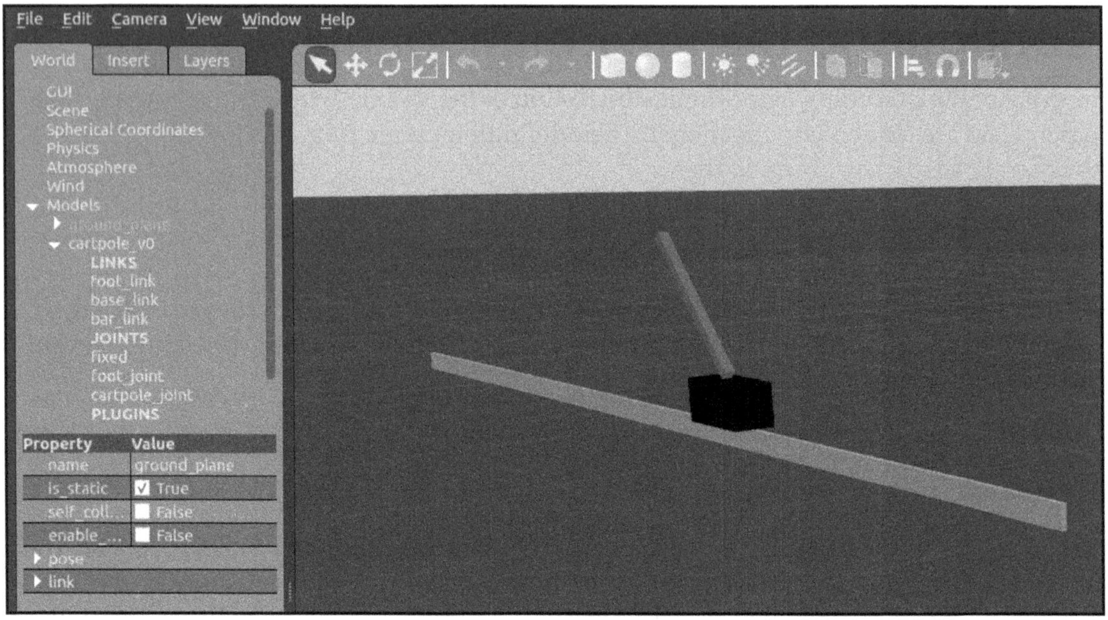

For the training process, we have the launch file in the other ROS package, that is, `cartpole_v0_training`:

```
T2 $ conda activate gym
T2 $ (gym) roslaunch cartpole_dqn start_training.launch
```

Be aware that before running the launch file, you have to activate the `gym` Python environment, which is where you installed OpenAI Gym.

You will see a live plot of the evolution of the training process that shows, in real time, the reward obtained in each episode. After the training concludes, you should obtain a graph similar to this one:

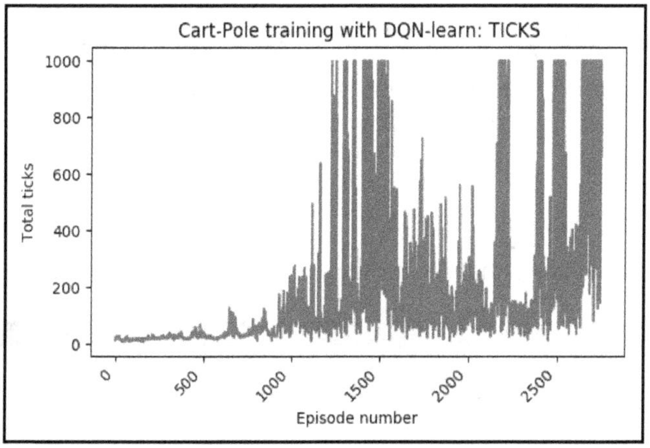

Bear in mind that for every tick of the cart pole, a reward of +1 is given. Hence, the graph also represents the total number of rewards per episode. To have a measurement of the convergence it is more useful to plot—for every episode—the average number of ticks (= reward) over the last 100 episodes. For example, for episode 1,000 this means to take the reward (number of ticks) of episodes 901 to 1,000 and calculate the average of these 100 values. This result is the one plotted for episode 1,000 in the following graph:

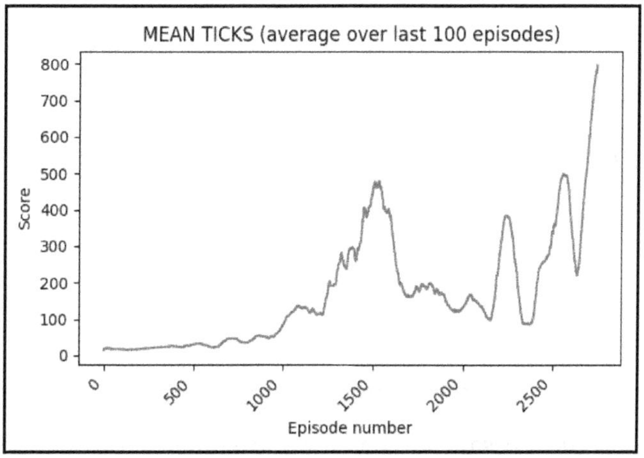

In fact, the criteria for the convergence is to obtain an average reward greater than 800 over the last 100 episodes. You may check that the curve experiments with a boosting after 2,600 episodes and quickly reaches the criteria.

In the second part of this section, we will present a friendly way to access the ROS console log to follow the training process in detail.

Checking your progress with the logger

As you may have observed, the log output is huge and runs at a very high speed. ROS provides another `rqt_tool` to easily follow the log of the session. To access it, launch it from a Terminal:

```
$ rqt_console
```

This should display a window that is similar to the following screenshot:

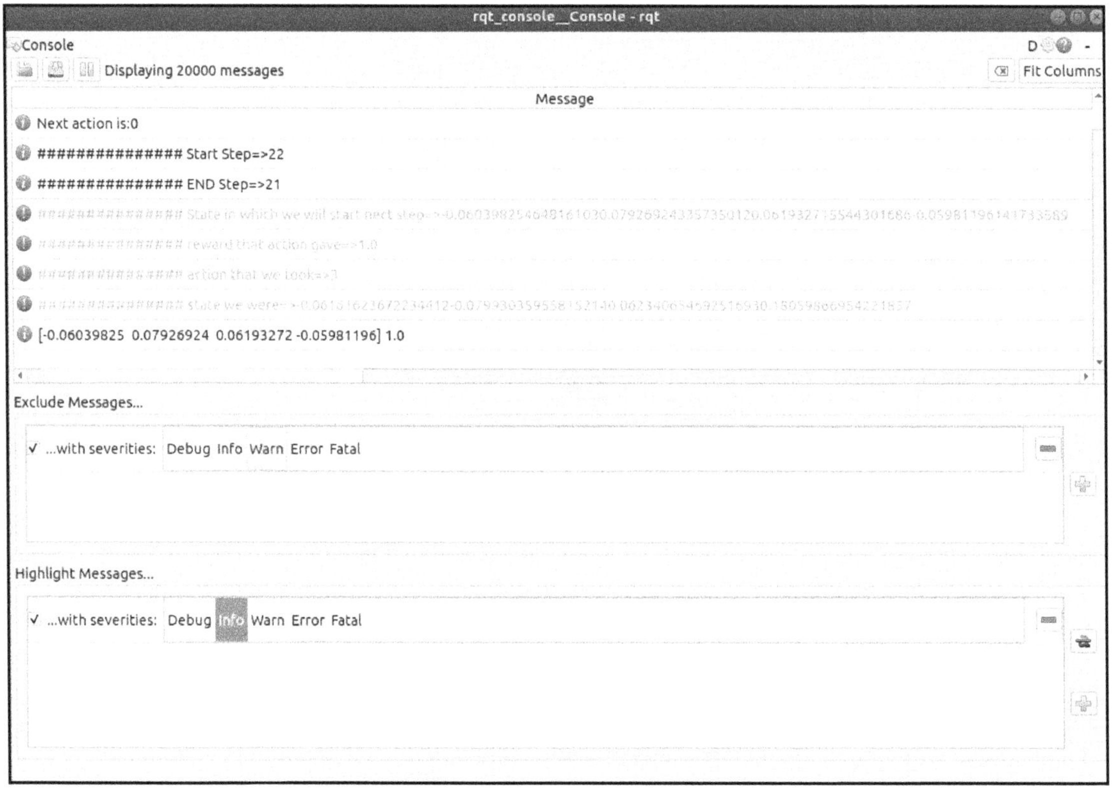

In the two boxes below the message feed, you can exclude or include messages based on your own criteria. If you want to change the log level of the node, run the `rqt_logger_level` utility:

```
$ rosrun rqt_logger_level rqt_logger_level
```

The following screenshot shows the log level of the node:

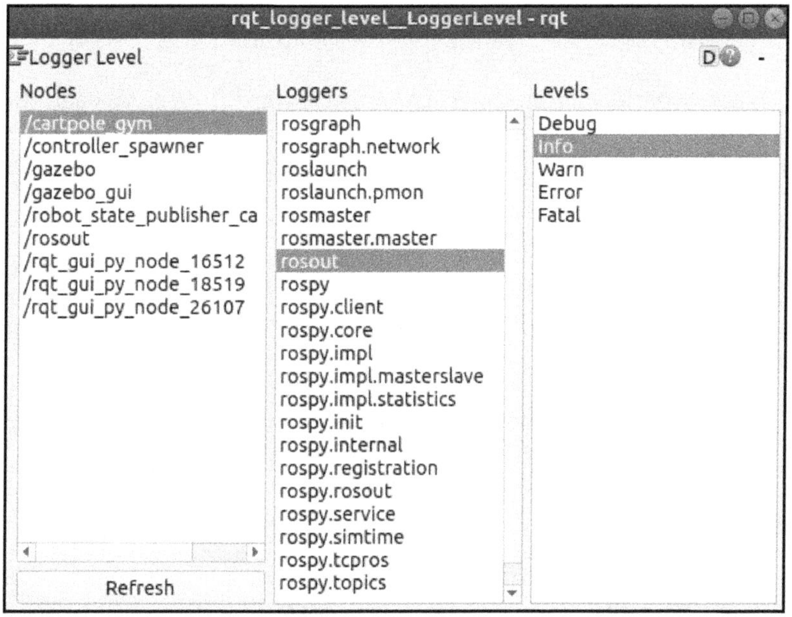

The `rqt_console` tool allows you to both follow the log in real time and save it to a file for offline analysis.

Summary

This chapter provided you with the theoretical background that you need to apply RL to real robots. By dissecting the simple example of the cart pole, you should now understand what happens under the hood in classical RL tasks.

Additionally, by doing this first with the native OpenAI Gym framework in Python, and afterward, inside ROS, you should have acquired the basic skills to perform an RL process with a real robot, our GoPiGo3. This is what you will learn to do in the final chapter of the book.

Questions

1. How does an agent learn following the RL approach?

   A) Via the experience that it gets from the reward it receives each time it executes an action.
   B) By randomly exploring the environment and discovering the best strategy by trial and error.
   C) Via a neural network that gives as output a q-value as a function of the state of the system.

2. Does an agent trained with RL have to make predictions of the expected outcome of an action?

   A) Yes; this is a characteristic called model-free RL.
   B) Only if it does not take the model-free RL approach.
   C) No; by definition, RL methods only need to be aware of rewards and penalties to ensure the learning process.

3. If you run the Q-learning algorithm with a learning rate, alpha, of 0.7, what does this mean from the point of view of the learning process?

   A) That you keep the top 30% of the pair state-actions that provide the higher rewards.
   B) That you keep the 30% of the values of all the elements of the Q-matrix, and take the remaining 70% from the result of the new action.
   C) That you keep the top 70% of the acquired knowledge from every iteration step to the next one.

4. If you run the Q-learning algorithm with a discount factor, gamma, of 1, what does this mean from the point of view of the learning process?

   A) That the agent will only be interested in the immediate reward.
   B) That the agent will only be interested in the goal of the task.
   C) That the agent will only be interested in achieving the goal once.

5. If you run the Q-learning algorithm with an exploration rate, epsilon, of 0.5, what does this mean from the point of view of the learning process?

   A) That the behavior of the agent will be similar to that of an agent that selects random actions.
   B) That the agent will choose a random action in 50% of the steps of the episode.
   C) That the agent will choose random actions in 50% of all the episodes.

Further reading

To delve deeper into the concepts explained in this chapter, you can refer to the following sources:

- *Reinforcement Learning: An Introduction*, Sutto R., Barto A. (2018), The MIT Press, licensed under the Creative Commons Attribution-NonCommercial-NoDeriv 2.0 Generic License (`http://www.andrew.cmu.edu/course/10-703/textbook/BartoSutton.pdf`)
- *Machine Learning Projects*, Chapter: *Bias-Variance for Deep Reinforcement Learning: How To Build a Bot for Atari with OpenAI Gym* (`https://assets.digitalocean.com/books/python/machine-learning-projects-python.pdf`)
- Reinforcement learning with ROS and Gazebo (`https://ai-mrkogao.github.io/reinforcement%20learning/ROSRL`)
- Testing different OpenAI RL algorithms with ROS And Gazebo (`https://www.theconstructsim.com/testing-different-openai-rl-algorithms-with-ros-and-gazebo/`)
- *Extending the OpenAI Gym for robotics: a toolkit for reinforcement learning using ROS and Gazebo*, Zamora I., González N., Maoral V., Hernández A. (2016), arXiv:1608.05742 [cs.RO]
- *Deep Q-Learning with Keras and Gym* (`https://keon.github.io/deep-q-learning`)

12
Achieve a Goal through Reinforcement Learning

After the background on reinforcement learning that we provided in the previous chapter, we will go one step forward with GoPiGo3, making it not only perform perception tasks, but also trigger chained actions in sequence to achieve a pre-defined goal. That it is to say, it will have to decide what action to execute at every step of the simulation to achieve the goal. At the end of the execution of every action, it will be provided with a reward, which will show how good the decision was by the amount of reward given. After some training, this reinforcement will naturally drive its next decisions, improving the performance of the task.

For example, let's say that we set a target location and instruct the robot that it has to carry an object there. The way in which GoPiGo3 will be told that it is performing well is by giving it rewards. This way of providing feedback encourages it to pursue the goal. In specific terms, the robot has to select from a set of possible actions (move forward, backward, left, or right), and select the most effective action in each step, since the optimum action will depend on the robot's physical location in the environment.

The field of machine learning that deals with this kind of problem is known as **reinforcement learning**, and it is a very active topic of research. It has surpassed human performance in some scenarios, as in the recent case of **Alpha Go**, `https://deepmind.com/blog/article/alphago-zero-starting-scratch`.

The following topics will be covered in the chapter:

- Preparing the environment with TensorFlow, Keras, and Anaconda
- Installing the ROS machine learning packages
- Setting the training task parameters
- Training GoPiGo3 to reach a target location while avoiding obstacles

You will find in the practice case how GoPiGo3 learns by trying different actions, being encouraged to select the most effective action for every location. You may have guessed that this is a very costly computational task, and you will get an idea of the challenge robotics engineers are facing nowadays to make robots smarter.

Technical requirements

In this chapter, we will make use of the code located in the `Chapter12_Reinforcement_Learning` folder: `https://github.com/PacktPublishing/Hands-On-ROS-for-Robotics-Programming/tree/master/Chapter12_Reinforcement_Learning`.

Copy the files of this chapter to the ROS workspace, putting them inside the `src` folder:

```
$ cp -R ~/Hands-On-ROS-for-Robotics-
Programming/Chapter12_Reinforcement_Learning  ~/catkin_ws/src/
```

As usual, you need to rebuild the workspace in the laptop:

```
$ cd ~/catkin_ws
$ catkin_make
```

Once you have the code for the chapter, we dedicate the next section to describing and installing the software stack for the practical project we will develop.

Preparing the environment with TensorFlow, Keras, and Anaconda

Together with **Anaconda**, which you were instructed to install in the previous chapter, you will now install the machine learning tools **TensorFlow** and **Keras**. You will need them to make the neural networks that are required to solve the reinforcement learning tasks:

- **TensorFlow** is the low-level layer of your machine learning environment. It deals with the mathematical operations involved in the creation of neural networks. Since they are mathematically resolved as matrix operations, you need a framework that is effective at solving this algebra, and TensorFlow is one of the most efficient frameworks for that. The name of the library comes from the mathematical concept of a *tensor*, which can be understood as a matrix with more than two dimensions.

- **Keras** is the high-level layer of your machine learning environment. This library lets you easily define the structure of the neural network in a declarative way: you just have to define the structure of the nodes and edges, and TensorFlow (the low-level layer) will take care of all the mathematical operations to create the network.

> TIP
>
> Here, we will make use of the isolation feature that Anaconda provides. Remember that in the previous chapter you created a **Conda** environment called **gym**, inside which you installed **OpenAI Gym** together with TensorFlow and Keras. Now you will be instructed to work in a different Conda environment, where you will install only the modules you will need for this chapter. This way, you keep the code for each chapter isolated, as they apply to different projects. In fact, you will install specific versions of TensorFlow and Keras that may be different than the latest versions that were used in the previous chapter. This is a common way to proceed in Python projects.

Once we have clarified what each component provides, let's install each of them.

TensorFlow backend

First, create a dedicated `conda` environment called `tensorflow`. It consists of a virtual space that lets users isolate the set of Python packages you will use for a specific project. This has the advantage of making it straightforward to replicate the environment in another machine with minimal effort:

1. Let's run the following commands:

```
$ conda create -n tensorflow pip python=2.7
$ conda activate tensorflow
```

   The second line produces the activation and binds the next installations to this `tensorflow` environment.

Conda enviroment are isolated buckets that contain the python modules you need for a specific **project**. For example, for **tensorflow** environment, every Python module you install with either `conda install` or `pip install` will be placed at `~/anaconda2/envs/tensorflow/bin`. The **activation** means that whenever a Python scripts needs to import some module, it will look for it at such **project** path.

2. Now you can proceed to install TensorFlow:

```
(tensorflow) $ pip install --ignore-installed --upgrade
https://storage.googleapis.com/tensorflow/linux/cpu/tensorflow-1.8.
0-cp27-none-linux_x86_64.whl
```

3. Additionally, you should also install `matplotlib` and `pyqtgraph` in order to draw graphs of the results:

```
(tensorflow) $ conda install matplotlib pyqtgraph
```

4. Then check for the versions:

```
(tensorflow) $ conda list | grep matplotlib
(tensorflow) $ conda list | grep pyqtgraph
```

These last two commands have been added to give you practical examples of common `conda` commands.

Deep learning with Keras

Keras is a high-level neural network API, written in Python and capable of running on top of TensorFlow. You can easily install a specific version with this command:

```
(tensorflow) $ pip install keras==2.1.5
```

We have specified version 2.1.5 to make sure that you run the code in exactly the same environment we tested it in. The latest version at the time of writing is 2.3.1.

ROS dependency packages

To use **ROS** and **Anaconda** together, you must additionally install the ROS dependency packages:

```
(tensorflow) $ pip install -U rosinstall msgpack empy defusedxml netifaces
```

You can check the version of any of them by using `pip show`:

```
(tensorflow) $ pip show rosinstall
```

In the next section, we will describe the machine learning package of the code for this chapter, which you should have already cloned to your ROS workspace, as per the *Technical requirements* section.

Understanding the ROS Machine Learning packages

The code for this chapter implements the classical reinforcement learning methodology of training a neural network. This neural network is mathematically similar to the one we introduced in `Chapter 10`, *Applying Machine Learning in Robotics*, stacking layers of (hidden) nodes to establish a relationship between the states (the input layer) and the actions (the output layer).

The algorithm we will use for reinforcement learning is called **Deep Q-Network** (**DQN**) and was introduced in `Chapter 11`, *Machine Learning with OpenAI Gym* in the *Running an environment* section. In the next section, *Setting the training task parameters*, you will be given the operational description of states, actions, and rewards that characterize the reinforcement learning problem that we are going to solve with ROS.

Next, we will present the training scenarios, and then we will explain how the files inside the ROS packages are chained to launch a training task.

Training scenarios

This section is devoted to explaining how the reinforcement learning package – the content of the code sample provided with the book repository – is organized.

First, let's take into account that we are going to train the robot for two scenarios:

- Scenario 1: **Travel to a target location**. This scene is shown in the following image and consists of a square limited by four walls. There are no obstacles in the environment. The target location can be any point within the limits of the walls:

- Scenario 2: **Travel to a target location avoiding obstacles**. This scene consists of the same square plus four static cylindrical obstacles. The target location can be any point within the limits of the walls, except for the locations of the obstacles:

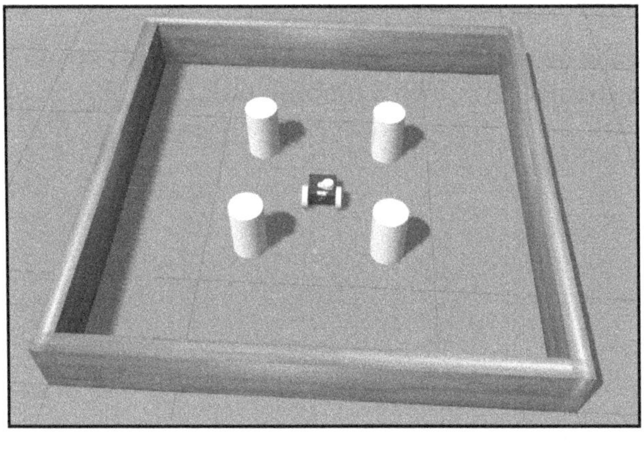

Now that we have presented the training scenarios, let's describe the ROS package that we will use for reinforcement learning for GoPiGo3.

ROS package structure for running a reinforcement learning task

The stack of code for this chapter is composed of the following packages:

- `gopigo3_model` is the ROS compilation that allows us to visualize GoPiGo3 in RViz using the launch file `gopigo3_rviz.launch`. The robot configuration is the familiar 3D solid model that we have used in the previous chapters. More precisely, it corresponds to the GoPiGo3 complete version, which includes the distance sensor, the Pi camera, and the laser distance sensor, that is, the model that was built in `Chapter 8`, *Virtual SLAM and Navigation Using Gazebo*.
- `gopigo3_gazebo` is built on top of the previous package, allowing us to simulate GoPiGo3 in Gazebo using the `gopigo3_world.launch` file. The URDF model that this file loads is the same as the one in the visualization in the `gopigo3_model` package.
- `gopigo3_dqn` is the specific package for carrying out the reinforcement learning task with GoPiGo3. As it is ROS, it is modular, and the decoupling we provide by separating model, simulation, and reinforcement learning makes it straightforward to use this same package to train other robots.

In this ROS package, we use the **DQN** algorithm to train the robot. Remember that DQN was introduced in the previous chapter, in the *Running an environment* section. In brief, what DQN will do is establish a relation between the *states of the robot* and the *actions to execute* using a neural network, where the *states* are the **input layer** and the *actions* are the **output layer**.

The mathematics behind reinforcement learning theory is complex, and it is not absolutely necessary to learn how to use this technique to train simple robots as GoPiGo3. So, let's focus on the configuration of the training tasks, abstracting the specific implementation in Python of the example that supports the practical elements of this chapter.

Setting the training task parameters

At this point, we are briefly going to introduce the three essential concepts in reinforcement learning: **states**, **actions**, and **rewards**. In this section, we will give you minimal information so that you can understand the practical exercise in this chapter. In this case, we are applying the strategy of *focus on the practice to really understand the theory*.

> This method of *focus on the practice to really understand the theory* is especially required for complex topics that are better understood if you follow an empirical approach with easy-to-run examples. This preliminary *practical success* should provide you with enough motivation to get deeper into the topic, a task that in any case will be hard both in the algorithms and in the mathematics behind them.

So, let's proceed to define these core concepts involved in the learning task of the robot:

- A **state** is an *observation of the environment*. Thanks to the data streaming from the LDS, the state is characterized by the range and the angle to the goal location. For example, if you get LDS measurements with a one-degree resolution, each state will be a set of 360 points, each value corresponding to every angle in the full circumference of 360º. As the robot moves, the state changes, and this is reflected in the new set of 360 range values provided by the LDS. Remember that each range value corresponds to the distance to the nearest obstacle in that specific direction.
- The **action** is what the robot can do using its motors to move in the environment, that is, translate and/or rotate to approach the target. By executing an action, the robot moves and changes its **state** – defined by the new set of range values coming from the LDS.
- The **reward** is the *prize* you give to the robot every time it executes an action. The prize you give for each action in every possible state is called the **reward policy**, and it is an essential part of the success of a reinforcement learning task. Hence, it has to be defined by the user (the *trainer*). In plain words, you will give a greater reward to an action the robot performs that is more effective in achieving the goal.

For the practical case, we are going to run the reward policy as follows:

- If the obstacle is in the forward half space of the robot (180° angle covering left to right in the forward motion direction), it obtains a positive angle-based reward ranging from 0 to 5. The maximum value (5) corresponds to the case in which the robot is oriented in the target direction. We specify this half-space by the relative angle being between -90° and +90° (in this angle the reward is the minimum, that is 0). The reference direction is the line crossing the target location and the robot.
- If it is in the back half space of the robot (180° angle covering left to right opposite to forward half space), the obtained reward is negative, ranging from 0 to -5 (linear dependence with respect to the angle: 0 at 90° and -90°, and -5 at -180°).
- If the current distance from the goal is above a preset threshold, the agent obtains a distance-based reward >2. If it is below this threshold, the reward is lower than 2, approaching the minimum value of 1 as the robot gets closer. Then, the **approaching reward** is the dot product of the angle and distance-based rewards = **[a]** * **[b]**.
- If the robot achieves the goal, a **success reward** of 200 is given.
- If the robot crashes into an obstacle, a **penalty** of 150 is given, that is, a negative reward of -150.

The reward is cumulative, and we could add any of these terms to the reward at every step of the simulation:

- Approaching reward
- Success reward
- Obstacle penalty

A **step** in the simulation is *what happens to the robot between two consecutive states*. And what happens is, that the robot executes an action, and – as a consequence – it moves, changing its state and obtaining a reward based on the policy defined in this section.

After this task configuration is understood, you are ready to run the training of GoPiGo3 in the two scenarios that have been defined.

Training GoPiGo3 to reach a target location while avoiding obstacles

Prior to running training in the scenario, we should note the adjustment of a parameter that dramatically affects the computational cost. This is the horizontal sampling of the LDS, since the **state** of the robot is characterized by the set of range values in a given step of the simulation. In previous chapters, when we performed navigation in Gazebo, we used a sampling rate of 720 for LDS. This means that we have circumferential range measurements at 1º resolution.

For this example of reinforcement learning, we are reducing the sampling to 24, which means a range resolution of 15º. The positive aspect of this decision is that you reduce the **state** vector from 360 items to 24, which is a factor of 15. You may have guessed that this will make the simulation more computationally efficient. In contrast, you will find that the drawback is that GoPiGo3 loses its perception capability, since it will only be able to detect objects whose angle coverage with respect to the point of view of the robot is larger than 15º. At a distance of 1 meter, this is equivalent to a minimum obstacle width of 27 cm.

> On a positive note, as the robot gets closer to an obstacle, its discrimination capability improves. For example, at a distance of 10 cm, an arc of 15º means it can detect obstacles with a minimum width of 5.4 cm.

The horizontal sampling is set in the URDF model, in the part of the file that describes the LDS, located at `./gopigo3_model/urdf/gopigo3.gazebo`. The number to specify for obtaining rays with 15º spacing is as follows:

$$360^{\circ}/15^{\circ} + 1 = 25\ samples$$

> Since LDS covers from 0º to 360º, to get 24 equally spaced rays, you have add one more sample, making it 25, since 0º and 360º are actually the same angle.

Then, the LDS part of the URDF file has to be modified as follows:

```
<gazebo reference="base_scan">
    <material>Gazebo/FlatBlack</material>
    <sensor type="ray" name="lds_lfcd_sensor">
    <pose>0 0 0 0 0 0</pose>
    <visualize>true</visualize>
    <update_rate>5</update_rate>
```

```
    <ray>
    <scan>
        <horizontal>
            <samples>25</samples>
          <resolution>1</resolution>
          <min_angle>0</min_angle>
          <max_angle>6.28319</max_angle>
...
```

By setting the `<visualize>` tag to `true`, the ray tracing is shown in Gazebo.

Is this sampling enough to ensure that the robot can be effectively trained? Let's answer the question comparing the number of rays for every case. This first figure shows the 0.5° actual resolution of the physical LDS. Rays are so close to each other that you cannot almost see the resolution. It provides very faithful sensing of the environment:

This second image shows the case of 24 samples and 15º resolution:

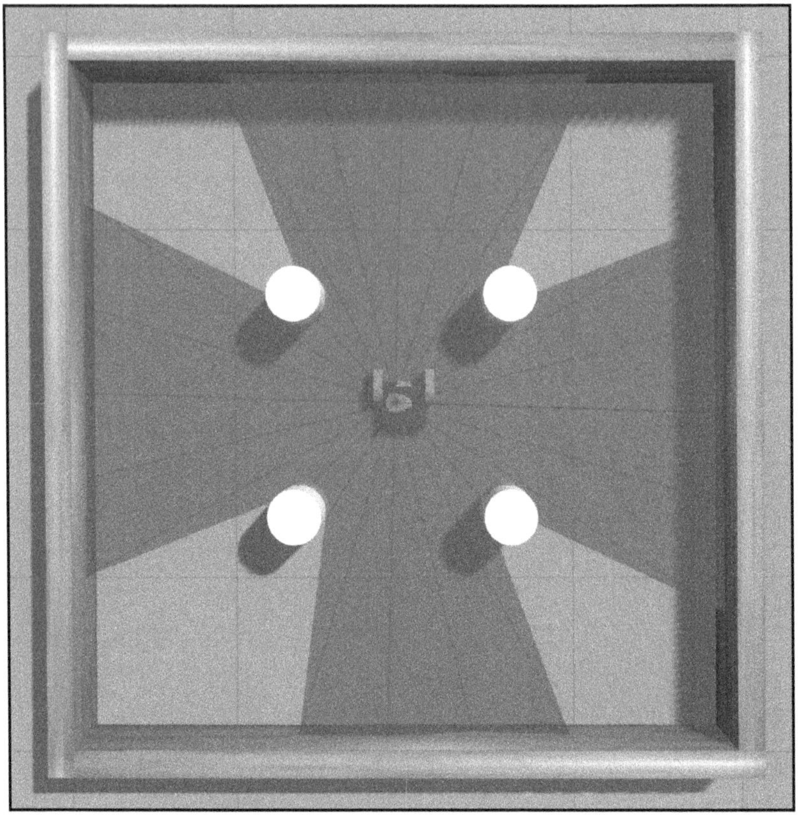

In this picture, the ray tracing shows that, even with so few rays, the obstacles are detected, since only one ray is needed to identify an obstacle. This fact helps to mitigate the loss of perception resolution. However, bear in mind that the robot will not be able to know the obstacle's width, only that it will be less than 30º. Why? Because you need three rays to detect an obstacle of finite width, the central ray detecting it and the extreme ones not interfering with it. Hence, this upper limit for the obstacle width is equal to twice the angular distance between adjacent rays, that is, *2 x 15º = 30º*. In some cases, this may be too imprecise, but, for the simple scenario we are using in this example, it should be precise enough.

How to run the simulations

Before beginning the training process for each scenario, let's recap what we learned in the previous chapter about visualization (RViz) and simulation (Gazebo) to establish a link with the learning process, which will make use of these tools and related scripts:

1. To launch the visualization in RViz, you have to simply execute the following command:

   ```
   T1 $ roslaunch gopigo3_model gopigo3_rviz.launch
   ```

2. To launch the simulation in Gazebo, you may proceed in a similar manner using this single command:

   ```
   T1 $ roslaunch gopigo3_gazebo gopigo3_world.launch
   ```

3. Finally, to run the reinforcement learning task you first have to launch Gazebo – as explained in step 2 – but with the selected training environment, instead of the general `gopigo3_world.launch`:

   ```
   T1 $ roslaunch gopigo3_gazebo gopigo3_stage_1.launch
   T2 $ roslaunch gopigo3_dqn gopigo3_dqn_stage_1.launch
   ```

   These two commands run the task in **scenario 1** described earlier. To perform the training for **scenario 2**, you only need to execute the corresponding launch files:

   ```
   T1 $ roslaunch gopigo3_gazebo gopigo3_stage_2.launch
   T2 $ roslaunch gopigo3_dqn gopigo3_dqn_stage_2.launch
   ```

   The first line loads the scenario 2 environment, and the second launches the training task for it.

The following two sub-sections show ROS in action by executing the commands in step 3.

Scenario 1 – travel to a target location

Follow the next procedure to make sure that the training process happens as expected:

1. First, launch the virtual robot model in Gazebo:

```
T1 $ roslaunch gopigo3_gazebo gopigo3_stage_1.launch
```

2. Then, you can start the training process. But first, you have to be in the `tensorflow` virtual environment:

```
T2 $ conda activate tensorflow
```

3. Now, start the training:

```
T2 (tensorflow) $ roslaunch gopigo3_dqn gopigo3_dqn_stage_1.launch
```

You might receive an error like this one:

```
inotify_add_watch("/home/user/.config/ibus/bus/59ba2b2ca56a4b45be932f4cbc9c
914d-unix-0") failed: "No space left on device"
```

Don't worry, you can solve it by executing the following command:

```
T2 $ echo fs.inotify.max_user_watches=65536 | sudo tee -a /etc/sysctl.conf
&& sudo sysctl -p
```

Hence, if you receive the error above, solve it as suggested and launch the training script again. Then subscribe to the relevant topics:

```
T3 $ rostopic echo get_action
T4 $ rostopic echo result
```

`get_action` is a `Float32MultiArray` message type whose data definition is as follows:

```
get_action.data = [action, score, reward]
pub_get_action.publish(get_action)
```

Let's see each component:

- GoPiGo3 always has a linear velocity of 0.15 m/s. The `action` item changes the angular velocity from -1.5 to 1.5 rad/s in steps of 0.75, to cover the integer range from 0 to 4.
- The obtained `reward` in each step is as was described in the *Setting the training task parameters* section.
- `score` is the cumulative reward that the robot obtains in each episode.

The corresponding ROS graph can be seen in the following figure:

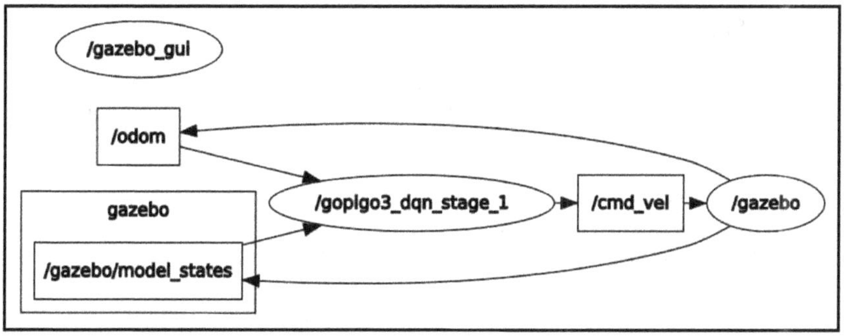

The key node in this graph is `gopigo3_dqn_stage_1`, which takes the robot state from the Gazebo simulation and performs the training task by issuing `cmd_vel` messages (remember that the velocity commands that drive the robot are published in this topic) and getting the reward for every new state GoPiGo3 achieves.

The episode record can be followed in the console log of terminal **T2**:

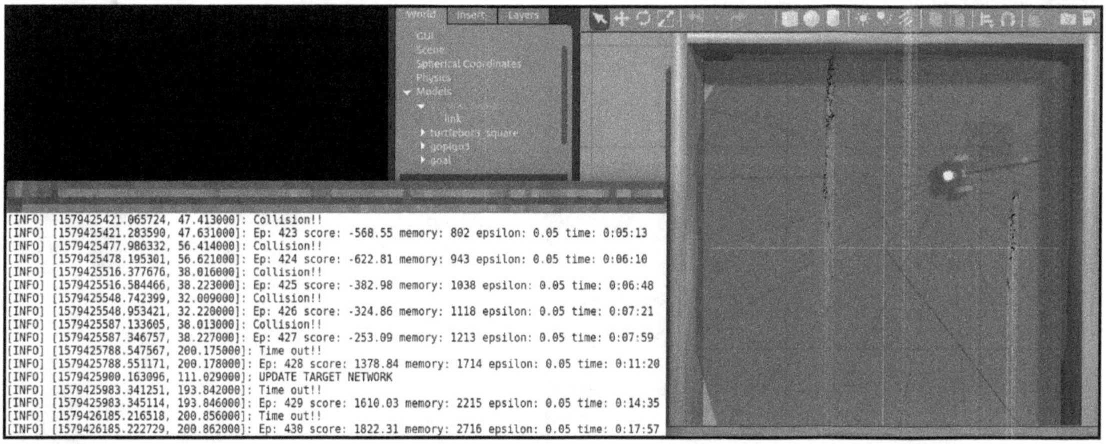

The red square is the target location and the blue lines are the LDS rays as described at the beginning of the section.

This first scenario aims to get you familiar with the training process in ROS. Let's move on to scenario 2, in which we will give quantitative information about how the training process improves through the episodes.

Scenario 2 – travel to a target location avoiding the obstacles

The procedure to start the training is similar to scenario 1:

1. We only need to change the name of the files and use the relevant ones:

```
T1 $ roslaunch gopigo3_gazebo gopigo3_stage_2.launch
T2 $ conda activate tensorflow
T2 (tensorflow) $ roslaunch gopigo3_dqn gopigo3_dqn_stage_2.launch
```

2. If you want to see graphically how the GoPiGo3 learning process is performing, execute the `result_graph.launch` file:

```
T3 $ roslaunch gopigo3_dqn result_graph.launch
```

The following screenshot shows all the content you should see on the screen of your laptop:

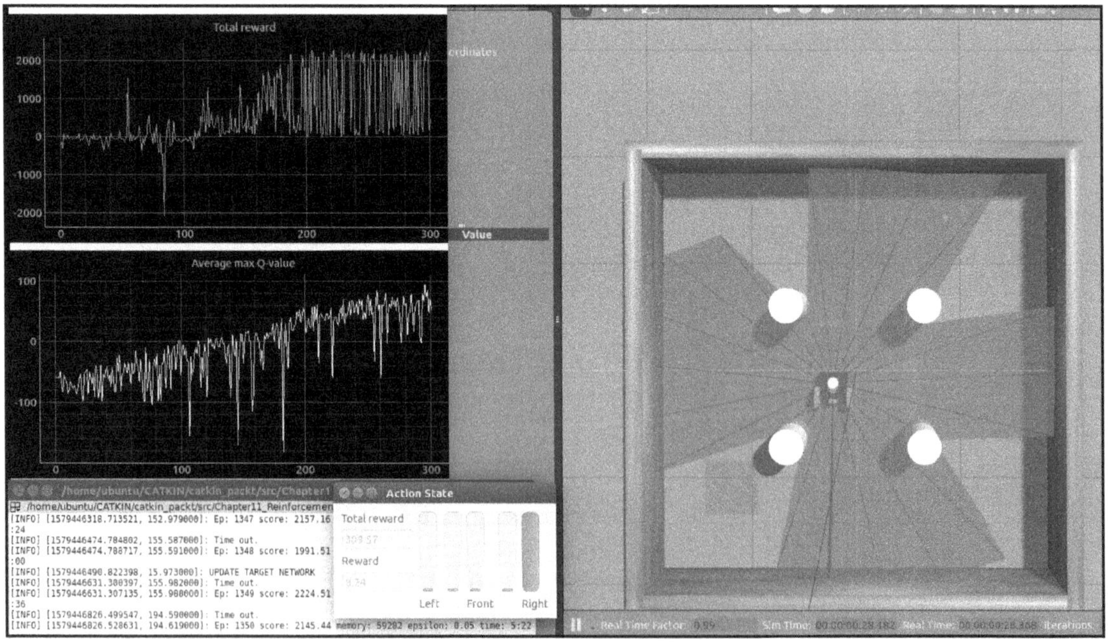

The red graph shows the **Total reward** obtained in each episode. Remember that an episode is defined as the sequence of steps that comes to an end when a criterion is met. In this problem, an episode finishes if the goal (the red square) is reached or if there is a collision with an obstacle. These graphs show the evolution in the first 300 episodes.

The green graph represents the average Q value of the trained model. Remember that this is the action-value function *Q(s,a)* that tells you how good it is to execute an action *a* in a given state *s*. This concept was explained in the previous chapter in the basic example of the self-driving cab in the *Q-learning explained* section.

You can see how, on average, GoPiGo3 is performing better as it accumulates experience. But how is it operationally using that experience? The answer comes from the reinforcement learning algorithm that has been applied, that is, by associating effective actions to every state given the rewards the robot has been receiving in that state during the training process.

Finally, we should note that in an execution environment like this, the ROS graph alternates between two states. One is when the robot executes an action by publishing a `cmd_vel` message that moves the robot:

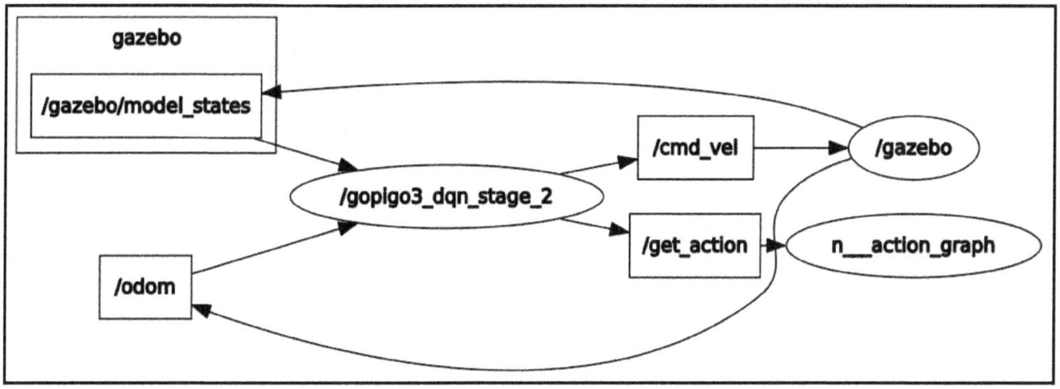

For clarity, in this graph we are excluding the nodes of the launch file issued in terminal `T3`.

The other ROS graph corresponds to the instants in which the agent computes the next state using the set of 24 values coming from the LDS in the `/scan` topic:

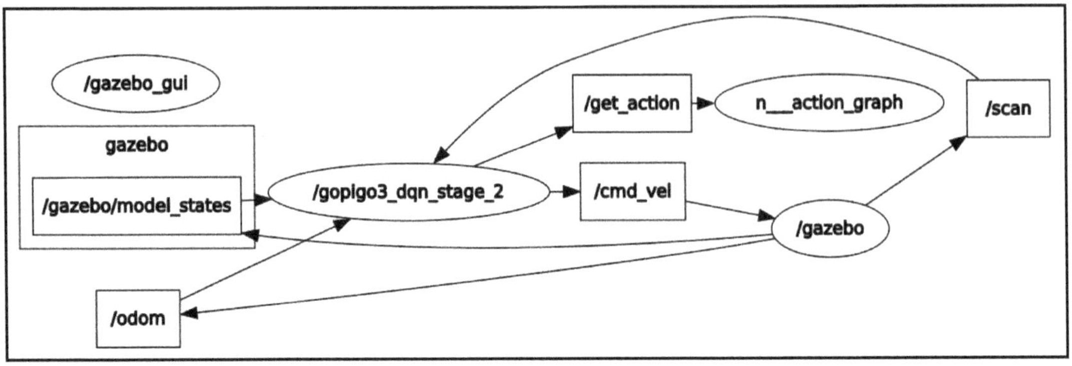

At this point, you have covered the end-to-end training process of GoPiGo3. The next challenge is to test the trained model.

Testing the trained model

Taking into account that we are using the **Deep Q-Network** (**DQN**) algorithm, what we have to save from the training process is the structure of the neural network and the weights of the edges. This is what the `gopigo3_dqn_stage_2` node performs every 10 episodes. Hence, you can find the saved models inside the `./gopigo3_dqn/save_model` folder, and the weights of the network are stored in the `h5` file type. Every file contains in its name the scenario (`stage_1` or `stage_2`) and the episode number. Follow these steps to evaluate the trained model:

1. Select the file with the highest episode number, that is, `stage_2_1020.h5`.

> Every `h5` file contains the weights of the DQN network as it appears at the end of the episode referenced by the filename. For example, `stage_2_1020.h5` refers to the network of scenario 2 at the end of episode 1020.

In order to use these weights, you basically have to use the same Python script of the training model (`./nodes/gopigo3_dqn_stage_2`), but initialize with different values the parameters marked in bold letters in the snippet below that reproduces the first lines of the `class ReinforceAgent()` definition:

```
class ReinforceAgent():
    def __init__(self, state_size, action_size):
```

```
        self.pub_result = rospy.Publisher('result',
Float32MultiArray, queue_size=5)
        self.dirPath = os.path.dirname(os.path.realpath(__file__))
        self.dirPath = self.dirPath.replace('gopigo3_dqn/nodes',
'gopigo3_dqn/save_model/stage_2_')
        self.result = Float32MultiArray()

        # Load model from last EPISODE
        self.load_model = True
        self.load_episode = 1020
...
```

Then, what each parameter provides is as follows:

- `self.load_model = True` tells the script to load the weights of a pretrained model.
- `self.load_episode = 1020` sets the number of the episode from which you want to load the DQN network weights, being the corresponding file `stage_2_1020.h5`.

2. Then rename the Python script as `gopigo3_dqn_stage_2-test` and generate the new launch file `gopigo3_dqn_stage_2-test.launch`, which will call the created test script:

```
<launch>
    <node pkg="gopigo3_dqn" type="gopigo3_dqn_stage_2-test"
name="gopigo3_dqn_stage_2-test" output="screen" />
</launch>
```

3. To launch the test process, follow the same steps as for running the training scenario, but using the test version of the launch file:

```
T1 $ roslaunch gopigo3_gazebo gopigo3_stage_2.launch
T2 (tensorflow) $ roslaunch gopigo3_dqn gopigo3_dqn_stage_2-
test.launch
T3 $ roslaunch gopigo3_dqn result_graph.launch
```

4. Remember that for `T2` you have to activate the TensorFlow environment with the `$ conda activate tensorflow` command. When it starts, you will see in `T2`, a message telling you that a model from episode 1380 will be used:

```
[INFO] [1579452338.257175, 196.685000]:
+++++++++++++++++++++++++++++++++++++++++++++++++++++
[INFO] [1579452338.258111, 196.686000]: STARTING TRAINING MODEL
```

```
FROM self.load_episode = 1380
[INFO] [1579452338.258537, 196.686000]:
=====================================================
[INFO] [1579452339.585559, 1.276000]: Goal position : 0.6, 0.0
```

5. If you plot the graphs for the first episodes (as per the command in terminal `T3`), you can confirm that the values are pretty good, that is, above 2,000 for the **Total reward** and above 100 for the **Average max Q-value**:

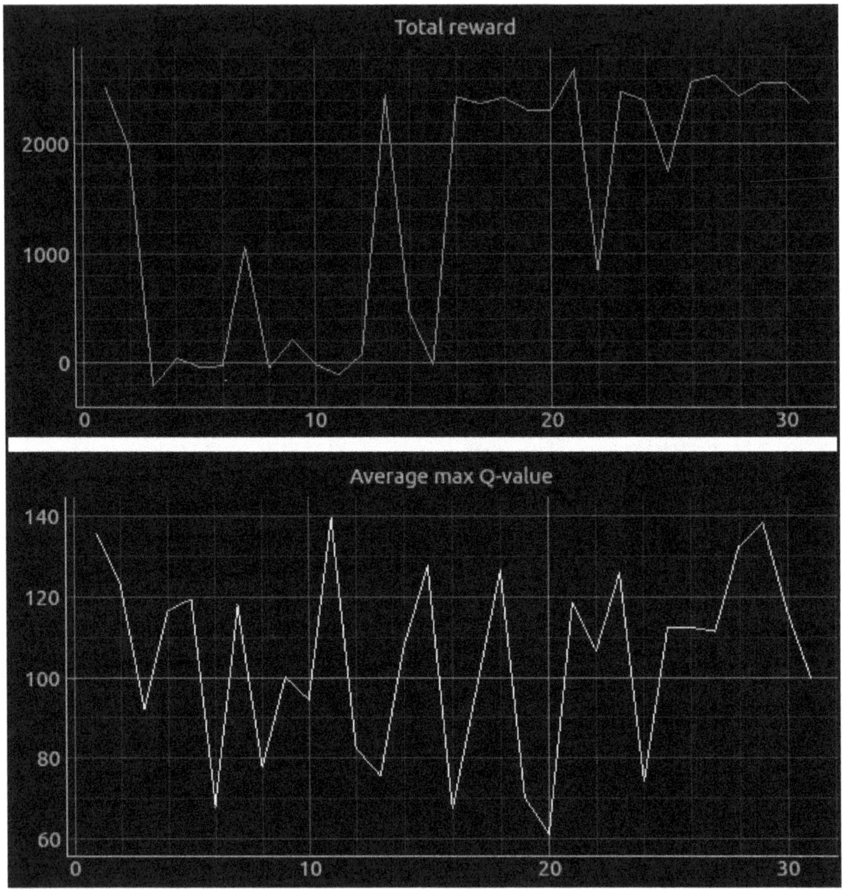

Although you are testing the model, every ten episodes the network's weights are saved to an `h5` file referencing the current episode number.

Summary

This chapter has been a quick and practical introduction to how you can apply reinforcement learning so that a robot can perform useful tasks such as transporting materials to a target location. You should be aware that this kind of machine learning technique is at the very beginning of its maturity, and there are as yet few practical solutions working in the real world. The reason is that the process of training is very expensive in terms of time and cost, since you have to perform thousands of episodes to get a well-trained model, and later replay the process with the physical robot to address behavioral differences between the real world and the simulated environment.

Be aware that the training process in Gazebo is not a substitute for training in the real world: a simulation necessarily implies a simplification of the reality, and every difference between the training environment (Gazebo) and the physical world introduces new states that can be missing in the training set, and hence the trained neural network will not be able to perform well in such situations. The solution? More training to cover more states, something that also means higher cost.

In the last part of the chapter, we have also covered the testing of a model using the same scenario in which the robot was trained. A more formal testing approach requires that you check how the trained model generalizes to different conditions in the scenario, such as having more obstacles or moving their positions. This is a complex topic, since reinforcement learning algorithms currently struggle to achieve generalization. Why? Because, when you introduce changes in the scenario, you are generating new states in the models. Since they are new to the robot, it will not know the most effective action to execute. Hence, new training is required to explore these new states.

Reinforcement learning is currently a very active field of research, and we should expect great advances in the years to come. What we should see is reinforcement learning being applied to real robots at a reasonable cost (that is, training a robot at a pace that doesn't require thousands of episodes) and providing techniques for the generalization of the models to environments other than those that were used for training.

This chapter closes the introduction to the application of machine learning in robotics. In this book, we have only scratched the surface of its potential, and, if you have followed the explanations you should have checked by yourself that this is a complex field where at some point you will have to master statistics, data analytics, and neural networks.

At the same time, it is a field where the focus is on experimentation. Instead of trying to model the reality with analytical formulas or computer-aided simulation, you observe the real world, get data from sensors, and try to infer patterns of behavior from them. Hence, the ability to successfully apply machine learning to robotics relies on being capable of streaming data continuously so that the robot can make smart decisions in real time. And the first step is to produce well-trained models. For this reason, a robot will be able to develop smart behavior in the medium and long term, as it accumulates experience that can be made available in structured trained models.

This is a challenging goal, both for the data scientist and the software engineer. They should work together to create mature robot frameworks that benefit from machine learning as much as common web applications and digital businesses are today.

Finally, many thanks for reading the book. At this point, you are challenged to explore advanced ROS topics, and we hope you can also become an active contributor to the ROS open source community.

Questions

1. What are the essential concepts of reinforcement learning?

   A) Robot actions and penalties
   B) Neural networks and deep learning
   C) States, actions, and rewards

2. Why do you need to use neural networks in reinforcement learning?

   A) Because the robot needs to use deep learning to recognize objects and obstacles.
   B) Because the robot has to learn to associate states with the most effective actions.
   C) We do not need neural networks in reinforcement learning; we apply different algorithms.

3. How do you encourage the robot to achieve the goal of the task?

   A) By giving it rewards when it performs *good* actions.
   B) By giving it penalties when it performs *bad* actions.
   C) By giving it rewards when it performs *good* actions, and penalties in the case of *bad* actions.

4. Can you apply the reinforcement learning ROS package from this chapter to other robots?

   A) Yes, because we have separated the robot model, the scenario and the training algorithm into different packages.
   B) No, because you have to rewrite the ROS package for every scenario.
   C) No: it is specific for training GoPiGo3.

5. Do you need to use the full data feed coming from a real LDS to train a robot?

   A) Yes: if you want to obtain accurate results; you have to use all the data.
   B) No: you have to decide the ray tracing density as a function of the typical size of the obstacles in the scenario.
   C) No: it depends on how much accuracy you require.

Further reading

To delve deeper into the concepts explained in this chapter you can follow the following references:

- *Practical Reinforcement Learning* from **Coursera**: `https://www.coursera.org/learn/practical-rl`
- Welcome to Deep Reinforcement Learning Part 1: DQN `https://towardsdatascience.com/welcome-to-deep-reinforcement-learning-part-1-dqn-c3cab4d41b6b`
- Simple Reinforcement Learning with Tensorflow Part 0: Q-Learning with Tables and Neural Networks `https://medium.com/emergent-future/simple-reinforcement-learning-with-tensorflow-part-0-q-learning-with-tables-and-neural-networks-d195264329d0`
- Simple Reinforcement Learning with Tensorflow Part 4: Deep Q-Networks and Beyond `https://medium.com/@awjuliani/simple-reinforcement-learning-with-tensorflow-part-4-deep-q-networks-and-beyond-8438a3e2b8df`

Assessment

Chapter 1: Assembling the Robot

1. C
2. A
3. C
4. C
5. B

Chapter 2: Unit Testing of GoPiGo3

1. C
2. A
3. B
4. A
5. B

Chapter 3: Getting Started with ROS

1. A
2. A
3. C
4. A
5. A

Chapter 4: Creating the Virtual Two-Wheeled ROS Robot

1. C
2. B
3. C
4. B
5. B

Chapter 5: Simulating Robot Behavior with Gazebo

1. C
2. C
3. C
4. B
5. B

Chapter 6: Programming in ROS - Commands and Tools

1. A
2. A
3. C
4. A
5. C

Chapter 7: Robot Control and Simulation

1. C
2. B
3. B
4. C
5. C

Chapter 8: Virtual SLAM and Navigation Using Gazebo

1. C
2. C
3. A
4. B
5. A

Chapter 9: SLAM for Robot Navigation

1. A
2. C
3. B
4. B
5. B

Chapter 10: Applying Machine Learning in Robotics

1. B
2. B
3. B
4. C
5. A

Chapter 11: Machine Learning with OpenAI Gym

1. A
2. B

3. B
4. A
5. B

Chapter 12: Achieve a Goal through Reinforcement Learning

1. C
2. B
3. C
4. A
5. B

Other Books You May Enjoy

If you enjoyed this book, you may be interested in these other books by Packt:

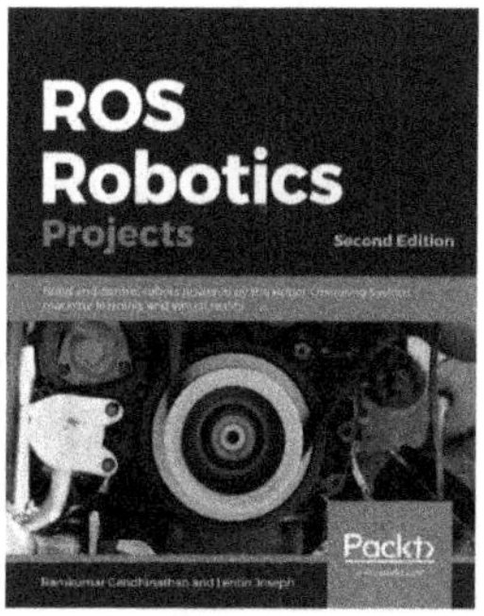

ROS Robotics Projects - Second Edition
Ramkumar Gandhinathan, Lentin Joseph

ISBN: 978-1-83864-932-6

- Grasp the basics of ROS and understand ROS applications
- Uncover how ROS-2 is different from ROS-1
- Handle complex robot tasks using state machines
- Communicate with multiple robots and collaborate to build apps with them
- Explore ROS capabilities with the latest embedded boards such as Tinker Board S and Jetson Nano
- Discover how machine learning and deep learning techniques are used with ROS
- Build a self-driving car powered by ROS
- Teleoperate your robot using Leap Motion and a VR headset

Learn Robotics Programming
Danny Staple

ISBN: 978-1-78934-074-7

- Configure a Raspberry Pi for use in a robot
- Interface motors and sensors with a Raspberry Pi
- Implement code to make interesting and intelligent robot behaviors
- Understand the first steps in AI behavior like speech recognition visual processing
- Control AI robots using Wi-Fi
- Plan the budget for requirements of robots while choosing parts

Leave a review - let other readers know what you think

Please share your thoughts on this book with others by leaving a review on the site that you bought it from. If you purchased the book from Amazon, please leave us an honest review on this book's Amazon page. This is vital so that other potential readers can see and use your unbiased opinion to make purchasing decisions, we can understand what our customers think about our products, and our authors can see your feedback on the title that they have worked with Packt to create. It will only take a few minutes of your time, but is valuable to other potential customers, our authors, and Packt. Thank you!

Index

H

I

J

K

L

M

N

O

P

R

S

T

U

V

www.ingramcontent.com/pod-product-compliance
Lightning Source LLC
Chambersburg PA
CBHW060648060326
40690CB00020B/4557
* 9 7 8 1 8 3 8 5 5 1 3 0 8 *